THE IRON CURTAIN KID

BY
OLIVER FRITZ

To my parents and grandparents

Cover Design by Edward Hellewell

Hazel and Ward, there would be no book without your inspiration and help. I owe both of you so much. Danke!

For an abundance of photos, jokes, recipes and interesting facts that will bring many episodes in this book to life please visit the website **www.ironcurtainkid.com.**

Copyright © Oliver Fritz 2009

ISBN 978-1-4092-7725-5

ironcurtainkid@hotmail.com

INTRODUCTION

If I had one wish, it would be to relive the night of 9 November, 1989 as I and thousands of other East Berliners broke through the Wall to join the party on West Berlin's famous boulevard, the Ku'damm. There was real champagne for free, souvenir editions of West German newspapers handed out, printed for the occasion, honking cars blocking the streets and everywhere one could see tears, tears, tears. East and West Germans were hugging and kissing each other. It was all a long, long way from the East Berlin where I grew up, just a few miles away yet worlds apart.

Looking back on it now, growing up in East Germany seems bizarre, surreal, like a weird dream. But at the time, it all felt perfectly normal. The German Democratic Republic was a member of the United Nations and had diplomatic relations with 150 countries. We citizens did not have to queue for absolutely everything, nor did we only communicate in hushed voices or were in constant fear of being randomly arrested. Churchgoers did not have their fingernails pulled out as a punishment, our dress sense and haircuts had evolved since the 1940s and as unemployment was unheard of poverty was a thing of the past.

Your media probably made you think otherwise. Just like our newspapers tried to convince us that the majority of the exploited workforce in the west was either unemployed or working for a pittance, always struggled to make ends meet, unable to afford proper healthcare and in constant fear of becoming homeless. Westerners never got the chance, like we had, to experience both systems. And a true experience "socialism in the colours of the German Democratic Republic" was.

This book is about my growing up in East Germany and along the way you will hear about the good, the bad, the bizarre and the surprising that happened to my family and me. But before I push the Iron Curtain aside for you, a brief lesson in history is in order.

THE FORTIES AND FIFTIES

LONG BEFORE MY TIME

February 1945. At a time when Hitler's armies still hoped that victory might just be possible, Roosevelt, Churchill and Stalin had already agreed on plans about a post-war Germany. During the Yalta Conference the decision was made to demilitarise the country and to divide it into individual zones of occupation. Once the Americans, British, French and Russians settled into their agreed areas, they would extract reparation by taking German assets from within their zones, and sending them to their homelands.

Because the Russians had suffered particularly badly at the hands of the German army, the Soviet Union was very ruthless when payback time finally came. Equity worth six billion Reichsmarks was sent eastwards by the Red Army. Entire factories, 2,000 in total, and nearly 12,000 kilometers of train tracks were disassembled in the process. Having already lost 50 per cent of its industry during the war, the part of the country that was to become the German Democratic Republic seriously struggled to have a future at all.

Germany's west however had only seen 20 per cent of its factories going up in smoke. All three western Allies together removed only 2.7 billion Reichsmarks worth of equity – not even half of what the Russians took. Furthermore, they pumped loans and aid worth billions into their zones. And what did East Germany get from the Soviet Union once the disassembling had stopped? A demand to send free goods. This way our economy lost another 34.7 billion marks over the years.

The beginning of the German Democratic Republic was very humble, but the determination of the people made the impossible possible: when our state vanished in 1990 it was among the 20 industrial leading nations of the world. Some economists even put it among the first ten.

THE IDEAL SOCIETY – ON PAPER

West German ex-chancellor Helmut Kohl led a ten-strong Hitler Youth group during the war, Erich Honecker, communist and East Germany's political leader from 1971 to 1989 on the other hand had spent ten years of his life in a nazi prison. It was precisely that clear break with the past, which made the East German experience of building a new state appealing to many people, especially in the beginning. The idealistic youth saw communism as the answer to all questions – a world of social justice freed from war and misery, a new and fairer society in which exploitation and money had both been abolished. Service before self for everyone.

Take for example an eager brain surgeon and a lazy welder. In communism the brain surgeon would go to the supermarket and say to himself: "Today I have operated on ten people successfully and I have done three hours overtime – I will take a lobster and some asparagus home for dinner. That's what I deserve because I have made a great contribution to society."

But the lazy welder would say to himself: "I was an hour late for work, I only finished half the jobs I was supposed to do and I was rude to my boss – today I will only buy bread and margarine because that's all I deserve."

To get everyone to think that way, after all, the human race has been "corrupted" by money for thousands of years, socialism was invented as a transitional stage – communism with money. Here the working class could try out their newly gained powers of ruling and owing the means of production while the people would metamorphose into altruistic individuals who only have one goal in life: the wellbeing of the society.

We East Germans never managed, which is why our country was stuck in socialism for 40 years – just like all the other east bloc states. Ironically, one of the first things done in East Germany in the process of the creation of this fairer society was to expropriate 14,000 companies and more than three million hectares of land in 1945. Oops!

SPLITTING UP

After the war all of Germany had just one currency. This changed in June 1948 when the western Allies replaced in their zones the old Reichsmark with a newly created currency called Deutschmark. The Russians followed suit and East Germany was given the mark as new currency. With two separate currencies in circulation the separation began to manifest itself.

A year later, on 23 May 1949, the West German state, the Bundesrepublik Deutschland (Federal Republic of Germany) was founded. East Germany's answer was the Deutsche Demokratische Republik (German Democratic Republic), which was officially declared on 7 October 1949. But there was hope on both sides that the two Germanys would soon be united again. And so the first four lines of the DDR national anthem were:

Risen from the ruins
and turned towards the future
let us serve you for the better
Germany, united fatherland.

Alone our politicians' dream of both countries eventually becoming one big socialist state never came true. Since it was even less likely to happen after the Berlin Wall was built in 1961 the lyrics were quickly dropped altogether. From then on our national anthem could be played and hummed but not sung – new lyrics were never written. East German pride had been done no favour with this decision.

MUM'S FAMILY

"We shall not capitulate...no, never. We may be destroyed, but if we are, we shall drag the world with us...a world in flames."

Adolf Hitler

The night sky was lit up like an angry red torch. Yet again the streets of Berlin were transformed into a blazing inferno as allied forces endeavoured once more to bomb Berlin's big train station, Schlesischer Bahnhof. In 1944 it was still a prime target, but it was never hit as the German *Abwehr* (defence) cleverly covered it in smoke during air raids to avoid detection and so once again it was the surrounding houses that were burning instead.

Alone in Berlin while her soldier husband, who had been conscripted a year earlier, was serving far away in Lower Saxony, a woman was struggling to get her two young children out of the danger zone having just lost their home in the air raid.

As she began to herd them past a house consumed by roaring flames, two toddler's arms suddenly grabbed at her legs, forcing her to stop. She looked down to see the anxious face of her three-year-old daughter staring up at her.

"What is it, Lulli? We must go this way."

"No mama no," her toddler insisted.

"But if we don't walk along this street, we must go a long way out of our way to get to safety."

Still Lulli refused to move, and while the woman bent down to lift her in her arms and carry her out of danger the house in front of them collapsed into the street. What had been home to at least ten families just a couple hours previously had turned to nothing but a huge pile of dangerous rubble, glowing red-hot right before their eyes. Had Lulli not refused to go any further, the little family would have been crushed to death, just like the people who had overtaken them during their unplanned stop.

The woman with the little guardian angel was my grandmother and the toddler with the sixth sense was my mum. Before the war finally ended they were to suffer a lot more trauma.

They were to lose their home twice more in the air raids and in the final days of the war my granny came upon her brother's corpse lying in the nearby park. Apparently he had been shot by the SS for not obeying an order, but she never found out the exact circumstances of his death as the only witness to the execution was killed in an air raid just the night before she was due to meet the lady.

But there were some faint rays of light. On my mum's fourth birthday, just a few days before Nazi-Germany finally surrendered she received a present that would last 20 years.

The allied bombers were once again dropping their deadly loads over the battered capital when Nan and the two kids were sheltering in the basement of their apartment building along with all the other tenants. A young German soldier, still half a child himself, took a piece of chalk and drew some gifts for my mum on the walls of the air-raid shelter. What a nice surprise that was for her. Though Mum could not take the presents with her the doll and pram the boy drew were there to stay until the mid-Sixties, when the building was finally renovated and the drawings painted over.

After the war had ended and before joining my grandfather in Lower Saxony, which later became the British Zone, my grandmother had a similar heartwarming encounter, this time with a Russian soldier. Seeing her with two young children in tow, he spontaneously gave her a wad of Reichsmarks. This helped a lot when it came to feeding the hungry mouths over the next couple of months. Other Russians however were anything but generous as my grandfather found out only a couple days later. He was determined to reunite with his family. In Berlin more houses were destroyed than Munich ever had, but he was confident he would find his wife and kids in the battered capital. Nearly 300 kilometres he managed without any incidents. Unfortunately, Grandad was unlucky enough to run into a Russian soldier just a few streets away from were he expected his family to be after they had lost the roof above their heads yet again. Looking down the muzzle of a Kalashnikov, Grandad had no other choice but to hand over his wedding ring. That the soldier promised to use it as part payment for a cow back in Russia hardly made up for the loss. Ever since then my grandfather was not particularly keen on backing the "inviolable friendship with the people of the Soviet Union", as proclaimed by our politicians over and over again. Who could have blamed him?

DAD'S FAMILY

While Mum was dodging falling buildings, Dad had troubles of his own. His family was from Pomerania, a northern part of Poland which used to belong to Germany. They owned a farmstead and were quite happy to stay there for the rest of their lives. But things were about to change.

Relatively early in the war, in 1941, my paternal grandfather was called up and sent straight to the eastern front, where two years later he was captured by the Soviet Army and became a POW. In 1945 at the tender age of four, Dad was about to have his own encounter with what Nazi Propaganda Minister Goebbels had branded the "Mongolian hordes" – the Russians. Even though the soldiers were very friendly to kids, his first memory of them is not a very nice one: Russians, passing through the area on their way to Berlin, nearly shot his grandfather in the courtyard. He had refused to hand over his livestock for nothing.

After the war, in 1947, Poland occupied Pomerania to make up for the land it had to give to Russia in the east, and all Germans who were not prepared to become Polish citizens had to leave their homes behind. Taking with them only whatever they were able to carry. The buttons on Dad's clothes were secretly replaced with fabric-covered silver coins. Everything else of value that could not be taken with them was put into creates or big industrial milk cans and hidden in the nearby swamp. My father's family was transported back to Germany in cattle carriages. The system used to evenly distribute people across the country was as sophisticated as possible at the time: whenever the train stopped in a station a certain number of expellees (or "resettlers" as they were called by East German officials) had to hop off. And so Dad ended up in Saxony, an area in southeast Germany. After living in a camp for a couple of months the family of nine (three kids and six adults), was given a two-bedroom flat. In those days you could not be choosy. They were tough times for many people, including my grandmother. She had to feed her kids and make ends meet without her husband, who was still a prisoner of the Russians. Food was scarce – so scarce, that my father once fainted from hunger in the local bakery.

In 1949 Grandad was released from captivity. Unfortunately, he did not return as a healthy man, and died ten years later. But my father, his brother and sister were happy indeed that they could finally see their father in the flesh – all three were far too young to remember what he had looked like.

Dad enjoyed school and being a smart boy he was even allowed to skip a grade. Yet all his good marks could not change the fact that when he finished school there were hardly any apprenticeships being offered by the companies in his small town. He began working in the nearby piano factory as a junior – a humble start to his successful career as a polisher and cabinet-maker.

BERLIN, THE MAGNET

By the mid-Fifties, my parents were living more than 300 kilometres apart in two different political systems. The chances of them ever meeting were very slim indeed. But things began to change in late 1956 when my maternal grandparents, both Berliners through and through, were fed up with being stuck in a small town far from what they still considered home – Berlin.

For 12 years this little family had lived in a tiny flat that consisted of a small kitchen, a living room and a loo in the courtyard. Things needed to change. Grandad started to look for a place and a job in Berlin; West Berlin to be precise. But the job search there proved difficult and he could not find anything decent, let alone an affordable place to live. So he checked out the job situation in the "Democratic Sector of Berlin" (East Berlin) and was immediately offered a job as a mechanic. Every day, hundreds of people from the Russian occupied zone were leaving their homeland for various reasons, so the communists were very eager to attract people from the west into their sector. In addition to a guaranteed job, East Germany also offered to pay for all removal costs and guaranteed to have a suitable flat ready upon arrival. This and the fact that both my grandparents were true East Berliners by heart (in a location sense), made it an offer they simply could not refuse. And they didn't. In spring 1957 after receiving written confirmation from East Berlin that the move has been authorised, my grandparents packed up their things in the British zone. Grandad accompanied the removal lorry on its way through the occupied zones; Grandma and the kids arrived in Berlin on a bus. Between 1949 and 1961 a total of 620,000 people packed their bags in the west and moved to East Germany.

When the removal lorry reached East Berlin the next day, all West German newspapers inside it were gone. DDR customs must have confiscated them when searching the lorry overnight (importing capitalist newspapers and magazines was forbidden). The two-bedroom flat my grandparents were allocated made up for the loss. The apartment was in good condition and nicely located. It had just been vacated by Joachim Herrmann and his family, a man who went on to become one of the few truly powerful politicians in East Germany. From 1978 to 1989 he was the Politburo member responsible for agitation and propaganda. To top it all, the new home even had a telephone! Unaware that private telephones were a rarity throughout the DDR's existence Grandma foolishly asked for it to be removed to keep the family's outgoings under control for a while. This was a huge mistake only a person coming from the west would have made. It wasn't until in 1990, some 33 years later, and after having been on a waiting list for ten years, that my grandparents again would have a telephone in their apartment.

To settle in, my grandparents were given 100 DDR marks welcome money each. Furthermore, they were issued temporary ID cards. This meant, in case they did not like their new surroundings they could pack up their things and move back to the west at any time – a right the normal East German citizen was denied. But those temporary ID papers also came in handy on other occasions. One day, my grandfather had just thrown a banana peel from a bridge into the river Spree, a grumpy police officer asked him for his ID. The expression on the policeman's face changed as soon as Grandad showed him his papers. In a flash he became friendly, chatty and apologetic – a scene, my grandfather was to witness a few more times. Sadly, three months later the honeymoon-period was over and my grandparents received normal East German papers.

The late Fifties did not only turn Mum's life upside down. After having been approached at work by people promoting a career in the armed forces, Dad felt that he was ready for an adventure. Prepared to leave the small town behind, he voluntarily signed up for a three year service in Berlin. Being able to live and work in Berlin might not sound like a big deal but, unlike Mum's family, the average East German could not just pack up at home, order a lorry and move to the capital. If you wanted to take up residency in Berlin you either had to find someone who wanted to swap flats with you, marry a Berliner/Berlineress, or wait for the city to call on you. Certain professions like construction workers for example, or in my father's case soldiers, were often desperately needed and big recruitment drives brought the necessary people in. The only drawback was that when the employment ended, people usually had to go back to where they came from unless their personal circumstances had changed in the meantime. But Dad was carefree when he stepped down from his army lorry on a hot summer day in Berlin in 1958. He was 18 years young and all he wanted then was to make the most out of his stay in the metropolis.

In the beginning Dad wasn't too impressed with Berlin's level of cleanliness. In any case, he soon found out that being in the army meant that he had to spent most of his time in the barracks, rather than being able to go to places after duty. To guard against a sudden attack on the republic by the enemy, only ten per cent of the country's soldiers were allowed leave at any one time. The rest had to stay put. Though this policy applied to the armed forces right up until the DDR ceased to exist, the irony is that it still did not prevent the state's takeover by West Germany.

During his holidays or on the two afternoons a week when Dad was free to leave the barracks until midnight, he either went dancing, to the pictures or checked out the sights. He did all the things you would expect a teenager to do. Did he also go to West Berlin? No, though the Berlin Wall hadn't been built by then, regular inspections were already carried out in the streets and on trains to West Berlin to prevent smuggling. Soldiers were strictly forbidden to cross the border, an act that could have easily been interpreted as desertion, even if all a soldier wanted in West Berlin was to go to the pictures to see the latest Hollywood production.

The Cold War was already in full swing and East German media regularly quoted West Berlin politicians who called their part of the city the "cheapest nuclear bomb" or the "stake in the flesh of the Soviet zone", in reference to its location right in the middle of the DDR, 150 kilometres away from West Germany. According to DDR newspapers, 80 different espionage and terror organisations resided in the capitalist part of Berlin. Up to half a million people passed the border between the two Berlins each day. Yet any East German soldier caught entering or leaving West Berlin could expect to be court martialled. Dad was not prepared to take this risk. One evening, a friend of his overslept in an overground train and missed the last stop in East Berlin. When he woke up and realised he was in the west he quickly took off his hat and jacket, making sure all DDR insignias and emblems were out of sight. He crouched between the seats and urged fellow passengers to not draw attention to his presence. At the next station he quickly jumped on the first train homewards. He made it back safely – wearing an East German uniform in the west (and vice versa) wasn't a wise thing to do in those days.

East German soldiers kept no civilian clothes in the barracks and so they always had to leave and return to the barracks in their uniforms, which consequently got a lot of wear. The one my father had initially been given was made of the standard thick felt and ill-fitting. His modest upbringing meant he was hardly spoilt, but even so, he wanted to wear a comfortable uniform in his spare time. Dad chose to spend a month's salary to have one tailored for him. My father's decision was triggered by his assignment, during which he was allowed to wear an officer's uniform (which was of better quality) even though he was just a common soldier. He belonged to a guard's regiment where one of his duties was to be an *Ehrenwache* (guard of honour). Him and another soldier had to stand at the entrance to Wilhelm Pieck's, East Germany's only president, working residence, the Palace Niederschönhausen, in the north of Berlin. Not that the president did much work in those days – he was well over 80 years old by then. Every other day he would arrive in his big Russian car to disappear inside the building for an hour or two. If the weather was nice he would go for a walk in the surrounding park with his nurse who, God bless, usually carried some pillows for him in case he decided to sit down somewhere.

Pieck was very popular with the people because of his unpretentious, down-to-earth attitude. It was said that he always had a hammer in one of his desk's draws to remind him that he used to be a carpenter. Regardless of whether that was true or not, my father was proud to work so closely to the country's president.

The downside of this job was that on other occasions he also had to guard the boundaries of the grounds, which was no job for scaredy cats. Picture this: It's night and you're standing guard in the woods in total darkness to somehow ensure that no intruder climbs the wall on the 150-metre-long stretch you are responsible for. To make matters worse, there is no communication link between you and any of the other guards. Dad improved conditions on night duty slightly by taking his private torch with him, but a feeling of unease remained whenever he heard steps nearby. Luckily any person approaching him always turned out to be a fellow comrade rather than an intruder. Once, he fell asleep leaning against a tree while on duty. He woke up minutes before an officer checked whether the guards were bright-eyed and bushy-tailed. Following the standard three-hour-guard/three-hour-sleep routine for 24 hours was very draining, but anyone caught sleeping on duty could not expect leniency.

A couple of months later it was love that made Dad come close to facing disciplinary action. By then he was dating Mum and occasionally at dawn he would help himself to some of the abundant daffodils in the palace garden. DDR florists' hardly ever had cut flowers left in the afternoon and Dad felt that the girl of his dreams deserved something better than pot plants. So once in a while he smuggled presidential daffs in his jacket, first to the guard's house and then, at the end of the day, to the barracks. But on one occasion a passing officer saw the daffodils standing in a vase in the guard's house.

It must have been obvious where they had come from. He immediately asked: "Who do those daffodils belong to?". Dad certainly did not own up and as none of his comrades denounced him either, the officer stormed off in a huff. Half an hour later he was back with a couple of soldiers still demanding answers. The only problem was that by then the floral evidence had disappeared. The soldiers conducted a search for the missing bouquet, but left empty-handed and none the wiser. Yet Mum still got her bunch of daffs that evening – no one had bothered to look inside Dad's spare pair of shiny guard-of-honour-boots.

A regular duty for Dad also was to guard the boundaries of the sealed off area where the DDR's leaders, the members of the government, and members and candidates of the Politburo and their families lived in rented houses that were practically, rather than luxuriously furnished. Though there was an abundance of bodyguards and secret service people patrolling on the gate and inside the compound itself, the surrounding walls and fences were guarded by Dad and his comrades – only ten men at any one time. Every soldier may have had a gun and some ammunition but during daytime their weapons had to be unloaded. None of them would have stood a chance had they ever had to face an armed intruder. Soldiers had to be reasonably good at maths, too. Passwords involved two figures being added up to correspond to a different number that changed daily: A guard hears someone coming his way at night and shouts "17", the invisible person in the darkness replies "Four" and all would be hunky-dory if the number of the day was 21. Anyone replying with a wrong number could easily have found themselves to be the proud owner of a potentially lethal gunshot wound. And what did the guards get in return for their special duty? The only perk that came with protecting the DDR's elite was the ability to visit the grocery shop that supplied the privileged residents and their families. It did not look much different to any of the shops outside the compound, but it did stock a couple of exotic items from other socialist states that at the time weren't available anywhere else in the country. My father still remembers that he bought his first tin of mandarin segments there – it had come all the way from the faraway People's Republic of China.

Mum on the other hand wasn't too impressed with her new *Heimat* (homeland). Sure she had no problems making friends, but it showed that she had spent most of her childhood and teenage life in the west. There individualism, rather than collectivism, was the educational goal, and she found it hard to adapt to the East German way of life. On top of that in the beginning, Mum hardly understood any of the socialist gobbledygook used in the media. And the fact that she stood up for herself if she wasn't happy with something also raised a few eyebrows with some people. Mum had her first confrontation with an East German policeman just a couple of weeks after the move.

She went to her friend Helga, a colleague who had also moved from the west to the east. Reading a West German film magazine (which East German customs officers had failed to spot when snooping around the removal lorry at the border) as she was walking, Mum was approached by a policeman. He was in his early twenties, fairly small and boyish-looking – the kind of person who makes women of any age feel maternal. "Excuse me" the police officer addressed Mum, speaking softly, "Is this a western magazine you are reading?" – "Yes" Mum replied innocently and somewhat bemused. In the west no policeman had ever taken an interest in her reading material. Straightening his jacket and with a slightly firmer voice, the constable informed Mum that according to the laws of the German Democratic Republic the possession of such press was illegal and that he would have to confiscate the magazine. Putting on a smile, Mum held the magazine behind her back and refused to hand it over. "Please hand me the magazine!" she was ordered, yet it sounded more like a plea. Mum still refused and instead replied, "You know what I will do instead? This!". She hadn't even finished the last word when she began ripping up the film mag. "Do you still want it?" she offered the constable the torn pieces with both hands. He didn't. So Mum threw the pieces to the ground and walked off. But the policeman still must have had an interest in the ripped up glossy. When Mum checked out the "crime-scene" ten minutes later with her friend Helga, the magazine's remains were gone. Only in Berlin could a publication that was legally sold in one part of the city cause such a stir in the other part.

In the rest of the republic, the border to the west had already been closed and guarded since 1952. In Berlin however, and only due to its allied status, people were still free to cross between the two sides as they pleased. In 1957 more than 150,000 East Germans pretended to just visit West Berlin when really they had no intention to return – leaving the country illegally was a punishable offence called *Republikflucht* (fleeing the republic). It attracted a prison sentence of up to three years. But far more common than emigrating was smuggling. It is estimated that approximately 200,000 marks worth of goods were smuggled to the west every year. Yet in 1958 alone, DDR customs confiscated, among other things, 213,000 eggs and 47,000 kilos of meat that were destined to be sold illegally in West Berlin markets.

By the late Fifties West Germany was meeting most consumer needs, while East Germany was concentrating its efforts and limited financial resources on building its infrastructure and establishing industries. Production of consumer goods was important too, but for the time being it wasn't a priority. Naturally this led to shortages or inferior quality items. So what did people do? They went to West Berlin and bought what they needed – whether it was zippers, oranges or pantyhoses. The money for these shopping sprees was supplied by West Berlin's bureaux de change. East Germans, who earned much less than their West German counterparts, got there one Deutschmark for four, five or sometimes even ten DDR marks which they had to smuggle out. Quite a rip-off but what could one do about it? Most people accepted that they just had to be very selective when going shopping in West Berlin.

Because my grandparents had brought a couple of hundred Deutschmarks with them when moving, they never had to resort to smuggling money or goods from the east to the west in those days before the Wall was built. If one of the kids had a cold, Nanna could easily afford to go to the west and buy a few lemons, which then were nearly impossible to get in the DDR. Or she would buy apricots, plums or bananas to boost the family's vitamin intake whenever fruit was in short supply in the east. The west was good for just window shopping, too. Mum's wedding dress looked exactly like one she had seen in a West Berlin shop, but thanks to my grandmother, a seamstress by trade, it was a lot more affordable than the original.

But travelling between the two political systems also had its risks. One day my grandma and my mum were on one of their fruit purchasing trips, sitting on an overground train going westwards. As usual at the border, customs officers walked through the carriages to check a few bags here and there. Nothing suspicious was found. But when the train approached the first station in the west, the friendly couple sitting opposite them suddenly reached under Grandma's and Mum's seat to fish out a sewing machine, and a plump bag that contained God knows what. Had the customs officers spotted the contraband, no one in the carriage would have admitted possession of the items and it would most likely have been Mum and Nanna who would have been frogmarched out of the train. Smugglers were considered to be saboteurs, willing tools of the enemy and if caught they could expect a heavy fine or prison sentence.

Though Mum wasn't into bootlegging, she knew some people who regularly earned West German Deutschmarks on the side by smuggling geese. Bought cheaply in East Berlin, the birds were either hidden in the pram (with the baby in it) or in their older daughter's doll's pram and sold for good money in the west. Others did not bother with peanuts like that and instead took up a job in West Berlin. A friend of the family was one of those guys. While Mum slaved away six days a week in the East Berlin factory he only worked two days a week in West Berlin. But because he exchanged all his earnings into DDR marks at an inflated exchange rate he always ended up with twice as much money as her at the end of the month. How unfair was that? Up to 60,000 East Germans worked in West Berlin but continued to benefit from subsidised prices as well as free education and health service in the DDR. Supporting these people cost our economy annually 2.5 billion marks (one billion dollars). Many DDR citizens thought that something needed to be done to put a stop to this abuse. Fellow countrymen working in the west were viewed as parasites, just like benefits cheats are today. But the real problem for the DDR was the constant flow of people leaving the country westwards – around 560 refugees every single day in 1958 alone, 2.7 million people between 1949 and 1961. The DDR government had to act, sooner or later, if it did not want the country to bleed to death.

THE SIXTIES

DANCING THE NIGHT AWAY

One year after Mum had started her job in the East Berlin clothing factory Fortschritt (Progress), a few of her friends persuaded her to join the company's folk dancing group. Like Fortschitt, many corporations had *Kulturpläne* (cultural plans) in place, which were defined as "working programmes for the planned furtherance of communal and individual activities to systematically increase the cultural and educational level of socialist personalities". Usually, the bigger an enterprise was, the more money they spent on supporting cultural activities within their organisation, where like-minded employees could get together and express their creativity. Culture for the people, by the people. There were choirs, groups for painters, photographers or film makers and, in my mum's case, a folk dance troupe, where 20 boys and girls in their late teens and early twenties learned traditional dances that they would perform in pensioners' clubs, retirement homes or at the company's own Christmas parties. Once the weekly training session had finished, the whole group would go to the Musikbox (Jukebox), a nearby bar, where to sounds from a jukebox, more modern dances were performed. All in all, the dancers enjoyed each other's company, and my mother was quite happy to have found so many friends in such a short time.

Unfortunately, the socialist machinery was out to spoil the fun for Mum in an episode that left her with a bitter aftertaste: One day the FDJ-*Sekretär*, the company's representative of the communist youth organisation, asked her during working hours into his office. He offered Mum a seat in one of his comfy armchairs and some sparkling wine before asking her: "Wouldn't you be interested in joining the FDJ, the Free German Youth?" Mum, never having heard of this organisation replied that she would think about it and get back to him – hoping he would forget about it. He didn't. After a couple of weeks, he asked her again to see him. This time she had to see him after work and was only offered a cup of tea. Wanting to be left alone Mum made it clear that she wasn't interested in being politically active: "I have no intentions of joining any organisation," was her straightforward reply as she left, thinking that this was the end of the matter. It wasn't. A couple of days later the representative wanted her to see him again. This time she was not offered a drink, nor a seat but given a "choice": "Become a member of the Free German Youth or leave the folk dancing group." Mum wanted to stay with the troupe, so she joined the youth organisation.

Once in, Mum hardly was a model member. She and Gisela, one of her friends, were chosen one day by the very same FDJ-*Sekretär* to (illegally) distribute propaganda leaflets in West Berlin. At first, the two girls were quite enthusiastic when stuffing the fliers into people's letterboxes, but after having done a few apartment blocks the excitement quickly faded and both became increasingly bored and tiered. "Sod it" they said to themselves, dumped the leaflets and went into a nearby department store instead. After her friend had stolen some ornate buttons from an expensive coat on sale (East German buttons were far too plain for those teenagers who wanted to look different) they called it a day and went back home. The next day, Mum and her friend were praised for having done such a marvellous job distributing the leaflets and though both had to stifle their laughter throughout the eulogy, they were not caught out. Eight months later Mum finally had enough – she quietly stopped paying her monthly membership fee and never heard from a Free German Youth official ever again.

Joining the Free German Youth hadn't been a totally pointless waste of time for my mother, though. In fact it turned out to be the best decision she ever made – it was because she was able to stay in the dancing circle that she was about to meet Dad. For a few months the group had a severe shortage of men. The majority of the guys in the factory had no interest in joining, so the troupe had to look elsewhere for suitable young and fit men. In late summer of 1959 a "Looking for..." note went up on the notice board in Dad's barrack. He could not see himself prancing around on a stage in costumes, but his army buddy Herman, convinced Dad to give it a go. Also was the additional evening leave to attend rehearsals and performances not to be sniffed at. So he joined the group, and once the good-looking blonde there had caught his eye, he knew for sure that he had made the right decision.

Mum, still blond and beautiful to that day, had naturally noticed the newcomer's interest in her but did not feel it necessary to rush things. Many boys had made advances to her but she wanted more than awkward kisses and a quick fumble. Commitment and trust were more important to her. Assuming that anyone interested in one thing only would quickly lose interest if no progress was being made, Mum played the patience game. This way the cowboys were separated from the gentlemen.

After weeks of obvious mutual attraction Mum finally allowed Dad to bring her home one evening. Dad was a bit surprised to see his dream girl quickly covering her mouth as he tried to plant a goodnight kiss on her lips. Yet the shyness did not bother him. He was happy to wait and to prove that his intentions were genuine. On the ensemble's New Year's Eve trip in 1959 Mum finally lowered her defences. The whole group had gone down south, where many fell ill with food poisoning, Mum being one of them. It might have been the worst New Year's Eve she ever had, but seeing how caring Dad was had finally convinced her that he was indeed the knight in shining armour she had been waiting for. That evening, he got his kiss. My parents engaged in 1960 after the return from a folk dance festival and married a year later. They are happily married ever since. Hip, Hip, Hooray!

A DAY TO REMEMBER

"To stop the hostile activities of...militaristic powers in West Germany and West Berlin, such control will be introduced on the borders of the German Democratic Republic, including...Berlin, as it is common in...every sovereign state. It is to warrant on the West Berlin border a reliable guard and effective control... As long as West Berlin is not transformed into a demilitarised neutral Free City, citizens of the capital of the German Democratic Republic will require special permissions to cross those borders. Visits to the capital of the German Democratic Republic (the democratic Berlin) by peaceful West Berlin citizens are possible."

Law Gazette Part II Number 51

This resolution was published on 13 August 1961 after 14,500 armed and uniformed men had started to secure the border to West Berlin shortly after two am. The few hand-picked workers who had printed the public announcement posters the previous day had been kept in custody after their shift had finished to stop them revealing the government's intentions early.

Sunday 13 August 1961 promised to be just another nice day. It was eight o'clock in the morning, most of the night's clouds had already cleared and Dad, on weekend leave from the army until Monday morning, had a bit of a lay-in with Mum who by then was seven months pregnant with my brother. Once more they were talking excitingly about how life would be different once the baby had arrived. Then Mum got up to quickly pop over the road to buy the daily milk in the corner shop – in those days fridges were luxury items. My parents could not afford one. While my father started to lay the table and to prepare breakfast, my mother quickly threw on a cardigan, grabbed the empty milk-can and nipped out. But once in the street Mum did not go very far. Something just wasn't right out there.

My parents' flat was 500 metres away from the border to West Berlin. Not only was the street leading to the west completely sealed off but also the side streets were filled with tanks. The whole area was buzzing with uniformed members of the *Kampfgruppen* (Fighting Groups), a paramilitary organisation of volunteers who were supposed to protect factories and public institutions in war-like situations. Was war to break out? Milk was now the last thing on Mum's mind. Storming back into the flat, or at least as much as a heavily pregnant woman is capable of storming, she asked Dad to quickly switch the little transistor radio on. Glued to the loudspeaker they both listened to a few of the many special announcements made throughout the day informing everyone that with the exception of 13 checkpoints the border to West Berlin had been sealed off. East Germany hailed the stunt as a guarantor of peace in Europe, West Germany condemned it as an act of imprisonment. The truth probably lay somewhere in the middle and many East Germans liked to hear both sides of a story.

Thankfully my parents were not that much effected by the closing of the border. Neither of them had immediate relatives in the west. But what was going to happen next? Would the Americans feel their allied rights had been violated? Were they going to send tanks to tear the barriers down? How would the Russians retaliate if such an attempt was being made? Whichever way you looked at it, the whole thing seemed to spell one thing: W-A-R. Mum and Dad quickly had a bite to eat, and then left their flat to go to my grandparents' place – my mother wanted to be together with her family in such an uncertain time. While catching the nearby tram my parents saw that the streets of East Berlin were fairly deserted. Most people out there were gathering around the specially printed public announcement posters, nodding in agreement as they read through the text. Hardly anyone spoke. Though there were some protests in East Berlin close to the border, with people demanding to be let through to the west, my parents only witnessed one heated discussion between two men, gesticulating wildly.

But they also spotted the occasionally odd person (usually males in their twenties) carrying a couple of suitcases heading hastily in the general direction of the border. First it did not register with Mum and Dad what was happening there. Only when a very distressed woman in her forties was struggling down the street with two oversized bags, wearing a fur coat in the height of the Berlin summer, did it finally click. By four pm 800 East Germans had managed to make it across the frontier. It took our authorities a few days to discover and block all secret paths to the west.

Gloom was in the air. East Berliners feared the day's events were about to start a military conflict between east and west. So the majority of them stayed home – just in case. And whoever wasn't listening or watching the news hovered around their house entrance and asked passers-by for their eyewitness account. As soon as Mum and Dad had walked into the stairwell in my grandparent's apartment block, a woman from one of the two ground floor flats quickly emerged. "So, what's happening in the streets?" she asked. My parents calmed her down and continued their way up, only to have the same encounter with one of the first floor neighbours. As they finally reached my grandparents' flat there was relief on both sides. Mum and Dad had made it without being caught up in riots or any military action. My grandparents were the first ones in their building to have a TV set. After lunch everyone, including the next-door neighbours, gathered around the box and watched the latest political developments unfolding. By the evening 193 roads and 48 train stations had been sealed and the Cold War still hadn't turned into a hot one. Relieved, my parents went home to get on with their lives.

It seems odd that at no stage was Dad ordered back to the barracks on that Sunday. Instead he was able to continue his leave until Monday morning as planned, while the armed forces up were practically in a combat-ready state. Wasn't he worth calling on? Maybe he wasn't considered trustworthy enough because his wife had grown up in the west.

Whatever the reason, my father was quite glad he didn't have to stand in the front line. But his joy was short lived. Only a couple weeks later he too had to contribute to the erection of what DDR officials publicly called *Antifaschistischer Schutzwall* (Antifascist Protection Rampart), known to everyone as *die Mauer* – the Wall. Though this straightforward name is very deceptive. There was more to this structure than just a single wall (we are talking German efficiency here). It started in many places in the early hours of 13 August 1961 with nothing more than some hastily unreeled lines of barbed wire attached to quickly erected stakes. Sometimes even just soldiers standing next to each other and forming a human wall. But all that would develop into a nearly impenetrable structure with signalling fences, watch towers, dog guarded sections and ditches, all sandwiched between two approximately four-metre high concrete walls on either side. In the final stages of Berlin's division, the border fortifications were so well lit at night, apparently they could be seen from space.

But the first generation of the *Mauer* was very basic indeed. In fact so basic, that on their weekend walks in autumn that year at some places my parents were still able to get fairly close to the fence marking the actual borderline. People just strolled alongside it. Mum however, rebellious as ever, liked to tease the border guards. She would stop, stand really close to the fence and wave at an imaginary friend in the west. At that time it was quite popular for separated families to meet at a certain time near the border and just wave at each other. Our border police did not like this custom one bit. They never used to say anything to my mother whenever she provoked them in this way, responding only with foul looks. Once, though, a border guard barked at her: "Move on please!". Finally Mum's time had come. She looked him in the eyes, said loudly "Yeah, yeah, keep your bloomers on." and strutted off. Mum was never to be spoken to by a guard again.

In early September 1961 it was Dad's turn to work on the border fortifications. His army unit was ordered onto lorries and driven to a stretch of the frontier nearby. They had to dig a ditch parallel to the borderline and put some anti-tank barriers up. West Berliners waved their fists in anger at the soldiers or took pictures of them working. If someone in the west was too persistent with their camera, the soldiers had fun by getting a mirror out and temporarily blinding the person with the sun's reflection. And thankfully that was as violent as it ever got during my father's brief stay at the border. He did not witness any desertions, and no shootings. Neither did any of his army friends seem to think: "Oh my God, we've walled ourselves in."

The truth is that for the majority of the East Germans, who were fairly happy with their life and had no intentions of fleeing, the Berlin Wall came as a relief. Now things could improve in the DDR: no more doctors heading off to the west and leaving their patients behind, no more missing workers slowing down the production of much needed goods and no more external acts of sabotage to the economy. The Sixties were a time when most DDR citizens still believed that as well as being progressive and socially fairer, their country would one day also become the economically stronger of the two Germanys. Yes, those were the days were everything seemed possible.

I AM BORN

"It is the right and chief duty of the parents to bring up their children as healthy and life accepting, proficient and universally educated people – as patriotic citizens."

GDR constitution Section 2, Chapter 1, Article 38

September 1967 was a warm autumn month. A lazy sun threw long shadows onto East Berlin's streets. On one afternoon, Mum shut the door on the family's oven heated, one-bedroom flat in the Greifswalder Street and took my six-year-old brother to celebrate her father's fifty-seventh birthday.

Mum had a jolly good time at my grandparents' place, which must have made me curious about the outside world, because as soon as she got home she went into labour with me.

I got my bottom slapped at 2:55 the following morning. Nationality: German, Citizenship: DDR – would my ID card later state. When Dad saw me for the first time being held by a nurse on the maternity ward he tapped his finger gently on the glass that separated us. I immediately began wobbling my little head trying to find out where the noise was coming from. It looked like I was destined for a career in the secret service.

Eleven days later Dad picked Mum and me up. I looked absolutely ridiculous as we headed home. Being a big boy (with a birth weight of 4.5 kilos and a height of 57 centimetres), my jacket and hat did not fit and had to be laid on top of me. At least none of the baby-girls saw me half dressed like this.

Thankfully between my brother's birth, six years earlier, and mine, life for DDR citizens had changed for the better. In 1961 Mum had to bribe a shop assistant 20 marks (eight dollars) just to be considered the next time a delivery of prams was being received. Colour and style could not be chosen. In 1967, my parents looked in four or five shops before finding a pram they liked. Politicians had done their homework and were by then paying more attention to the production of consumer goods to keep the masses happy.

VITAMIN C

Food wise, the situation had also improved since the early Sixties. If in 1962 Mum had to buy packets of soup vegetables just to get hold of carrots for my brother, in 1967 vegetables were freely available. It was also helpful that one of our neighbours was the guy who owned the greengrocer's around the corner. A tip now and then, and me looking at him with my big saucer-eyes, ensured that we were getting our vitamins not just from the omnipresent apples but also from bananas and oranges.

Having the right connections in East Germany meant that you could nearly get everything – provided you could afford to bribe people or repay their favours with other sought-after goods. Anyone else had to rely on family members or friends being in charge of distributing services or goods. Knowing the right people was called having "Vitamin B" – the B standing for *Beziehungen*, which means connections, so in English it could have been "Vitamin C". One popular saying was: Socialism without connections is like capitalism without money. That sums it up nicely.

BATTLING THE BUREAUCRATS

If all the friendliness, tips and connections failed to get you what you wanted, a GDR citizen had two powerful weapons at his disposal. One was to write a complaint to a more powerful institution, like a ministry.

Another, and probably more fearsome, weapon was to threaten government bodies with the refusal to vote on election day. Not that it mattered much whether one voted or not, as throughout the existence of the DDR election results always turned out to be 99.something per cent. But refusal to vote, or even just the threat of refusal, worried local officials. They had to meet targets for voter participation and so had an interest in making sure that as many people as possible in their district went to the polls on election day. Sorting out a voter's previously ignored problem suddenly was the lesser evil.

However, threatening not to vote was a very drastic step to take and not done willy-nilly. It could easily make you look like a troublemaker and even might have put an end to your climb up the career ladder. So the underlying problem that would lead to a person making such a threat would have to be very serious. It wasn't enough just to be unhappy with the selection of fresh fish in your local supermarket. It had to be caused by something like an unsuitable place to live, politically motivated unhappiness or perhaps a lack of refusal by the authorities to grant permission to attend your grandmother's funeral in West Germany.

Mum once wrote a complaint to Walter Ulbricht, who was the leader of our Communist Party back in the early Sixties and then the most powerful man in the country. She was eight months pregnant with my brother and my parents felt that the one bed- cum living room flat with a leaky roof was neither spacious enough nor the right environment for two adults and an infant. So Mum went to the local housing office, since the majority of flats in apartment blocks were managed and distributed by government bodies. The member of staff she spoke to immediately rejected her request for a bigger place. Mum asked to see the manager. She should not have bothered. He told her rather rudely:

"As far as I'm concerned you can sit there until you give birth – you will not get another flat."

My mother threatened in return: "If you are not prepared to help me then I will have to send photos of the poor living conditions in our flat to West German magazines. Maybe that will bring the desired results."

"You should be careful of what you are saying," came the ominous reply.

Fed up with the treatment she had received, Mum decided to write a letter to Walter Ulbricht. But as many people decided to write directly to the top dog, only a few complaints actually made it to Ulbricht's desk. Aides forwarded the majority of letters for actioning to regional offices.

A few weeks later, Mum was invited back to the Housing Office. She was met by a rather nasty woman in her fifties.

"Mrs Fritz," she said triumphantly, "You can write to whoever you want but in the end your letters will come back to me. I am the one distributing the available flats and I can tell you that you will not be considered."

But did that discourage my mother? Far from it. Instead, she started to visit the housing office on a weekly basis and wrote another complaint letter. This time to the head of the district council who, obviously fed up with such a querulous person, advised her in his reply to have a look at a flat in the Greifswalder Strasse which was about to become vacant. And twelve months after her initial request Mum had finally succeeded. Her little family moved into a bigger flat that did not have a leaking roof – if you wanted results, patience and determination were the two most beneficial virtues a DDR citizen could posses.

TIME WARP

The rent for this hard-won one-bedroom flat, where I learnt to walk and spent the first five years of my life, was 46 marks (18 dollars). To put this into perspective, my father's monthly salary at the time was 570 marks (228 dollars), which was about the average wage in the late Sixties. As the GDR was a state ruled by the working class, blue-collar workers like my father were only taxed five per cent of their earnings, whereas white-collar workers had to cough up 20 per cent income tax. So much for socialism being the fairer society!

But regardless of the tax rules, the rents were incredibly cheap for all because they were frozen at a 1936 (pre-inflationary) level. Just like the prices for coal, gas, water, basic food and transportation. Set in the late Fifties, these prices stayed the same for 30 years! A single bus, tram or underground ride cost an adult 20 pfennigs (kids paid half that amount) in 1959, and it cost the same thirty years later when the Wall fell. The price for a kilogram wheat and rye loaf remained constant over the years at 1.05 mark (42 cents) and a bread roll was always a snip with its price tag of five pfennigs, even though in 1989 it cost ten pfennigs to make.

Most of our politicians grew up under capitalism in poor living conditions with food being scarce and parents worrying how to pay the rent. So the thinking behind this rather uneconomical pricing policy was that in socialism no one should need to worry about being unable to afford food or rent, regardless of the costs to the state.

"Marx discovered...the simple fact that people have to eat, drink... and dress first before they can go into politics, science, the arts or religion."

Friedrich Engels

On a rainy evening in autumn 1968 after having been out shopping with Mum, who had spent some of the 700 marks (280 dollars) she had received from the government for giving birth, the doorbell rang. It was a neighbour who was a member of the Communist Party and he wanted to talk to Dad, who was ill with a cold. When Mum wanted to know what the visit was about, she was told: "I don't have to tell you that. In fact, I could even ask you to leave the flat while I am talking to your husband." Now, that was too much! For seconds Mum was lost for words. But she gained her speech back quickly and gave the guy a good piece of her mind: "I don't believe what I have just heard. You want me to leave my own flat? That will be the day!" The neighbour was thrown out and avoided Mum ever since. She could live with that.

The Communist Party – the Sozialistische Einheitspartei Deutschlands (United Socialist Party of Germany) was the biggest party. It had more than two million members. Nearly every eighth citizen was a "comrade", as party members addressed each other officially. The other four DDR parties were: the National Democrats, the Liberal Democrats, the Christian Democrats and the Farmer's Party.

The SED was running the country. Every individual with real political, economical or military power belonged to it, or rather, had to belong to it. The Communist Party held 60 per cent of the seats in the parliament. To keep it that way, its leading role was written in the constitution:

"The German Democratic Republic is a socialist state of the workers and farmers. She is the political organisation of the working population... under the leadership of the working class and its Marxist-Leninist Party."

Allowing the other parties to exist was supposedly living proof that the Deutsche Demokratische Republik was indeed what its name suggested – democratic. And even though none of the other parties was able, or at that time willing, to change the political status quo, they still served a purpose: giving people the opportunity to be politically active without too much surrounding communist hoo-ha. The National Democrats in particular attracted people with titles – dukes and counts (yes we had them too). Master craftsmen, private business owners and the intelligentsia usually joined the Liberal Democrats. However, if you wanted to further your career in any of the state-owned companies, you had no choice but to become a member of the SED.

But at the age of two or three I had other things on my mind than politics. Having mastered the skill of walking without falling over, I wanted to discover the world and play with my toys.

What did I care that in 1969 Cambodia under Prince Sihanouk ignored West Germany's policy to withdraw its ambassador from any country which recognised the DDR and that Cambodia became the first non-communist country to take up diplomatic relations with the state I was living in? Or that our brand-new second TV station occasionally transmitted in colour – the TV set my parents had bought the same year for nearly 2,000 marks (800 dollars) was only a black and white model. Mind you, the 365-metre tall TV tower that opened in the heart of East Berlin, also in 1969, to mark the twentieth birthday of our republic was a magnet for people. I don't think any other building in the country had a revolving café, let alone such magnificent views over West Berlin.

When I began talking I invented my own language, where money was "ebt" and chocolate was "rarara" For hours I would babble away to Püppi, my sleeping doll. Dad had bought it for me when once I had a nasty cold and felt very poorly. But 1969 was a hard time for him as well, because he was working at daytime and studying in the evenings. My father was relieved when evening school finished in 1970 and he was handed his managerial degree. Finally he could get more responsibility and a better pay package. The company he was employed by specialised in prestigious interior wood furnishings, decorations and floors and mainly carried out work in hotels and public buildings. They were regularly called in on to improve the interiors of the three most important buildings in the German Democratic Republic – the Central Committee Building, the State Council Building and the complex of the Ministry of State Security (secret service), the Stasi.

The Central Committee Building, once the headquarters of the German Reichsbank, was, as the name indicates, the building where the Central Committee of the United Socialist Party of Germany (SED) resided. The highest authority of the SED strangely was an event – the Party Conference – which took place every four to five years. The Central Committee's purpose was to make sure all resolutions made at the conferences were realised. But really powerful were only 20 odd people (numbers varied over time): the Politburo. Its members were running the country and included the General Secretary of the Central Committee, the Minister of State Defence, the Chairman of the Cabinet Council (the Prime Minister), the Minister of National Defence, the President of the People's Chamber and other high ranking officials. And in case you wondered, the People's Chamber was neither the prison service nor a chain of public lavatories, but East Germany's parliament. Every Tuesday this illustrious group of Politburo members got together to deal with the country's latest problems. On the agenda was anything and everything from the seasonal price of cauliflower to whether it was wise to agree to a particular UN resolution. The government only followed the Politburo's decisions.

When external workmen were needed in the "Big House", as people called the Central Committee Building, companies had to prepare lists with workers names before a project was to commence. Those lists were checked by the secret service. Sometimes workers had to be replaced. But, all in all, security was not as tight as you might imagine.

When Dad turned up at the Central Committee Building in the mornings, he had to hand over his ID card to the uniformed porter, who cross-checked his name against a list and issued him a visitor pass for the building. But his bag, for example, was never searched. Nor were there any metal detectors for visitors to walk through. When Dad left the building in the evening he just had to collect his ID card and was free to leave, once again without a bag search. A normal pass gave him access to the entire building, except the second floor, where the members of the Politburo had their offices and meeting rooms. If work was to be done there, he was given a pass with a diagonal red stripe. But he never saw any of the Big Shots as renovating was always done when the country's elite was not around. One thing Dad was quite surprised about when he went to the Central Committee Building for the first time was that the whole place looked disappointingly plain. There were dark corridors due to the lack of natural light, lino floors and mismatched office furniture for the employees. Naturally the corridors, offices and assembly rooms for the Politburo were more comfortable, with their light-coloured carpets and wood panelling, but by no means could they be described as luxurious – functional would be more apt.

One might think my father and his colleagues were constantly guarded while working on the Politburo's floor, but this wasn't the case. They had to show their building passes a second time to enter this executive floor but, once in, they could do whatever they wanted. When Dad's *Brigade* (team) was putting wood panels on the walls in one of the assembly rooms, some security person would pop his head in the door once in a while to check that everything was alright. Yet no one watched the workers permanently. It would have been so easy for any of them to put a listening device or a mini bomb behind one of the panels, because once those were fixed, they were fixed for good – after all, we are talking here about German workmanship.

My father particularly liked working at the Central Committee Building because of a little grocery and bookshop inside which were both preferentially supplied. One day he brought home a copy of the much sought-after *Struwwelpeter* (Slovenly Peter), a kid's book of 150-year-old cautionary tales, which was hard to get. I particularly liked looking at the old-fashioned illustrations. A highlight always was if one of my parents red me a bedtime story from the book. Sweet memories! Just like the ones of Dad coming home with chocolate tree decorations from the Central Committee grocery shop in the run-up to Christmas. Rare to find in the high street sweet shops the two pounds of decorated chocolate rings he usually bought never lasted very long.

The security procedures in the complex of the Ministry of State Security (secret service) and the State Council Building were the same as in the Central Committee Building. Mysteriously, some of the assembly rooms in the Ministry of State Security could not be closed or opened from the inside, as the doors only had (West German!) door handles on the outside.

The State Council Building on the other hand was home to a weird institution – the Staatsrat, (State Council). The first East German president (Dad was his guard of honour during his National Service) died in 1960, and it was decided that his role as Head of State would not continue. Copying the Russians a collective organ – the Staatsrat – was founded. Now a total of 22 people, elected every five years, could all call themselves Head of State. What were they thinking to come up with such a daft idea? In the end common sense prevailed. One person was chosen to officially represent the DDR, and given the title of Chairman of the State Council.

The State Council Building was the place where foreign dignitaries were welcomed, citizens honoured and diplomats schmoozed. The floors and wall panels were made with proper wood veneer – none of that cheap wood effect laminate used in so many other buildings. The veneer needed to be refurbished on a regular basis, so my father and his colleagues were often called in to work in the building. What they always looked forward to with anticipation was having lunch in the State Council's canteen. Dad's company did not have a kitchen and the meals there, delivered in big containers by an out-house catering firm, often arrived too early or with open lids. At lunchtime workers were regularly served lukewarm schnitzels or meatloaves. And even when a meal was still hot it was nothing to boast about. The machines peeling the potatoes usually missed little areas, vegetables had a tendency to be overcooked and the gravy always tasted artificial. Having lunch in the State Council building on the other hand was almost like eating in a self-serve restaurant. There was a choice of three main courses as well as various starters and desserts on offer. The in-house kitchen cooked fresh meals that looked and tasted yummy. Whether it was goulash with red cabbage and dumplings, fried liver with onion and rosti or carrot hotpot Dad always had a look at other people's steaming white plastic plates first before deciding what to go for. If he was lucky there was even a peach or an orange for dessert. If not, he was quite happy to settle for a rice pudding with applesauce or a chocolate blancmange with custard. But not only were the meals on offer there of a higher quality, they were also much cheaper than elsewhere in the country.

At one mark (40 cents), lunch in my dad's company was hardly exorbitant, but in the State Council Building, where the average salary was much higher, a meal only cost 70 pfennigs (28 cents). Somehow this did not seem right but it was hardly the thing to start a revolution over.

One day Dad was in the building there was a big hoo-ha. A colleague was working in a conference room and busy with an electric saw near a newly installed doorframe when accidentally cutting the utility cables running underneath it. The moment this was reported to the Building Supervisor, the place was swarming with security people. The poor guy wasn't quite whisked to the Ministry of State Security for questioning, but he had to do a lot of explaining about how the incident happened. In a situation like this the worst case scenario was almost always assumed – sabotage.

There were other, less serious, incidents. Once a 20-something year-old greenhorn, Udo, who worked in my father's team, discovered that the soap in the building's bathrooms was not a DDR brand, but imported from the "enemy of the working class", as capitalists were called by our propaganda. He grabbed the bar of Lux soap, and showed it to all his workmates, loudly expressing his surprise that domestically manufactured soaps were obviously not good enough for the delicate skins of DDR politicians.

Many people in the building heard his comments but nothing happened as a result of his big mouth. However, that changed later in the week when Udo did something very surreal.

He decided it would be super cool to pretend to be a stuntman and to fall down the red-carpet-covered stairs in the main entrance hall. Crouching behind the metal handrail, shooting with his fingers at an imaginary enemy and shouting things like "Boom", "Take that, bastard" and "Gotcha" he finally rolled down the most prestigious flight of stairs in the whole country.

The workers had a good laugh but the next day Dad's company got a call from a clerk in the State Council, requesting Udo to be replaced by someone else. They did not want to see him there ever again. Fair enough, Buckingham Palace would probably have done the same to one of its contractors. But what is worth mentioning is that under no circumstances would Udo have lost his job as a result of that joke. The "Right of Work" was constitutionally guaranteed:

"Every citizen of the German Democratic Republic has the right to work. He has the right to a working place and its free choice in accordance with social requirements and his personal qualifications."

Impressed? Sure, it's truly progressive stuff. Which western government would be prepared to guarantee work for everyone? But before we all go onto the streets and start demonstrating for the resurrection of the DDR, let's have a look at the second paragraph of this particular section:

"Socially useful activity is an honourable duty for every able-bodied citizen. The right to work and the duty to work form one unity."

We East Germans did not only have the right but also the duty to work. Of course, no one forced the average housewife to take up a job but work-shy people were classified as *asozial* (antisocial). Their "endangering of the social harmony and public order" usually led to the imposition of a range of educational measures. Most popular was "work education" – a closed environment where individuals were supposed to learn the necessity of earning a living by means of work.

Thank God, at the age of three I already had a very clear idea of what I wanted to be as a grown up. Actually I came up with two, equally liked, jobs, which unfortunately, due to their rather unconventional nature, never materialised. East Germany followed the international practice by not recognising "Prince" and "Black Guy" as professions. Bastards!

THE SEVENTIES

A QUICK BUCK

In the early 1970s the DDR government introduced a number of changes that signalled an improvement in the lives of many East Germans. In 1971 the telephone lines between the two parts of Berlin were de-blocked for the first time, since August 1961. Berliners could now stay in touch much easier with friends or relatives in the other part of the city. When Erich Honecker took over as party leader in the same year, his concern was "the happiness of the people". At the Eighth Party Conference in June 1971 he declared the "unity of economic and social policy", meaning that the material and cultural living standard of the people should be increased by shorter working hours, more holiday entitlement, higher salaries and pensions, and by building lots of new flats. What a programme!

This was definitely good news for everyone, including the Fritz family, whose living standard dramatically increased in early 1973 as a direct result of this new policy. But before this came about, we had to adapt first to a few changes in 1972.

Many East (and West) Germans who live in apartment blocks in cities, have and had an allotment. Ours was off the beaten track near the Leninallee (Lenin Boulevard) in the borough of Weissensee. As in the UK, the German tradition of allotments too goes back to the early twentieth century, when the labouring poor received small parcels of land to grow their own food. However unlike in the UK, Germans are allowed to have little houses on their allotments. DDR citizens collectively enjoyed heading to their beloved bungalows and gardens on the weekends. Here they could relax, be with Mother Nature and grow their own flowers, fruit and vegetables. In 1984, two million hobby gardeners managed 124,000 acres of soil. This wasn't necessarily a lot, considering that 15 million acres of land were being farmed commercially. But when the DDR ceased trading five years later, 50 per cent of its population had an allotment!

People could also benefit financially from their land by selling produce to the wholesale trade. On summer and autumn weekends, nearly all of the allotment areas had places where gardeners could bring their excess fruit and vegetables to be weighed and exchanged for cash. This way, people were encouraged to help the state supply the masses with a variety of foods. In the Eighties, 13 per cent of all vegetables and 22 per cent of all fruit sold in our shops was supplied by private gardeners. When I was older, I regularly increased my pocket money this way. One year I collected and dried rosehips which I sold to a pharmacy, another year I gleaned green beans walking behind the harvesting machine on a field of an agricultural co-op, which I then sold to our local supermarket. Naturally there was a difference between the purchase and the retail price, but not in the way a capitalist consumer might think. The same green beans that I sold at the goods entrance I could have bought back five minutes later in the same shop for a fraction of the money I had been paid! One year I made a killing with tomatoes this way. Any of the 15,000 weighing stations paid ten marks (four dollars) for a kilo. In the shops a kilo tomatoes only cost a fiver. Another year I profited from selling gooseberries. Their retail price was 1.80 mark a kilo but supermarkets bought them from private suppliers for four marks a kilo. As strange as it sounds, the purchase prices for fruit and vegetables were set an average 100 per cent higher than the selling prices. Sometimes the difference was even greater. Plums were bought from gardeners for 1.50 mark a kilo (60 cents) but sold to the public for only 30 pfennigs (12 cents) a kilo. With livestock the pricing structure was very similar.

For farmers, like my uncle Klaus, it was common practice to sell their eggs to local grocery shops, only to buy them back cheaper the next day. When he bred geese and sold them live to the wholesale trade, he received 90 marks (36 dollars) for one bird but in the shops a goose, dead, plucked and ready to cook, cost only 30 marks (12 dollars). It was the same with milk. The retail price for a litre was less than 70 pfennigs (28 cents); nonetheless farmers were paid 1.70 mark (68 cents) for it. It sounds mad, but providing people with moderately priced and affordable groceries was undoubtedly a very humane policy. Unfortunately, selling products for less than their production cost was uneconomical and encouraged waste. Because food was cheap, people often bought more than they needed then threw what they didn't consume away. In my uncle's village it was normal practice for small farmers to buy six to eight loaves of bread a day each to feed them to their animals – proper animal feed was not subsidised and more expensive than bread. Every seventh loaf was eaten by an animal – a total of 200,000 tons annually. Crazy!

GETTING ORGANISED

There were 30,000 allotments in East Berlin alone, usually on a 99-year leasehold. Our plot, 200 square metres big, once belonged to Grandad's cousin who had moved to West Germany well before the Berlin Wall was built. My parents paid roughly 65 marks (26 dollars) rent a year. This money was paid into an account held at the State Bank of the DDR. Whenever this cousin visited East Germany he could withdraw money and spend it as he pleased, as long as it stayed in the country – it was strictly forbidden to export the DDR mark. Even though I was very small at the time, I can still remember the tarry smell that the roofing felt released into the house when the hot summer sun was shining and I was about to have my lunchtime nap inside. When awake, playing on the swing that was hanging on a branch of our huge plum tree, was one of my favourite pastimes. Just like running, at least once a weekend, with 50 pfennigs (20 cents) and a little blue bucket to the nearby pub to buy a litre of orange-flavoured fizzy lemonade. The barmaid in there was a busty blond in her late forties with a roaring laugh. For me she always had a smile and a free lollipop. Once I fell on my way out and spilled the entire contents of my bucket because its lid had become loose. I was given words of comfort and a free refill. Unfortunately, in early 1972 it all came to an end as the land occupied by the allotments was needed to build apartment blocks. We were given a new allotment slightly further out. At 500 square metres it was double the size of the old one, but still had a very reasonable annual rent of 90 marks (36 dollars). We happily moved on.

The problem was, now we needed a new bungalow, and building a house was not one of the easiest tasks in East Germany. Concrete, gravel and bricks were fairly easy to obtain with a waiting period of only two to three weeks. But as for other materials, you never knew when Lady Luck would be on your side. Your best bet to "organise" material was to go at six o'clock on a Monday morning to a building material supplier. By the time it opened at eight you would have secured a good position among the 30 or so other people in the queue. This way, Dad got his much-needed sacks of cement. For other items, such as tiles, patience was needed. To get your hands on them you had to put your name and colour preference on a waiting list in a building material depot first. With a little bit of luck, you got a notification card eight to 12 months later asking you to pick up the order. If you were unlucky, you had to wait for two years, or even longer. And there was no guarantee that you were allocated your ordered quantity or colour.

The construction of our bungalow went along nicely without any major hickups. Dad got the roof beams from a friend who worked for a company that salvaged them from demolition buildings and the window frames he made himself. As for building the house, he relied on elbow grease, family members, friends, colleagues and our neighbour in the Greifswalder Strasse who, conveniently, was a bricklayer. Though every bungalow in the allotment was built to the same plan, I found our house the most beautiful. Dad's finishing touches included colourful three-dimensional geometrical shapes attached to the white pebble dash and concrete tiles with imprinted chestnut leaves decorating the lower parts of the walls. He had seen them first at a nursery but because they were not available to buy Dad simply made them himself. He copied the original design onto paper, carved a wooden mould and then churned out one tile after another.

Inside the house, which consists of a kitchen, bedroom and living room (WC and shed are in a second building nearby), Dad made the most of the space available by building a bed in a wardrobe. Every year we stayed a few nights at the bungalow.

MUMS, KINDERGARTENS AND A
VERY MELODIC PEOPLE'S POLICEMAN

Until 1972 I had been quite privileged, because I had always stayed at home with my mum. She had made the decision to spend as much time as possible with me and my brother while we were small, which did not make her a typical DDR woman – 90 per cent of the female population had a job Thirty per cent worked on a part-time basis.

> "Man and woman have equal rights and have the same legal status in all areas of social, public and personal life. The furtherance of the woman, especially in the professional qualification, is a social and national task."
>
> GDR constitution

This policy against sexual discrimination helped ease the shortage of workers caused by the labour-intensive production methods of our industry. Women were actively encouraged to take up a career. Companies set up *Frauenbrigaden* (women-only teams), where help and understanding for mothers juggling family and work were guaranteed. Many women enjoyed the social aspect of work, the responsibility, the respect and the self-confidence that came with a job, not to mention the pay packet at the end of month. Growing female confidence also showed in another statistic: In East Germany twice as many women filed for divorce than in West Germany. But just like Mother's Day in the west, East Germany too had one day dedicated to acknowledge the hard work that women, and not just mothers, did day in and day out. The country honoured its female population officially once a year on 8 March – International Women's Day. It was the one day on which mums, girl-friends, wives, aunts, grannies and female colleagues were pampered at home and at work. They received flowers (the government always made sure florists had enough stock in the build-up to it), kids made small presents, male family members took care of the housework and companies handed out awards and organised festive hours or office parties. For our women this was a much-welcome break from the daily routine but even in the DDR one thing had not changed since the dark ages – most top positions were occupied by men.

The government at least tried to make life as easy as possible for women who worked and had a family: every month they were given a paid day off, the so-called *Haushaltstag* (Household Day) on top of their four-week holiday entitlement. Furthermore, mums had fewer working hours, were granted paid maternity leave for 12 months (18 months after the third child), and could return to their job knowing that their children would be looked after in a national network of affordable crèches and kindergartens. The East German state sponsored 85 per cent of the cost for bringing up a child! The birth money alone, paid to parents upon arrival of their offspring, cost the state a whopping 300 million marks (120 million dollars) annually. For the first child parents received roughly the equivalent of a month's salary – 1,000 marks (400 dollars). For the second baby, they got 1,500 marks (600 dollars) and for each consecutive child, 2,500 marks (1,000 dollars). And for anyone not wanting to go through with a pregnancy, the Pill was prescribed free of charge and abortions were possible up to the 12th week. Over 80 per cent of all kids went to crèches. Just to recoup costs the state would have had to charge 340 marks (136 dollars) a month per child. Instead, parents only paid 20 marks (eight dollars) towards food and drinks. This whole social net may not have made a working woman's life stress-free, but it made it easier to have both a family and a job. In fact, it was so easy that even my mum eventually wanted to get out of the house more and started looking for a job again, one that would still allow her to be there for me during the day and for my brother after school.

A kindergarten near my grandparents' house had a sign in its window advertising for a part-time teacher's assistant. This was a typical DDR way to look for employees – bigger companies even had huge "We employ" signs at their entrances, listing all their available vacancies. Mum applied for the job and got it. So her and I both joined this kindergarten.

Like most things in East Germany, kindergartens too were well organised. Over 90 per cent of all kids visited one and a typical day in there looked like this:

6:00 to 8:00 – Children arrive (most people started work between 6:30 and 7:00)

8:00 to 8:45 – Breakfast with food brought from home and milk/cocoa from the kindergarten

8:45 to 10:00 – Learning Hour (drawing, craftworking, singing)

10:00 to 12:00 – Playground activities outside (weather permitting)

12:00 to 13:00 – Lunch (with a visit to the toilet afterwards)

13:00 to 14:30 – Collective midday rest followed by another toilet visit

14:30 to 15:00 – Snack brought from home with milk/cocoa provided

15:00 to 18:00 – Playtime and parents picking up their kids (work usually finished between 16:00 and 16:30)

18:00 – Kindergarten closes

All three to six year olds at kindergarten were divided into groups of 16 and parents had to pay about 20 marks (eight dollars) a month for a place, which included food and drink. We were taught the basics of hygiene (hand washing before eating and after the loo), learned to have responsibility (helping to set and clear the table for meals), were encouraged to be tidy (putting our clothes on hooks) and challenged to learn new things. There were separate doll and car play corners and when it was someone's birthday, the child celebrating brought in a cake, received a little gift in return and all the other kids sang a song.

As positive as it was having this nationwide network of childcare places (DDR kindergartens could accommodate up to 785,000 children), they were also the first step in the process of forming "socialist personalities". The following song was my favourite:

Song of the People's Policeman

I stand on the roadway
with cars on the go
I don't dare to cross it
to go to and fro.

The people's policeman
who lends us a hand
he walks with me over
he is our friend.

I have lost my way
the town is so big,
my mum will be waiting
I must find her quick.

The people's policeman
who lends us a hand
he brings me safe home
he is our friend.

And when I am grown up
I say now to you
such a people's policeman
I will become too.

We help all the people
every chance we will seize
protect all the children
as people's police.

Though we never had to march around in formation, and were not told that guns are great, we were certainly made aware that there were soldiers on our border who safeguarded us and our parents so we all could live in peace. Sometimes we sang this policeman song (it had a very catchy tune), at other times it was the equally toe-curling song of *When I'm Grown Up I Will Be Joining the People's Army*. Occasionally we even had to draw all the things a soldier can protect. East German kids started their political education early.

Kindergartens were a Mecca for talent scouts. Film producers liked to pop in if they had to fill roles and sports clubs regularly invited youngsters to their training centres, to assess whether they might be future champions. The foundations for many illustrious East German sporting careers were laid at kindergarten-age. Katarina Witt, the Olympic ice skating champion was nick-named "Ice Princess", and had circumstances been a bit different, I could have been the "Ice Prince" East Germany never had...

One day the kids from our kindergarten were invited to a training centre where some coaches gave us all skates, so we could try our luck on the ice. I had never been skating before, but I got on the ice and sped off effortlessly while the other kids, struggling to keep upright, hardly made any headway. At the end of the exercise, the coaches thought that I, along with two other boys and one girl, had the best potential to become "diplomats in track suits" as DDR media referred to our top sportsmen. Because of my long arms and legs and my natural ice-skating talent, I was to be trained either as a figure or speed-skater. If that didn't work out, the back-up plan was to turn me into a rower. Although the "sport functionaries" tried very hard to convince my parents to give their approval, none of the plans materialised. The training centre was just too far away from where we lived and it was simply impossible for Mum to take me there a couple of times every week.

Would I have become East Germany's best known sportsman? Who knows, but by foregoing a professional sports career I definitely spared my body years of exposure to power enhancing drugs. No doubt I, like many who did join the training programmes, would also have swallowed the "vitamin supplements" handed out by trainers.

SURPRISE, SURPRISE

If the events in 1972 were exciting for me, 1973 must have made our politicians ecstatic. The DDR joined the Vienna Convention and became a full member of the United Nations. Finally our little country was properly internationally recognised. Among the 17 new countries that established diplomatic relations with East Germany were France and the UK. News on a smaller scale was that the world's "progressive youth" was invited to East Berlin for the Youth World Festival: a big propaganda event which the DDR used to boost its image. 1973 was also the year in which East Germans were for the first time allowed to legally possess foreign currencies such as US dollars or West German Deutschmarks. Money that could be spent in Intershops – little shops selling western goods for hard currencies. Also did the Communist Party announce in 1973 that it would dramatically improve the living conditions of ten million people by building or renovating three million flats between 1976-1990. When the DDR collapsed 17 years later, a total of 225,700 apartment blocks had been built as a result of that policy.

Our family certainly needed an improvement in housing conditions. Like my brother and parents, I hated the weekly baths in a zinc tub, which was usually put in the kitchen and had to be filled and emptied with bowls. In early 1973, this inconvenience did not seem to bother my father any more. Strangely, one bitterly cold weekend he got on his "Swallow" moped and announced he was off to the allotment. We waited six hours for his return. A couple of times, the following week, he came home from work unusually late. Something was brewing, but we did not know what.

The next weekend he suggested we all go for a walk. We went to Köpenick, a borough which is a bit further out with lots of nature, and as we walked to the woods we passed an area of newly built apartment blocks. We joked about how nice it would be to live in one of those new flats, when Dad suddenly said: "Why don't we see whether any of my keys fits? Maybe we could have a look into an apartment". Naturally, Mum was shocked by such a suggestion. She could not believe what she had just heard, but Dad, encouraged by my brother and me, went to the entrance of one building and opened the front door. Mum told him to stop immediately, but her protests fell on deaf ears as we three disappeared into the house. She had no other option but to follow.

Walking up to first floor, Dad rang a bell. There was no reply. So he got out his bunch of keys again and fumbled at the lock. I can still feel the tension that was in the air then, interrupted only by my nervous sniggering and Mum's hushed attempts to reason with Dad. When the door suddenly sprang open there was an eerie silence. Never in my life have I seen my mother so petrified. Dad quickly rushed us all in, switched the light on, and there was a big sign, in my father's handwriting, saying: "Welcome to our new flat." What a surprise that was. We were now the tenants of a spanking new one-bedroom flat with a proper bathroom – how luxurious.

After we had all praised my father's organising skills, nothing was able to hold us back from putting that bathtub to use. Dad had even thought of a bottle of bubble bath and some fresh towels.

How did he get hold of the flat, we wanted to know. His company gave it to him. In East Germany it was common for sought-after commodities like flats, cars and package holidays, to be allocated to companies, which in return offered them to hard working members of their staff.

The incentive for the people was not the chance to get a freebie, as whatever was dished out still had to be paid for in full, but the opportunity to get something faster or with less hassle than the rest of the population. And so we did not beat around the bush and quickly moved into our new home. It may have been a bit on the small side and far from the city centre, but for the time being my parents did not mind those little disadvantages. Though I could easily have done without getting up at four-thirty in the morning when Mum had her early shift and we had to be in the kindergarten by six o'clock. At least on those days we were back home at around two o'clock, but when Mum had her late shift, which started at noon, we only returned at seven pm, and my brother would have been on his own all afternoon. It soon became clear that it wasn't going to work, and my parents decided that we'd all be better off if Mum quit her job.

So she did, and immediately we had more time available for visits to my grandparents. Hooray! I loved playing with cotton reels at Nan's feet while she was busy on her motorised Singer sewing machine. It was even better when Mum allowed me to stay overnight. I could sleep in my grandparents' bed and be spoiled rotten.

DDR DOCTORS

Not such a highlight for me, however, was a visit to the doctor. I never looked forward to being examined by a person in a white coat. The free-of-charge health system in East Germany was organised in a similar way to the NHS. Anyone with a problem went to a GP who, if necessary, would refer the patient to a specialist. Hospitals had waiting lists for major operations. Medical staff were constantly faced with problems over insufficient supplies of materials and the latest medical equipment.

The DDR health system employed 500,000 members of staff, including more than 60,000 doctors and dentists. There were more than 3,000 individual surgeries and smaller health centres, but the DDR was best known for its *Polikliniken* (polyclinics) – large out-patient health centres that had to cover at least four different medical fields. Although most polyclinics included all of the following: GP's, paediatricians, ear-nose-throat specialists, dermatologists, eye-doctors, urologists, gynaecologists, internal specialists, orthopaedists, neurologists, physiologists, psychiatrists, surgeons, diabetologists, dentists and dental technicians, a laboratory, pharmacy and an X-ray facility. All parties involved benefited from the polyclinics – doctors were able to work closely together, the health service saved money through several doctors sharing the same administration/facilities and the patients were glad to have everything under one roof. Today there is a revival of these polyclinics in Germany.

When Mum had to take me to a polyclinic once, the nurse, who was filling in a few gaps in my medical record, asked her where she worked. When Mum explained that she was a *Hausfrau* looking after her kids, the astonished nurse asked quite sharply, "You don't work?" Mum's reply was even sharper and consequently she was never asked this question again. What she did not know at the time was that a decade later she would be managing a team in a polyclinic herself. Being East German did not mean you had to live a monotonous life. Just like in the west, you were able to change your life completely – provided you were prepared to take the necessary steps.

AND THE WINNER IS...

One dream never materialised for my parents – winning big in the lottery. Even, or especially, in a worker's paradise such as East Germany, people still dreamed the dream of having a carefree life with lots of cash. The most popular lottery was called Tele-Lotto in which, as the name suggests, the numbers were drawn on telly. Since January 1972 every Sunday at seven pm, a different, more or less famous, person hosted the half-hour programme, talking about a specific subject and drawing the numbers as they go along. The lotto machine was what impressed me most on this programme. It was made of blue fibreglass and dome shaped with a hole in the middle (just like a crater). When the host pushed a button, a skittle ball slowly emerged out of the hole, then rolled down in a spiralling groove to the bottom where it would hit one of 35 skittle shaped wooden cutouts that surrounded the dome on a revolving ring. The skittle flipped back on a hinge and revealed the drawn number while the ball disappeared back into the machine. Quite sophisticated for then! I thought it was the most amazing machine ever built.

To make the show more interesting, and to stretch it to fill the half-hour slot, every number coincided with a different theme. If, for example, 35 (which stood for "Circus") was drawn, then it was followed up with a short circus-performance-related film clip. When skittle 24 (Easy Listening) was hit by the ball, we were shown some artist singing a song, and so on. I liked the crime-story film clips most (skittle 19), but naturally players were more interested in hitting the jackpot, for which they had to get five out of five numbers right – this game had no bonus ball. And even though 60 per cent of the stake were handed back in winnings, the maximum amount a lucky player could get was half a million marks, later reduced to 250,000 marks (100,000 dollars). That might not sound like a huge amount of money today, but back then the annual average salary only was around 12,000 marks. And so, every week punters filled in five million coupons and handed over 20 million marks to the 13,000 lotto-kiosks nationwide, just to be in it to win it.

One particular visit to a lotto-kiosk I still remember very well. It was on a hot summer day, when Mum and I on our way home from a shopping trip nipped into the place to play Tele-Lotto. At first, everything seemed normal – the shop assistant was chatting to a construction worker while Mum went about finding the correct coupon and ticking off her numbers. After a minute it became apparent that something was not right. The conversation between the two men had stopped. Mum had put her pen aside. All three looked at each other. That was the moment when I too detected the distinct lingering odour of farts. No verbal accusations were made but Mum, not impressed by the smell, looked at the builder with such disgust that he felt it necessary to defend himself. "Don't look at me. All I had for lunch was a beer," he muttered. But that didn't convince my mother in the least. After she paid we left very hastily. Only at home did we realise that she had done the poor guy an injustice because it was actually us who had caused the stink. At the bottom of her string bag was a very smelly cheese we had bought earlier in town. Mum was so embarrassed by this incident, she was never able to go back to that lotto-kiosk again.

Even more embarrassing was New Year's Eve 1973. I was only six years old at the time, but I was helping Mum with the preparations for the evening, as Dad had to work for half the day. My brother had a friend over and they were playing in the bedroom with our DDR version of Scalectrix. Getting the novelty hats out, decorating the rooms with paper streamers, lending a hand in the kitchen – I loved doing all that. Jam-filled doughnuts are traditional for New Year's Eve in Germany. Part of my kitchen duty was to inject mustard into one of the many doughnuts that we had bought fresh from the bakery that morning. I can't speak for other areas in Germany but in Berlin this mustard-in-the-doughnut joke has made people laugh for nearly a hundred years now and is still going strong.

Once I had accomplished my mission, I put the specially prepared doughnut back with the others and mixed the whole lot up until I had lost track of the one to avoid. Later in the evening, with the whole family, including my grandparents, together, mum finally brought the big doughnut-platter in. Everyone knew the name of the game and tried to avoid any suspicious looking doughnuts until only the last few were left. I became more and more impatient as the doughnut numbers dramatically dwindled without the mustard-filled one turning up. With only one doughnut left and everyone else being full, I sacrificed myself. I closed my eyes, had a big bite and – surprise, surprise – there was no surprise. To my disappointment this doughnut had only a plain raspberry filling, just like the rest. What had happened to my mustard? Where had it gone? It took us a while to figure it out but in the morning my brother and his classmate had a doughnut each and his friend must have picked the mustard doughnut without saying anything. What must he have thought about our hospitality? He came over a few more times but funnily enough ever since then, whenever he was offered something to eat, he always declined.

IT'S SCHOOLTIME

1974 was a turning point for me as I was now nearly old enough to go to school. In the few months before starting school, I would occasionally spend time trying to read and can remember feeling very frustrated at not being able to make sense of all those letters. Like all East German kids, before I could go to school and start learning my ABCs properly, I had to have my physical and mental fitness assessed. First a doctor certified my physical suitability. Then an official from the Educational Ministry visited the kindergarten and judged the mental development of us older kids. I had to build and draw something and was encouraged to show off my counting and spelling abilities. I passed with flying colours, even though, when I had to colour in different animals with their appropriate colours, I gave what should have been a plain grey donkey a much more interesting zebra-look. Well, I had never seen a donkey before. When the official explained to me how the colour should have been applied correctly I was angry with myself for being so stupid. A pre-school defeat, perhaps, but my anger turned into pride on the day I was enrolled in elementary school.

Enrolment Day is a cause for celebration for kids and parents all over Germany. In the DDR, the new school year always started at the beginning of September and enrolment day was on a Saturday. Quite early on my big day, grandparents, uncles and aunts gathered in our flat. We all left at nine-thirty am, heading for the big function room of a local company. I was so proud to carry my brand-new ligh-brown satchel and to wear the black patent leather shoes, which mum had allowed me to choose in the shop especially for the occasion. When all the school beginners arrived at the hall, we had to wait in the entrance hall while our families took their seats in the auditorium. One red-haired girl cried bitterly as she was separated from her family. A puny boy in *Lederhosen* and with matchstick legs slapped her in the face. It shut the girl up but only as long as it took her to realise that her nose was now bleeding. Streams of tears began pouring down her cheeks. Mixed with the blood dripping from her nose an interesting pattern began to form on her frilly white dress. "Hopefully she's not in my class", I said to myself while giving the *Lederhosen*-boy an agreeing nod. A teacher finally managed to calm the girl down. When both returned from a visit to the bathroom a couple minutes later all the bloodstains were gone from the girl's dress. Instead the fabric was now covered with huge wet patches. An elderly lady, wearing a heavy flowery perfume, ushered us all through a side entrance to the first few rows of the auditorium. Our families, occupying all other seats, applauded us as we walked in. Now even the girl with the wet dress smiled. Once we sat down the *Schuldirektor* (headmaster) said a few words, congratulating us on our big day. Then some older kids staged a little performance with songs and dances and, after another short speech by the headmaster, the teachers introduced themselves. Finally we were called one by one onto the stage to form the individual classes. Neither red-haired girl nor *Lederhosen* boy were in mine. I saw Dad taking photos as I was on stage and frantically waved at him. The teacher then led us to the nearby school for our first ever lesson.

In the classroom all our schoolbooks were laid out on the tables and, after we sat down, the teacher introduced herself again. She gave us our timetable, told us what we had to bring to school and how we would have to behave there. No one said a word. Though it was the first time the teacher had met us, she would already have been familiar with our strengths and weaknesses as the kindergartens had to write assessments on everyone who was starting school. After 20 minutes the bell rang and our introductory lesson finished.

We were greeted and congratulated by our families as we came out of the building. Finally our parents would give us the long-awaited *Schultüten* (school cones).

Schultüten are big decorated cardboard cones filled mainly with sweets, small presents and some school related items like rulers, pens and erasers. The *Schultüten* tradition goes back to the early nineteenth century when in some parts of Germany well-off parents began giving their children big cones filled with sweets, fruit and nuts to sweeten their first day in the new environment. In time, more and more regions of the country adopted the custom and for decades now every German child looking forward to starting school has been looking forward just as much to getting their cone – one without the other is simply unthinkable.

The school system in the DDR was very straightforward: There were no private schools, every child had to go to a General Educational Polytechnical Upper School for ten years. These schools were exactly what the name suggested – a place where kids received a sturdy, all-round education. You could not pick and mix subjects, instead you had to do it all, whether it was the natural sciences, P.E., Arts Education, languages or any other field. Naturally, not everyone was good at everything but the advantage this system had was that by the time kids finished school they had the foundations for a career in almost any industry. School education was free of charge and took place from Monday to Saturday, normally starting at eight o'clock. The 45-minute-long lessons were interrupted by five- or ten-minute breaks with two exceptions: a 25-minute "milk break" after the second lesson and a 45-minute "big break" for lunch after the fourth lesson. The milk (plain or with strawberry, chocolate, vanilla or yucky artificial banana flavour) and lunch were subsidised and very reasonably priced at 15 and 55 pfennigs respectively (six and 22 cents). Over 70 per cent of all pupils drank the school milk, while 80 per cent had school lunch, which always consisted of a main course and a dessert. The government Kids from families with three or more children received both free of charge. Each class had an average of 30 pupils (give or take a few) who stayed together from the first to the tenth grade, unless someone moved away or was so bad they had to repeat a year.

We did not have to wear school uniforms. Also, corporal punishment in school was strictly forbidden. Kids coming from families with three or more children received their schoolbooks free of charge. And so did every pupil going to school in Berlin. As to why Berliner children were privileged in that way, I don't know. Perhaps the government wanted to show how socially progressive it was, but could not afford it for the entire country.

To develop our handwriting skills, we were required to use only fountain pens in school. So classmates judged you by the kind of pen you had. The most embarrassing thing that could happen to any East German pupil was to have to make do with a DDR model, the Heiko fountain pen. It was a status symbol to write with a West German Pelikan pen. Also was the capitalist nib much more reliable than its socialist cousin. The only problem was that the Pelikans were not sold in the DDR and if you did not have anyone in the west who could send you one, you were screwed. Thankfully I was able to start school with my reputation intact – Dad had organised me a spanking new Pelikan pen through one of his colleagues.

In the first grade we had three or four lessons a day, consisting of reading, writing, maths, handicraft, drawing, singing and P.E, nothing too out of the ordinary there. But despite the benign nature of the subjects taught in them, schools were also institutions where the second phase of the process of forming "socialist personalities" took place.

"Every citizen of the German Democratic Republic has an equal right to education. The educational institutions are open to everybody. The standardised socialist educational system promises every citizen a continuous socialist upbringing, education and continued development.

The German Democratic Republic ensures that its people stride forward to a socialist community of universally educated and harmoniously developed individuals, who are imbued with the spirit of socialist patriotism and internationalism and who possess a high general and special education."

GDR constitution

BECOMING A PIONEER

When their children were in the first grade, parents were asked whether they would give consent for them to join the Pioneer organisation – a socialist version of the scouts. I, like all the other kids in my class, was very keen to become a Pioneer. Pioneers were always doing fun stuff and becoming one was definitely a highlight for any seven year old. A pity this mass organisation was very political. According to its statute, the organisation's aim was to ensure that "all Young Pioneers and pupils grow up to be trustworthy socialist patriots and proletarian internationalists", whatever that meant. Naturally over the years the fun factor decreased as the political part increased. But even as membership became more and more an unwanted obligation, the thought of leaving the Pioneers did not occur to the majority of 1.5 million kids who were members. For us, going to school and being a Pioneer simply went together, just like living and breathing.

On my first days as a Pioneer, I put on my special Pioneer shirt before going to school for the initiation ceremony. The uniform consisted of a dark skirt or pair of trousers and a white shirt. On one sleeve of the shirt was the Pioneer's badge – the initials JP (standing for the German words meaning "Young Pioneers") topped with the inscription "Seid Bereit" (Be Ready) and three burning flames. I don't remember much about the initiation ceremony, except that we had to promise to be good Pioneers and to act in accordance with the Ten Commandments of the Pioneers, which were:

We Young Pioneers love our German Democratic Republic.

We Young Pioneers love our parents.

We Young Pioneers love peace.

We Young Pioneers make friends with the children of the Soviet Union and all countries.

We Young Pioneers learn diligently, are tidy and disciplined.

We Young Pioneers respect all working people and help vigorously wherever a hand is needed.

We Young Pioneers are good friends and help each other.

We Young Pioneers like to sing and dance, play and do handicraft.

We Young Pioneers go in for sports, keep our body clean and healthy.

We Young Pioneers carry with pride our blue neckerchief.

Once that was out of the way everyone finally received what they were really after – their membership card and blue neckerchief (whose three corners symbolised the unity of the Pioneers, the school and the home). With our outfits now complete, we all left the school with our chests puffed out. I did my first good deed already on the way home when I saw an elderly woman in the street struggling with her shopping. I lent her a hand and she gave me a chocolate bar as a little thank you. Being a Pioneer truly rocked.

GREETINGS

Like most of the other first-graders, my main aim in life was to behave well enough or get a good enough mark to have a little bee rubber-stamped into my notebook. The more bees a child got, the more recognised, valued and encouraged they felt. Unfortunately, in 1974 there must have been a shortage of rubber stamps featuring bees. In my class we collected East German coat-of-arms stamps – a hammer (representing the workers) and set of compasses (denoting the intelligentsia) surrounded by a wreath of wheat ears (standing for the farmers) which was embraced at the bottom by a black, red and yellow band. Why our teacher couldn't just have substituted the bee stamp with another friendly animal will remain her secret.

No secret, however, was that at the beginning and end of each school year, and on special occasions in between, we had school assemblies. They always took the form of musters. All classes had to stand in the schoolyard in a horseshoe formation facing the head teacher, who would stand behind a microphone and in front of the flagpole with the DDR flag flying on it, making some announcement or honoring pupils. It was on occasions like these that we had to wear our Pioneer shirt and neckerchief. But as soon as a muster was over, shirts and neckerchiefs went straight back into our satchels. We were proud to be Pioneers, just not overly proud. Although the assemblies were militaristic orientated, their actual content wasn't. After all we were kids and no soldiers. There was no barking of orders or marching around; our head teacher then was a lovely old man, vaguely resembling an aged Peter Ustinov. He always had a friendly word for his pupils – no child would have rejected him as their grandfather.

But as nice as he was as an individual, he too made sure that we followed official procedures. At the beginning of each lesson we had to stand up, were greeted by the teacher and then allowed to sit down – quite normal. However, at the beginning of the first lesson of each school day the pupil responsible for carrying the class-register from classroom to classroom had to stand in front of the class, together with the teacher. Once everyone had calmed down, the pupil in front of the class would turn round and salute the teacher by placing his outstretched hand, thumb touching the scalp, like a cockscomb on the top of his head, and report: "Frau Arendt, class 1B with 27 pupils ready for tuition. Andrea Schulze and Viola Wehr are ill and not present."

For P.E. lessons the class had to line up facing the teacher and one classmate, who had to shout: "For the report to the P.E. teacher, eyes right", before addressing the teacher while doing a cockscomb salute: "Frau Singer, class 1B formed up and is ready for Physical Education."

After the command "Eyes front!" the reporting pupil joined the line-up and the teacher then opened the lesson with the greeting "Sport frei!" (meaning "sport, go ahead") to which the whole class had to repeat "Sport frei".

Yes, the cockscomb salute was very popular then. It originated from the official Pioneer greeting which was done in the same manner, with one person saying to a group of Pioneers "For peace and socialism. Be ready!" to which all the other Pioneers, also with hands on heads, would reply "Ever ready!". And it was exactly THAT greeting which got my brother for the first time on East German telly.

A CHILLY WELCOME

After Pinochet's putsch in Chile in 1973 and his overthrow of the left-wing, freely elected government there, the DDR not only offered 3,000 fleeing Chileans exile as an act of anti-imperialistic solidarity but also felt it necessary to honour Chile's assassinated president Dr. Salvador Allende. First the area to which our block of flats belonged became the Salvador-Allende-Quarter. Then the street in which we lived changed its name from Achenbach Strasse to Salvador-Allende-Strasse and as if that wasn't already enough, the school to which my brother and I went was now going to become Salvador-Allende-Schule. One day, prior to the school-naming ceremony taking place, which was due to be attended by Mr Allende's widow, my brother and two of his classmates were called to the headmaster's office during their German lesson. All three were wracking their brains on their way to the office trying to work out whether they had misbehaved recently. As they entered the *Direktor*'s office it became clear that there was nothing to be worried about. They were told to go home, put on their Pioneer uniforms and return quickly to school so a teacher could drive them to the airport. They had been chosen on behalf of all the Pioneers in the DDR to greet and hand over flowers to Mrs Allende on her arrival in the country. What child would not want to do that instead of sitting in a classroom? Unfortunately, the plane arrived three hours late and the excitement of being at the airport had turned into boredom. Shortly before the plane's arrival the kids had to take off their anoraks for the entire proceedings so their shirts and neckerchiefs would be visible (the uniform didn't include a jacket). It had been a coldish day, with blustery winds and, sure enough, two of the three, including my brother, caught nasty colds and had to stay at home for a week afterwards. On the plus side, and much to my family's excitement, my brother's welcoming committee made it onto the prime time news that day.

I don't remember much about the naming ceremony at school, but I would bet my old Pioneer shirt that it happened in the form of a muster. It would have been unthinkable to do it any other way. What I do remember is that we had to learn a song called *Venceremos* (Spanish for "we will be victorious") for the occasion, which was about the Chilean people fighting for freedom. The chorus went like this:

Venceremos, Venceremos,

break the chains of the nation, strike quick.

Venceremos, Venceremos,

freed from misery we will be big.

Not really the sort of thing for seven year olds to sing. For us it was just a song we had to learn. That we did not understand it did not bother us.

TELL ME YOUR STANDPOINT

Among the songs I did understand and enjoy, just like the rest of my family, were the tunes from Frank Schöbel, a very popular singer then and today, who you could say was the Cliff Richard of East Germany. Lots of his songs were hits, like *There was Gold in Your Eyes* and *I'd Go from the Northpole to the Southpole by Foot (for a Kiss from You),* to name just two. He was not quite as wealthy as Sir Cliff, and as such he lived at the end of our road – just like us in a two-bedroom flat in a newly built apartment block. Not very glamorous for a pop-singer but then, what pop-singer would tolerate teenage boys ringing his bell and shouting up to his windows: "Hey Frank. Leave your missus alone and come down, we're playing football."? At the time Frank was in his early thirties and going through a chubby phase. With his curly hair he always reminded me of a Roman marble cherub that I had seen on a museum visit. Of course, unlike the old statue, Frank Schöbel did not display himself to the public in the buff. To the envy of my brother he usually wore flared Levi's whenever we bumped into him in the streets. However, Frank's tops did not differ from what every other man was wearing at the time – brightly coloured shirts with long pointy collars, made of shiny, non-breathable polyester. What impressed me most was his attitude-free behaviour. Despite being a huge star he was always friendly and responsive whenever members of the public got near him. I must know. My parents bought a lot of his records but somehow it was always up to me to approach him in the street with a piece of paper or a record cover and ask for his autograph – everyone else in my family was too embarrassed to do it. I did not have such reservations and he came always across as a down-to-earth guy. Decades later Frank Schöbel is still singing and loved by his fans.

A group which called themselves October Club was considerably less popular. Their name was a reference to the Russian Great Socialist October Revolution of 1917. "Catchy" tunes like *Construct, Construct* or *Tell Me Your Standpoint* were not the kind of music we, as a family, considered worth buying. However, that did not stop me being excited when, one day, October Club turned up with a television crew at the playground opposite our flat, where they were filmed miming to a song that was blasting out of the loudspeakers. It was hardly MTV-material, but I was still thrilled to watch, for the first time, how television was made. What I did not know then was that just a couple of weeks later I would be seeing myself on national telly.

LIGHTS, CAMERA... AND ACTION!

Once a month on the Sunday children's programme at ten o'clock in the morning a show called *Mach mit, mach's nach, mach's besser!* (Join In, Copy It, Be Better!) was broadcast. It was a very popular hour-long programme, hosted by an enthusiastic ex-sportsman called Adi. The guy was black-haired, in his mid-thirties, had a friendly moon face and a pudding bowl haircut. Wearing a brown tracksuit was his trademark. We kids just loved him. Adi was short for Adolph, a name which you would have been well advised to change if you wanted a career in the German spotlight. The show involved teams from two different schools competing in various sporting tasks. One day this show was recorded in the gymnasium of our school. Not that I took part in the competition, I was only a spectator just like hundreds of other kids. But I made sure that I would be seen on telly by being in the front row where the huge, solid, old-fashioned cameras would be able to pick me up. Sitting there in my nicest Sunday outfit I wanted my first appearance on telly to be a hundred per cent perfect, and for some reason I got it in my head that I had to constantly make sure that there was no boogie on my nose. The programme was screened a week later, with me prominently and frequently in shot just as I had planned. I looked fine, except for one thing – the constant touching of my nose, which only I knew the reason for, had made me look like the DDR's champion nosepicker – all on national TV.

The Fritz family had one more claim to TV fame that year. One Saturday morning, spotlights and a camera were unloaded in front of our apartment building and filming for the popular TV series *Polizeiruf 110* (Police Call 110) began. The programme's name originates from the police emergency phone number 110. *Polizeiruf 110* was a very successful show with up to fifty per cent of the viewing public tuning into each episode. It was even exported to over 30 countries, including West Germany, Sweden, Italy, Afghanistan, Mongolia and all over eastern Europe. Since 1971, East Germans were able to watch a new 60 to 90 minute long episode every month, in which criminals were caught by the *Volkspolizei* (People's Police). Just like in real life the criminals did not carry guns, except for one episode where the beginnings of the story went far back to the war. Some of the perpetrators showed remorse, some did not, but you could always bet your last aluminium chip (East German slang for DDR coins), that a murderer would start a confession with the words: "I did not mean to..."

The series was not only about entertainment, but also had an educational task, which was to show that committing crime in a socialist society was wrong and did not pay. It speaks for the quality of the series that these days not only are the old episodes frequently repeated on German TV, but that the programme is also one of the very few to have survived the end of DDR television and is still in production.

On that day the *Polizeiruf 110* team came to our newly built neighbourhood, they had to shoot a simple scene – a pram, in which a baby had been kidnapped, was discovered by playing kids. I was excited when the film people asked us for a baby blanket and a small pillow to put in the pram because some props had been forgotten. Hours later they were setting up spotlights in our communal stairwell to film a man leaving the neighbour's flat in the search for the missing baby. The crew had been at it for some time when, suddenly, there was a knock on our door and we were asked whether we would object if they would film an actress opening our door and talking to the police. Of course, we didn't object! It didn't take long to shoot that little scene and back in school on Monday I proudly told everyone in great detail about our door making it onto national TV. I should have been more humble about the whole experience. It turned out our door scene did not make it into the final version of the film and was replaced by some other woman talking to the police at someone else's door. Bugger!

DECISIONS, DECISIONS

I was quite excitable as a child. So it was only natural that I insisted on tagging along when Dad went to the new *Kaufhalle* (supermarket) nearby for the first time. Imagine my amazement when I saw on the shelves there the most exotic items – shiny, golden imported tins that contained soups. But not just any old soups, oh no. Mysterious flavours such as turtle, alligator, kangaroo, shark fin and ostrich. The exoticism did not come cheap – with a price tag of five marks each (two dollars) the tins cost roughly five times more than the average "Made in GDR" soup. The writing on the labels was in English but thankfully accompanied by sketches of the animals they contained and I just could not make my mind up about which flavour I wanted to try first. Dad refused my request point blank. From then on, whenever I went with one or both of my parents to the supermarket, I constantly nagged, nagged, nagged for the soups. One day Dad finally caved in. I was so excited and went for the Kangaroo soup. Disappointment set in quickly when we saw that the tin was past its sell-by date. We checked the other soups but to no avail – the entire stock had exceeded its life span. Tears rolled down my cheeks. Dad told one of the shop assistants about their old merchandise and next time we went back to the *Kaufhalle* the whole lot was gone. To this day I can't understand why East Germany, always short of western currency, had to blow its US dollars on importing exotic soups that had to be thrown out in the end.

THE MOVE

Just as my first year at school was coming to an end, my parents were fed up with the remote location of our apartment. Instead they wanted to live closer to the city centre. Real estate agents were unheard of in East Germany, so they placed an ad in a newspaper looking for someone to swap their flat with. A suitable candidate was found but, because we had to move quickly and before the end of term it meant I would miss out on getting presented with my award for "Good Learning in the Socialist School". I was very upset about that, but it was nothing a big bag of lollies could not cure.

On the day of the move, my father organised a driver from his work to come around with a lorry. It did not save him money as he still had to pay his company for the use of both, but it saved him lots of hassle as he would otherwise have had to go through the state-owned removal firm Deutrans, which was usually unable to accommodate short-term requests.

Though I was very sad to leave my classmates behind (especially my girlfriend, Annette), at the same time I was also very relieved to see the back of Henry the notorious school bully. Not that he ever did anything to me personally, but we feared this particular boy from the fourth grade because of his erratic and selfish behaviour towards us juniors. One of my classmates once got punched for laughing when Henry slipped on the schoolyard, another first-grader was being spat at for wearing a green anorak.

On that very last morning in Köpenick, my parents and my brother were loading up the lorry while I was looking out the window watching the kids go to school, and who should walk past at just that moment? Of course, the bully. Seizing this last opportunity for revenge I shouted out his name and as he turned and looked up I finally did what I had always wanted to do – I stuck my tongue out as long as I could. "I'll get you later for that," he shouted. "Yeah, yeah" I replied, smiled and disappeared from the window, feeling very smug. I still had a grin on my face as we drove off in the lorry a couple hours later, but at the same time I was also a tad worried, not knowing what nasty characters I'd have to face at my new school.

SPIES AND LIES

In retrospect, I worried needlessly and quickly settled into my new school. But on the subject of nasty characters, Lichtenberg, the borough we moved to, had a bit of a bad reputation.

It was home to a sealed-off complex of buildings that formed the headquarters of the Ministerium für Staatssicherheit (Ministry of State Security). The Stasi, as this ministry was usually referred to by ordinary people, operated both inside and outside the borders of the German Democratic Republic. Hardcore communists liked to call it "The Shield and Sword of the Communist Party".

Surviving documents show that the Stasi had files on more than six million people. It was probably the most efficient secret service in the world. A dubious record, but what else would you expect when you couple German efficiency with a network of 90,000 permanent and up to 175,000 freelance employees. With a population of roughly 17 million people, around one in 60 people was part of this machinery that was nicknamed "The Company" or "Hear and Peer". And no one could apply for a job with the secret service. The Stasi contacted the people it deemed suitable for employment.

To be fair, it should be said that not every Stasi employee was a spy. The secret service looked well after its socialism-defending workforce, pampering it with in-house shops and holiday homes, for which cooks, hairdressers, cleaners, shop assistants, drivers, waiters and other harmless professions were recruited. 60 per cent of its full-time staff were backup or service personnel. It was the freelancers – in Stasi-speak the *inoffiziellen Mitarbeiter* (unofficial employees) – that you really needed to be careful of. Your flirty colleague, your retired neighbour, your trusted teacher or even your closest friend, anyone could have been living a double life as an informant. It was no accident that, in the first six months of 1976, for example, 365 out of the 455 people who had planned or attempted to escape through the border to the west were arrested before they got anywhere near the frontier.

In fact, most domestic investigations by the secret service were triggered by reports from unofficial employees. What motivated all those tell-tales? Surprisingly, not the prospect of earning extra cash, because most of them didn't. Of course, money did sometimes change hands, and the more valuable you and your information was considered to be, the more reward you would get. But the majority of voluntary informants received a pittance in recognition of their work – a medal here, a bottle of sparkling wine there, and if you were lucky (and a female), a bunch of flowers on International Women's Day. There were two main reasons for ordinary people to spy. The first was simply that they truly believed in socialism. The second was that they were opportunistic. It was much easier to make a career in your normal job knowing the Stasi was backing you.

The full extent of this spy-network was beyond most people's comprehension, but no one was so foolish to believe that it didn't exist. A popular joke at the time was this one:

A drunk walks into a pub, orders a beer and sits down. After one sip he asks his neighbour: "Do you know the difference between this beer and Erich Honecker? This beer is tasteless and Erich Honecker is useless."

The other guy replies: "Do you know the difference between you and this table? This table stays here and you come with me."

Despite the Stasi, it was not the case (as is sometime suggested by American spy films) that people spoke constantly in hushed voices or nervously turned around every five seconds to check who was standing behind them. Naturally everyone had friends, colleagues, neighbours or acquaintances who they might suspect of collaborating with the Stasi, and approach with caution. Yet the real spies were often the people you trusted most – a wife spying on her husband or a father writing reports about his son's activities. But there was no ambiguity about what could or couldn't be said when dealing with officials. While it was possible to complain to them about the inefficiency of civil servants, institutions or companies, to openly criticise the government, its politics or representatives was not advisable. Anyone doing so could have been locked up either for "subversive agitation" or for "public debasement of the state".

The first "crime" was covered by section 106 of the GDR's *Zivilgesetzbuch* (Civil Penal Code) which penalised criticism of the political system or its representatives with a prison sentence of up to ten years. For the second "offence", section 220 applied. It read:

"Anybody who brings into contempt or slanders the political order or the public authorities, institutions or organisations or their work or actions will be punished with imprisonment of up to two years, or probation or public censure."

The constitution guaranteed each citizen the right of free speech:

"Every citizen of the German Democratic Republic has the right to express their opinion in accordance with the principles of this constitution. This right will not be restricted by any contractual relation between employer and employee. No one may be disadvantaged when exercising this right."

Unfortunately, the reality looked different. This led most people to have two political opinions – an official one and a private, more honest, one. We school kids joked:

The teacher asks little Frank: "What is small, red and has a bushy tail?" Frank replies: "If my dad had asked me I would have said a squirrel but because it's you, the correct answer is probably Lenin."

Depending on what you wanted to achieve in life and how much you were prepared to compromise your beliefs, you would switch between opinions, in much the same way as you might refrain from telling your boss what you really think of him, while still moaning about him to trusted colleagues.

WATCH OUT

I became aware at the age of seven that there were some things that were better left unsaid. My parents urged me, for my own good, to pretend at school that we were not watching West German programmes at home.

Because of the proximity to West Berlin, we had no trouble receiving West German TV and radio stations. Over 80 per cent of DDR citizens were able to watch and listen to western programmes, thanks to 364 powerful transmitters which West Germany had strategically positioned along its border to us. Nearly 90 per cent of those installations were transmitting radio programmes, the rest were broadcasting television programmes. However, there was one area the West German signal did not make it to – Saxony.

Hence the reason why that part of the country was known as the "Valley of the Clueless". This south-west corner of the DDR, where my father's side of the family lived, was just too far away to receive the West German transmissions properly – much to the regret of my uncles and aunts. They were only able to watch West German telly when there were no atmospheric disturbances and the powerful Czech and Polish transmitters in the vicinity were switched off at around midnight. Even then, the action on the screen looked as though it was taking place in a sandstorm.

Some DDR citizens deliberately chose not to watch or listen to western programmes because it was against their beliefs. In my class was one girl whose father was a very committed communist. He would not allow his family to watch western programmes. So whenever he was out, my classmate and her mother would put on any old channel from the west and settle down to watch it, regardless of what rubbish was being shown. Local legend has it that they even watched the West German test pattern. Whenever the father came home earlier than expected both mother and daughter were able to change the channel back to a DDR station with incredible speed – let's not forget, we are talking pre-remote control days here. Forbidden fruit was even sweeter behind the Iron Curtain!

Of course, our leaders were not too happy about their citizens tuning in to western programmes, which were officially branded as "Mouthpieces of the Enemy of the Working Class". In the Fifties and Sixties, the first television sets to bear the mark "Made in GDR" did not even allow viewers to watch the three West German stations – the DDR had opted for the French SECAM transmission system, while West Germany used the American PAL system. When people began building their own PAL receivers, television sets were finally fitted with receivers for both systems. Instead the government resorted to bullying tactics and counted on its loyal youth to climb onto rooftop and readjust the television antennas, or to pull them down completely.

Later it adopted a more subtle technique by getting teachers to ask the kids nationwide in schools to hum the TV news theme to find out which stations were watched at home. The performance of the "wrong" melody resulted in the parents being invited to school for a clarifying chat. All that ended in 1973 when Erich Honecker wanted to show the world how liberal the DDR was. He mentioned in a public speech that the freely available West German radio and television programmes could be switched on or off by every DDR citizen as they pleased.

My parents remained cautious, hence their request to me to keep stumm about our viewing preferences at home. It may have disadvantaged my social progress by having admitted to watching western television.

Mum and Dad, both already established in their careers, did not have to be as cautious as me, and spoke freely to their colleagues about what they had watched the previous night regardless of which station it was on. Countless times, Mum would set the alarm clock to two o'clock in the morning, or some other ridiculous time, to watch Mohammad Ali boxing so she could analyse the fight with her colleagues at work the next day.

I, for many years, continued pretending to have accidentally missed the films my schoolmates were talking about the following day. Naturally as I got older, I stopped that practice, but the western programmes were still branded by our media as "ideological diversions" – tools of the capitalists, who were trying to encourage us DDR citizens to topple our government. According to our politicians, the capitalists were distracting us with nice music and other innocuous forms of light entertainment, and all the while slowly brainwashing us with subtle political messages.

While this might have been true to a certain extent (for example did the CIA support the West Berlin radio station RIAS, short for "Radio in the American Sector", annually with 54 million Deutschmarks – 21.6 million dollars), the real danger for our government was that DDR citizens could compare their lifestyle with that of a West German at the flick of a switch.

JUST KIDDING

East Germany had the highest living standard among the communist countries, but obviously it could not compete with West Germany. This made parts of the DDR population constantly disillusioned or dissatisfied. The daily task for the Politburo was therefore to permanently convince us, more or less successfully, that despite the colourful image of the west in its media, the DDR was actually the better and more humane place to live in. East Germans reacted with telling jokes like these:

Erich Honecker visits Leonid Breshnev in his Kremlin-office and sees that one telephone on the Russian leader's desk is padlocked. Curious about this, he asks Breshnev for the reason and is told that this telephone is a prototype with a direct line to hell. It needs to be locked to avoid misuse because the call rate is exorbitant. Doubting what he has been told, Honecker asks for a demonstration. Breshnev takes off the lock, lifts the receiver and both can hear a "Hello. Hell here. Who is there?" Breshnev hangs up quickly and asks his secretary to bring in the telephone bill for this call. Five minutes later the door opens, the secretary comes in and presents the anxious Breshnev a bill for 500,000 rubles. Honecker is gobsmacked but wants such a telephone too and immediately upon his return to Berlin asks his scientists to develop one.

Twelve months later a prototype is installed in his office. He lifts the receiver and, just like a year earlier, he hears a "Hello. Hell here. Who is there?" He hangs up quickly and asks his secretary to bring him the telephone bill. After ten long minutes the door finally opens, the secretary comes in and puts the bill on his desk. Honecker takes a deep breath, puts his reading glasses on, looks at the piece of paper and what does it say? Total cost: 20 pfennigs – local call.

Of course, life wasn't really hell (unless maybe you were in prison). If it had been that unbearable, people would hardly have waited for 40 years before storming the border to the west. So, just to be balanced about it, here's another political joke involving heaven:

Erich Honecker dies and goes to heaven. On arrival he meets God who asks him whether he would like to go into the capitalist heaven on the right or the socialist heaven on the left. Without hesitation Erich Honecker says he would like to go to the socialist heaven to which God replies: "Okay. Go through the door on your left, enjoy yourself, but for meals you will have to join the others in capitalist heaven – we are not going to open up the second kitchen for just one person."

Political jokes like these were a bit beyond me when I started second grade in September 1975 in a spanking new school set in a small park. The school was, in fact, so new that for a while we had to bring in dust cloths to wipe our benches every morning, as the nearby park was still under construction. The surroundings might not have been ready yet, but the school itself, like most, had very good facilities. Some classrooms being dedicated to specific subjects – the arts, chemistry, biology, physics or craft work – were fitted out with the relevant equipment. There was even a small medical room which was staffed occasionally by a GP or dentist. And just next to the school was the newly built gymnasium. But it did not do anything for me. I hated P.E.

CLASS ACTS

As in Köpenick, this school too wanted to have a proper name and so the 45th General Educational Polytechnical Upper School became the 45th General Educational Polytechnical Upper School – Vinzent Porombka. It was named after a member of the International Brigades who lost his life fighting

Franco's troops in the Spanish Civil War. The name-giving ceremony happened in the form of a roll call – with the deceased hero's widow in attendance, of course – socialism was so predicable.

And so was my new class, with its combination of goody-two-shoes, slow learners, braggarts, nerds, super cool kids and normal children. Where did I fit in? It hurts to admit, but sadly not in the cool kids category. Back then I wasn't too self-confident. Nor did I have any West German relatives who could regularly send me trendy western clothes. Sporting, for example, a nice pair of Levis or maybe a T-shirt with a character from the *Muppet Show* on it, was a great way to make other kids look at you with envy.

There is a stereotype that East Germans went around dressed in flares and pointy collared shirts made of acrylic and polyester. This stereotype was largely true in the 1970's when clothes made from non-breathable synthetics were the epitome of fashion in the DDR – just like in the rest of the world. For me, polyester was a short-lived phase and one I am determined not to repeat, as Berlin summers can be scorchingly hot. Ever since the early Eighties I have made sure that all my clothes were pure cotton and nothing else, making the occasional exception for a woolly item. It wasn't impossible to buy nice clothes in East Germany, it's just that our planned economy was for the most part simply unable to react fast enough to pick up fashion trends while they were still trendy.

Also was western fashion that was considered too outrageous and decadent toned down before being adopted by our industry. Not a single pair of pre-aged jeans, for example, ever made it into a DDR shop. So, if you lacked imagination and relied on the bog-standard clothes available without pepping them up a bit, you were doomed to run around wearing bad copies of last year's fashions. But that is as bad as it fashion-wise got.

Back in 1976 I did not care yet much about fashion. Instead I concentrated on getting good marks. I enjoyed going to school. At the end of grade two, 13 out of 15 marks on my report card were A's. The other two were B's. I certainly could have taken things a little less seriously than I did at the time. But even in socialism good school results were the ticket to a good job.

"Oliver pleases us with conscious, diligent learning. He works very independently and intensely, understands the importance of things and is able to think a problem through. His exemplary attitude towards learning, the conscientious handling of all his assigned tasks and the friendly behaviour towards his classmates have resulted in him being a respected member of the class."

Assessment on my second-grade report card

As soon as I joined my new class, I became friends with Lars, a smart, very honest and down-to-earth guy with floppy black hair. He was also somewhat cool. Thanks to supportive relatives in the west, Lars had clothes and toys from the other side of the Iron Curtain.

Every year I enjoyed going to his birthday party because his mum would spoil us rotten with chocolates, sweets and other treats from the west. I stumbled home one year having had the (non-alcoholic) fruit punch that contained exotic tinned pineapple pieces, believing that I was drunk. Thank God I did not have to go very far, we only lived 200 metres apart.

Nearly all of my classmates lived close by in newly built, pre-fabricated, ten-storey high apartment blocks of the type "QP71". DDR product types were usually easy to decode – "WM66", for example, was the name of a washing machine model, which was first produced in 1966. "QP" could easily have stood for "Quadratic Panels" or "Quality Prefabricated" but instead it was the abbreviation for an equally naff name: *Querwand-Plattenbau* (right-angle-walled prefabricated building). East German bureaucrats were ever so inventive in their quest for names. After all, they renamed blow dryers "hot-air showers" and referred to pocket torches as "pedestrian protection lamps".

FAB PRE-FAB FLATS

While the bureaucrats thought up silly names, it was up to the construction workers to fit together the above-mentioned panels in record time. They used between 32 and 38 of them for an average 58-square-metre flat with six doors and seven windows, which could be built in just 200 man hours. Built the old-fashioned way with bricks and mortar, the same sized flat would have taken 500 man hours.

Unfortunately, building quicker did not necessarily mean building better, it just gave construction workers more time to do their own thing. You hardly ever saw any of them constructing for socialism on Friday afternoons or whenever it was raining, regardless of the day. Unsurprisingly, the result of such attitudes was often sub-standard output. Our flat was fine, unlike the home of one poor classmate I visited on a rainy day. She lived on the top floor in an apartment block further down the road. There was a bucket in her room to catch the water that dripped from the ceiling – five years after the block had been built. Still, most people, including our family, were very happy indeed to live in the new flats with their central heating.

Our development housed 50,000 people in 15,730 flats. Yet the demand for new apartments was so big that nearby a 400-hectare satellite city called Marzahn was built. It would become home to 150,000 Berliners. Between 1977 and 1989 at the end of each working day 17 new flats were completed there, 60,000 in total. Disrespectful citizens nicknamed Marzahn's apartment blocks "snoring silos" or "workers deposit boxes".

The monthly rent for our apartment in Lichtenberg was 92 marks (37 dollars) and remained so from the time we moved in 1975 until the collapse of the DDR in 1990 (even though the average annual salary increased in this period from 800 to 1,000 marks). The flat belonged to a co-op, and as most of the co-op's assets were newly built apartment blocks, being a member was deemed very desirable. There was a long waiting list to join, and memberships were inheritable, making it even harder for new people to get in. We were lucky that a co-op member wanted to swap flats with us. This way the membership was just transferred. All Mum and Dad had to do in return was refund the couple their deposit of 2,000 marks (800 dollars). We were even spared the 200 hours of work for the co-op that each member joining via a waiting list had to do.

Our new flat may only have had, just like the old one, one living room and one bedroom, but my parents were still able to give me and my brother our own room. Thanks to his skill and ingenuity, my father devised and built a pull-down bed. During the day it was hidden in what looked like a normal wardrobe. At night it was pulled down to convert the living room into my parent's master bedroom. I could have made a handy sum if I had charged all my classmates eager for a look at this novelty a small fee. Over 30 years later Mum and Dad are still sleeping in the very same bed (though they have gone through quite a few mattresses since then).

I have always envied my father, and still do, for being a jack-of-all-trades and good at everything he turns his hand to. He can tile, wallpaper, paint, is a blessed gardener and can turn lumps of timber or plywood into almost anything he likes. Nearly every wooden item in our apartment owed its existence to Dad's hands. Whether it was the living room setting, desks and bunk beds for me and my brother, the fish-shaped wall clock in the kitchen, made-to-measure sideboards, shelves, chairs, candle holders or drink coasters; everything was individually made to my parent's taste. The only two things Dad did not make were the already fitted kitchen and the living room tabletop, which comes with a story. In the late Sixties, this had belonged to Walter Ulbricht, East Germany's party leader and Head of State under whom the Berlin Wall was built in 1961. My father rescued it from the scrap heap while his company were building and fitting a new interior in Ulbricht's home and office. Today, the table still serves my parents well in their garden hut.

Quite a few of Dad's workmates cashed in on their artisan skills by building made-to-order furniture for private individuals in their spare time. One of his former colleagues even quit his job altogether and opened a shop selling wooden knick-knacks like candle holders, bowls, statues and so on. Because of an overwhelming demand, he was not able to make everything in the shop himself but had to buy stock from professional wood carvers. They traditionally had their workshops in the south-eastern region of Thuringia. Unfortunately, for Dad's friend, those artisans were working mainly for export. Privately owned shops like his were last in the pecking order and only received whatever supplies were left after the state-owned shops had placed their orders. So, how did my father's ex-colleague get his hands on the desperately needed stock? Luckily for him, his shop was next door to a greengrocer's which regularly gave him boxes of bananas, which were not always readily available in our little country. He would load a few of those onto his car trailer and head south, where he was then able to secure new merchandise, from which, of course, the greengrocer also received his cut. My father once profited from this network of connections too. He mentioned to this guy that some gravel ordered for our allotment would take two to three weeks to deliver. "Leave it to me," was the ex-colleague's reply. A couple of days later Dad went to the allotment and nearly fell off his moped when he saw a big heap of gravel waiting for him next to the fence.

Dad's friend made an absolute killing from his shop but in the mid-Eighties it all came to a sudden end when he was allegedly caught with tens of thousand of DDR marks in his pockets trying to illegally cross the border to West Germany. This time, even his connections proved to be worthless, and he was given a jail sentence. His assets were confiscated by the state and the once-successful shop was a thing of the past.

ARE YOU BEING SERVED?

In 1975 Mum wanted to get back to work. In autumn of that year she began a part-time job as a shop assistant. For the next seven years she worked two-and-a-half days a week in a privately owned shop with the promising, yet slightly antiquated name of Chic & Elegant. The shop offered its female clientele mainly smart and smart casual clothes. Mum immediately got on with her new colleagues like a house on fire (everyone in the Fritz family is a very likeable character). Naturally it did not take very long for one of them to play a practical joke on her.

It was a busy day and my mother was with a customer when someone in a fur coat who had just walked into the shop caught her attention. She did not know what it was but something did not seem to be quite right about this person, who headed towards another colleague. A couple of minutes later the senior sales assistant asked Mum to take two dresses to a lady who was in the changing room. My mother opened the curtain slightly to hand in the dresses to find the woman she had spotted earlier half naked. The reason for Mum's odd feeling earlier suddenly became very clear – she was really a he. The man, a petit, grey-haired guy in his fifties, was a regular customer and had been buying clothes in this shop for ages. Like many colleagues before her, my mother sported a lovely pair of red ears for the next couple of minutes.

Contrary to popular belief, the shops in East Germany did not just contain empty shelves. Of course, due to our inflexible planned economy we had shortages here and there and the merchandise on offer might not always have been what people wanted or needed at any given moment of time but there were always goods in the shops. At least in Berlin. Big cities were better supplied than smaller ones, villages were the worst off. But in general one certainly did not constantly have to queue up for everything, as featured in many western films about East Germany.

True, if a shop was selling anoraks (maybe even imported ones) in an attractive design, people would line up. However, if you were just after a plainer, more average looking anorak you were able to get one without queueing. All prices for goods were calculated and fixed centrally by the Office for Prices, which meant an item cost the same regardless of where in the country it was being sold. In fact, most of the time the manufacturers printed the prices on the packaging. While fixed prices were definitely good news for the discerning consumer, they also meant that there were no such things as summer or winter sales, let alone buy-one-get-one-free or three-for-the-price-of-two offers.

In Mum's shop, previous seasons' collections still needed to be shifted. This led to scenes which could have come straight from an episode of *Are You being Served?,* as customers were occasionally sweet-talked into buying unsuitable styles or colours – ("Oh, yes, now that DOES suit madam") or even the wrong-sized garment if the right one was not available ("Don't worry, it will ride up with wear.").

Staff sometimes got a bonus for every old item sold, but even so, Mum never had the heart to palm unsuitable *Ladenhüter*, (old stock) off on unsuspecting customers.

The upside of being a shop assistant was that she was able to get her hands on much sought-after goods – and not only from within her shop. Close to my mother's boutique was a greengrocer's, a fishmonger's, a sports shop, a florist's, an arts and crafts shop and a draper's. Whenever one of them received a delivery, they would let the other shops know, so their staff could pop round and take their pick before the goods were put on display. This way

Mum was able, without hassle, to get regularly hold of *Erdnussflips* (a savoury snack made from ground peanuts), *gefüllte Oblaten* (big round wafers filled with roasted hazelnut pieces), *Schokoküsse* (chocolate covered soft meringue dollops on a wafer), *Dominosteine* (little chocolate covered cubes which are a Christmas speciality and consist of layers of gingerbread, jam and marzipan) and Nudossi (a brand of hazelnut chocolate spread). Other items she brought home were smoked eel, attractive looking trainers, oranges and bananas, reasonably priced bedding, nice cuts of meat such as pork loin, lead crystal bowls and tumblers – all highly desirable goods and in short supply. Sometimes things went a bit too far. For example, when a woman came into Mum's shop, saying she was the mother of one of the shop assistants in the draper's shop. She demanded loudly to be sold one of the few red dresses she knew were in the storeroom. This woman left empty-handed, as that sort of attitude did not get anyone anywhere in East Germany. Your chances of successfully securing the rare and desirable increased dramatically if you were a regular customer or had something to offer in return. It helped too, if a shop assistant took a liking to you. And if you were lucky enough to meet all three criteria, you could even, like Mrs Fishmonger, leave a lingering seafoody smell behind in the changing room every time you tried a garment on and still be welcome the next time round.

THE LIFTING OF THE IRON CURTAIN

In late 1975 the Iron Curtain lifted for my grandparents as they both retired that year (women at 60, men at 65) and were now allowed to travel westwards. From 1964, DDR pensioners were able to legally cross the border to the west; in the Seventies for up to 30 days in a calendar year, in the Eighties for up to 60 days. All Nanna and Grandad had to do was go to their local *Einwohnermeldeamt* (Population Registration Office) fill in some application forms, hand over two passport photos and pay a, 11 marks (four dollars) administration fee. Then a few weeks later they were able to pick up their blue passports with the DDR emblem on the cover, in which the East German authorities had stamped exit visas (available for an additional 15 marks fee), allowing them multiple visits to West Germany and West Berlin. A passport without an exit visa wasn't worth anything. The only tricky bit in the whole process was, that in order to get such a visa, you had to provide the *Einwohnermeldeamt* with the details of a person you wanted to visit in the west. In the Seventies this person had to be a relative, in the Eighties it could also be a friend. My grandparents came up with some very distant relatives in West Berlin but hardly ever visited them in reality.

It did not enter the authorities' heads that people might just want to do some shopping and sightseeing. Instead passports for private travel were issued purely for humanitarian reasons – something of an acknowledgement, at least, by the DDR government that the 1,548 kilometre-long border through Germany divided hundreds of thousands of families. Thankfully, things relaxed somewhat in 1972. From then on also non-pensioners could apply for visits to the west, and in the mid-Eighties the privilege was even extended to members of the Communist Party, who had previously been excluded. But there was one hitch – travel was only allowed if immediate family members – parents, grandparents, siblings or grandchildren – in West Germany had requested their presence in an urgent family matter. This could be a birth, christening, confirmation, communion, marriage, death, life-threatening disease, a sixtieth, sixty-fifths, seventieth, seventy-fifth birthday, or any birthday thereafter. Cheating was virtually impossible as every application had to be supported by official documents. Unlike senior citizens who could slip through the Iron Curtain whenever they felt like it, everyone else was given non-negotiable dates for their travels. Also to make those people think twice about defecting, the state normally dictated that the travellers' dependents had to stay behind.

Only pensioners and a small number of VIPs could keep their passports at all times, other private or business travellers had to hand theirs back upon their return. The "normal" DDR citizen did not have a passport at home and did not need one either. To visit other socialist countries, the ID card was sufficient. Many East Germans therefore just had one goal in life: reaching retirement age and getting this little dark blue booklet bearing the word *Reisepass* (passport) in golden capitals on its front cover.

"The Ministry of Foreign Affairs requests that the holder of this passport travels freely and is granted any protection and assistance that they might require."

A DDR passport's first page

Although I was only a child, I already understood that having a passport meant my grandparents were able to go somewhere that I could not. The older I got the more I began to think about this. Over the years I asked them countless times to let me have a look at their passports. I imagined how cool it would be to have one of those myself so I could walk through a border checkpoint without any hassle.

At one stage, I must have been nine or ten, I even thought seriously about replacing Grandad's passport photo with one of mine so I could go with Nanna to West Berlin and check out the toy shops for some action figures that I had seen advertised on western telly. Eventually I decided against this cunning plan. It had dawned on me that no checkpoint passport inspector would be so stupid to mistake me for an old man. I was really upset that I wasn't a pensioner yet – life just seemed so unfair.

My earliest recollection of there being two Berlins separated by a guarded border was when I was about seven or eight years old and my father showed me some sights in the city, including the Brandenburg Gate. It stood on East German soil, but because it was just 50 metres from the *Staatsgrenze* (state frontier) a railing prevented us from getting within 150 metres of the iconic monument. Straight ahead, on the western side, some people were standing on a viewing platform, taking photos. Between us and them was just a big empty space – No Man's Land – and not more than three or four visible border guards. Dad explained to me that we couldn't get closer to the Brandenburg Gate because we would get stopped by a guard or even shot at.

"But," I asked, "what if all the people standing here suddenly climbed the railing and quickly ran towards the border?"

"They would also not get very far", he replied, "because there are more border guards with guns nearby." That made me think for a while.

"But Dad," I insisted, "What if lots and lots of people came here and stormed the border, surely they would overrun the guards, wouldn't they?" Thinking about his answer for a few seconds my father pointed out that the police would probably have stopped the people well before reaching this area. "But otherwise you are right", he continued, "there isn't a lot the border guards here could do if hundreds or thousands of people would run to the other side at the same time." Wow, what a revelation. I had outsmarted the border troops.

The first time I remembered this conversation was when the Berlin Wall came down in 1989, and lots and lots of my fellow countrymen did exactly what I had suggested some 14 years earlier.

Before the border checkpoints finally opened to all East Germans, only about two million individuals a year were able to check out the shops of the "rotting capitalism" (Lenin) for themselves. And over 99 per cent of those privileged travellers returned to their fatherland, though our government would not have minded in the least had all pensioners stayed on the other side. It would have saved our state a pretty penny not having to pay their pensions any more. After all, pensioners were a financial burden. Each retiree was paid around 300 marks (120 dollars) a month, roughly one third of the average national salary. Life's basics such as food, rent, electricity, water and transportation were cheap, healthcare free of charge and a place in a *Feierabendheim* (retirement home) only cost 80 marks (32 dollars) a month all inclusive, but being a pensioner still meant you had no money to waste.

Furniture and electrical items were quite expensive. A new fridge, for example, would have set you back a whopping 1,100 marks (400 dollars).

It never even occurred to my grandparents not to return home after a shopping trip to West Berlin. How they could afford going shopping in West Berlin on a regular basis, when East Germany only allowed every traveller to change 15 DDR marks into 15 Deutschmarks once a year? To a great extend they relied on the western authorities which granted them free transport and handed out free money once a year. In the Seventies, the doled out *Begrüssungsgeld* (welcome money) was 60 Deutschmarks (24 dollars) per person, in the Eighties it increased to 100 Deutschmarks (40 dollars). But regardless of how modest and financially resourceful someone was, 100 Deutschmarks was not enough money to see anyone through 12 months of visits. And it was officially forbidden to export DDR currency for the purpose of converting it in a western bureau de change into Deutschmarks. So my grandparents did what most of our geriatric travellers did – they smuggled money from the east to the west and forbidden goods from the west to the east.

SLIPPERY SENIORS

I loved to listen to my grandfather telling me his border crossing stories about how he and Nanna had tricked our customs officials over the years. Not only did our family have requests but my grandparents were also approached by friends or ex-colleagues who wanted things they had seen advertised on West German telly. Most of them only had DDR marks to pay for the things they wanted. So my grandparents had to smuggle out the money to exchange it into Deutschmarks (usually at a rate of four or five DDR marks for a single Deutschmark). Only then were they able to hit the department stores to make their friends' and family's dreams come true. You had to be canny to avoid having your shopping money confiscated.

Normally it was up to my grandpa to put the banknotes into his handkerchief or underneath his insoles when crossing the border. He never got caught. Sometimes Nan helped out by tucking Karl Marx (his head was on 100 mark banknotes) or Friedrich Engels (50 mark note) into her bra. It was pure luck she wasn't "on a mission" when one day she was picked out by a sour-looking customs official to have her clothes and handbag searched. She even had to strip to her slip. Apparently Nanna, by then a woman in her late sixties, only escaped a rectal examination because the female customs officer appreciated my grandmother's level of cooperation throughout the procedure and did not deem any further probes necessary. Some members of the East German border police still had a heart behind the stern expressions which seemed to be a pre-requisite for getting a job at the border.

The border regime on the way back was no less rigid. Any East German travelling privately was well advised to hide any Deutschmarks they might have acquired in the west. If you had more than 15 Deutschmarks in your wallet, customs were so "kind" as to arrange the mandatory conversion of your money into DDR mark at the official exchange rate of one to one.

"All foreign currencies that have been imported into the DDR... have to be offered to the State Bank of the DDR for purchase within seven days of entry into the country."

Official leaflet

Western foreigners bringing Deutschmarks into the DDR were welcome to turn up with as many western banknotes as they desired – no questions asked. The same policy applied to everyone entering the country with western goods. The DDR was quite happy for its citizens to turn to the west for goods whenever our economy could not cope with particular demands. However, importing western magazines and newspapers was definitely a no-no. But that didn't stop people bringing them back, including my grandparents. Nanna, a seamstress, had a go with some fabric on her old Singer sewing machine and came up with a little device that she called the "Inside-Trouser-Belt". It allowed Grandad to slip a newspaper into one of his trouser legs and kept it firmly in place when crossing the border. Thank God Nanna's craftmanship never let him down – if he'd been caught my grandfather could have waved goodbye to his passport.

All this was peanuts compared to the stunt my grandparents pulled at the end of each month when all immediate friends and family members wanted the latest West German TV magazine, covering the programmes for the coming month. On average, 40 to 50 magazines were needed to satisfy all requests. A feat that Grandad managed once again with the help of my grandmother who constructed another one of her devices, this one dubbed the "Over-the-Shoulder-Magazine-Holder". It consisted of two pouches – one for the chest, one for the back (to balance the load, presumably) – made from a soft fabric and connected by two shoulder straps. There was only one drawback – the magazine-filled pouches gave Grandad two very suspicious looking square lumps underneath his shirt, which he had to hide under a loose-fitting jacket every time when on a mission. As years went by the magazine requests became too much and in the early Eighties my grandfather finally pulled the plug after his greatest-ever smuggling triumph – 100 TV magazines hidden on his body in one go. That must be a world record!

Only once did he come close to being caught. As he arrived at the border, carrying his usual haul of magazines, he could see that the DDR customs officers were more diligent than usual. Everyone in front of him in the line had to open bags and jackets for inspection. Being a quick-thinker, he pretended to have heart troubles. It did not take very long for a helpful border policeman to bring him a chair and a glass of water. So he sat comfortably with his contraband, monitoring the situation carefully from a safe distance, waiting for the right moment to make his move. After about ten minutes, his time finally came. The bottleneck at the customs counter had caused such a build-up of people at the checkpoint that a safety-conscious border police chief gave the order to immediately stop all searches. As soon as the first few people started going through customs unsearched, Grandad jumped off his seat and made sure he reached the exit before things changed again. God knows what the friendly border guard who had offered chair and water made of this sudden recovery.

Some checkpoint personnel were friendly and courteous, while other members of staff were nasty and horrible. Once Nan bought me a little Matchbox car in West Berlin. Being a law-abiding citizen (apart from when she was smuggling magazines and money through the Iron Curtain) she dutifully declared it as "car" on her customs declaration form. My grandparents arrived from the west by underground at the station Friedrichstrasse, which had an integrated checkpoint. Among the customs officers on duty was one woman who was a really nasty piece of work. After reading my grandmother's customs declaration, the woman started to look around wildly. "What happened to the car?", she demanded to know, crossly. When Nanna tried to explain, showing the toy in her handbag, Mrs Customs Official had a hissy fit. "You have tried to mislead the security organs of the German Democratic Republic," she accused my grandmother. Thankfully, Nan managed to stay calm, amended the form to the women's liking, promised never to make such a terrible mistake again and was eventually free to enter her homeland.

WHEELS ON FIRE

In 1976 I wasn't the only one in our household getting his hands on wheels. One of my father's colleagues had bought a new car and approached Dad to see if he was interested in his old one? What a question – of course, he was.

In East Germany you could not just walk into a shop and buy a new car. Oh no, no, no. Instead you had to step into an Auto Salon to register your interest in buying a new car. Though you were able to choose a preferred make, colour and type of car – a saloon or a hatchback for example – there was no guarantee that the car allocated to you in the end was the one you wanted. Once the application was out of the way, all that remained for you to do was wait for the notification card to arrive. This would tell you the date and time you could go to the depot for the actual purchase and collection of the car. The average person waited between 12 and 17 years before the postman finally delivered their notification card – the demand for cars outstripped the supply many times over. Getting a driving licence was slightly easier – most people were able to join one of the scarce driving schools within two years, a waiting time hardly worth mentioning.

Q: Why are there no bank robberies in the DDR?

A: Because you have to wait 15 years for a getaway car.

Lots of people, like my father, therefore looked for private sellers instead if they were after a car soonish. The classifieds were full of people wanting to buy or sell old bangers, but the convenience of getting your four wheels without the wait came at a premium – as soon as a new car left the Auto Salon's depot it doubled in value. To calculate the (black) market value of an old car a private seller would, as a rule of thumb, deduct 1,000 marks (400 dollars) from this inflated price for every year the car had been on the road.

The madness did not stop there. People were even happy to pay you 3,000 or 4,000 marks just for your car application, depending how soon the notification was due. This was especially tempting for anyone who had applied for a car many, many moons ago but still had no money for such a status symbol – DDR banks did not offer personal loans to their customers.

Despite the problems of buying a car, as the years went by more and more people owned one: while in 1975 only 26 per cent of households were mobile, by 1989 this figure had increased to 57 per cent. And though we did not have the west's diversity on our roads, there were still a fair amount of car types to choose from – Trabant and Wartburg (DDR), Skoda (Czechoslovakia), Lada, Volga, Moscvich and Saporoshez (USSR), Polski Fiat (Poland), Dacia (Romania) and Zastava (Yugoslavia). And for whoever could afford it, we even imported VW Golfs, Mazdas, Volvos and Citroens.

By far the most popular car with the people was the omnipresent Trabant. This funny car with its 26-horsepower two-stroke engine and a body made of fibre glass was East Germany's answer to the VW Volkswagen and is even today THE symbol of the DDR. After all, more than three million Trabants were built over the decades. Mind you, it was also the butt of many jokes:

An American car-collecting millionaire hears that in the German Democratic Republic a car named Trabant is built, which apparently is so exclusive that people have to wait more than ten years to get one. In a bid to secure such a rarity for his collection, the next day he sends a $500,000 cheque together with a request for some information to the East German car manufacturer. Happy about the unexpected windfall, the manufacturer doesn't bother sending out a brochure but ships this guy his own brand-new Trabant instead. A couple of months later the millionaire meets his friend again. Asked what progress he had made with his car application the millionaire replies: "I haven't been given a delivery date yet but if the Trabant is as superbly built as the fully functional life-size cardboard model they have supplied me with in the meantime, it will be worth the wait."

A Trabant and a cowpat meet in the street. The cowpat looks at the Trabant and asks: "What the hell are you?" – "I'm a car," says the Trabant. "Yeah, right," replies the cowpat. "If you are a car, I'm a pizza."

Q: How do you double a Trabant's value?

A: You fill up its petrol tank.

It is true, by international standards the Trabant could not be taken seriously. It was small, lacked sufficient suspension and was rather noisy once it reached the maximum national speed limit of 100 kilometres per hour (62 miles per hour). Because of its compact size (slightly bigger than a Mini) and its rigid plastic fibre shell, the Trabant had no such thing as a crumple zone. A serious car accident was, therefore, better avoided if one wanted to hang on to life. Nevertheless, the Trabi, as it was nicknamed, had then (and still has today) a loyal fan base. People accepted it for what it was – a set of wheels at a reasonable price. With a price tag of around 10,000 DDR marks (4,000 dollars) in an Auto Salon (roughly a year's salary) the Trabant could not necessarily be considered cheap but it was still a good "no frills" option because other, proper, cars cost at least twice as much.

The shop price for a new Lada was around 28,000 DDR marks (11,200 dollars), while a new Volvo, if you were lucky enough to get one, would have set you back a whopping 42,000 marks (16,800 dollars), or 85,000 marks (34,000 dollars) on the black market! How anyone was able to pay that sort of money is something I still can't get my head around. My fellow countrymen were baffled too. Hence the popular interpretation of the letters "IBM" which were allocated to all Berlin-registered Volvo licence plates – "Ich bin Millionär" (I am a millionaire).

Because we Fritz's weren't millionaires, Dad had settled for the eight-year-old Trabi his colleague had offered him for 8,500 marks (3,400 dollars); the price the guy had paid when he got it new. It was still in good nick but we were not too keen on the mousey grey colour. So Dad mixed a few paints together until he got the shade he was after; a bold, signally kind of green which resembled a colour called "Ravenna Green" he had seen at a colleague's place, who had brought it back from a trip to the west.

Dad had one more ace up his sleeve. When he varnished the car himself one weekend at work, he added a big white stripe above a small white one around the car's length for that special touch. Voila, our personalised *Rennpappe* (racing cardboard – yet another nickname inspired by the Trabant's flimsy bodywork) was ready. And believe me, THAT colour made all the difference. It was a real head turner, people constantly approached my parents in the street asking them where they got the car paint from and what the shade was called.

My father loves driving so we made good use of our Trabi. We took it on trips to the Baltic Sea, Saxony, Poland and Czechoslovakia, to name just a few destinations. If it was only me and my brother in the back everything was fine. But a full car on a long journey was torture. There was hardly enough space on that back bench for three people and regardless of how much I loved my grandparents, it still makes me feel a bit funny thinking about how unpleasant the squeezing was – especially in summertime.

The coolest Trabant moment for me was when once my parents, my brother and I were driving home after a day at our allotment. All the windows were open, my brother had his big chunky wooden DDR radio and cassette recorder on his knees, playing the siren from the opening sequence of the Sweet's hit *Blockbuster* at maximum volume. It was enormous fun to see overly obedient drivers quickly pulling over to the kerb mistaking us for a police car.

1976. The East German Schmidt family goes to the Auto Salon to apply for their Trabant. The clerk tells them that they can pick up their new car at three pm on 10 May 2006.

The father asks: "Could we maybe get it in the morning? Because in the afternoon I have already made an appointment with the company delivering the freezer we ordered last week."

That old chestnut might have been a slight exaggeration. We did not have to wait until 2005 to get our freezer, though just like in the joke, we happened to get one in the same year as we got our Trabi. Mum "organised" (a term often used in the DDR) for us to get this sought-after item which hardly made an appearance in the shops. One of her colleagues with Deutschmarks and the right connections was getting a big deep-freeze chest from the west and was looking for someone to take her two-year-old DDR freezer cube. At 800 marks (320 dollars), the shop price for a brand-new unit, it did not exactly come cheap, but having a freezer meant we could finally stock up on easily perishable treats like prime cuts of meat. Vegetarianism never really made it to East Germany.

PLACE 12

Thankfully the same cannot be said about comic books. The most popular one by far was called *Mosaik* and was about three boys who travelled the world in different centuries. They'd always have great adventures and be smart enough to fight sinister characters like dangerous pirates or plotting courtiers. It was published monthly and if you didn't manage to get hold of a copy on the day it came out, or weren't on good terms with your local newsagent, you would miss an issue. My collection had quite a few gaps. *Mosaik* was such a success it was even exported and translated into Finnish, English and several other western languages.

Bummi was about the adventures of a teddy and his friends targeted at kindergarten kids or first-graders, and *Atze*, a flimsy little number had one ever-changing main story and two regular cartoons about a couple of adventurous mice and a time-travelling guy named Pat. Readers could win prices for spotting an out-of-period item hidden in a Pat story. Even more popular than East German comics were, of course, West German comics, although it was forbidden to bring them into the country. But in my brother's class were the children of several African diplomats who could travel freely to West Berlin without having to succumb to searches. Thanks to them I was able to read my first *Superman*, *Mickey Mouse*, *Lucky Luke* and *Fantastic Four* comics back in 1976. I just loved them – so much so that I still have them to this day. It was a sacrilege to throw away or recycle any newspapers or magazines from the west. Normally they were handed down to relatives, colleagues or friends who, once they had finished with them, would continue to pass them on to their relatives, colleagues or friends and so on.

One thing I never did was take western comics to school. If caught, my parents would have had a lot of explaining to do to the head teacher.

Every class register had one page reserved for teachers to write in the dates and results of bag searches for "trashy and filthy literature" – western magazines and newspapers with a decadent, anti-peace, anti-democratic or indecent content.

But in the ten years I went to school, I never witnessed such a search myself. However, the possibility of one taking place at any time was always there. Other searches were more popular with the authorities:

"Secrecy of the post and secrecy of the telecommunications are inviolable. They can only be restricted on a statutory basis, if required by the security of the socialist state or a prosecution."

GDR constitution

While the majority of East Germans communicating with westerners by post were realistic enough to suspect that their mail was screened by the Stasi (despite assurances to the contrary), the full extent of the efficiency of our mail snoopers far exceeded people's imagination.

Only after the Wall came down did the public learn that all main district post offices up and down the country had sealed off areas called "Place 12". There nearly every letter, every postcard, every parcel going to or coming from the west was either read, copied, photographed or X-rayed by Stasi employees. A never-ending task, considering that 25 million parcels alone were posted every year.

The secret service had even automated the letter opening and resealing process. While a skilled person was able to open up to 400 letters in an hour, specially built machines managed 600 letters. The glueing machines were yet even more efficient, they could close up to 800 letters in an hour. Unfortunately, the reading itself slowed things down a bit as it could not be delegated and still had to be done by humans who each "only" managed 800 letters or postcards in one shift. Despite that particular bottleneck the secret service still set their prying eyes on 90,000 postal items every single day! And as the security of our socialist state required such action, the Stasi did not violate the constitution. Ingenious! To be fair, the West German BND, short for Bundesnachrichtendienst (Federal Intelligence Service), also got its hands dirty. It had 2,000 members of staff to open and read letters. In other words a private and rather personal letter sent either way through the Iron Curtain might well have been secretly read twice before being finally received by the intended addressee. No wonder the post took ages to arrive. DDR citizens joked:

An East German writes to a West German relative: "Dear uncle Paul, Many thanks for your last parcel. The gun and the ammunition have arrived safely.

I have buried both in the garden, as suggested." One week later a second letter follows: "Dear uncle Paul, The Stasi has just dug over my garden, you can now send me those Dutch tulip bulbs."

I remember one incident in 1976 when part of my grandad's birthday parcel from a friend in Hamburg must have ended its journey at "Place 12". Being a numismatist, Grandad had asked for a few West German coins for his collections. Knowing that like stamps, it was not allowed to send currency in or out of the DDR, he had suggested to the sender to wrap them up in aluminium foil, hoping that they would not be detected by the customs' X-ray machine.

Unfortunately, the trick did not work. When the parcel arrived, instead of the desired coins Grandad found inside a copy of the East German official party newspaper *Neues Deutschland* (New Germany) and a *Teil-Einziehungs-Entscheid* – a document informing him that the coins had been confiscated. If he wanted, he could lodge a complaint against the decision within four weeks. He did but could have saved himself the hassle. The coins were gone for good.

"Place 12" was also vigilant when it came to preventing forbidden goods leaving the country. Once my grandmother received a small parcel (one that had not been opened by the Stasi or customs) from an old classmate who lived in Munich. She wanted to reciprocate the gesture, like every self-respecting East German who did not like being portrayed as a needy charity-case by the West German media. Nan knew that heavily subsidised goods like meat products, shoes or kids' clothing for example, were not allowed to be sent to the west, and as her friend was a smoker she opted instead for a nice chunky ashtray. A few other stocking fillers were bought, everything was wrapped up nicely, put in a box and taken to the post office. Unfortunately, a week later the parcel came back. A little piece of paper informed Grandma that the DDR customs administration had returned the item, because part of its contents violated against decree blah blah blah, regulation blah, blah blah. The ashtray, made of pressed lead crystal, was not allowed to leave the country westwards. As with porcelain, the state wanted to officially export those products for hard currency. The drip feeding of such goods as presents to westerners was therefore forbidden.

Next, Nanna described the ashtray in the customs declaration as being made of plain glass and sent the parcel off again, hoping that it would fool the officer on duty. Sadly it didn't and the parcel was returned once more. Fed up with the hassle Grandma replaced the ashtray with a comfy pair of slippers. Off the parcel went once more only to be returned for a third time – slippers fell into the category of shoes and were not allowed to leave the country. Nan gave up and wrote her friend a letter describing the problems she had encountered. Her words were met with disbelief. Suggesting that Nanna had made it all up, the reply postcard read: "You might as well have written that my parcel was eaten by a dog." Their friendship never recovered from that incident but the big chunky lead crystal ashtray stood the test of time, as my grandparents, both non-smokers, used it for two decades as a little sweets bowl on their living room table. It is now in my possession.

What made the whole process of getting presents in and out of the country so unpredictable, was the human factor. To keep its options open, the state deliberately worded parts of the customs regulations vaguely. Enforcing individuals had to decide what goods were falling into which categories.

The import of a record was only permitted when the music was either part of our cultural heritage or "a truly cultural piece of contemporary work". The problem was, that music taste differs. What one customs officer considered cultural and contemporary, another one branded rubbish. Were Boney M truly cultural? And what about AC/DC? Difficult decisions needed to be made. To be on the safe side, many customs officers were overzealous and if not sure, confiscated rather than letting items slip through.

Several times my grandparents were stopped at one checkpoint with western records but had no problems crossing the border when trying their luck at a second checkpoint. I have also heard of cases where records were confiscated from western parcels even though licence copies of the same albums were sold in DDR shops (you just had to be lucky enough to be there at the right time). The authorities' irrationality and inconsistency made it easy for people in the east and the west to conveniently blame DDR customs whenever a promised parcel did not arrive – even if nothing had been posted.

MISCALCULATIONS & COMPLAINTS

Not every westerner was as rich or well off as they pretended to be and able to afford sending regular goodie-parcels to East German friends or relatives. But rather than simply saying how things really were, some people came up with the most bizarre stories in an attempt not to lose face. A West German friend of my parents' for example, claimed to have sent us an abundance of parcels over the years containing chocolates, coffee and sweets. But mysteriously none of them ever arrived. How likely was it that every single parcel would have been confiscated?

In the mid- to late Seventies, pocket calculators were the latest must-have accessory all over the world. Even though the first models were made for really big pockets, could only manage basic arithmetic and cost an arm and a leg (nearly half an average monthly salary in the DDR) people were still keen on them. And as with many popular goods, the demand in East Germany far outstripped the supply. It happened that in one year my brother's birthday coincided with the East Berlin visit of the aforementioned friend whose packets we never received. When told that his present had to be gotten from the car, my brother understandably got very excited. He shouldn't have. To the words: "I did not know whether you already had a pocket calculator, so I got you this..." he was handed a family-sized bag of Haribo's mixed assortment – not really what he had hoped for. But there is a happy ending to this story because a couple of weeks later he got his much-wanted calculator, a Japanese brand. My grandparents bought it for him in West Berlin.

While my brother was quite pleased that his wish had finally come true, other people weren't so happy. Something happened in 1977 to make it a year in which the feelings of many East Germans ran high and lots of people wrote letters of complaint. As already mentioned, this was a very popular way for DDR inhabitants to voice their anger if they felt they were being disadvantaged or treated unfairly in any way.

"Every citizen can address petitions (suggestions, comments, requests or complaints) to representatives of the people, their delegates or the political and economical organs. Exercising this right must not be detrimental to them."

GDR constitution

Unlike the articles in the constitution about the right of free speech and the secrecy of the mail and telecommunications, this one was for real. Whether you thought a temporary unavailability of loo paper was a disgrace or felt the health care system had let you down, writing a complaint was the solution for most East Germans. Complaints were also written if, for example, a civil servant behaved inappropriately, or someone had their application to visit their West German aunt on her sixtieth birthday rejected by the authorities. There was certainly no shortage of cause for complaint. This system even worked on a smaller scale: should you have received poor service in a shop or restaurant you simply asked for the Customer's Book and were able to write your grievance down on numbered pages on the left hand side. The duty manager then had to reply to you on the right hand side pages within 15 days. Naturally, the whole process worked the other way around as well. You also could inform a manager about an extremely helpful member of staff or send a letter to a ministry applauding them on new legislation they may have passed, though not many used this system for praise. Even fewer people did so in 1977 when the DDR was hit hard by the coffee crisis.

THE BALLOONING BEAN BUDGET

The Seventies had been very kind to us East Germans. Since Erich Honecker had come to power the living standard of the DDR population had steadily increased, which in return had lead to an increased consumption of non-essentials such as alcohol, tobacco, cakes, sweets, chocolates and, of course, coffee. Even though 20 per cent of our country's total coffee demand was satisfied privately by West Germans sending goodie parcels to their East German relatives or friends, 50,000 odd tons of beans still had to be legitimately imported. But because of drastic price hikes on the world market in 1977, the DDR suddenly had to cough up 300 million US dollars for those imports – four times the amount needed in 1975. Spending that much money on coffee beans seemed more than just a tad excessive to the Politburo, so it hit the emergency brake and decided that national coffee consumption had to be reduced, quickly. Restaurants were reminded to make sure they only used 6.5 grams of coffee per cup as indicated in guidelines, companies were advised to serve tea instead coffee during meetings. But the most efficient way of achieving lower import figures seemed to be an increase of the retail price. Secret plans were drawn up to discontinue all existing coffee brands and replace them with a new, more expensive one, costing 60 marks (24 dollars), rather than the usual 35 marks, for 500 grams. Meanwhile, people had become aware that coffee seemed to be harder and harder to find in the *Verkaufsstellen* ("selling places" was the official East German jargon for shops). Panic buying became widespread.

The Politburo hesitated to increase prices, instead a new product called Kaffee-Mix was launched. It cost 24 marks per 500 grams and contained a mixture of ground coffee beans (51 per cent) and other filler ingredients, including chicory, barley, rye and peas, to stretch the available coffee stock as much as possible. As these other ingredients, were not individually listed on the packaging, people started to smell a rat. Two very popular jokes from that time reflect what people thought of this new invention:

Q.: What is the difference between a film star and the new Kaffee-Mix?

A.: A film star has got fans.

Erich Honecker wants to visit the west and applies for a passport at his local registry office. His application is rejected on the grounds that he is a bearer of secrets – only he knows all of the Kaffee-Mix's ingredients.

East Germans may have accepted a lot of things but having their beloved real coffee taken away was not one of them. Up and down the country, well-behaved yet outraged DDR citizens sat down at home and wrote petitions demanding a change back to the old-style coffee. After all, coffee is a German's most favourite hot drink. And because East Germans spent more money in a year on coffee than they did, for example, on furniture or shoes, the government had no choice but to give in to the pressure from the man in the street. The plan to introduce the new, more expensive brand never materialised. The despised Kaffee-Mix was reduced in price by one third in an attempt to generate at least some interest, but without success – shoppers still shunned it. Eventually production stopped. Our economists only breathed a sigh of relief when in the following year coffee prices on the international markets sank by 30 per cent and East Germany's spending on coffee beans was once more in line with the estimated budget.

MY BRUSH WITH THE COUNCIL OF FRIENDSHIP

As I was only nine years old in 1977, the Coffee Crisis went way above my head. I had problems of my own! According to my much-liked class teacher, Frau Arendt, I had a sense of duty, engaged actively in after-school events and took on little jobs for the class. So far so good. Unfortunately, it was that combination of qualities that made my classmates elect me onto the school's Freundschaftsrat (Council of Friendship). Only the best Pioneers became members in the council. At first I was proud as punch. But what was supposed to be an honour soon turned into endless boredom. As the sole representative of all the school's third-graders, I regularly had to meet up with the representatives from the other grades, while my friends were out playing. And meetings were no fun. We third-graders despised the "babies" from the second grade, and so I didn't bother talking to their representative. Likewise, the girl representing the fourth-graders ignored me. Hardly anyone talked to each other. The whole thing was a total nightmare and I hated every second of it. Yet we still had to make it work somehow because the Council of Friendship was quite an important institution. Its members represented the school's Pioneers who, according to the statute, were supposed to be "at ease and happy to learn and work together". To achieve this, the Freundschaftsrat had to set tasks for the Pioneers to fulfill, such as organising cake sales in aid of struggling Third World countries or meetings with war veterans to find out how hard life for communists was back in the old days.

But did I care? Not a sausage. As the year went by I preferred more and more to be "at ease and happy" with my classmates instead and I attended fewer and fewer council meetings. The best thing was, I never had to face the music for my half-hearted input. The assessment on my year-end report card read: "Oliver fulfilled his function in the Friendship Council with conscientiousness." If my disgraceful behaviour had been a shining example of conscientiousness, I can only imagine how dedicated the other members must have been.

UNION TALK

The DDR union movement, the FDGB, short for Freier Deutscher Gewerkschaftsbund (Free German Association of Unions) had, like the Pioneers, a large number of members, too. Although nearly ten million of the 17 million East Germans belonged to it, the FDGB's desire to truly represent its members interest was unfortunately somewhat limited. The top union boss was also a member of the Politburo of the Communist Party and consequently the workers' ultimate bargaining tool, strike action, was not allowed to even be considered.

Just like any other union in the world, the FDGB had to rely on monthly contributions to finance its work. Unionists paid 2.5 per cent of their gross salary in membership fees and my father, being a union member too, sometimes had to pick up the membership stamps for his company from the union headquarters.

Membership stamps came in different denominations, just like postage stamps, and were given to people as receipts for their contributions. One day, Dad was on his way back from the union headquarters on his motor bike when he noticed that the briefcase containing stamps worth 50,000 marks (20,000 dollars) was no longer on the bike's carrier – it must have fallen down somewhere along the way. Panic-stricken, he quickly turned around and drove back the way he had come. A kilometre down the road in the dust next to the kerb he thankfully found his brown leather case, untouched. The average person would have had to work five years to earn 50,000 marks before tax, so if that briefcase had been lost for good my father would have been in a lot of trouble.

The pensioners were an envied group of union members. Their monthly contribution was the price of a fruit-flavoured yoghurt: 50 pfennigs (20 cents). Dad's company threw them a nice Christmas party every year. The costs for the party alone exceeded the annual contributions made by the oldies. On top of that every pensioner was given 30 marks for Christmas. For a union member to get back sixty times the amount paid in a year was one of those things that were only possible in the German Democratic Republic.

But throwing parties for senior citizens wasn't all the union was about. It did other things too. You could call them as intermediaries if you were unable to come to an agreement with your boss about a work-related problem. The union was also interested in hearing from anyone who had an idea about how to save material at work or how to make internal production processes more efficient. Employees who came up with good ideas received one-off cash payments if their proposals were realised. Union reps also had a say in which teams or individuals would receive cash bonuses in recognition of fulfilled or exceeded set performance targets. But for most people, union membership meant they were able to get hold of the very popular and extremely moderately priced group holidays or holiday accommodations in union-owned houses. All union holidays were subsidised by 75 per cent and almost always attracted more applicants than there were places available.

HAPPY HOLIDAYS

East Germans cherished their annual holiday. Although it was possible to travel to other socialist states, most preferred the cheaper option of going somewhere in the DDR instead. But our country wasn't exactly blessed with an excessive supply of hotel rooms, especially in the tourist hotspots near the Baltic Sea in the north or the ski resorts down south. You could not just turn up at a hotel and ask for a room. Even trying to book one a couple of months in advance was difficult as regular hotel guests would often reserve rooms when leaving a hotel in the previous year. Private accommodation was equally hard to come by. Locals, especially near the Baltic Sea, made small fortunes by becoming part-time B&Bs and converting chicken sheds and basements into bedrooms. Even obtaining a camping permit was difficult – you had to apply a year in advance if you wanted to be considered.

In less popular destinations there was a much better chance of finding a place to stay, but you were still well advised to make a reservation a few months in advance. If you were after an independent holiday, your safest bet was to stay with friends or family members. The main reason it was so hard to find accommodation was a lack of investment by the state, which spent too much money on subsidising people's holidays.

To relieve some pressure, hotels were under strict instructions to not accept guests if they lived in the same town. I still remember how as a child I watched an episode of Dallas in which J.R. had a row with Pamela and stormed off in a huff to spend the night in a hotel. I imagined how funny it would have been had the receptionist said: "I am terribly sorry Mr Ewing, but I cannot give you a hotel room. Please try your luck in another city."

The FDGB operated its own hotels and guesthouses, which were purely there for the benefits of its members. Though they also had a limited supply of five-star accommodations available, the majority of their rooms was more one, two and three star material. You had to make your own way to the hotel but with a full-board stay costing 140 marks (56 dollars) per adult for a fortnight (30 marks for kids), no one quibbled. The union also organised travel abroad but our family had never been lucky enough to snap one of those deals up. We did not rely too often on the FDGB's travel service anyway. On most of our holidays we either stayed with family members or managed to secure reservations for one of the holiday homes Dad's company owned in various locations around the country. It was quite common for firms and institutions to have their own accommodation. Usually the bigger a company was, the more places they offered their employees. Acquisition of those holiday homes did not always take place by conventional methods: My father's firm, for example, once received a request from the Deutsche Reichsbahn (German Reich Railways) to build a skittle alley in one of their holiday complexes. Being satisfied with the speedy execution of the job and the quality of work delivered, the Reichsbahn not only paid the money due but also gave the firm's workers sole use of one of their holiday homes. (East Germany's national train company was still called German Reich Railways – the Antifascist DDR had not renamed Hitler's train running network fearing it would otherwise lose the operational rights for West Berlin, which were granted to the Reichsbahn by the Allies immediately after the war.)

On another occasion Dad's company was asked by the FDGB to renovate some of the union's holiday homes at the Baltic Sea. This time their reward would be the ownership of a couple of run-down holiday accommodations which they could renovate for themselves. With seven million holiday-makers yearly, the Baltic Sea was the number one DDR holiday destinations. Acquiring the leasehold to a property there was like being given a licence to print money.

Barter deals did not only take place on a national basis, they also played a role in international trade relations. This was especially the case when the DDR was dealing with countries which, like us, had national currencies that were not popular on the world financial markets.

Over the years Dad's company did quite a few barter deals. A ground-floor self-contained apartment in a converted old house, up north in the charming seaside town of Bansin was the result of one of them. And one year we were able to stay there. Boy, was I excited when packing my little suitcase with toys and books the day before (Mum took care of the clothes). My first trip to the Baltic Sea! After we arrived I went straight to the beach to taste the seawater. Dad had told me earlier that it would be salty and I did not believe him. Of course, he was right and I got a yucky surprise.

Just thinking of our Baltic Sea holidays puts a smile on my face. Over the years we went a few times to Bansin, staying at various places. I can still see us going to the FDGB hotel for breakfast in the mornings and heading down to the beach afterwards. Never having been too keen on the sun, I usually played or read in the shade. I collected shells, built sand castles, went for dips in the lukewarm, murky water and had the occasional jelly fish fight with other kids while my parents worked on their sun tans. Sometimes I would put my kiddies traffic police outfit on (consisting of a white PVC cap, belt and cuffs) and regulate imaginary traffic on the promenade. Some years I even had little lady friends. There was Anne, a skinny, black-haired girl I met on the beach. Not only did I share my sweets with her, but we also made some money. We picked wild flowers from a nearby meadow, made little bunches and offered them to holiday-makers at one mark a bunch. If I was well behaved (which most of the time I was) my parents would give me some money for giant marshmallow-filled wafers from the nearby supermarket. The ones half covered in chocolate were my favourite.

On each holiday I was allowed to buy one souvenir. It usually took me several days to decide what to get: "Shall I buy the wooden sailing ship or the pirate doll? Or what about the picture frame made of shells? On the other hand wouldn't it be much cooler to have the miniature bottle ship? Or should I go for the plastic treasure chest-cum-moneybox instead?" Thankfully the merchandise did not change very much over the years. This way I ended up with the wooden sailing ship AND the pirate doll AND the picture frame AND the miniature bottle ship AND the treasure chest. Plus a selection of miniature books with photographs of all the towns we visited on day trips, and a big pile of postcards.

In the afternoons we often went to the ice cream parlour, which was further down the promenade near a stage where orchestras regularly played. The first time we sat down on the terrace overlooking the Baltic Sea I ordered ice cream with tinned lychees. The waitress unwittingly called them *Glitschies* (glitschig in German means slippery). Those lychees just looked and tasted so exotic, I immediately fell in love with them. But a rival tinned fruit soon won over my affections.

The day I discovered them it was wet and windy. Outdoor activities were out of the question so we went to the ice cream parlour out of pure boredom. The gusty winds were fiercely throwing raindrops onto the full-length glass windows when the waitress brought my order – a selection of different ice cream flavours garnished with arbutus. Arbutus are the rough-textured fruits of the Asian strawberry tree. They looked like cherries with goose pimples, had an earthy taste and hairy stones. What a novel fruit! I was so excited about my new discovery I convinced Dad to take a few stones with him so we could grow a strawberry tree in our garden. As he predicted, those seeds were as dead as seeds from preserved fruit can be. The spot in the garden where I had imagined myself harvesting bumper crops of exotic Asian arbutus was shortly afterwards given over to an apple tree, which is still going strong today.

The omnipresent apple was not what I was after. There were 17 million apple trees alone in the main apple growing region around Berlin – statistically at least one tree for every single DDR citizen. Fifty per cent of all fresh fruit sold was apples – the only fruit available all year round. Sadly, fresh arbutus did not feature in our shops at all. After our holiday I looked out for the tinned version whenever I went into a *Kaufhalle* (supermarket) or an *Obst- und Gemüseladen* (green grocer). And though I was quite often lucky and got the tinned lychees, I was not to see tinned arbutus again for some 12 years. For that to change the Wall had to come down.

But our holiday at the Baltic Sea not only acquainted me with strange fruit, it was also the perfect place for my parents to explain to me why only the sea was visible on the horizon. Only sometimes if the weather conditions were perfect, a very, very fine sliver of land would be visible in the faint distance – Denmark. Imagine how disappointed I was when Mum rejected my suggestion of trying to see whether we could paddle there on our air mattress.

There was no barbed wire on the beach or helicopters flying low to keep visitors in check. It was a normal beach that could have been anywhere in the world, with kids screaming, sun-seekers enjoying themselves, swimmers dipping into the sea and lifeguards making sure that there were no nasty accidents. But despite all the normality this beach was still different to others. The whole area was off-limits at night. Diving and boating were not permitted at any time and neither was venturing past the 150-metre zone in the water, marked out by buoys. If by mistake or intention someone went any further, maybe even on an air mattress, and was caught by a patrol boat, they would have had a lot of explaining to do. *Republikflucht* (fleeing the republic) as it was officially known, was a punishable offence. Section 213 of the DDR penal code regulated "Illegal Frontier Crossings" and anyone found guilty could expect a prison sentence of up to eight years. Even the mere preparation of an "Illegal Frontier Crossing" was punishable. In fact, just being suspected of attempting a *Republikflucht* was a good enough reason for imprisonment on remand.

The risks associated with such an attempt were an effective deterrent but, contrary to western Cold War films and novels, the majority of East Germans did not constantly think about how to escape through the Iron Curtain.

Of course, there was a curiosity and interest to see this big wide world that was inaccessible to most of us. Forbidden fruit is the sweetest, and many would naturally have jumped at the chance to see maybe Stockholm, Sydney or San Francisco with their own eyes. But how many Brits, for example, also have never left their own shores and still live normal, happy lives?

Living conditions in the German Democratic Republic might have been far from perfect, but for the majority of us, life was not unbearable.

A secret opinion poll done for the Politburo in the Seventies even found the vast majority of DDR citizens associated the words freedom, social security, democracy and humanity with life in East, rather than West Germany. Hardly the findings one would expect to get from a population that, according to the western media, was suppressed by the governing Communist Party.

Though the Iron Curtain narrowed our choice of worldwide travel destinations, it also protected us from the harsh winds that tend to blow in capitalist countries when it came to things like crime, poverty and unemployment. Because of this deliberate isolation, life in the east was somewhat comfy and cushy. Many people found their niche. The secured border to the west was an unalterable fact of life, and by the looks of it, one that was likely to remain in place for a very long time indeed. So most DDR citizens blanked out the western border altogether and got on with their everyday lives.

OBEYING THE LAWS

At the beginning of the fourth grade in September 1977 my classmates and I were looking forward to leaving the Young Pioneer phase behind us. We were eager to reach the next milestone in our socialist education – the becoming of *Thälmannpioniers*.

Ernst Thälmann was a historical figure who became the leader of the German Communist Party in 1925. In 1933 he was imprisoned by the Nazis and killed in a concentration camp in 1944. By wearing his name, swapping our blue neckerchiefs for red ones and paying a monthly fee of ten pfennigs (four cents) we were supposed to become, just like him, class-conscious socialists. After we had solemnly promised in a ceremony that Ernst Thälmann was our role model and we would learn to work and fight like him, we were handed our new neckerchiefs. We were also given guidelines on how we had to behave as Thälmann Pioneers:

The Laws of the Thälmann Pioneers

We Thälmann Pioneers love our socialist fatherland the German Democratic Republic. With words and action we will always and everywhere side with our state, which is an integral part of the community of socialist states.

We wear our red neckerchief with pride and treat it with respect. Our red neckerchief represents the working class's flag and it's a great honour to wear it as a sign of our close ties with the cause of the working class and its party.

We love and respect our parents. We know that we owe our parents much. We follow their advice and help them always. We want to become conscious creators of the socialist society.

We love and protect peace and hate warmongers. We strengthen socialism and help peace-loving forces all over the world by learning diligently and doing good deeds. We will face always and everywhere the agitation and lies of the imperialists.

We are friends of the Soviet Union and of all socialist countries and maintain friendship with all children in the world.

The friendship with the Soviet Union is integral to us. The Lenin Pioneers are our best friends.

We acquire thorough knowledge and skills and stand up for tidiness, discipline and cleanliness. We encourage everyone to learn without cheating, to use their knowledge and to make sure that words match action. This way we prepare for life and work in the socialist society.

We love to work, respect work and all working people. We learn from workers, farmers and other members of the working population and we lend a hand wherever help is needed. We protect public property.

We love the truth, are reliable and friends with each other. We always aspire to recognise the truth and stand up for socialism. We accomplish assigned tasks and give our word of honour as Pioneers. We ensure that our Pioneer group will become a team of comrades and we will help other pupils.

We make ourselves familiar with engineering, study the laws of nature and get to know our cultural treasures. We are interested in the latest developments in science and technology.

We Thälmann Pioneers keep our body clean and healthy, regularly take part in sports and are cheerful.

The laws were certainly quite a mouthful and it is only now that I have bothered reading through them in detail. Though they were printed in our membership booklets they never made an interesting read. In everyday life, being a Pioneer meant to us kids two things: trying to get good marks in school and helping others.

I, for example, was very good in German and so I gave after school lessons on a one-to-one basis to classmates with grammar or spelling difficulties. Once or twice a year the class would hold a cake bazaar, to which everyone brought in a home-made cake. During the breaks we then sold the slices to other kids, raising money for starving children in Nicaragua or some other good cause. Alternatively, we raised cash by bringing in old newspapers, empty glasses, bottles or tins, which the school then sold to the national recycling company. The possibilities of doing good deeds were endless.

SAVING THE ENVIRONMENT

"In appreciation of the achieved results when competing with other schools in the collection of secondary raw materials as an important resource for the national economy, the 45th Polytechnical Upper School – Vinzent Porombka is honoured with a financial reward."

Certificate, awarded to my school in 1977

As the DDR wasn't exactly overflowing with natural resources, recycling was constantly promoted. People were encouraged to hand in their *Sekundärrohstoffe* (secondary raw material) at special collection points by being offered money. For a kilogram of old newspapers and magazines you received 15 pfennigs (six cents). Glasses or bottles, depending on their shapes and sizes, earned you between five and ten pfennigs. Sparkling wine bottles may have weighed a ton, but at 15 pfennigs each they were real cash cows. Recycling was a great money generator for kids. Normally, if children wanted to boost their pocket money, they would bring to the collection point whatever glass or paper they could find at home. If more money was needed, kids did the rounds, going from door to door asking people whether they had any bottles, glasses or old paper they wanted to get rid of.

During the summer holidays I did that quite often, too. It was hard work lugging all that stuff to the collection point but I often made seven, eight or even ten marks (four dollars) in a day. Someone had even written a Pioneer song called *Don't You Have Old Paper*:

Don't you have old paper,
dear granny, dear grandpa?
Ding-dong, a Pioneer,
ding-dong, stands here.
Don't you have old paper,
bottles, glasses or scrap metal?
Ding-dong, please give it to me,
before the Free German Youth takes it away.

People tended to hand over more recyclable goods to kids who were collecting for their school. Therefore I, like many others too, pretended to be on official Pioneer duty when in fact all I wanted was to bump up my pocket money so I could buy an action figure or a car I had seen in a toy shop.

Even toys were given a second life. We were regularly asked by our teachers to donate things we did not play with any more, to go to kids in poorer countries. Twice our class expressed their solidarity by sending off parcels, once to Vietnam and once to Poland during a very cold winter. I found it a bit weird that we had to send things to other socialist countries when we were always told it was the workers in the capitalist countries who just scraped by, but I did not let those thoughts dampen my enthusiasm.

THREE IN A BOAT

Enthusiastic I was also about my classmate Cordelia. Lovely Cordelia with her long blonde hair and those cute little freckles around her nose in summertime – I always had a soft spot for her ever since I joined this class after our move to the borough of Lichtenberg two years earlier.

Early in the fourth grade I plucked up all my courage to finally ask Cordelia the one question I had meant to ask ever since I laid my eyes on her. It was a sunny autumn day when we were walking down the road to the nearby adventure playground which had a wooden climb-on fort and a rope-bridge. Going through a public garden on the way I plucked Cordelia a rose from one of the many flower displays. With my heart pounding like a pneumatic hammer I only managed to get out a, "Do you want to be my... " My shyness prevented me from finishing the sentence. In desperation I resorted to the game "Hang Man", and put eight little horizontal lines for the word *Freundin* (girlfriend) with my shoe in the sand.

Cordelia, equally embarrassed, pretended at first that she didn't know which word I was after. Only her bright red ears betrayed her. That was so sweet. Finally after a couple of seemingly endless minutes she shyly nodded her head. I was on cloud nine. So much so, that a couple of weeks later I even came close to fighting for her.

By then I had noticed that Rene', one of our classmates, who, to make matters worse only lived six floors below Cordelia, seemed to be around her a lot at school. One day during the first break I took Rene' aside and told him something about three people in a boat that only fits two makes it one person too many on board, suggesting whoever joined last should leave first.

God knows why I came up with such an elaborate story when all I wanted to say was: "Oi! Back off Cordelia, she is mine."

My little talk still did the trick. First Rene' looked at me as if I had a screw loose. He clearly did not know what to make of it all, yet instead of giving me a smack and starting a fight, as I had expected, he just walked off and Cordelia was left alone from that day on. Mission accomplished!

But my joy was short-lived. Rene' had his revenge a couple days later. He told Cordelia about our conversation. She took me aside and asked with a frown and disbelief in her voice: "Three people in a boat are one too many?"

I wanted the earth to open up and swallow me.

MONITORING THE CLASS

Maybe it was this willingness to confront problems head on that prompted my classmates in the autumn of 1977 to put me up for election for the post of *Gruppenratsvorsitzender*. At least I like to think so, but the real reason behind it was most probably that no one else could be bothered to take on that role. *Gruppenratsvorsitzender* translates roughly as "Chairman of the Group Council". But what sounds quite impressive was only the East German equivalent of the class monitor.

Each class was considered a separate Pioneer group and needed a Group Council. A council consisted of a cashier to collect the monthly membership contributions, an agitator to keep everyone politically informed and last, but not least, a chairman who officially represented the class and who had the overall responsibility for everything class-related. Every month our Pioneer group, like all the others, had a big meeting to discuss any problems that needed to be tackled. If someone had problems with their schoolwork, a classmate with good marks had to be found to give them after-school lessons.

If someone had played truant, they had to explain themselves and we had to take action to stop it once and for all. If someone had behaved inappropriately, we had to make sure it would not happen again. But it wasn't just about problems. Classmates who had done good deeds were praised in front of everyone and others were encouraged to follow their example. We also used the meetings to organise cultural after-school events, agreed on where to go on class trips and when to hold class discos.

At first I felt honoured to be elected class monitor. Unfortunately, after doing the job four years in a row the selection process amounted more and more to something like: "Why don't we vote for Oliver again to get it over and done with as quickly as possible". Holding the position was something to be proud of, but it was also a thankless job in which I was constantly caught between two sides. The teachers put me on the spot if individuals or even the whole class did not behave. But I also did not want to turn my classmates against me or even worse, lose good friends.

On a couple of occasions lessons throughout the day were cancelled due to teachers being ill, though the very last lesson was still on. Usually it didn't take very long for some smartarse to come up with the idea that the whole class should skip the last lesson. As *Gruppenratsvorsitzender* I could not sit back and allow this to happen. So I tried to make everyone see that playing truant for one lesson wasn't worth the possible consequences of getting an official reprimand on their school record. If that did not work (and sometimes it didn't) then I really was in trouble, because one of my responsibilities was to carry the class register from lesson to lesson. So I had no choice but to go back to school and hand it to a teacher who would be waiting for a class that wasn't going to show up.

I put the emptiness in the classroom down to a mass-misunderstanding and promised that I would have a word with the rest of the class the following day. Of course, I didn't but my pleading was always accepted and our class was never subject to any disciplinary action. Phew!

If in doubt, behaviour deemed worthy of a Pioneer could always be checked in the annual Pioneer calendar. I still have the edition from 1978 which promises "a book that contains many stories, serious and funny which will surely give you pleasure". A promise that remains largely unfulfilled when you look inside at the table of contents: *A Visit to the Cuban Pioneers* (dull), *The Discontented Commander* (yawn), *Dear Soldiers* (snore), *We Hold a Learning Conference* (oh, please!) and *Soldiers with the Red Star* (a boring piece about the glorious Soviet Army). There are also other, more appropriate stories, riddles and jokes for kids, but, for my liking, far too few.

The last 16 pages of the book are also disappointing. Next to pictures of different types of mushrooms, fish and locomotives are illustrations of badges from other Pioneer organisations around the world. The UK is represented with the Woodcraft Folk – "a progressive child organisation in England". On other pages readers can familiarise themselves with pictures of the insignias of rank for the DDR army forces, together with a drawing of what goes where in a soldier's locker. Our state made sure it used every opportunity trying to get us young boys interested in a military career.

HIGH FLYERS

In the Cold War days, east and west, both constantly tried to impress each other. However, it was pretty obvious to every East German that we, the puny DDR, were not able to compete with the mighty West German economy. So our government regularly organised propaganda events. Celebrating big always turned the ugly duckling of the two Germany's into a beautiful swan – at least for a few hours.

When it comes to victories in the propaganda war, the 26 August 1978 deserves a mention as one of East Germany's finest hours. On that day, DDR Wing Commander Sigmund Jähn boarded the Russian spacecraft Soyuz 31 in Vladivostok and became the first German in space. What a success that was for our leaders – the tiny German Democratic Republic had beaten the mighty Federal Republic of Germany in the space race. Mind you, the propaganda victory lost some of its impact when only four days later another GDR citizen, Detlef-Alexander Tiede, also lived out his ambition to fly to the unknown. He hijacked a plane from the DDR airline Interflug (Interflight) during a flight from Warsaw to East Berlin and forced it to land in West Berlin instead. Nine other quick-thinking passengers made the most of the situation and also decided to not return to their socialist fatherland. The whole incident was such an embarrassment for our secret service, who seemed to have been caught off-guard by the successful escape, that from then on all Interflug flights between East Germany and Poland, Hungary and Czechoslovakia were accompanied by two plain-clothes Stasi employees. No further hijacks of DDR planes were ever reported. Mind you if it hadn't been for West German telly and radio, the DDR population would not even have known about this one successful hijack. Unsurprisingly our media did not consider the story to be worth reporting. Putting yet another Siegmund Jähn special on telly or in the newspapers was a much safer bet for our journalists.

And as the government did not want a single cloud to overshadow its space race success in any way, it went for the whole caboodle when Siegmund Jähn and his Russian flight companion Valerie Bykovski arrived nearly a month later in Berlin for the big PR finale of the mission. Around 300,000 people lined the streets as the two cosmonauts made their way from the airport to the city centre on Thursday 21 September. How did the organisers get nearly one third of East Berlin's population, to wave little flags in the streets on a normal working day? As always, when important guests of the state arrived, companies, institutions and schools were asked to send greeters. Those occasions must have cost our economy thousands and thousands of marks in lost productivity. We kids certainly were always thrilled if halfway through the day we were told to pack our things and leave school to line some street. Unfortunately, it did not happen that often. As far as I can remember we went cheering three times in ten years – for the Soviet party leader Leonid Breshnev, the cosmonauts Jähn and Bykovski, and an African politician, whose name I cannot remember. The Jähn greeting was the biggest one ever staged in East Berlin. The officials had even thought of 500 temporary snack kiosks and 300 orchestras to entertain the masses. A true festival atmosphere had been created and Siegmund Jähn was a hero, our hero.

MAKE-BELIEVE

What followed the staged celebrations was cosmomania. Every child in the country wanted to become a second Siegmund Jähn and fly to the stars in a rocket. And in 1979 we kids could do exactly that. Not for real, but the Cosmonaut Centre in the newly opened *Pionierpalast* (Pioneer Palace) in Berlin, (yet another building Dad had worked on), was the next best thing. This activity centre for kids boasted a gymnasium, a pool, a big playground as well as lots of other facilities for us kids to learn, play and make handicraft things. But the Cosmonaut Centre was its biggest attraction – a large room with a number of machines to swirl you around for cosmonaut training, overshadowed by a huge shiny rocket in the middle that could be entered once training had been completed. After you had put your space helmet on, there was a countdown, then "take off" and finally the "flight" itself. None of us kids cared that the "space" passing by on the windows was only a moving screen. We were truly in heaven and once we had "landed" we would quickly run back to the end of the queue to start the process all over again.

My fantasies weren't limited to just pretending to be a cosmonaut. I had many more ideas up my sleeve to keep me and my friends entertained. In the fifth grade I claimed that my brother was working for a radio station and that he had asked me to present an impromptu kids programme later in the week, for which I needed the help of my classmates. I planned to "record" the show in front of the *Dienstleistungswürfel* (service centre) which housed the local youth club, post office, newsagent's, florist's, dry cleaner's, hairdresser's and beauty salon in our area.

Before the "recording" could start, I had to come up with an idea for the programme and, most importantly, get hold of a microphone that looked the part. The first task was the easy bit. I looked through my parents' bookshelf and found a book called *Laugh and Let Laugh* that contained a mixture of funny stories and poems. Many of these were just right to be read "live on air". My search for a professional-looking mic however was somewhat harder. The only real microphone we had at home was a small, square, grey plastic one. Its flimsiness would not have fooled anyone. No, I needed one of those round, shiny mics that singers on telly used. As the real thing was out of the question, I looked around at home for a good replacement. A few minutes later I had found it – my trusty metal pocket torch. Off came the head and out came the light bulb but somehow it still did not look like a professional microphone, more like a pocket torch with its head and bulb missing. There was no doubt, more work on the design was needed, but what could I possibly change? Searching through my parents' wardrobe I found the answer – a thin, square brown leather string. This knotted around the base of the torch resembled, in my eyes anyway, a cable and I now considered my creation complete. I wondered whether my "microphone" would be convincing enough to fool my classmates.

Funnily enough, it was. Naturally some of the 15 guys and girls who turned up had doubts about the whole thing being for real and did not hesitate to voice their concerns, but because I carried on with the show regardless no one could be a hundred per cent certain that they were right. Ines, one of the cool kids in class, shouted: "It's not a mic, it's just a torch with a leather string around it". Yet, when I approached her and asked her to say a few things to the listeners, she ran away. I chased after her, with the "mic" in my hand and the leather string flying high in the wind, but I could not get her to say a single word into my torch. By the time the "broadcast" finished, everyone, including Ines, wanted to know when the programme would be aired so they could listen to it at home. Imagine their disappointment when I told them that this had been a live broadcast.

Some classmates even looked forward to me doing a second show, but I decided against it – a mock radio show, like a magic trick, could only work once with the same audience. I knew this for certain, because by then I was spending most of my pocket money in East Berlin's only shop selling magic tricks and props. Whenever I passed the shop I would stand outside and look at its window display for ages, mulling over which magic trick I should spend my money on this time. No book explaining magic tricks was safe from me. Though in theory I could have made an elephant disappear, in reality I concentrated my efforts on more useful tricks. Predicting the word to be picked by an audience member from a randomly chosen book or making coins, cards and rings vanish in thin air were my bread and butter, magic-wise. The pièce de résistance was my finger guillotine. Two holes in this otherwise concealed handheld device allowed the audience to see the moving blade. I regularly put carrot pieces into both holes before pushing the blade down to prove the seriousness of the device. Consequently I always encountered a certain reluctance when asking for a volunteer. When a brave audience member was finally found, they had to put their finger into the top hole while another piece of carrot went into the bottom hole. Upon pushing the blade down the finger was mysteriously spared while the carrot fell down to the floor cut into two pieces. The audience could inspect the device immediately but never figured out how the impossible was made possible.

I loved performing my magic at family birthdays or even at our *Pioniernachmittagen* (Pioneer afternoons). These were occasions when the class would get together and do fun things like hold a disco, make little presents for family or friends in the run up to Christmas, visit an exhibition or go to a play in the *Pioniertheater* German Titow, a theatre which catered solely for kids. Even more exciting than seeing a kid's play was when the *Pionierhaus* (Pioneer house) near us had a *Tag der offenen Tür* (open day). Pioneer houses were places where kids with special interests could form little groups with other like-minded children and indulge in their hobbies under the supervision of adults. Unfortunately, they did not have a circle called "Young Magicians". Instead I joined the group "Young Paramedics" which I considered to be quite interesting and useful. Shame it all came to an abrupt end for me when we were shown slides of different kinds of wounds – I had not known before that the sight of blood would make me squeamish. But the "Young Traffic Helpers" were equally happy to have me. There I learnt the meaning of all traffic signs, and could even, equipped with a fairy-light belt and a traffic baton (a 30-centimetre long, hollow and illuminated tube with black and white markings) be the East German equivalent of a Lollipop-Lady. When on duty, I had the power to stop the oncoming traffic when smaller kids were approaching the zebra crossing. Having the cars at my mercy, I felt so grown up!

Sometimes during our annual eight-week school breaks in July and August I pretended to be a security guard and went to the school to check that everything was alright. Imagine my surprise when on one of those visits I noticed that the school's front door was unlocked. I went a couple of steps inside, shouted a few "Hello, hello is anyone there?" into the dark entrance hall and stairwell. There was no reply. How exciting! But what was that? Didn't I just hear a noise coming from the second floor? In my mind a number of shady and ruthless characters were wandering through the building, stealing whatever valuables they could lay their hands on. They clearly had to be stopped. Quickly! I ran out of the building to the nearest police station a couple minutes away and, totally out of breath, reported what I had discovered. The *Polizist* (policeman) on duty took my name and address, thanked me, and said that a car will be sent there in due course. But surely he did not think that he could wave me away just like that?! Or did he? After all, I had provided the police with some valuable information for their fight against crime. So I put a droopy face on and asked the officer whether I could get a ride to the crime scene in the police car. This would so have made me the envy of my friends. But his answer was "no". Quoting regulations and orders the *Polizist* seemed to forget that I was just an 11 year old who was looking for an adventure.

By the time I arrived back at the school, the police were already there. Apparently a quick search inside did not reveal anything unusual and when the caretaker, who lived nearby, arrived it emerged that he simply had forgotten to lock one door when he left the previous day. My vigilance had caused a lot of commotion for nothing.

Cordelia was not so much into real-life crime prevention. Her interest laid more in admiring the characters of a TV detective series, that was shown on West German telly at the time – *The Avengers*. She was so impressed by their canny fight for justice, that she decided to call herself after her idol Emma Peel. I was offered the chance to become John Steed but declined as I found it silly to adopt a fictional name. So another classmate stepped in to fill that space and for years to come Cordelia signed cards and letters with the initials C.E.P. Cordi's quirky traits were part of what attracted me to her. The bubbly personality, the beautiful face and most of all her complex and interesting character definitely did it for me. I have never met anyone else who called a collection of hundreds of chocolate wrapping papers their own.

Cordelia was always up for a laugh. One practical joke we played that I particularly liked, was when we sneaked into an apartment block, attached a cord to the doorknobs of two opposite flats and rang both bells. We were in stitches as we watched the people trying to open their doors. When the cord was about to snap we quickly did a runner. On another occasion I looked up in a dictionary the Latin names for the common frog (Hyla Arborea) and toad (Bufo Bufo) before we approached unsuspecting members of the public. Armed with pen and paper we told our victims that our Pioneer group had set us the task to find out the meaning of those words and asked them to assist us in our research by having a guess, as every clue, however small, was welcome. All answers were written down by us diligently, and though I still remember that some of them were quite hilarious and that we cried tears with laughter when we went through them again afterwards, those sheets of paper have unfortunately vanished over the years. The florist in the *Dienstleistungswürfel* (service centre) nearby came closest to guessing the meaning of the words. Quite correctly she noticed the Latin origin of the names but was wrong in assuming that they stood for flowers. The old lady in the newsagent's was probably the one whose answer was furthest from the truth. Her suggestion that those words might be in connection with a visit of an African leader in the DDR at the time was for us the weirdest one. A political association was the least likely we expected anyone to make.

COWBOYS & INDIANS

The Cold War was still in full swing when Soviet party leader Leonid Breshnev, who arrived in Berlin for the festivities of the DDR's twentieth anniversary in 1979, announced that the USSR was to reduce its forces stationed in East Germany by 20,000 men and 1,000 tanks. Though this initiative still left some 400,000 Red Army soldiers, 6,000 Russian tanks and 2,000 Russian aircraft in the DDR, for the majority of East Germans any number, however small, of Russian soldiers leaving was good news. Unlike the American, British and French armies in West Germany and West Berlin, the Red Army never bonded with the Germans in their zone. The Russian generals did not approve of close contact with the civilian population. For the average Soviet soldier, who earned a humble 20 DDR marks a month (eight dollars) life outside his barracks and compound with its Russian shops, Russian cinemas, Russian theatres and Russian hospitals did not exist. The American, British and French forces in the west also had national "ghettos" surrounding their barracks. They and their families too could live everyday lives without needing to ever speak a single word of German. But while those soldiers could get out of their enclaves whenever they wanted, the common Russian soldier was not so lucky. He was not granted leave from the barracks for private reasons. That right was strictly reserved for officers and civilians. And should a solider have been allowed out of the military area for some purpose, he would have to be accompanied by an officer. In public, Russian soldiers were only ever seen in groups. Perhaps their generals feared that individuals might try to escape to the west. Allied military personnel in uniform could cross the border between the two Germanys freely and unhindered by car – the inside of an allied car, like all allied military installations, had an extraterritorial status.

Our army could not even prevent western allied vehicles from approaching East German military installations on reconnaissance missions. And we had a lot of military installations. One third of the DDR's territory was off-limits for one reason or other. Big signs warned potential intruders: "Prohibited Area. No entry to unauthorised persons! No photography! Violations will be punished." American, British and French soldiers just laughed off the warnings. After all, what could the East Germans possibly do to stop them? Officially nothing, but of course there were ways around it. One summer, the Americans tried time and time again to get some intelligence on an East

German army base that was hidden in a forest. Each time they tried, it was the same story: An American military vehicle drives down the narrow forest road. Having been spotted by our guys, a stationary lorry around a bend in the road blocks the way ahead. Trying to reverse back, the Americans notice that their car can't go anywhere as a second lorry has in the meantime crept up behind them, blocking the escape route. Boxed in, the Americans sit tight. And what do the East German soldiers do? They put a huge black tarpaulin over the immobilised enemy car and wait, letting the summer sun do the work for them. Eventually the American car's air conditioning unit can't handle the heat any more and out of their extraterritorial space come the GIs, stepping onto East German soil in a prohibited zone. Our boys hand them over to waiting Russian officers who take them to their base for questioning before releasing them at the border. After this scenario had played out a couple of times, American and East German soldiers apparently greeted each other with handshakes and parted by saying: "See you again, soon". At a time when politicians in east and west expected the other side to start war at any time, American and East German soldiers were playing cowboys and Indians in a DDR forest. They tried to outsmart each other without firing a single shot and even kept their sense of humour. Well done, boys!

FROM RUSSIA WITH LOVE

The Red Army had a very negative image among us East Germans. We had not forgotten that it were Russian tanks that had rolled in the streets when people demanded political reforms in the DDR (1953), Hungary (1956) and Czechoslovakia (1968). The Soviet regiments in the DDR were recognised by us for what they were – watchful guards rather then defenders of freedom. East Germans joked:

Carter, Breshnev and Honecker sit together and argue about whose country is the biggest. Carter boasts: "The United States is so big, it took the fastest American runner two months to get from the east to the west coast."

"That's nothing," replies Breshnev. "Our Russian world champion in cycling was on the road for six months when crossing the Soviet Union in its entire width."

"Gentlemen," says Honecker. "Impressive as these facts may be, I don't think any of you can compete with the DDR. Russian soldiers marched into our country in 1945 and they still haven't come out."

The suspicion that many East Germans felt towards the Russian soldiers did not stop them from building genuine friendships with Russians they may have met in other circumstances, for example, when travelling to the Soviet Union. I, too, had a Russian friend. It all started in grade five after we had our first compulsory Russian lessons. I decided during an open day in the Pioneer house that I wanted to befriend a Russian Pioneer. Someone handed out letters written by Lenin Pioneers who were looking for German pen pals and I, like most of my classmates, made sure that I got hold of an envelope. We all sat down and looked excitedly at the strange stamps and the letters inside. Mine also contained a poor quality and slightly out of focus photo in sepia that showed a boy about the same age as me. He had fair hair and was dressed in shorts, standing next to a massive sofa that had been decorated with a crocheted blanket. From the letter I could make out that the boy's name was Aljosha and that he lived in Orenburg. Orenburg is a town in Russia's south-west, nestled on the Ural Mountains close to the Kazakh border. From there it is roughly 1,250 kilometres to Moscow and 2,850 kilometres to Berlin, about the same distance as between London and Ankara. It seemed a very long way indeed. Some of my classmates were just after the stamps on the envelopes and threw the letters away, but I decided that I wanted to make this friendship work. So over the years, with my Russian vocabulary increasing, the letters became longer and we got to know each other better. On birthdays or Christmas we exchanged small presents; to this day I still got a little decorative samovar I received from him one year. The only snag with this long-distance friendship was that the Russian mail did not provide an airmail service. A posted letter took three to four weeks to arrive. As we got older, the letters were written less regularly but the contact remained – after all, we had been communicating with each other since 1979. Then, it must have been in 1986, I stopped hearing from Aljosha. I put it down to him having moved on to a new stage in his life. Two years later I sent him a letter to find out how he was doing. After a couple of months I received a reply, but this time from his mum. In her letter she thanked me for having been Aljosha's pen pal for all those years before telling me that he had been conscripted to military service in 1986 and sadly did not return from his posting in Afghanistan.

I could not believe what I was reading. I even double-checked the words in my Russian dictionary to make sure I hadn't made a mistake in the translation, but the letter still said the same. I was in shock – there was no Aljosha any more. While I was enjoying my late teenage years worrying about what to wear when going out on the weekend, Aljosha had been put in a uniform, given a gun and sent into a real war to die at the age of 19. For me, only people in the news and in far-away countries I had no connection with died in wars, not someone from another socialist country and certainly not someone I knew. But it had happened. The war in Afghanistan, which had started in the same year as Aljosha and I had started our letter-friendship, had claimed him. His death did not make any sense then and seems even more pointless today.

TALKING SHOP

Back in 1979 I had no interest whatsoever in politics. What captured my imagination more than anything else was how good our summer holiday trip to the Mecklenburg region in the DDR's north would turn out to be. Mecklenburg was our country's equivalent of the English Lake District. Dad had been lucky enough to secure us accommodation in this popular area and once again we had to thank his company for it. We still had to pay for our bungalow, but to holiday in such a tourist hotspot was a privilege. By offering another company to complete the wooden interiors in their twelve newly built bungalows near a lake, Dad's company was given the right to use one of the bungalows whenever they wanted. And so in summer 1979 it was the Fritz family's turn to holiday for two weeks in this part of the country. There was loads to do. We watched bison in a nearby enclosure, went for swims in the lake, made use of the rowing boat and did some fishing. Unfortunately, we did not catch anything and my brother ended up posing for a photo with bought herrings. A couple of times we climbed into our fluorescent-green Trabant and drove the 120 kilometres to the Baltic Sea for a fun day at the beach. It was in a supermarket there, that I bought my very first western-style bubble gum.

Chewing gum was no stranger to East Germany. Little white cubes, made of sugar, flavour, starch and talcum powder, wrapped in silver foil were available virtually everywhere at a price of ten pfennigs each. It's just that they weren't too popular with us kids because of their consistency. DDR gum had a tendency to be hard, required lots of chewing effort and if you had it for too long in your mouth it would disintegrate into crumbs. In the west, such a product would not have lasted five minutes on the market. Hence, DDR kids tried to get their hands on real chewing gum whenever possible. An easy task if you had relatives in the west who would send you stuff. I however had to rely for years solely on my grandparents, bringing home Hubba Bubba and multi-coloured gum balls, which were sometimes even filled with sherbet, from their trips to the other side of the Iron Curtain. Things became easier for us kids in 1979 when the government invested 30 million marks (12 million dollars) in a so-called *Gestattungsproduktion* (permitted production). A DDR factory began to produce western-style gum under the West German licenser's name O.K. Pinneberg with western technology and packaging for the East German market. What a great concept. The individually wrapped and strawberry-flavoured Big Babaloo chewing gums (55 pfennigs each) even had little *Otto & Alwin*-comic strips included. Millions of kids were already familiar with those two characters. Otto, the green-coloured gorilla, and his friend Alwin, the penguin, appeared together for the first time in 1976 in the monthly kids magazine *Frösi* (short for *Fröhlich sein und singen* – to be happy and sing). *Frösi* contained a mixture of stories and comics but also surprised its readers every month with its freebies. Whether it was flower seeds, an advent calendar or something to build out of cardboard, the latest issue of *Frösi* usually sold out in the newsagents' very, very quickly. Each issue also included a reproduction of a popular painting, but this hardly got any kid's heart racing. It was a nice idea to make children familiar with art, but probably slightly too ambitious. Which child would get a kick out of analysing an old master?

The sale of proper bubble gum wasn't the only western influence which had manifested itself in our supermarkets. Since 1977 we could also buy, among other things, Pepsi Cola – a 330-millilitre bottle of this thirst quencher cost one mark (40 cents). Mum bought it once but none of us liked it. We remained loyal to Club Cola, a DDR brand. It was a less-sweet version of Coca Cola. And with a price of only 65 pfennigs for half a litre (26 cents) it also was considerably cheaper than its western cousin. In 1980, Pepsi disappeared from our shops due to a lack of demand. Our family's taste buds seem to have been in line with the rest of the DDR population.

Unfortunately, this also applied when it came to such things like tomato ketchup, spiced plum jam, honey, marzipan, sponge fingers, liquorice sticks or *Salmiakpastillen*. All these food items had in common was that the demand for them regularly outstripped the production capabilities. *Salmiakpastillen* were a personal favourite of mine – little rhombus-shaped pastilles made of flour, sugar, ammonium chloride and liquorice, intended for people with colds who wanted to keep a phlegmmy throat under control. Liquorice enthusiasts like myself bought them because they tasted nice. The problem was that because *Salmiakpastillen* were a niche product, they were in even shorter supply than any of the other hard-to-get food items. Sometimes I had to go without my beloved pastilles for a year or even longer! The last time I was able to get hold of them in the DDR was in 1987, two years before the Wall came down. I got lucky in a little private drugstore just opposite the cinema Rio in Berlin and bought their entire stock of 80 packets. As a DDR citizen you were wise to constantly carry your chequebook or a supply of cash with you. Lady Luck could strike any time and you never knew when you would come across a sought-after item. People also never left home without bags or stringnets – another DDR phenomenon, as most shops did not provide customers with bags to get their shopping home. This policy, dictated by economic reasons, might not have been very consumer friendly, yet the environment thanked us for it.

Admittedly, shopping the East German way could be quite frustrating when looking for an item that was in high demand, but I still enjoyed going to the shops. Every visit was a mini adventure – you never knew whether you were going to get something special or not. And if you did, the feeling of satisfaction that followed was tremendous. The closest experience today is going to a market. The greengrocer's stall might not have the rhubarb you were after but they do have those red Egyptian potatoes you so desperately looked for two weeks ago. You get two kilos of those (God knows when they will have them again) and just as you want to go home you see on the food stall a very interesting looking selection of Spanish biscuits. Out of curiosity you buy two packages and as you turn around you may as well ask (again) on the cheese stall whether they now have had another delivery of that really delicious smelly, French cheese you had bought there a month ago. They haven't so, you settle for a piece of mature Somerset cheddar instead.

DDR shoppers had to be flexible and needed to think ahead – it didn't hurt to always have a few things in the larder. And our supermarkets made it easy to stock up on foodstuffs. They were not as glamorous as their western counterparts but the layout was similar: fruit and veggies first, then meat refrigeration units, frozen food and dairy refrigeration, followed by beer and soft drinks. Next were tinned food and preserves, dried foods, bread, baking ingredients, special diet food, alcohol, sweets and then things like stationery, kitchen utensils, cleaners and personal hygiene articles. Many supermarkets also had counters for meat/delicatessen, cheese, patisserie and cosmetics.

What was different however where the shopping trolleys. As there was no need to lure unsuspecting shoppers into buying more than they intended DDR trolleys were only half as big and half as deep as the ones most people in the west are familiar with. Though our trolleys served their purpose, looking back they seemed flimsy, like some kind of oversized doll's trolleys. The hardest workers of all in a DDR supermarket were the girls on the tills. With no conveyor belts, they had to shift people's purchases, however small and big, or light and heavy, with their left hands from one trolley to another, while their right hands keyed the prices into the tills. Despite the job requiring such a lot of physical effort, the cashiers were surprisingly fast. What probably helped was the fact that the majority of prices had not changed for decades, so the cashiers knew them by heart. If they didn't, prices were printed on the packaging anyway. This well-oiled machinery regularly came to a sudden halt when someone had an imported item in their trolley. With no pre-printed price on the label and some dimwit from the supermarket staff having forgotten to scribble the price on, the search for the correct EVP (short for *Einzelverkaufspreis* – individual retail price) was on.

First the item in question would be inspected a couple of times from all sides. If no progress could be made that way, colleagues on the other tills were shouted at, with the mystery article held up high in the air. If that did not get results, the worst case scenario would unfold. The cashier would leave their workstation, either to have a look at the shelve herself or to ask someone in the stock room. That, and some shopper slowly writing out a cheque at the till, were the most dreaded moments for anyone queueing at peak periods in the supermarket. My aunt and uncle developed a system in which the length of the queue indicated to them how long it would take to reach the till: 25 minutes if the queue stretched to the margarine section, 40 minutes if the last man standing was by the cheese counter further down.

The lowlight of a trip to the *Kaufhalle* (supermarket) was getting fresh milk. Milk was sealed in one-litre polyethylene bags and the bags were piled into plastic crates. Each crate usually contained some bags that had not made it, so if you were buying milk late in the day, you would have to fish around in murky milk to find an undamaged bag. At least it kept the kids entertained. But arriving late in the supermarket could also be a distinct advantage. If you were lucky, it would allow you to travel in time. If bread had sold out early and more had to be ordered, the loaves arriving in the late afternoon would already bear the next day's manufacturing date – the bakeries changed their date stamps at four pm. Only in the DDR could tomorrow's bread be bought today at yesterday's price!

COUNTING THE BEANS

Unfortunately, the ketchup producers weren't as progressive as the bakers and always lagged behind. When shop assistants in a *Kaufhalle* (supermarket) wheeled out a whole pallet of ketchup bottles to unsuspecting customers, what would have lasted weeks in a West German supermarket barely survived an hour. And who can blame eager shoppers for grabbing four, five, six or even ten bottles at once, in an attempt to have a stable supply of ketchup until the next purchasing opportunity would arise? Our family was no exception, we too hoarded hard-to-come-by products, food or non-food items alike. At home we always had a stash of UHT milk, which was normally hard to get hold of. The same applied to paper tissues and toilet paper. Yet considering the limited storage space in our one-bedroom flat, we could never be too greedy. Though to a certain extent, we too stocked up on other things we did not necessarily need at the time. Items could always be swapped with someone else.

Dad kept spare parts for the car in the box room. Once he was in need of a new exhaust pipe. The shops did not sell any at the time, not for money nor any amount of persuasion. A friend was happy to hand over the exhaust pipe he had been hoarding, but only in return for an equally sought-after trailer coupling. Thankfully, Dad had bought one speculatively earlier in the year. The next morning, both men were owners of the parts they really needed.

But swapping was not always so straightforward. One of my uncle's colleagues once bought a couple of smoked eels from a friend, which he used to bribe a greengrocer to reserve him a few kilos of bananas, which in return worked wonders with a shop assistant at his local electrical retailer. She had a small daughter who loved bananas very much. As soon as the shop got its next delivery of colour TVs "Made in DDR", my uncle's colleague became the proud owner of a new set.

Hoarding was a national sport and ran in the blood of every East German. It scarred me for life. I still can't escape the iron grip of the urge to stockpile. The shelves in my larder are already buckling under the weight of the myriad of tins and glasses containing preserved fruit, vegetables and sauces. Yet every time I go to the supermarket something in my brain tells me to get a few more. At least I will be prepared when the great tinned fruit shortage of the second millennium rears its ugly head (or the spaghetti sauce shortage, or the gherkin shortage...)

Because certain items only appeared rarely in our shops, people maintained a stash of them at home. Had people not hoarded so much, these goods would probably not have been in short supply at all. On one occasion the production line at the country's main toothbrush manufacturer came to a standstill for a couple of months, because of a fire. With no toothbrush deliveries for a number of weeks, some shops sold out of their existing stock. This triggered a nationwide chain reaction. Having heard from friends, colleagues or family members that toothbrushes seemed to be in short supply, people began stocking up on them. Our family too got sucked into the hype. We ended up with twelve toothbrushes neatly stacked up in the bathroom cabinet. To calm the situation, short-term imports from China were arranged. As soon as the toothbrushes were back on the shelves, shoppers lost interest in them. A popular joke from that time goes like this:

A man walks into a shop and asks: "Do you have toilet paper?" The shop assistant replies: "No, the shop next door is the one where you cannot get toilet paper, we are the shop with no aluminium foil."

The products in the joke were interchangeable. But in reality, most of the time shopkeepers and shop assistants tried to be fair and wheeled out their scarce goods in small batches several times a day, rather than offering them all in one go. This way, the working population would not miss out. On other occasions, shoppers were given a limit on how many units of a product they could take each. For example, while plain, unflavoured yoghurt was widely available, fruit yoghurt often had a sign next to them in the chiller cabinet asking shoppers to please only take two pots at a time. On those occasions, long-standing family members pretended to not know each other when queueing at the till. Husband, wife and kids all pretended to be individual shoppers and so were able to bring home four or five times the allowance. If you were on your own when something scarce was available, you would buy your allowance of the items, then go back for more and queue at another till. Sometimes shopping could take hours...

Oh yes, us East Germans were not short of ideas when it came to getting the things we wanted in adequate quantities. The first step was always letting your extended family know what you were after. If you were not lucky enough to be in a shop when corn flakes, for example, were sold, some family member probably was. In our family we also made use of "Vitamin C" – the connections that the country's economic life thrived on. Brigitta, the wife of one of Dad's colleagues, worked in a butcher's shop. This meant we regularly could get hold of premium cuts of meats which were in short supply in the DDR because the government made a quick Deutschmark by selling those to the west. It's important to say though, that essential food items were never in short supply. East Germany was not a second Romania, where people had to queue hours just to get hold of some bread. In the Deutsche Demokratische Republik we did not starve. Our dissatisfaction had more to do with not being able to buy grapes or peaches throughout the year because DDR shops sold only seasonal fruit and vegetables – no strawberries for us in wintertime. Instead the average citizen gobbled up nearly 100 kilos of meat, the same quantity of vegetables and flour, 40 kilos of sugar and 100 litres milk a year. And with an average yearly butter consumption of nearly 15 kilograms per capita, we even beat the West Germans. Our diet might not have been the healthiest, but underfed we were not. Twenty per cent of men and 40 per cent of women were overweight.

The state did get food companies to cut corners here and there to save money on expensive imports. Bakers were supplied with "candied lemon peel" made from green tomatoes. An imitation marzipan, called Persipan, was made of ground peach and apricot kernels or cherry stones instead of expensive almonds, and the popular Schlager Süsstafel (Sweet Bar Hit) looked and tasted like a normal bar of chocolate with peanuts, but contained only a minuscule amount of cocoa.

As with coffee, the import of cocoa gave our economists headaches. It wasn't necessary from a nutritional point of view, yet it had to be brought into the country because people craved chocolate whether cocoa was cheap on the world market or not. To keep the costs for imports as low as possible, manufacturers were instructed to invent new products to make the cocoa beans last longer. Products like Bambina (a bar with a thin coating of chocolate containing a chopped nut, milk & caramel filling) or Knusperflocken (little chocolate drops containing crumbs of crisp bread) were conceived. They soon became firm favourites with the people so much so that they are still available today. Even the cheap and cheerful Schlager Süsstafel has made a comeback, though these days it contains a lot of cocoa and hasn't got that much in common any more with its predecessor, except for the smell when you open the packaging for the very first time.

DDR chocolate was moderately priced. While the nearly cocoaless Schlager Süsstafel was sold for 80 pfennigs (32 cents), a 100-gram bar of the real thing cost three or four times as much. At all times the cocoa content of chocolate remained a secret. The law did not require it to be stated on the packaging and our politicians preferred to keep it that way. On average, products contained only seven per cent of cocoa. Naturally it did not take long for rumours to spread that the brown colour in DDR chocolate was achieved by adding lentils. I doubt that this was really the case, yet the average East German consumer was aware that the majority of our chocolate was only of mediocre quality. After all, many of us knew what proper West German chocolate looked and tasted like. Our shops sold capitalist 100-gram bars for 7,50 marks (three dollars).

Only the more expensive upper-end DDR products were able to compete with chocolate from the west. Many people who had money to spare would treat themselves to the proper stuff. I too appreciated the West German chocolates I got on a regular basis from my grandparents, but overall I wasn't that choosy – as long as something was sweet, I liked it. Two of my preferred products were mint fondant and sugar foam fruits. But I just as happily sucked on a ball-shaped lollipop with a chocolate filling or munched on a Bon chocolate bar (East Germany's version of a Bounty), a Fetzer (Milky Way) or a Joker (Snickers). Yummy!!!

CASTRO'S REVENGE

While we in Berlin were reasonably spoiled for choice when doing our shopping, my paternal grandmother as well as my aunts and uncles from my dad's side of the family unfortunately weren't. Their Saxonian hometown of Neugersdorf (12,000 inhabitants), nestled close to the Czech border in the south, suffered the fate of many smaller cities and villages in the country –

patchy deliveries of shops. Berlin and other big cities were always allocated the lion's share of goods and resources to prove to the legions of foreign visitors what a success story German socialism was. The rest of the country had to make do with less. The smaller a place was, the less priority it had. A joke from the time goes like this:

During a state visit, Erich Honecker and Leonid Breshnev talk about the distribution of goods in their countries. Breshnev says: "Following years of extensive research, our economists have developed a distribution formula to ensure that all shops in the country offer an adequate supply of goods. Moscow, for example, receives eight per cent of the total national production, while Leningrad only gets five per cent." Erich Honecker replies: "We have come up with something much more simple and efficient. Everything is being delivered to Berlin and people just pick it up from there."

With the exception of eel, which was a rarity in the DDR as most of it was exported for hard currency, it was fairly easy to get hold of fish in Berlin. However our Saxonian relatives were not as lucky. The fish shop in their town only received one delivery a week, every Wednesday, and sometimes not even then. On those occasions, fish lovers there could only hope that the lorry would show up in the following week. If it didn't, tough luck.

Or take bananas. The state spent 8.5 million Deutschmarks (3.5 million dollars) a year on importing bananas, hardly a trifling amount. But it wasn't enough to satisfy the demand. The average DDR citizen ate three kilograms of the yellow fruit each year, twice as many as the Greeks but only half of what the West Germans scoffed down. In Berlin you had to queue to get them (a kilogram cost five marks – two dollars) but at least you could get them fairly regularly. In small towns and villages, however, exotic fruit only made an occasional appearance in the greengrocers'. Even then, people could not buy as many as they wanted because shop assistants rationed them. If your family consisted of three people you were given three bananas, if you were single, you could only buy one. Naturally, the constant shortage of bananas resulted in masses of jokes:

"Did you know that the DDR got an entry in the Guinness Book of Records? It is the country where one banana has to be shared by the highest number of people."

Q: How can you tell east from west without a compass?

A: Peel a banana and put it on top of the Wall. East is where someone has taken a bite from it."

Two little boys, one on the eastern side, the other one on the western side stand opposite each other on the Berlin Wall. The western boy eats a banana and shouts at the sad looking eastern boy: "Na, na, na, na, na, I got a banana and you don't." The commie kid yells backs: "Na, na, na, na, na, we got socialism and you don't." Western boy thinks for a while and shouts: "Na, na, na, na, na, soon we will have socialism too." Eastern boy triumphantly replies: "Na, na, na, na, na, then you won't have bananas either."

But if bananas were hard to get, navel oranges were an even rarer commodity. They were only sold for four to five weeks a year, with the first selling day always being the beginning of December. This way, parents could give their kids an extra vitamin C boost, as well as the traditional chocolates and sweets on 6 December, St Nicholas Day. In Germany, children traditionally leave a pair of polished shoes in the hallway before going to bed on 5 December. By the time they wake up the next morning, St. Nicholas has visited them and whoever had been good throughout the year can expect to find their footwear filled with goodies. Anyone else can only look forward to a bundle of branches – St Nicholas' warning to be good in time for the Christmas present delivery. Once the festivities were over and the new year had arrived, kids and adults alike took comfort in the knowledge that in less than 12 months the next lot of navel oranges could be carried home. Hooray!

A little girl asks: "Mummy, what are queues?"

The mother replies: "A queue is where people line up behind each other, for example when buying oranges."

The girl thinks for a few seconds and asks: "Mummy, what are oranges?"

Unfortunately, out of the average 90,000 tons of oranges especially imported for the festive season (five kilos for every citizen) a high percentage consisted of the dreaded Cuban harvest. In our family we referred to them as "Castro's Revenge". Although those oranges were sweet like their navel cousins and contained lots of juice too, their flesh was extremely stringy and the outside an unappealing mottled brown, green and yellow. Very good for juicing, but unsuitable for eating. At one stage, to entice the discerning shopper to buy a kilogram or two, little leaflets were produced informing the consumer that Cuban oranges were a healthy addition to one's diet, despite their looks. The campaign made little difference. DDR shoppers continued to shun Cuban oranges. Again, it was lucky for our family that we lived in Berlin. Occasional queueing here and there ensured that every year in December our larder would be stocked with several kilograms of Spain's finest oranges. That was something our Saxonian relatives could only dream of. If their greengrocers were lucky enough to get oranges and did not ration them as they did with the bananas, people were forced to accept tie-in sales: purchase two kilos of Cuban oranges and you'd get to buy one kilo of Spanish oranges. With a price tag of five marks a kilo for both varieties it was not the most consumer-friendly way to get rid of unwanted stock, but somehow greengrocers just had to shift the unloved fruit.

My parents did all they could, to ensure that our relatives down south also benefited from Berlin's preferential supplies. A couple of times a year, we drove the 250 kilometres to Saxony. On those trips our car boot was always packed to the brim with in-demand non-essentials such as UHT milk, tinned fish, savory snacks made of peanuts called *Erdnussflips*, fruit gum bears and whatever else was in seasonal short supply at the time outside the capital. We are a big family and in the days leading up to a departure our flat usually looked something like Del Boy's place in *Only Fools and Horses*. About 50 half-litre cartons of UHT milk, 60 bags each of *Erdnussflips* and *Gummibären* (gum bears) as well as the large quantities of all other requested items would be piling up everywhere. Sometimes there was so much stuff that we could not even fit it all into the car. On those occasions Dad borrowed a trailer from work and with our 23 hp Trabant engine straining under all the weight, we would snail along the motorway at a top speed of 80 kilometres per hour. Whoopi-do!

PLANNING AHEAD

Someone growing up in the west might find it hard to get their head around why DDR factories did not produce more of an item if it turned out to be in high demand. Things weren't that simple. Modern machines, which made production lines efficient, had to be imported from the west for yen, dollars or Deutschmarks. The DDR had to earn this money first by exporting goods such as chemical products, household items, optical instruments or textiles to the west. Unfortunately, the communist equivalent of the European Union, the Rat für gegenseitige Wirtschaftshilfe (Council for Mutual Economical Help), had decided that 75 per cent of all DDR exports had to be sold for roubles to other communist countries. And with limited hard currency funds, only limited investments could be made in our economy. The problems continued even when money was not an issue. We could not buy all the equipment we needed for our factories from the west because the NATO committee, COCOM (Coordinating Committee for Multilateral Export Controls), prevented western technology exports to eastern bloc countries, in order to disadvantage them economically. As production lines became more and more automated, endless numbers of machines were out of reach for us because their electronic components appeared on the COCOM embargo list. As intended, the boycott forced us to reinvent the wheel. Instead of importing PCs from the west for 1,000 Deutschmarks (400 dollars) each, we had to manufacture them ourselves at an exorbitant cost. The DDR retail price for an East German PC was 28,400 marks (11,360 dollars). Only 8,000 of our 84,000 robots used in production came up to international standard. Once machines were imported from the other side of the Iron Curtain replacement parts too had to be paid for in hard currency. And some production lines only worked with imported raw materials. The ever present UHT milk shortage in the DDR, for example, was mainly due to the fact that the imported packaging machines could only be used with genuine TetraPak cartons, which also had to be imported from the west.

But the biggest millstone around the neck of our industry was the planned economy. Unlike the west with its free economy the DDR had followed the Soviet example. Centrally devised five-year plans outlined the general development of the economy. Based on those, one-year plans were drawn up, under which every company was allocated material for its production and set an output target. And as all plans were based on figures from previous years, our industry was not able to set a trend but would always follow it instead – and even then only with some delay. Due to the rigid organisation of the economy, production lines could not be switched quickly enough from one product to another whenever consumer demand changed. If, for example, the population suddenly bought more slips than anticipated, there were no additional raw materials or production facilities available to remedy the situation in the short term. Unplanned imports of slips had to be made. As a result, the production of slips in the following year would increase, yet by then people's interest might have shifted to another item of clothing. And just as the country was about to be drowned in a sea of variously shaped, sized and coloured slips "Made in GDR", it might have been socks that were suddenly in high demand. Unplanned sock imports would have been necessary. So in the following year our industry would churn out more socks than ever, only by then consumers might have taken a particular liking to belts. And so on, and on, and on.

This inflexibility was the planned economy's Achilles heel. Centrally made decisions on what was going to be produced and in what quantity also were creativity killers. When companies were given targets to manufacture an x-amount of *Nickies* (T-shirts) or *Niethosen* (jeans), no further requirements would be made. Our politicians main concern was to get as many goods produced as possible. For example, in 1975, 8.7 million men's shirts were manufactured. In 1981 it were 9.3 million. The design of the goods was secondary. It's easy to imagine what the result of that was. In most cases, very basic, or shall we call it "classic", patterns and styles, which were economical to produce, but hardly the height of fashion. The most prominent example was the DDR jeans industry. No self-respecting DDR teenager wanted to be seen in a pair of Boxer, Wisent or Shanty jeans (all East German brands), even when they were made from imported fabric. They just did not look right and were never in the same league as a pair of jeans made by Levi's, Wrangler or Lee. Hence, if you had a pair of the real McCoy, you wore them until they virtually fell off your legs. Even Jinglers, C&A's own brand, was considered a thousand times more desirable than any of the DDR's own creations. Thanks to my grandparents I can proudly say that I never owned a pair of East German jeans. And the same goes for corduroy shoes. Yes, corduroy shoes! When were corduroy shoes fashionable? Were they ever? One day Dad came home from shopping, proudly waving a shoe box at me. Knowing that I did not want to be one of mob and liked experimenting with clothes, he had bought me a pair of poo-brown corduroy shoes as a surprise. And what a surprise that was! He had meant well, God bless him, but those shoes definitely did not do it for me.

I rejected them outright: "Dad, not even in the deepest province would anyone wear those kind of shoes." I was wrong. As my father could not be bothered returning the pair to the shop, the next time we took another load of UHT milk and peanutflip snacks down south to our relatives, we also took the shoes with us. Unbelievably, my uncle Klaus took an immediate liking to them and got years of use out of them – even though he only wore them when feeding his animals.

OLD MC FRITZ HAD A FARM, EE-EYE, EE-EYE, OH.

Because of their warmth, hospitality and down-to-earth attitude I have always been very fond of Uncle Klaus, my dad's brother, and his wife, Aunty Christel. For many years both worked in a local textile mill before deciding that what they really wanted was to leave the rat race behind and make a living from their 4,000 square-metre farm. To begin with, Uncle Klaus registered a part-time hatchery in his name while still staying in his old job. He was granted a business licence but was not allowed to take on employees. Fine, he never intended to anyway. And thanks to him and his wife still getting their regular salaries at work, any financial rough patches in the beginning were easily ridden out. However, after a few years both felt the strain of "dancing at two weddings" as we say in German. Being in the factory during the day and working at the farm every evening, weekend and even during their annual holidays was an arrangement that had to come to an end sooner than later. To keep the financial risk low Uncle Klaus handed in his resignation first, while Aunty Christel continued on at the factory.

Because he was in a highly regarded managerial position the company did not like to see him go and tried to persuade him to stay. Every trick in the book was used to make him change his mind, however when all the sweet talk did not have the desired effect, company officials tried to ridicule him: He was asked whether he, as a man, would enjoy sponging off his wife's earnings should the business fail. But Uncle Klaus did not budge under the pressure, so a promise was made to him. Pity, it was one he could have done without. The managing director openly told him: "I will do all I can do to make your life as a business man as difficult as possible." So when Uncle Klaus finally got his full-time business licence one of the conditions imposed on him was: He had to build feeding dispensers for chickens, yet was not allowed to obtain any material for the production from either wholesalers or retailers. That problem was easily taken care off. A friend bought in his name whatever material was needed and then sold it privately to my uncle. As soon as the hatchery was properly established, Uncle Klaus decided it was time for revenge. He handed in his membership resignation from the Communist Party, the SED. And that was the moment when the "fun" started. My uncle was asked to attend one party meeting after another to explain himself and his reasons. Comrades from the party headquarters in Berlin arrived to convince him to retract his resignation. All to no avail. He had made up his mind and stood his ground. The SED had no choice but to let Uncle Klaus go. Though the Communist Party gave itself the right to expel members, people leaving it in protest did not fit in with the official picture of a picture-perfect country full of happy citizens.

In most cases having your own business in the DDR was not an opportunity to become filthy rich. The government considered privately owned companies as somewhat dubious and levied income tax of up to 90 per cent on their profits. Yes, 90 per cent! To make things even harder private firms were only allowed a limited number of employees and offered salaries had to be lower than in state-owned companies. In the late Eighties, East Germany only had 2,000 private businesses employing just two per cent of the total workforce.

But the high tax burden did not dampen uncle Klaus' entrepreneurial spirit. He regularly came up with new money-spinning ideas. Feathers the peacock had lost were sold to florists for extra decoration in bouquets. For Easter, little fluffy chicks were coloured in to get kids to nag their parents to buy them some and one year when DDR furriers needed more supplies, Uncle Klaus started to raise beavers. Not only could the skin be sold, the meat was snapped up by speciality butchers and their prominent orange front teeth made perfect keyring pendants, which were sold privately.

I always liked going down south to Dad's relatives. At least once a year we visited Uncle Klaus and Aunty Christel at their farm. A real highlight for me as a city child was being so close to all their animals. The only one thing I liked more than just being there was being there when the *Schiessen* was on. The *Schiessen* was the annual local fun fair at which my aunt and uncle used to supplement their income by running a beer tent, just like the ones that can be found at the *Oktoberfest* in Munich. It was fun helping them clearing tables or handing out the deposit money for returned glasses; drunken punters always gave me a tip. One year I decided it was time to make serious money. Dad supplied me with wooden candlesticks he had made in his spare time and in true artisan style. I had manufactured some very Eighties earrings out of triangular pieces of white plastic which I decorated with stripes of coloured foil. Some copper wire from my electronic construction kit for the hook completed the design and off I went selling the stuff from a little table in the beer tent. I can't remember how much money I made with my merchandise but unlike Uncle Klaus I wasn't doing a roaring trade and so I went back to clearing tables and handing out deposit money the next year.

"Nothing comes from nothing" has always been Uncle Klaus' motto. He will stand up for his rights and never take anything lying down. But sometimes not even that approach brought him the desired results and he would have to resort to plain cheekiness. In the Eighties my uncle and aunt decided they wanted some deer on the farm but the problem was finding the space for them. So Uncle Klaus felt it was about time to reclaim some of the 2,000 square metres of land at the back of their property which had been ceded to the state in the Fifties for use by the local collectives which dominated DDR agriculture. The land used by those *Landwirtschaftliche Produktionsgenossenschaften* (Cooperatives of Agricultural Production) still technically belonged to the individual farmers. So my uncle was quite hopeful as he went to the local council to ask for some of his property back. He should have known better. A snooty woman advised him that "as the soil is actively worked, the current co-operative's use of this land reflects the best possible interest for society and therefore outweighs any personal use". Uncle Klaus was denied access to his own land. Fed up with the authorities, he took the law into his own hands and with Dad's help, secretly moved his fence a few metres. A few years and a few more fence movements later, Uncle Klaus had reclaimed all the land he needed through the backdoor. Unlike the DDR, he and his deer are still going strong.

Mum (1959)

Dad (1960)

My first Christmas (1967)

First day in school (1974)

Dad's picturesque hometown of Neugersdorf

My Saxon nanna

In search of the unusual – a Czechoslovakian shopping street near the German border

Me, the Baltic Sea and a DDR compact camera without zoom

Showing off my new sunglasses and paramilitary uniform

Mum's parents: Nan

Grandad – in the background Dad's disguised pull-down bed

View over the Wall – from West to East Berlin

For more pictures please visit www.ironcurtainkid.com

As nice at it was to see our relatives in the countryside, whenever we left Berlin it became obvious that our economy was not as strong as the newspapers tried to make out.

The roads weren't as good, and many towns we drove through were far from being attractive. Many buildings were in dire need of repair or refurbishment. Apartment blocks from the turn of the century were in especially poor condition. Big patches of render had fallen off over the decades exposing the underlying brickwork. Sometimes we were spared this depressing sight – when the lingering smog from industrial areas covered the buildings with a veil. On those occasions, we were particularly glad to live in the spoilt capital and be able to fill the car with stuff which mysteriously only ever seemed to find its way to Berlin.

While many city dwellers like us took the nationwide distribution of rare goods into their own hands, it didn't mean that Berliners were welcomed with open arms by everyone in the country. People with no friends or relatives in the capital had a grudge against us. For them, the Berliners were arrogant. There were even tales that in the provinces stones were hurled in anger at cars with Berlin licence plates. Luckily nothing like that ever happened to us but the people's rage was understandable. Not only did we in the capital get a wider assortment of goods more often, but we also pulled in workforces and resources from other areas. At one time, Neugersdorf, the small town my paternal grandmother lived in, was to get a public swimming pool. The planning was done and the building materials were delivered to the site but just as work was about to commence, the construction workers were transferred to Berlin to build something else. Construction projects in the capital had priority. Work on Neugersdorf's pool never started.

The town's newly built apartment blocks were another example. At first glance they seemed like run-of-the-mill, five-storey apartment blocks we had seen a million times in Berlin. Nothing special. It was only when Uncle Klaus pointed out the unusual little chimneys on the roof that we realised the flats did not have central heating, but were heated by stoves in each room. A connection to the local thermal power station would have been too costly. If new apartment blocks in East Berlin had been built like that, people would have rioted – a risk that could not be taken with the capitalist enclave of West Berlin and its horde of nitpicking journalists on the doorstep of our capital. However, far away in a small town out of the limelight, no politician seemed to care. The clocks ticked differently in the countryside, as even the locals happily admitted. When going to the hairdresser's in Saxony for a wash and cut, my hair was strangely cut dry and washed afterwards. Timidly pointing out that in Berlin hair was washed first to make cutting easier, I was swiftly advised: "That's Berlin for you – everything is different there."

One day my Saxonian nanna asked me to get some meat from the butcher's shop. I found myself in a shop that was empty except for fresh mince, salamis hanging from the walls and stacks of tinned pate on the counter. Where was the choice of meats I was used to in Berlin? The butcher, seeing my bemused face, shrugged his shoulders: "We didn't get a delivery this week." At 12 years old, I had never seen such an empty shop. I felt like I was in a different country.

Still, on the way back to Berlin our car was never empty. We always found something to bring back, whether it was some local food items, maybe a new nightie for Mum or a nice pair of shoes for Dad. My brother got lucky a few times, getting hold of some books that were sold out in Berlin and as for me, I could never walk pass the local toy shop without spending a few marks in it. Czechoslovakia, only a few kilometres away from Neugersdorf, also featured regularly on our shopping itinerary. There we stocked up with nice glass or crystal items. Even the Czech drugstores were fertile hunting grounds. Perfumes with real flowers stuffed into the bottles made nice presents. But my favourite shop in Varnsdorf, the nearest Czech village to the border, was the local grocer's shop.

A trip to another country was never complete without a good rummage in the local supermarket. In Czechoslovakia I discovered things like coloured sugar cubes, sweetened, evaporated milk in different flavours (chocolate was my favourite), tinned mussels (imported from Spain) and lots of interesting looking sweets and pastries. The only drawback to many of those shopping trips was that we had to fund them in ways, which DDR law defined as illegal. Under a bilateral agreement between the two countries, East Germans could only change 20 marks (eight dollars) per person (half of that for kids) into Czech kronas at our state bank for each day of an intended stay – neither country wanted to give other commie tourists too much shopping power. That meant if my parents and I wanted to go to Czechoslovakia for one day (by 1979 my brother was already holidaying with his friends), we were only allowed to carry with us 50 marks (20 dollars) worth of kronas, plus change from previous visits. On longer trips, costs for meals and accommodation had to be considered. Such a paltry sum made it impossible to have a decent holiday. But there was a way around it – like everyone else, we too, greatly exaggerated the length of an intended stay when changing money. When we returned earlier, having spent all of the money, there was nothing customs could do about. On day trips we resorted to smuggling leftover Czechoslovakian banknotes from previous trips. Thankfully in twelve years, our car was only searched once, and even then only half heartedly. Nothing was found. Dad's rolled up shirtsleeves and my ID card's protective cover were very reliable hiding places for contraband banknotes.

The same hiding technique was used on our day trips to Poland. The Poles might not have had enough to eat, but their entrepreneurial spirit was second to none and the flea markets with their leather goods, bold glassware, fake designer clothes and other fashionable items on offer were irresistible to DDR people. I regularly invested my zlotys in novelty lollipops and (illegally) reproduced rubber characters from *The Muppet Show*. Unfortunately, once again, only a small amount of money could be officially exchanged per person and day. If more money was needed, you had to resort to changing additional DDR marks with dodgy looking Poles who tried to avoid police detection by loitering casually in house entrances.

One day, being short of zlotys, Dad and I were changing 50 DDR marks (20 dollars) with a creepy guy who had a mouth full of silver teeth. Having distracted us with his bling-smile, "Jaws" short changed us by counting some Polish banknotes twice by rolling them around his middle finger. As the exchange rate was something like 15 zlotys for one mark there was so much paper in his hand that we did not notice his little trick at first. By the time we realised he had already vanished in thin air. Bastard!

CHAPTER 4: THE EIGHTIES

ROBERT MAXWELL, BURGEONING FEELINGS
AND A GOULASH WITH A TWIST

In 1980 the Poles were very close to having more Germans come to them then they bargained for. The independent union Solidarnosc (Solidarity) had been founded and the DDR, together with other neighbouring countries, was concerned that political unrest might spread and destabilise socialism in Europe. So plans were drawn up for an invasion of Poland, which thankfully never took place. German soldiers crossing the so-called border of peace and marching into Poland would have been a sight no one was keen on – once in a century was more than enough.

Someone who got quite a lot of wanted media attention in 1980 was Honnie (as our Erich Honecker was often referred to by us people) when he had his autobiography published by the late Robert Maxwell. Apart from *Erich Honecker – From My Life*, other titles in Maxwell's *Leaders of the World* series were *Nicolae Ceausescu – Builder of Modern Romania and International Statesman* and *Todor Zhivkov – Statesman and Builder of New Bulgaria*. But to do Honnie justice it should be mentioned that Breshnev and Carter also had their lives featured. It was vanity publishing on a glitzy level and, no doubt, a nice little earner for Maxwell. Surprisingly, Honecker's book, unlike so many others, was never affected by a limited print run caused by paper shortage. Funny, that.

For anyone else, publishing a book in the DDR was fraught with difficulty. All of our 78 publishing houses had to apply for printing permits prior to the publication of titles. This process enabled the authorities to censor a title – with the excuse of paper shortages any work or author considered not worthy of being distributed in the DDR was rejected. Yet even with such a procedure in place, our bookshops were far from empty – every year 6,500 new titles were published. Despite this being only one tenth of the West German annual output at the time, it still amounted to an impressive 130 million copies annually. The average DDR household was home to more than 140 books.

Going into any of the DDR's 900 bookshops was usually a very straightforward affair. There was a small section dedicated to specialist and non-fiction literature, the remaining and by far the biggest area belonged to poetry and novels for kids and adults. Those tables and shelves were regularly scanned by the customers for little gems – books that seemed to be interesting despite being from run-of-the-mill or unknown authors. But no reader would ever expect to find a sought-after title this way. For that you either had to queue or build a relationship with a bookseller through regular visits, so he or she would reserve you a copy of a rare title on delivery day. The next time you then popped in the shop the assistant would say: "Your order has finally arrived", protecting your book from the prying eyes of other jealous customers by waving a wrapped package in your direction.

Classic authors such as Maupassant, Dumas or Tolstoy were more or less readily available, while Marx, Engels, Lenin and their complete works were (surprise, surprise) omnipresent in our bookshops. One author who was very popular with DDR readers was Jules Vernes. Mum regularly queued up to get me and my brother the latest published title. If East Germans could not see the world for themselves, they at least wanted to read about it. This explains why other international writers published in the DDR were also extremely successful and incredibly hard to get hold of. Samuel Beckett, William Faulkner, Gunter Grass, James Joyce, Jerome D. Salinger and John Updike, just to mention a few, were some of the authors our family sadly had to miss out because we weren't at the right place at the right time when their books were sold. With other authors we were luckier. DDR editions of *Father Brown* (G.K. Chesterton), *The Little Prince* (Antoine de Saint-Exupery), *Travels with my Aunt* (Graham Greene), *Roots* (Alex Hayley), *Malevil* (Robert Merle) and *Gone with the Wind* (Margaret Mitchell) still form part of my personal library to this day.

But spring 1980 is not a time, which sticks in my mind for literary reasons. Rather, it's because of a four-day class trip to the Baltic Sea at the beginning of May that this year is chiselled into my memory. Every year we did two class trips, always staying in a youth hostel for three to four days. East German youth hostels were cheap as chips – kids, apprentices and students paid 25 pfennigs a night (ten cents), everyone else twice that amount. Even with the extra charge of 2.50 marks (one dollar) for hiring the bed linen, accommodation costs hardly broke the bank. And I am not talking about filthy and flea-ridden dormitories here. The hostels received generous subsidies from the state and all of the ones we ever stayed at were spotless.

On this particular trip to the Baltic Sea our accommodations were little bungalows near the beach where boys and girls, separated of course, shared two houses each. I even managed to take a few photos using the 1950's camera I had borrowed from my nanna.

Unfortunately, zooms were not common then. I would not have minded being slightly bigger than a centimetre in the photo which I got Lars to take of me. I even hid the camera bag behind my back while the photo was taken thinking it might ruin the composition. One shot from this trip, though fairly blurred, I regarded very highly – the first photograph of my girlfriend Cordelia. She was only identifiable by her long blonde hair flying in the wind. I did not care. I was 12 and madly in love.

It may have been too cold for a swim, but those late afternoon strolls along the seashore with Cordelia looking for shells and fossils were unmissable. It was all very sweet and innocent. We both were incredibly shy. I still remember our embarrassment when a flint stone that I had found on the beach and given to Cordelia for good luck turned out to have a pencilled heart on it. A classmate discovered it while rifling through Cordi's stone collection and naturally it did not take very long for remarks like "Oliver loves Cordelia" to start. The two of us were so mortified that we stayed well clear of each other for a day to stop the gossiping.

But no gossiping could stop us dancing together at the youth hostel disco in the early evening the following day. I remember that Wishful Thinking and Racey were on the playlist. Those two English bands had made it into the West German charts at the time. Because of the influence West German media had in the DDR it did not take very long for their music to be played by our radio stations and disc jockeys.

Racey even performed their song *Some Girls* on one of our Saturday evening TV variety shows and had their single released in the DDR. *Hiroshima* by Wishful Thinking was for a long time THE song for slow dancing at the end of an evening. Naturally, as soon as it came on I asked Cordelia for the dance. At first she coyly said no, but it did not take too much persuasion to make her change her mind. And even though there was no kissing or hanky-panky, that evening I was on cloud nine.

The next day the class trip was over. We all packed our bags, did a little bit of shopping in the city centre and boarded the train back to Berlin after having lunch in the station restaurant – goulash with dumplings and red cabbage for the whole class. Yum!

At home I spent most of the evening in the bathroom. A fate, it turned out, I shared with my fellow classmates. We all had the runs. Instead of seeing each other at school the next day, we bumped into each other pale-faced in the nearby *Poliklinik* picking up miniature spoons and little glass tubes in small wooden cases. To rule out an epidemic, we were required to hand in stool samples within 24 hours. God knows what we had been served the previous day at the train station; some classmates suggested it might have been Goldie, the DDR's answer to Pedigree Chum. A health inspector was apparently dispatched immediately to the restaurant to investigate the case, but we were not informed of his findings.

A Romanian explained to me how under Ceausescu's reign people thought themselves lucky if they managed to get hold of chicken feet, pigs trotters or fish fins once a week – all proper animal cuts were exported to pay off the national debt. I'm not even sure that any of these by-products were considered safe for human consumption in East Germany. Although some of the things we enjoyed in our family might get a raised eyebrow from snotty gourmets, the difference between us and a Romanian family was that we had a choice. We went for things like kidneys, livers, chicken stomachs or cow brains because we felt like it, not because we had to. While the kidneys and chicken stomachs were braised, the livers and brains were fried (fried brain has the consistency of soft scrambled eggs). Thankfully the DDR was free of BSE. Since reunification, brain no longer features on the family's menu. But Mum still makes the best chicken stomach goulash in town, though. For anyone crazy enough to try fried brain, here is the recipe:

Take 500 grams of the finest cow brain available. Remove any membrane, coagulated blood and look out for little pieces of bone. Heat some margarine in a pan, add the brain and a large finely chopped onion. Fry for seven to eight minutes. Turn down the heat, season, add fresh herbs to taste and serve with boiled potatoes. Bon Appetit!

A hard-to-get item, and one we also loved, was tongue. Whether it was from a pig or a cow did not make any difference. Preparing the tongue was a lot of hassle because first it had to cook for ages and then you had to peel it, which was a bit on the yucky side. These days it's much easier to satisfy such a craving – 200 grams of lunch tongue from the local supermarket usually does the trick for me.

In a way, traditional German cuisine is very much like olde-worlde British cooking: a piece of meat, vegetables and potatoes. Probably the most traditional German dishes are pan-fried black pudding and onion with sauerkraut and potatoes, as well as finely chopped spinach mixed with cream and spices spooned over two eggs and potatoes. Yum...

Being an adventurous shopper at a very young age, a couple of times I bought Mongolian tins of cow's heart. Heated up, they were quite nice – unidentifiable pieces of meat in gravy. But I liked cooking much more than opening cans and heating their contents. So I invested 5.80 marks (2.30 dollars) in the best-selling cookbook ever East Germany had to offer – *Wir kochen gut* (We Cook Well). First published in 1968, by 1980 it was in its twentieth edition. It contained lots of down-to-earth recipes, information on herbs, spices and food preservation as well as advice on healthy eating. It explained different cooking methods in great length and even told you how to lay a table. *Wir kochen gut* did for the DDR what Delia Smith did for Britain. The only drawback with such a long-running book was that some of the recipes might have been okay in 1968 but were rather un-PC in 1980, quite apart from the fact that some of the ingredients weren't even available any more. But then, would I really have enjoyed eating whale goulash? I don't think so. Or what about cow's udder? According to my parents, who ate it in the Sixties, udder tastes like schnitzel. For anyone being interested in the preparation of this culinary delight, here is Mum's old recipe:

Wash one kilo of udder thoroughly and let it soak in water for a couple of hours. Dispose of the water. Add stock cubes to fresh water to taste and let it boil for four to five hours on a medium heat. Once the udder is cooked, cut it into finger-thick slices. Dip those into a seasoned egg-and-breadcrumb mixture and fry in a pan until golden brown. Serve with potatoes and vegetables of your choice.

The only weird thing I ever saw in a butcher's shop was tripe. Its rubbery look, combined with the knowledge that it was also used for making pet food, ruled it out for human consumption in my eyes. But I did not have any such qualms about *Lungenhaschee* (hash of lung).

We normally bought it ready-made in a jar, but at one time there must have been a shortage of lungs, jars or lids (or maybe all three) because for quite a long time you could not get hold of it. So one day when I was in a butcher's buying some cold meat I had a flash of inspiration – we will make our own *Lungenhaschee*. The price wasn't an issue. A pound of lung cost less than 50 pfennigs (20 cents). I bought two kilos. When I came home with my purchase Mum, like me, could not bear to touch the lungs. Their redness combined with the spongy consistency gave us the shivers. Dad had to come to the rescue. Though he wasn't too keen either on handling my purchase, he washed the lungs and put them into our pressure cooker. After 15 minutes he checked whether they were cooked. When he opened the lid an endless stream of lung came towards him – during the cooking the lungs had soaked up all the water, which led to a massive expansion in their size. Red goo soon covered the whole stovetop and part of the adjoining working surface. It was a disgusting sight. Dad continued the cooking regardless, but even when the lungs started to shrink back to a consistency we were familiar with, somehow we all had lost our appetite and ended up chucking the whole lot in the bin. I haven't eaten hashed lung since and don't think I ever will again.

Sometimes my parents shook their heads in pure disbelief about the state of my taste buds. One weekend we went mushroom hunting and found a fair number of ceps. Most of them were used for dinner on that day; the rest my parents wanted to dry. They painstakingly cleaned the mushrooms and cut and dried them in the oven on a low heat for hours. A very elaborate process but worth it, as you could not buy dried mushrooms in the DDR. However, one evening, watching telly on my own, I felt like a savoury snack. What did my eyes see first when I opened the kitchen cupboard? The big jar with the dried ceps. Out of curiosity, I tried one and quite liked the taste. So I had a few more there and then. A couple of weeks later the jar was empty – I had munched my way through our entire stock. No one noticed until a month later when Dad reached for the jar to add some flavour to a sauce. Though my parents saw the funny side of it, the next lot of dried mushrooms was hidden from my prying eyes.

My eating habits were also questioned when I snacked on some Früchtewürfel (fruit cubes) – a laxative. I saw the packets lying in a supermarket shelf. "Früchtewürfel" sounded interesting so I had a look at the ingredients list. Fig was listed as the main ingredient. Dried figs (imported from Turkey or Greece) and dates (imported from Iraq) only made an occasional appearance in our shops, usually in November and December, but I craved them all year round. And as this was in spring I decided to try the cubes, just to see whether they would be a suitable alternative. Back home I helped myself to a cube. It had a nice figgy taste. To be on the safe side, or at least so I thought, I waited for ten minutes before reaching for the second cube, which I consumed like a chewing sweet. Believing myself to be immune from the laxative, I felt encouraged to have a third as well as a fourth cube, exceeding the recommended dosage by 100 per cent. A couple of hours later I had to pay for my greediness when I had to run to the bathroom and arrived not a minute too late. What followed were 24 hours of pure hell, accompanied by the worst stomach cramps of my life. Since then I have never felt the need again to satisfy my fig craving with a laxative, however tasty it might be disguised.

CARRY ON DOCTOR

A doctor visited our school at least once a year to check the general health of every pupil. We kids did not mind. Queueing up in the basement at the GP's meant missing a lesson. One by one we were always called into the consulting room. Our height and weight was measured, and our ears, tongue, sight, pulse, blood pressure and reflexes were checked.

The only embarrassing part for us boys was when the doctor asked you to cough while having a peek into your undies to check whether your balls had dropped. Though normally I received a clean bill of health, when I was twelve years old a rather overzealous doctor, nicknamed "the veterinarian" by us kids because of her brusque attitude, felt it necessary to refer me to an adiposity specialist. I was devastated. True, at that time I still had some puppy fat, but when I turned up at the specialist's doorstep and sat in the waiting room, I felt so out of place. I was a dolphin among whales. A view shared by the doctor. As soon as he saw me I was asked why I had come there. "You're the skinniest patient I've had in years," he said, sending me straight home. That restored my ego and thankfully in the following years "the veterinarian" was replaced by a more sympathetic paediatrician.

We also received all necessary immunisations in school. Polio was by far the most popular one. It did not come in the form of a jab, instead the serum was dripped onto sugar cubes we could suck on.

The school also sent whole classes for dental check-ups to a surgery nearby. I was never particularly worried about having my teeth checked – I brushed them regularly with Putzi (Brushy), the bubble gum-flavoured toothpaste for kids. On top of that I went to see our family dentist at least once a year. And a true family dentist she was: my maternal grandparents as well as my parents had been her patients since the Sixties. Me and my brother had already climbed into her dentist's chair before we both even had teeth. Her expertise and craftsmanship have stood the test of time – some of those DDR amalgam fillings have been with me for more than three decades. There is no question I was in very good hands there, yet I never felt at ease in that dental chair. The dentist always had a distinct air of authority and wore her dark hair in a Sixties-style bun. Her nurse, a serious, matronly spinster, who was nearing retirement age, did not help ease the atmosphere either. The only thing I looked forward to on my appointments was spotting the dentist's pencilled-on beauty spot – it was never in exactly the same place twice.

But the worst nightmare for me always was getting a new filling. In those days, it was unheard of to get a local anaesthetic for such a simple procedure. Countless times I sat on that dentist chair clutching a handkerchief in my left hand when the drill accidentally hit a nerve. Ouch!

While the dental care provided was generally very good I still blame the DDR for my many fillings. Though we had fluoride in our drinking water, our toothpaste was lacking this useful additive. Probably the worst paste available was a Bulgarian import made of coarse salt or sand. If you brushed your teeth with it for a few years you wouldn't have had to worry about them any more – they would have been reduced to stubs. As I got older I looked for an alternative and found it in Czechoslovakia. A well-known West German brand was manufactured there under licence. Whenever we paid our neighbouring country a visit I stocked up. Since starting doing this, I can count on five fingers the times I needed a new filling.

CAMP RESCUE

Every year in September when we returned to school after our eight-week summer holiday, I had to listen to my classmates' tales about the adventures they'd had in holiday camps. I usually spent the summer time with my parents or grandparents, but as I became older I decided to give a holiday camp a try. Once again I had to see a doctor, the dreaded "veterinarian", who thankfully certified that I was camp-fit. With this confirmation I could get Dad to book me in for three weeks into his company's holiday camp. Forty holiday camps nationwide, offering kids 40,000 places, were run by the state. But the majority of the children, like myself, went to holiday camps that belonged to companies. Most businesses had set up their own camps, to which employees could send their kids. Each year around one million children spent part of their summer holidays this way. And it cost parents next to nothing. Dad had to pay five marks a week (two dollars) for my stay – a ridiculously low amount for a full-board holiday. Many companies with large social funds at their disposal did not even bother charging such token amounts and offered employees free summer camp stays for their children.

Companies usually turned one of their properties away from home into a camp during the summer. The one I went to, near Berlin, was located in a forest, on a lake with a beach. It had some brick buildings for the girls and tents for us boys. All the kids were divided into groups of ten and specially trained company employees were the minders. Martin, a guy in his early twenties, was looking after my group. Whenever he had a free minute he would chat up the women who were responsible for the girls, although most of the time he was busy doing fun stuff with us. On an excursion to the nearest town he handed out sweets to everyone who could prove that he was a master in something. Being all boys, naturally some of the abilities displayed were gross. One guy could fart on demand, another one swallowed a living fly. I got my sweets for making a coin appear from Martin's ear. It was a hot day and when we reached the town we all wanted to head to the nearest ice cream parlour. But Martin told us that because of Health and Safety regulations we were not allowed to buy any ice cream – not even packaged one from the supermarket. We were so mad at him. But our grudge did not last long. By the time we started our scary night walk through the forest that evening, we had forgiven him already. Equipped with pocket torches we walked through the woods telling ghost stories. Occasionally some of his friends jumped screaming from behind the trees and scared the living daylights out of us. An afternoon at the lake was equally entertaining. We held swimming competitions. The boys chatted up the girls who, in return, made fun of the guys who had to sit on the beach in their undies because they had forgotten their swimming trunks at home. On other days we had quizzes, played cowboys and Indians or went on walks with someone explaining to us the local plants and wildlife. The open-air disco one evening unfortunately had to be cut short because of a sudden mosquito invasion. Yet the bonfire a night later, was a roaring success. In a combined effort, all us kids had gathered wood during the day and put potatoes into aluminium foil, so they could be put into the fire as an evening snack. It was quite romantic sitting round the flames and singing songs (including the ever-popular *We Shall Overcome*) while one of the minders played the guitar. Nothing can beat that campfire feeling, where your front gets really hot while your back is absolutely freezing...

I got on well with the other guys in my group. One day we were even responsible for the security at the main entrance, making sure that no one entered or left the camp without permission. Naturally, no one did but we felt grown up walking up and down that gate. The meals were very enjoyable. For breakfast we had fresh bread rolls with jam or cold meats, a piece of cake for afternoon tea and sandwiches for dinner. The hot dish at lunchtime was welcome too – as long as the outside temperature did not reach 30 degrees centigrade. The only hot day that we did not lose our appetite on was when every East German kid's favourite dish was served: noodles with tomato sauce and little pieces of *Jagdwurst*, a smoked sausage. Mmmm.

As one would expect, we also played pranks. Once we got up in the middle of the night to put toothpaste on the doorknobs in the girls' buildings. In return, the girls tried to pull our shorts down in public. When we put toads into their rooms the whole camp could hear the screams as yet another one was discovered hopping around on a bed. The following evening some guys found their pyjamas sown up.

All in all, the first five days were fun and very enjoyable indeed. Mind you, we could have done without the trumpets playing through the loudspeakers, waking us at seven o'clock every day, and the morning gymnastic session afterwards, but that was all part of the experience.

And then the big rain started. On the first day it was welcome, as the downpour meant the dreaded open-air gymnastics were cancelled. We just stayed indoors and played games. But then it rained for a second day. And a third day.

Gusty winds caused the temperature to drop significantly and the constant downpour turned the camp into a giant mud pool. Tiptoeing to the canteen became a lottery. Everyone would ask themselves before every mealtime: "Will I make it without slipping?" There were always kids who didn't. Covered in mud, they would have to detour to the showers instead. The rain prevented us from going anywhere. Confined to our cold tents, us boys got on each other's nerves. We began bickering and fighting about petty things, like who's turn it was to get some hot tea from the canteen. We took it in turns to spend time with the girls in the brick buildings, just to warm up a little. First it was only our clothes that were damp, then it was our duvets too. Covering yourself at night with a soggy blanket was hardly a dream come true. Most of us got the sniffles, despite constantly wearing four layers of clothes. If you listened very carefully at night, you could hear some boys quietly sobbing in bed. Things got even more depressing when our tents could not take the battering of the elements any longer and began leaking. Sleeping in a top bunk bed, I had raindrops hitting my head and pillow.

After four days of constant rain, I wrote a desperate card to my parents, asking them to please pick me up on the weekend, because I'd had enough and wanted to come home. It was such a relief to see them arrive with my grandparents in our Trabant car a couple of days later. Naturally my departure was the talk of the camp, but instead of being called a *Memme* (wimp), which is what I expected to happen, other kids asked whether they could go home as well.

Ralf, one of my camp friends, said: "I envy you so much," looking at me with his brown eyes that filled with tears. He shook my hand and quickly disappeared back into the cold tent while I walked away to an afternoon of pampering in the warmth. The rain stopped the following day but as far as I was concerned the chapter entitled "holiday camp" had been closed in my life once and for all.

WINTER WEEKENDS

Many parents complained about their children having to attend school on Saturdays but Margot Honecker, Erich Honecker's wife and the Minister for Education, was having none of it. Quite a few of my friends regularly suffered mysterious Saturday illnesses that prevented them from coming to school on that day but my parents hardly ever wrote me a bogus sick note. If they wanted to go somewhere with my brother and me, most of the time they waited grudgingly till around noon when we came home. I regularly tried to convince them that it would be much better if we drove off in the morning, but they would not listen. Damn!

Because of school on Saturdays, I especially cherished my Sundays, even more so in wintertime when it was too cold to leave the house. On Saturday evenings I would usually watch a big entertainment show like *You Bet* or *Generation Game*, followed by a film on a West German station where classics such as *The Poseidon Adventure, Westworld* or *The Towering Inferno* were regularly shown. On Sunday mornings I would sleep in. If I was particularly lazy I would get out of my bed just to climb into my parents' pull down bed in the living room which conveniently stood right in front of the telly and watch the box all day long. Could life get any better?

Yes it could! On some Sundays we skipped our usual healthy continental breakfast for fried bread. Mum would use up a whole kilogram loaf making it – we just could not get enough of it. The dessert after the Sunday roast lunch was usually blancmange or, even better, a big jar of home bottled fruit from our allotment – plums, pears, apples or gooseberries. And if we felt peckish in the afternoon, out would come the waffle iron for some Belgian Waffles. Later, as we sat down to have our sandwiches for dinner (according to a German saying, you should eat breakfast like an emperor, but have dinner like a pauper) we, like so many DDR citizens, mentally exited our country by tuning into a West German TV station. The most popular series in the prestigious Sunday evening slot over the years included *Bonanza*, *Gunsmoke*, *Star Trek* and *The Waltons*. I always looked forward to Hoss, Festus, Captain Kirk or John Boy joining us at our Sunday dinners.

PIONEERING WORK

Grade six came to an end in early July 1980 and all classes lined up in the schoolyard for the obligatory last assembly in that school year. It did not take very long to hear my name called by the *Direktor* (head teacher) asking me to step forward and pick up my "Certificate for Good Learning in the Socialist School". This was a familiar call. Because of my good marks, I got this particular award every single year. After receiving the certificate, I went back to join my classmates. Then I heard my name again. I made my way to the *Direktor* and this time I was given a "Recognition for Enthusiasm in Handicrafts". I said "Thank you very much" as the head teacher shook my hand and quickly headed back to my class. A few minutes later I heard my name called out for the third time. I was handed a certificate and matching badge honouring my achievements in Science and Technology. I did not really know why I got it but who was I to argue. Lost in thought, I traipsed back to my classmates. Having hardly reached them my name came out of the loudspeakers for the fourth time. Embarrassed and with a tomato-red face I turned around again. This time I was presented with a badge and certificate for my achievements during the realisation of the Pioneer order: "Make socialism stronger, mate – learn for our peace-loving state."

Pionieraufträge (Pioneer orders) were mottoes issued by the Pioneer headquarters. Every year there was a new one, to keep us kids engaged. One year we were asked to focus on collecting recycling material, another year we had to demonstrate our support for developing socialist countries. Teachers monitored our activities and awarded particularly enthusiastic kids with certificates and books. Others were chosen to be delegates to festivals, which our media declared as "enthusiastic manifestations of the bond between the young generation and the politics of our party". In reality these events were just giant fun get-togethers with a few political slogans thrown in. If something was organised in the name of peace, friendship, socialism and anti-imperialist solidarity it was much easier to secure funds and make things happening. But no one went to those festivals because they wanted to save world peace. World peace, my arse! All the kids and teenagers were after was having a fab time and seeing their favourite DDR bands for free.

STARTING YOUNG

Grade seven, starting in September 1980, promised to be a very demanding year. In the previous grade only one more subject (Physics) had been added to our timetable, now we were faced with another six new subjects – Chemistry, Introduction to Socialist Production, Technical Drawing, Productive Work, Civics and either French or English.

Neither French nor English were compulsory. But for some reason our school particularly pushed the French lessons. A letter, sent by the head teacher, to parents read:

"Foreign language skills are urgently needed as a communication tool in a time of growing international cooperation on the basis of peaceful coexistence. French is a major language, mother and business tongue for 75 million people in all continents. The German Democratic Republic entertains diplomatic relations with 30 French-speaking countries. We take the opportunity to remind you that in the years to come, French-speaking staff will be in high demand."

I chose English because it seemed more practical, but Cordelia went for French because of its sexy sound. First I had problems getting my head around the language but things improved quickly. The English textbook introduced us to "A Weekend in New York", "Jerry in Glasgow" and "A Trip to the British Countryside". There was even a school programme shown on DDR television called *English for You*. Although the episodes, made in the late Sixties, seemed a bit dated, fashion-wise, accompanying Anne, Mary,

John, Mr Winter or Mrs Green to a cinema, hotel or train station during our English lessons was always a welcome diversion.

Civics class had to make do without an associated television programme. Here we learnt all about the history, development and organisation of the German Democratic Republic. In the first year we covered such subjects as "Ourselves and Our Time" and the "Socialist GDR and Imperialist FRG – two German States with Opposite Social Systems". As the years went on things became more philosophical and we tackled "The Socialist State and Socialist Democracy", "The Rights and Obligations of Socialist Citizens", "Communism – The Goal of the International Workers Movement" and "The Rudiments of the Socialist Point of View and Moral". Whatever the topic, it was always wise to be up to date with the current national news when attending Civics lesson because a recent party resolution or new law would often be used to illustrate a point. Although the teacher assessed you on your knowledge about the DDR and not your attitude towards the state, I played it safe and followed the herd by displaying the "correct" public opinion in the lessons. Only once did the teacher, Frau Szopinski, give me a disapproving look when I referred, without thinking, to our Berlin border as the Wall. I was quickly reminded that its proper name was Antifascist Protection Rampart. Next we were lectured for the umptiest time that our border fortifications were not there to stop people leaving our country but to ensure that hostile people stayed out. Sure, Miss Szopinski.

In grade seven, our handicrafts lessons were replaced with three new subjects – Introduction Into the Socialist Production, Technical Drawing and Productive Work. No more making presents like candle holders and letter openers, now we were expected to work in a socialist production environment. It was intended to prepare us for the life ahead.

Each school was allocated a company and every fortnight we would go to the firm to do very basic jobs, always under the watchful eye of a teacher. In the first year we were sent to Elektro Apparate Werke, an electronic instrument and machine making company, which was located very close to the Wall. We were not part of the normal production line but worked in a special room, the *Lehrkabinett* (teaching cabinet), where we made tips for soldering irons. The process was fairly simple: First the tip of a copper blank had to be flattened in a huge press, then the burrs had to be filed away. We were given targets and, before we went home, everyone's work was marked based on the quality and quantity of the tips produced. The more organised you were, the more tips you would produce and the better your mark would be. Most of the teachers in these companies were just normal workers who had undergone a short teaching course. Not being proper pedagogues, the majority of them were very direct in their approach. If you produced rubbish and wasted material, they would let you know without beating around the bush. While a normal worker usually knows how to deal with constructive criticism, we were still very sensitive and required a more diplomatic approach. Working life hadn't toughed us up yet. I wasn't afraid of our Productive Work teachers, but Cordelia was always terrified of doing something wrong and being told off. One day she broke a soldering iron tip on which she was working. I could see the fear in her eyes as the tip snapped. Every pupil was accountable for the number of blanks they had been given at the start of the day. So her first thought was to swap the broken tip secretly with someone else's without them noticing. But Cordelia was not that ruthless. Instead she quickly hid the evidence of her careless moment in the right pocket of her pink-laced pinafore (everyone had to bring their own protective clothing from home). As the clock ticked away and the working day came to an end, the teacher started his round to collect and judge everyone's output. As he got closer and closer Cordelia prepared herself to argue that she had never been given a full set of blanks. But Lady Luck was on her side. Just as the teacher approached her neighbour the bell rang. Our Productive Work lessons had finished for the day. The immediate rush of everyone tidying up their work station, packing their stuff together and trying to get out as quickly as possible created mayhem that worked in Cordelia's favour. Together with half a dozen other pupils she hastily forced her tips and leftover blanks into the teacher's hand and got out of there in a flash. No prizes for guessing who's shoddy workmanship I blamed when Dad's soldering iron, bought a year later, packed it in just after a couple of uses.

The following year we had to attend work in a clothing company that made uniforms and camouflage gear. We assisted with the production of winter jackets and it was our responsibility to ensure that each workstation always had an ample supply of padding. I briefly considered buying a camouflage jacket for 50 marks (20 dollars) but eventually decided against it. Wearing DDR army clothing in the streets wasn't very cool. A jacket from the West German Bundeswehr or any other western army would have been highly prized by us youths, but our military gear somehow did not cut the mustard. How things have changed since then. Today, many young people on the streets of Berlin and London sport coats, jackets and tracksuit tops once belonging to our Nationalen Volksarmee (National People's Army).

In the final two years of school we had to traipse to yet another firm: Fortschritt (Progress). This was the very same clothing company Mum had worked for in the Sixties and which had brought my parents together through its folk dancing group. The girls in our class were given crash courses in how to operate sewing machines. Not being professional seamstresses, they were only entrusted with churning out grass-collecting bags, made of fabric, for an electric lawn mower named Trolli. We boys on the other hand had a very laid-back work experience. Our responsibility was to get finished suits ready for dispatch – putting them first onto hangers and then onto rails. Of course, we teenagers would discuss among ourselves how unfair and exploitative it was, having to work for free. We never admitted that working in a factory every second Wednesday for four hours was really a welcome change from the normal school routine. We saw how companies were structured and, most importantly, we were able to decide whether factory work was for us when we finished school. Those Productive Work lessons taught me that under no circumstances did I want to end up as a factory worker.

Progress, like many other East German companies, also produced for export. Suits destined for West Germany had to be put under a layer of clear plastic by us boys, but suits going to the Soviet Union had to make do without this protection. Quality-wise, there was a huge difference between a suit being shipped to a socialist country or heading to a capitalist retailer. The West German importer had chosen a light wool mixture in blue, grey and black, while the Russian buyer had ordered a stiff, shiny brown, embossed fabric, made of 100 per cent polyester. I was familiar with this DDR polyester fibre called Präsent 20 (Gift 20), which was invented in honour of the DDR's twentieth anniversary in 1969, but frankly I had never seen it woven into such a hideous fabric.

It was quite common for companies to "put presents onto our republic's birthday table", either by exceeding production targets or by dedicating new products to the state. The last invention involved in this dedication circus was a TV set known as "Colour 40". Developed in 1989 it was an extremely heavy monstrosity costing 8,500 marks (3,400 dollars) that, despite the weight and price, was far from being luxurious and still had a plastic casing. Our politicians were proud of their brainchild, the plastic industry. There was never a shortage of plastic coffee filter holders, butter dishes, eggcups or household containers, manufactured mainly in three colours: red, orange and yellow. Even better if plastic could also be used to dress people. Präsent 20 must have seemed like a godsend to our economists. Consequently, many DDR suits in the Seventies were made from this easy-care, non-breathable, man-made fibre. Usually suit designs were reasonably decent, yet this 1981 delivery for the USSR was appalling. The fabric was so plasticky stiff, when I tried on a jacket for a laugh I could hardly bend my arm. Just touching the fabric made my flesh crawl. The labels in the Russian suits proudly proclaimed "Sdjelaju v GDR" (Made in GDR), but the nice suits heading to a major West Germany catalogue shopping company had no reference in regards to their origin. Many items produced in the DDR for consumption in the west did not carry the country of origin, at the request of the importers.

It was also while working at the Progress factory that I was confronted with western affluence – the majority of the suits we sent to capitalist countries had two pairs of trousers. I had never seen anything like it before.

When lorries heading westwards arrived at the factory and my rails full of two-trouser-suits were loaded on, I sometimes imagined smuggling myself on board. Just a dream, especially as two uniformed officials from Customs and Excise monitored every single rail that went into the back of the lorry before sealing the tray following a final inspection. Even if it would have been possible to sneak out of the country that easily, what would I have done all alone in West Germany?

Other kids must have had similar thoughts, judging by a speech a teacher at Fortschritt once gave us: "Here in the company we are very proud of our products that are being exported all over the world and represent the DDR wherever they may go. So we were disappointed when a pupil recently slipped a note into a suit pocket with his name and address asking the buyer of the suit to send him a parcel with sweets and chocolate. Imagine what this would have done to the DDR's reputation had our agent in the Federal Republic of Germany not found this piece of paper before forwarding the delivery to their client. The western media would have loved the story, probably saying something like: East German child has to beg for food to avoid starvation. Now, would that be a true reflection of the DDR?" (Disagreement from us kids) "Do any of you have to starve?" (Disagreement from us kids again) "Can you buy chocolate and sweets when you want to?" (Agreement from us children) "OK, so I hereby ask you officially to not put any notes whatsoever into our clothes. Not only will they be found by the obligatory checks here and behind the border, but because of the potential implications, we will also have to report any such incidents to the police. And I am sure, no one wants to get into trouble for something silly like that!"

Whether that story was true or not, it served its purpose. None of us wrote any begging notes. But once I could not resist putting an old tram ticket into a suit's inside pocket. Just to be on the safe side fingerprint-wise I touched it only with another piece of paper. I don't know whether my old ticket made it to the west but the irony of it is that I never would have put anything in a suit if the teacher had not given me the idea for it in the first place.

When we were not busy doing menial jobs in the manufacturing industry we went to the nearby education centre to sit through lessons in Introduction to Socialist Production (ISP) and Technical Drawing (TD). Here real teachers taught us. It was a pity the lessons were so boring. Some of the "fascinating" subjects we covered in ISP were "Three-Phase Current", "Mechanical Technology", "The Rudiments of Production in Socialist Companies" and "The Economic Importance of Electrical Engineering". Yawn!

Technical Drawing was much more interesting. Time always flew when we got our rulers and pencils out and got working on graph paper.

One day at home I mentioned the name of the head teacher at the education centre. My parents looked at me first, then at each other and next old photo albums were taken out of a cabinet. Soon I was surrounded by 20-year-old photos of the head mistress. It turned out she was the one who ran my parents' folk dance group. What a small world the DDR was.

FUN, THE SWEDISH WAY

I did not care how well the DDR did in the 1980 Moscow Olympics. Nor did I engage in any sports after school. But I liked roller-skating and swimming. While the first was a rather exhausting affair, the latter always seemed a bit boring when not performed in a lake or the sea. All that changed in spring 1981. For three years, several Swedish and DDR companies had worked together on a building, which was going to become Berlin's Sport und Erholungszentrum (Sports and Recreational Centre), shortly called SEZ. Dad's company was responsible for all the wooden bits of the interior. When the SEZ was inaugurated in March 1981, all participating workers and their partners were invited for a party prior to the official opening a couple days later. Mum and Dad were on the invitation list too. I waved them goodbye as they left the apartment in the late afternoon and prepared for a nice evening in front of the telly. A few hours later Dad turned up and asked me to quickly grab a towel, my swimming trunks and bathing cap. "And get a move on!" I was hurried along. What was going on? How could a public bath possibly be so exciting that it prompted my father to come home, pick up his bathing costume and get me to do the same? All became clear when, 20 minutes later, we arrived at the SEZ. This wasn't a run-of-the-mill public bath. The bathing area consisted of no less than six pools, one for plain swimming, one for diving, a water gymnastics/beginners basin, a cascading pool with massaging jets of water, a heated outdoor basin and the pièce de résistance, a giant wave pool. Suddenly going for a swim was fun! But the building had more to offer than just getting wet: bowling alleys, sports halls, a skating rink, billiard and chess tables, a gym and other keep fit rooms as well as a number of bars and restaurants. The whole complex was so ahead of its time. If an exact replica was built today it would not seem dated, except maybe for the heavy use of orange in the interior décor.

Once the building was open to the public, people were queueing up for two hundred metres just to get to the pools – what had been designed for a capacity of 8,000 swimmers attracted 20,000 visitors daily. The queues for the skating rink were slightly shorter. But it wasn't as bad as it may sound, because a stay in the rink or bath was limited to just two hours, so the queues were constantly moving. The bowling alleys operated a strict reservation system to manage the masses. Booking requests were accepted up to six months in advance. Thankfully East Germans were experts in planning ahead (and remembering their bookings half a year later).

FUN, THE DDR WAY

East Berlin only had three bowling alleys, but there was an abundance of skittle lanes in the DDR. The only snag was, being seen at one of those was considered social suicide among us teenagers. Mind you, it was different if an alley was not open to the public. Dad's company had transformed one of their building's basements into a skittles alley with attached bar and, away from my friends' critical eyes, I was quite happy to skittle away.

It was very common in the DDR for colleagues who worked together and were a *Kollektiv* (team), to meet after work on a regular basis and do things together, with or without their partners. Whether it was for a short trip to another town, a theatre visit or a cosy evening in a nice restaurant, each team-member paid a set monthly contribution into a cash tin, which took care of most of the costs. Many companies supported this sort of socialising by making extra contributions. And to make sure everyone in the team would remember the event, one person was usually set the task of making a commemorative entry in the team's diary. Witty texts and pictures ensured that the book, like a treasured family photo album, would evoke memories in the years to come.

Schools kept children happy with one-day excursions to interesting places or manoeuvres, on which the class was split into two groups and each one had to try to capture the other team's flag. Just like in Tag, you had to drop out of the game once an opponent had touched you. One thing I wasn't too keen on was the school sports carnival. Normally we would go to a stadium nearby to do all the required races, jumps and throws. As well as the shot put, we were also judged on our hand grenade throwing skills. The further it flew the better the score. Thankfully we did not throw live ones. Had we done, I would have died many horrible deaths – my grenades always flew high, high up into the sky, only to just land a few metres in front of me. If height instead of distance had been marked, I would have been the best hand grenade thrower the school ever had!

Another East German idea of fun was a *Subbotnik* – a kind of community "busy bee". The word *Subbotnik* is an import, derived from the Russian word for Saturday, *subbota*. The "fun" thing we did while being at *Subbotniks*, (which always took place on a Saturday, hence the name), was voluntary work. If your classroom or work place needed a very thorough clean once in a while, or even a mini revamp with a lick of paint, a *Subbotnik* would take place. If the front garden of the apartment block you lived in needed tending, another *Subbotnik* would be scheduled. Your local sports club was in urgent need of a new clubhouse, but the council would not allocate any builders because they were needed elsewhere? Club members would build it themselves during a string of *Subbotniks*. Although attending a *Subbotnik* was entirely voluntary, socialism worked on a tit-for-tat basis – if you contributed to the state, the state showed its appreciation and contributed to your development. You were therefore well advised to get your priorities right. Attending a *Subbotnik* at work, for example, was always far more important than going to one that had been called by the local council to clean up a park. If you could not be bothered to go to either, the best excuse was to pretend you had already committed to another *Subbotnik* elsewhere.

It would be unfair to say that these voluntary work Saturdays were a regular occurrence – most people attended one or two a year. Even hardcore communists preferred to spend their weekends at home with their families.

1981

For communists and non-communists alike, 1981 was a mixed bag of events. In our neighbouring country of Poland, the independent union Solidarnosc gained too much momentum for the Polish government's liking, so martial law was declared to avoid a Russian "let's-sort-it-out-once-and-for-all-style" invasion. As a result Poland was taken off our travel maps for quite a while. A West German chancellor officially visited East Germany for the second time. Furthermore, it was the year in which the last death sentence was carried out in the DDR. A captain of the Stasi had been convicted for treason and was executed with a single gunshot to the neck. In total, nearly 200 people were executed in the DDR. The majority of them were murderers, but since the Seventies most victims were ex-members of the secret service who had betrayed their last employer. In 1987 the death penalty was taken out of the penal code. The DDR was the only communist country to do so.

When Ronald Reagan was inaugurated as president in January 1981, our media portrayed him as a sabre-rattling, sad, has-been actor who was the voice of the US monopolists. Our politicians were worried that he might be stupid enough to end 35 years of peace in central Europe.

"Carter's intelligence was praised. A quality that Reagan is lacking. He often gives off the impression that he hasn't done his homework..."

Zwischen Dallas und New York by Ingrid Deich (Urania Verlag, 1986)

Unlike Jimmy Carter, Reagan was not very popular among East Germans. His "Star Wars" plans frightened many, including me. With the DDR on the geographical frontline of the communist/capitalist divide, East Germans could imagine how a nuclear war would leave central Europe – uninhabitable for the next thousands of years, which was not exactly a nice prospect!

The must-have item in 1981 was the Rubic's Cube. I was over the moon when I got mine. Because our economists had been unable to predict the success of this toy when production/import plans were drawn up for that year, I had to rely, once more, on my grandparents. They bought me the original Hungarian cube in West Berlin. I'm not even sure Rubic's Cubes ever made it into DDR shops at all. If they did, it was most probably only after they were yesterday's news in the west.

A number of DDR citizens did, however, manage to get Japanese cars without major delays. Erich Honecker went on an official state visit to the land of the rising sun in May 1981, where he signed a contract for the importation of 11,000 Mazda 323s. When offered the chance of having their original car application for a Lada or Polski Fiat upgraded to a Japanese model, many people did not think twice and happily swapped. Only in later years did they realise their mistake as the state did not like to spend dollars or yen for western car spare parts.

But the Fritz family profited nicely from all those people switching to Mazdas. The Lada we had on order was ready for collection five years earlier than expected. Our Trabant was quickly sold for the same price we had paid in 1976 and, with a little financial help from my grandparents, we were soon the proud owners of a "proper" car. The Lada's red bodywork wasn't necessarily to my parents' liking but they had no real choice, it was the only colour available at the time. That was socialism for you.

Typical of our form of socialism was also the *Rotlichtbehandlung*, which translates as "infrared treatment" and was disrespectful slang for any sort of politically motivated get-together that exposed participants to prolonged communist indoctrination. No one in a job or in education was safe from it. Especially in the seventh grade we kids received a fair share of "infrared treatment". Moving on to the next level in our personal development, the state felt it necessary to prepare us for leaving the Pioneer organisation behind and becoming members of a two-million strong organisation called the Free German Youth.

In get-togethers we were told by teachers and officials how our active membership in the youth organisation will enable us to build the socialist state we all were assumed to strive for. Blah, blah, blah, waffle, waffle, waffle, b-o-r-i-n-g! Unfortunately, non-participation was not an option. To make time pass faster we held secret doodling competitions. Whoever managed to doodle most during those meetings was declared winner on the way home.

FREE GERMAN YOUTH

With the beginning of the next school year in September 1981, the political indoctrination we were subjected to earlier seemed to have paid off – the whole class joined the FDJ, the Freie Deutsche Jugend (Free German Youth). This organisation, aimed at 14 to 25 year olds, was founded in 1946 when people were trying to build a true alternative to Germany's war-blighted past. But for my generation, that political enthusiasm from the immediate post-war years was no longer there. Thankfully, over the decades, the Freie Deutsche Jugend had partially evolved in an attempt to keep its members interested. In my time the FDJ organised youth festivals and concerts and entertained members and non-members alike in 10,300 youth clubs and 5,000 discos. Its original political message, however, remained ever-present and seemed dated for the Eighties. Everyone I knew, except for some hardcore communist kids perhaps, just wanted to do the fun things, and not sit in courses and get acquainted with the Marxist-Leninist philosophy, or the biographies of Marx and Engels. But you could not have one without the other.

"The politics of the Marxist-Leninist Party of the working class... show the youth of the DDR the way to a communist future. The FDJ considers it an honour to prepare its best members for admission as candidates into the Communist Party. The FDJ sees its main task as... to ensure its members... develop and hold an unshakeable socialist standpoint..."

Statute of the Free German Youth

But not every 14-year-old East German became an FDJ member. Each year, roughly five percent of pupils refused membership for religious or political reasons. It might not have done their careers any favours, considering that membership in the youth organisation was a pre-requisite in most jobs. At least it saved them from having to sit through the membership meetings in which participants were subjected to more *Rotlichtbehandlung*.

Members were required to wear their FDJ shirts on all official get-togethers. The shirts were cobalt blue and had the organisation's emblem on the left sleeve: a rising yellow sun (indicating the dawn of a new day) above the letters FDJ. How uncool! Everyone I knew put their shirt loosely over their normal clothes just a minute before an event started, only to take it off immediately after the do had finished. No fashion-conscious teenager wanted to be seen dead in it.

BEING IDENTIFIED

Moving from one mass organisation to another was not the only highlight in the life of a 14-year-old DDR citizen like myself. A much more anticipated one was being issued with an ID card.

"Citizen of the German Democratic Republic, this identity paper is your most important document. You have to carry it with you at all times, prevent its loss and hand it over on demand to the security organs of the German Democratic Republic or show it to other authorised persons."

The first page of a DDR ID card

ID cards have been mandatory in Germany since well before the DDR existed. Even the reunited Germany continues the practice today. Our East German identity paper was a 12-page booklet. The vital statistics (name, date and place of birth, marital status, children) were spread over two pages, followed by the signature and photo, in semi-profile. The rest of the booklet was made up of empty pages for entry and exit stamps. The document doubled as passport when travelling to other European communist countries like Hungary, Czechoslovakia or "the Mallorca of the east", Bulgaria.

Shortly after my fourteenth birthday in September 1981 I finally received the long awaited letter from the local *Einwohnermeldeamt* (population registration office), inviting me to the handover ceremony of the document. When I and 30 other teenagers arrived at the office, which was housed in a police station, the atmosphere among us was expectant but also tinged with disappointment. The room we were asked to assemble in had iron-barred windows which hardly made it an uplifting location. And the handover ceremony matched the drab surroundings perfectly. First some uniformed official told us in a monotonous voice about the importance of the ID card then everyone was individually called to the front of the room to sign their document in black ink. The ID cards were dished out with quick handshakes and then we were free to go home.

My ID card number was A1280164. Not very catchy but the really good numbers were already taken by our top politicians: Number A0000003 had been issued to the President of the Volkskammer (our parliament), number A0000002 was held by the Prime Minister and who may have owned ID paper A0000001? Of course, the General Secretary of the Central Committee of the Socialist Unity Party, the Head of State Council and Head of Security Council, Erich Honecker. It was issued to him when new-style ID cards were introduced in the Seventies, though he had not requested this number.

But ID card numbers weren't really that important. It was the Personal Identification Number which made you an open book to the authorities. Equivalent to the National Insurance Number in the UK or the Social Security Number in the US, every DDR citizen was issued a *Personenkennzahl* (Personal Identification Number). It was noted in your ID card and gave away your date of birth, gender and responsible registration office. Your entire life was linked to this number, whether it be your employment contract, further education or medical treatment.

LESSONS IN LOVE

September 1981 marked the beginning of grade eight. It was a time when most of us 14 year olds experienced the hormones kicking in, giving us a taste of adulthood. Sex-related stories started doing the rounds. Like the one about a classmate who had offered other girls the chance to hide in her wardrobe at home and watch while she bonked her boyfriend on the couch. Five girls took her up on the offer. According to Andrea, one of the invited spectators, the wardrobe was so full she hardly fitted in. Someone had even brought a camera. Naturally, the boyfriend discovered the spectators as soon as they opened the wardrobe door to get a piece of the action. I always wondered what must gone through the poor guy's head as he saw ten pairs of eager eyes steering at him from the inside of that wardrobe. Apparently first there was an eerie silence. And then, so I have been told, it was broken by a "click" – the girl with the camera had decided to take a snapshot. That proved to be too much. The guy jumped up stark naked, ripped the film from the camera and threw the girls out.

The year 1981 was a time when the girls began gaining womanly curves and we boys began being turned on by it. More and more often, the air was filled with sexual tension and innuendo when I got together with classmates in the afternoons at our most favourite hang-out spot, the table-tennis tables close to the nearby playground. Previously innocent boy-girl friendships began to take on another dimension, though hardly anyone I knew had full-blown sex. For most of us it was a quick kiss and fumble behind the school's sports hall. My parents had given me East Germany's sex education bible,

Man & Woman Being Intimate, so I had become familiar with the theoretical ins and outs of human reproduction and everything that goes with. For anyone with prudish parents, the subject was also covered in biology that year. I still remember our teacher's unease when explaining how babies were made. The 20-minute film that followed answered all the questions we could possibly have. Surprisingly the entire class behaved rather maturely while the film was shown, but I think it had more to do with the teacher threatening to throw out anyone who made rude remarks during the screening.

I had no intentions of having sex at that time, yet I was still disappointed that I did not make any progress, however limited, with Cordelia. We shared jokes, played pranks on unsuspecting people and could, like all teenagers, talk about anything for hours, but that seemed to be it. As much I enjoyed her presence and bubbly personality there was never a moment or gesture that would have opened the way for me to give her a kiss the way a boy ought to kiss a girl. And without a signal from her I decided to sit tight and wait for the day where we could be more than just friends. In the meantime, I made do with scratching a little heart containing Cordelia's and my initials in the black paint of a pillar near the local playground. I was in desperate need of some self-affirmation about my attractiveness to the opposite sex and decided to test the waters by putting an ad in a monthly youth journal. The four lines stating my vital statistics, hobbies and address attracted 50 to 60 letters, most of them rubbish. I considered only a few worthy of a reply. So as not to look like the novice I was, I pretended in my replies to have split up with my previous girlfriend. After receiving the requested portrait photos, I sat down again and decided on two finalists – Jaqueline and Antje received the thumbs up, the rest of the shortlisted candidates landed in the waste paper basket. But I realised quickly that my heart wasn't in it. The one and only girl I really wanted still was Cordelia. When, after months of delaying, I finally agreed to meet Jaqueline at the Weltzeituhr (World Time Clock) in East Berlin's city centre, I arrived an hour late because I had made an impromptu detour to a bookshop where I had decided to queue for a rare title. Of course, Jaqueline did not wait that long for me – I never heard from her again. Antje too wasn't very happy with my stalling technique. We only lived 15 tram stops apart, yet incomprehensibly to her, I never made a move to arrange a meeting. One day she finally had enough and sent me a dumping letter. One sentence in it made me smile:

"To me you don't appear to be too socialist, but your humour is strange."

In my previous letter to Antje I had asked whether I gave off the impression of being too communist. Nowadays it seems an odd question, but everyday life in the DDR was very political and I did not want it to rub off on me and ruin my image. Politics and coolness just don't go together. British politician William Hague is living proof. As a 16-year old he held a speech at the 1977 Conservative Party Conference. Girls were not driven crazy by it.

CASH IS KING

Five marks pocket money a week (two dollars) may not sound very much but then I hardly had to buy anything for myself. My parents bought my clothes and school-related items and whatever money I did not save, I spent on magazines, books, the occasional ice cream (who could possibly resist a Mr Whippie?) or visits to the cinema. Watching a film on the big screen only cost the equivalent of 60 cents.

But even with low prices like these, additional money was always welcome. Being 14 years old when our four-week winter holiday started in February 1982, meant I was allowed to work for one week during that break. Having a sweet tooth I applied for a job at an export/import company dealing with sweets, chocolates, alcohol and tobacco and was given the green light a few weeks later. The DDR only had one company specialising in the import and export of those non-essential food items, and I would be working for them. Hooray!

"In socialism, foreign trade is conducted and planned by the socialist state under the leadership of the communist and workers parties."

Political Economy for the Foreign Trade Merchant

Foreign trade, just like the rest of the DDR economy, was centralised. DDR companies were generally not allowed to do their own importing and exporting. All international trade was realised by *Aussenhandelsbetriebe* (foreign trade companies) of which each one specialised in a different field. One company only dealt with electronic goods, another one just with health-related products and so on. Centralisation meant the state always knew exactly how much money made from exports was available for imports. After all, our currency was not accepted on the international markets.

For one week's work in the foreign trade company I was about to earn 110 marks (44 dollars). Not bad. For that sort of money I could buy quite a few elaborate tricks from my beloved Magic Shop. My first day at work was a crispy winter's morning. The temperature was minus five degrees centigrade and the streetlights beautifully illuminated the virgin snow that had fallen overnight. Snowflakes were still tumbling down when I made my way to the nearby tram stop. About 45 minutes later I reached my destination – a part of the city centre that was very close to the Wall and the Brandenburg Gate. The company occupied a building which was once a wing of the famous Hotel Kaiserhof (Emperor's Court), a hotel that for decades after its opening in 1875 was Berlin's most luxurious accommodation. Unfortunately, the hotel had not survived the war intact – in 1943, bombs reduced the main building to rubble. And whatever was left of the remaining wing could hardly be described as glamorous. White painted corridors with fluorescent lights and linoleum made the place look dull. Hotel rooms had become offices and with their lino, generic DDR wallpaper and office furniture, you only had to look into one room to know what the rest looked like.

But the drab surroundings did not dampen my spirit and I quite enjoyed going to work and doing the company lawyer's admin. He was a pipe-smoking, bow-tie-wearing guy with a beard in his forties. Whenever I read a term I did not understand in the papers I was sorting, he took the time to explain it to me in layman's terms. His humour was very dry and I could have killed him on the very first day for dwelling on the fact that my voice hadn't broken yet. But after that we got on like a house on fire. A pity that when I worked for the company again the following year (by then my voice had broken), I was assigned to assist the company's handyman on his various missions throughout the building. At least this way I got to know quite a lot of people and everyone I met on my rounds seemed very friendly indeed. I remember one woman in particular who was so impressed by the speed with which I replaced her desk lock, that she gave me a big bag full of yummy nougat as a "Thank You", wishing her sons were as dexterous as me. It was hardly rocket science to unscrew a broken lock and slot in a new one, but who was I to argue.

What also boosted my ego were the occasions when I was mistaken for a proper adult. Like the time when I had to put a new letterbox at the entrance to the company's reception area. After I finished the job the receptionist asked me whether I wanted a beer. Being offered a beer at the age of 15! I felt so grown up. A pity I did not like beer. Declining the offer without losing face I screwed my nose up and mumbled: "I can't drink alcohol." "Oh, sorry," was her reply, "do you come by motorbike to work?" I muttered a yes and was offered a coffee instead. I didn't dare say that a nice cup of hot cocoa would have been much more up my street.

Class trips were naturally the highlights of any school year. In the eighth grade we went away three times. Two trips were day excursions. The third, and most anticipated, tour was a four-day trip to a small village called Eisenberg, 300 kilometres south of Berlin in Thuringia. When Mum accompanied me to the train station on a warm, sunny, April Thursday morning she slipped me a 20 mark note and said out of the blue: "Behave! We don't want you to be sent home." Instead of a reply I rolled my eyes and tutted. No one had ever been sent home early from a trip. And I, the class monitor, was surely the least likely candidate to suffer such a fate.

As we arrived in Eisenberg some hours later we had to schlepp our bags a couple of kilometres through a forest before reaching our hostel, an olde-worlde-timber-framed building. We boys made ourselves at home in one big dormitory style room, while the girls were split into groups occupying three smaller bedrooms. Everyone seemed happy with the arrangements and the afternoon was spent with exploring the surrounding area and playing table tennis. Dinner was a bit of a disappointment – slices of cold meat with brown, bent edges made us lose our appetite. But overall the whole class was in a jolly mood, looking forward to an evening of playing games. Nighttime brought the usual school trip shenanigans. All of us boys were in bed but no one wanted to close their eyes yet. So a mixture of scary stories, jokes and sexual fantasies were told until one by one dropped out of the conversation and fell asleep. As one of the last ones to stay awake, I decided to go for a quick wee before calling it a night. On the way to the toilet, I was joined by my classmate Silvio. When we walked past one of the girls' rooms we hit on the idea to say hello. Silvio opened the door slowly but instead of hearing from Viola, Andrea, Katrin and Heike the expected: "Come on in." we were greeted by their snoring. What a let down! Just as I was shutting the door we heard a sharp: "What are you two doing there?" behind our backs. An accompanying parent had followed us secretly. Silvio and I mumbled something about just having had a peep. We were promised by the classmate's foul tempered father that he would have the two of us on the carpet the following day.

The next morning, after everyone had finished breakfast and was about to leave the dining hall, our teacher, Frau Conrad, asked Silvio and me to stay behind. Bushy-haired Marion was sent to get the train timetable. It looked like we really were in trouble. Someone obviously had gotten up on the wrong side of the bed that morning. Silvio and I were standing with our heads down as our teacher accused us of entering the girls room with such a vigor, that it felt like we had planned an assassination attempt on the poor girls' lives. The truth, that we had only looked and not gone into the room was rubbished. We were ordered to pack our bags immediately. Apparently the next train to Berlin was ours. The class could not believe it when they heard of our imminent departure. Of course, there were quite a few smug smiles behind our backs. Goody-two-shoe Oliver being sent home from a class trip was the kind of news that triggered a lot of gossip starting with "Can you imagine...".

Having arrived back in Berlin and with Mum and Dad at work, I made my way to my grandparents. As one would expect, Nanna was very understanding. She tried to cheer me up with a nice hearty meal, comforting words and some West German chocolate. I wish the deputy head teacher at school, to whom Silvio and I had to report to the next day, had been equally sympathetic. Instead she greeted us with a sarcastic: "Well, well, look who we got here!" We had to sit with another class for the next two days. But Silvio and I were somewhat rehabilitated a couple of years later when our teacher Frau Conrad apologised for having overreacted by sending us home. Forgive and forget has been an integral motto in my life ever since.

WE WILL ROCK YOU

Like any other class, ours was far from perfect. Teasing and arguing among us happened on a daily basis and if a teacher was not well liked we gave them a hard time too. The most popular stunt was for someone to shout during a lesson: "Wow, what's that over there?" and point to something outside the window. This gave the rest of the class the chance to jump up and watch an imaginary event in the schoolyard, ooohing and aaahing. When the teacher would then storm out to get the head teacher, everyone quickly went back to their seat and started diligently reading or writing. By the time the *Direktor* showed up, we were the most well behaved class the world had ever seen. Our Russian teacher was often at the receiving end of our cruel games. We either ignored her or gave her so much grief that she was sometimes close to tears. Sadly, that gave us even more reason to be nasty to her. Poor Mrs Mollenhauer, I really felt for her and often tried to defuse situations, but then she would have moments where she ridiculed herself. On one occasion she insisted that Mickey Mouse really should be pronounced Mikey Mouse. The entire class laughed at her. To gain at least some control over us, she allowed one pupil a week to do her job for one lesson. I volunteered once, because at that stage I was still considering whether I should become a teacher. She briefed me a couple days beforehand about what vocabulary, grammar and exercises had to be covered from the schoolbook and the rest was left to me. The lesson did not go too well. Afterwards I asked myself why anyone would want to earn a living by teaching other people's offspring.

Several times a year our class would organise a disco. Those took usually place in our class room, with someone bringing in their tapes and tape player, someone else contributing loudspeakers and a third person organising the light show. The rest of the class took care of food and drinks. Naturally the older we got, the longer those events extended into the evening and the more snogging took place. But we also had musical get togethers outside school. The apartment block that Cordelia lived in had a party room in the basement and some classmates regularly celebrated their birthday there. Those parties were extremely popular. Mostly starting at around four pm, they usually went on until eight or even nine o'clock in the evening and were a great source of gossip: "What, he did not get an invite this time?" – "Did you see who she had danced with?" – "How embarrassing, she rejected him!"...

The most anticipated part of such a get together was the slow dancing toward the end of an evening. I liked to share this moment with Cordelia. Provided I had the guts to ask her for a dance, that is.

In the Seventies and Eighties disco dancing in East Germany was pretty much the same as everywhere else in the world. Thankfully by then we had moved on from the politics of the Fifties and Sixties when our then party leader, Walter Ulbricht, publicly declared: "Do we really have to copy all this western rubbish?" Indirectly referring to the Beatles he continued: "Comrades, my opinion is that we should put an end to the monotony of all this 'Yeah, Yeah, Yeah' or what ever it's called." Dancing to Rock'n'Roll was frowned-upon by our officials in those days. Consequently, two DDR dances were invented – the Orion and the Lipsi. The latter was to become the most famous one. Choreographed by two dancing school teachers it was introduced to the public in 1959, together with the *Lipsi Song*:

Today all young people dance

with Lipsi-steps, with the Lipsi-steps.

Everyone likes the dance at once.

They join in doing the Lipsi-steps.

Rumba, Boogie and Cha Cha Cha,

have long been around.

Therefore quickly overnight

this new rhythm saw the light.

Tonight we'll go out dancing.

Every time it's so much fun,

this dance is enjoyed by everyone.

I dance all night

but I only do the Lipsi-steps.

This musical "marvel" in six-four time was specially composed for the occasion but, even with TV promotion, the socialist dance alternative did not take off. Youths wanted to shake their bodies wildly to the Twist and not hold hands while moving their "left foot to the left, tap with the right foot to the left, move the right foot to the right and tap with the left foot to the right".

The Lipsi was as much of an embarrassment as were my first dance moves 23 years later. I practiced them in front of our full-length mirror at home. Tapping the right foot behind the left one, bringing it back to the front, followed by the left foot tapping behind the right one and bringing it back to the front made me look as if I was constantly curtseying. If it had not been for my arms moving up and down at the same time no one would have ever guessed I was dancing. Thankfully I acquired more sophisticated moves pretty quickly.

And with the dancing experience from the school and the party basement under my belt I felt ready to go to a proper commercial disco for the first time. Close to where we lived, a huge area was home to the company VEB Elektrokohle, which manufactured industrial carbon products, such as electrodes, heating elements and engine brushes. And a dirty business it was. Every second or third day, mum had to sweep our balcony to get rid of a fine layer of soot. Leave the laundry out for too long and you had to wash it again. Although the DDR had environmental protection laws too, it was often the case that the necessary money to implement them fully wasn't available. VEB Elektrokohle had imported filters in their chimneys, yet to make them last longer they were turned off as soon as the sun had set. Sometimes the shutdown happened a bit too early, and one could see thick dark smoke being released into the environment when usually at daytime it was just innocent fluffy white clouds that blew out.

But Elektrokohle's lax environmental policy aside, its *Kultursaal* (cultural hall) was greatly appreciated by the youth. It was only a hall with a stage, but several times a month the company hired a DJ and opened the place to Joe Public. Some of my classmates had raved about how good the disco there was. So, on Wednesday 4 April 1982, I finally followed their advice. I put on a light-blue shirt, a pair of dark blue corduroy trousers, my beloved pointy brown shoes and black fake leather jacket and made my way to the disco at half past three on a sunny afternoon. After paying the entrance fee of one mark (40 cents), I entered the dance hall and was immediately blown away. The loudspeakers were blasting Queen's *We Will Rock You* and 20 odd teenagers, sitting in a circle, bent forward, to hit the floor with their hands twice, then raised their upper bodies, to do one clap in the air and bent forward again to hit the floor. This went on throughout the entire song and I thought that was so cool. There were roughly 200 teenagers, all around my age. The majority of them wore velvety jumpers in various colours – THE fashion item at the time. Thankfully my carefully chosen outfit made me stand out from the uniform appearance of the others.

I noticed that a group of girls 20 metres away were giving me coy looks. A chubby brunette approached me: "My friend over there likes you but she is really shy. Would you dance with her?". A quick glimpse revealed that the secret admirer looking at me with hopeful eyes was twice my size, and I was already on the chubby side. I declined the offer by pretending that my girlfriend was turning up any minute and quickly made my way to the other side of the packed dance floor. Trying to take the atmosphere in I noticed the high ceiling of this Fifties building and the tall, but narrow, windows. The drawn curtains were not too effective in keeping the sunlight out, which ruined the atmosphere slightly but was great for checking out the crowd. Suddenly I felt like a fool. Everyone, but me, seemed to be there with friends. Maybe I should have been less snotty and danced with the fat girl? In desperate search for a familiar face a girl from school caught my eye. She also seemed to be there on her own. That was my chance! I asked her for a dance just as the DJ put on *The Lion Sleeps Tonight* by Tight Fit. After the song her boyfriend took over again. He had only been to the loo. Oops! My next victim was a soft-looking, skinny girl with long black hair who I approached while her girlfriends were busy talking to a group of boys. We danced to Soft Cell's *Tainted Love*. For Kim Wilde's *Cambodia* I picked a curly blond and round-faced beauty named Anne. We even danced together cheek to cheek during the slow songs. Her hair smelled of (West German) apple shampoo – by then the DDR had not yet discovered fruity-smelling shampoos. If the place had had a bar, I would have invited her for a glass of lemonade. When the music stopped at six pm we promised each other to be there for the next kiddies disco. Lying awake in bed that night reliving the afternoon I was well pleased with the progress I had made with the opposite sex. I didn't get a single rejection when asking for a dance!

Over the years I went back to Elektrokohle for many more discos, where I met many more girls. But Anne, with her apple-shampooed hair, never showed up again. Sigh…

While I started to get hooked on discos, some of my classmates were taking up a more serious habit – smoking. Tobacco and cigarettes might have only been available to anyone being over the age of 16, but if you knew someone who was that old or if you looked older yourself, it was a doddle to get hold of that stuff. Thankfully I never got addicted to smoking.

I must have been 14 when my parents, both non-smokers, called me into the living room. With a packet of cigarettes, an ashtray and some matches at the table Mum said: "Oliver, you know that smoking is dangerous. We would prefer if you didn't take this habit up at all. However, what we want to avoid is you smoking behind our backs. But before we continue we want to ask you first whether you have smoked already?" I did not know what to make of it all and honestly shook my head. "Good," Mum continued, "now light a cigarette and tell us whether you like it." After a nervous fumble with the matches I finally managed to light the damn thing. I did a few puffs before Dad asked me to inhale properly. And that was what did it for me. I started coughing my lungs out and had a horrible taste in my mouth. Truthfully I could say that smoking was not for me. Okay, as I got older I sometimes pretended to smoke, but I never inhaled. Most of the time I just held cigarettes or cigars to look distinguished, with occasional micro puffs thrown in to make it look genuine.

Smokers and non-smokers alike were keen to get hold of western cigarettes. A few packets slipped to a plumber ensured he would go the extra mile for you. A few more packets given to a shop assistant pretty much guaranteed that she would think of you the next time a delivery of imported winter jackets came in, and so on. But the majority of smokers had to make do with a DDR brand, whether it was the filterless Karo at 1,60 marks (65 cents) for a packet of 20 cigarettes, the very popular Club for four marks (1.60 dollars) or one of the many other brands in between. We had no tobacco advertising and rather than choosing a brand to make a statement about themselves, people smoked what they felt tasted nicest. And the export/import company I had worked for during the school holidays was the firm that imported all the tobacco used.

Once I gave chewing tobacco a try. You could buy 14 small brown pieces in a little green and yellow cardboard box for 40 pfennigs (16 cents). The instructions on the inside of the package read: "Put a piece of chewing tobacco between cheek and jaw. Do not chew on it, but let the piece of tobacco just lay in your mouth and in a short time you will notice that chewing tobacco tastes delicious and is a stimulant with a refreshing, thirst-quenching effect."

I followed those instructions to the letter, yet somehow I never experience the promised refreshing and thirst-quenching effect. The only thing I noticed was, that the stuff tasted vile – I spat it out and chucked the rest.

Probably the strangest brand name for a tobacco product made in GDR, was the "Speechless" brand of cigars. What a name! A packet of 20 was sold for 2,40 marks (96 cents) and whether it left the discerned smoker lost for words because of their exceptionally good or incredibly poor quality, is anyone's guess.

LET'S DEMONSTRATE, MATE

Every year in the DDR, there were two big demonstrations – the first on May Day, the International Fighting and Celebration Day of the Working People, and the second on 7 October, the National Holiday, to celebrate the inauguration of the DDR in 1949.

On both days the *Partei- und Staatsführung* (party and state leadership) occupied two hastily erected stands in the heart of East Berlin, in the early years at Marx-Engels-Platz (a huge square) and later at the Karl-Marx-Allee, our capital's most prestigious boulevard. The event on 7 October traditionally started with a military parade at nine am sharp. Rehearsals usually took place a few nights prior. One year in early October, we Fritzes were on our way home late at night from a birthday party. Driving along East Berlin's deserted streets in our Trabant we suddenly heard a cacophony of metal on asphalt. A seemingly endless convoy of tanks came down a sealed-off road, heading towards the city centre for the parade's dress rehearsal. What an eerie encounter. The sight of the tanks combined with the noise gave me the creeps. Thank God we did not live near that road. Twice a year angry, sleepless residents must have cursed the otherwise convenient location of their flats.

The televised events on 1 May and 7 October always followed the same pattern: Berliners would walk past the stands, accompanied by music and chanted slogans from loudspeakers ("A hip, hip, hooray to our party and state leadership!"). The media in return would label these processions as "powerful illustrations of the bond between the people and the party and state leadership". These demonstrations took place virtually in every town and village up and down the country, though the military parade was exclusive to the capital. Elsewhere people just walked past regional state and party officials who were waving back from stands. Yet what all demonstrations had in common was that most participants aimed for one thing only: Saving most of the day by finishing the march as quickly as possible.

The marches were joined by up to ten million people around the country. Not bad for a population of roughly 17 million, hey? The large number of attendees is even more surprising considering that many companies honoured exemplary individuals or teams the day before each event with bonus payments. The booze-fuelled celebrations that followed often went on into the early hours of the next morning. So, how did the organisers get the masses onto the streets? It helped that in most years we had lovely sunshine on those parade days. Grandad joked many times that the good weather could only mean one thing: "God is secretly a commie." Unlike our Russian comrades, DDR jets never sprayed clouds with silver iodide or frozen carbon dioxide (dry ice) making them release rain before they reached the capital. When sprayed into clouds both chemicals kick start the formation of heavy ice crystals. The crystals fall down and melt while the empty clouds move on. Today 25 countries worldwide use cloud seeding to benefit their agriculture yet, I believe, Russia was the only state that relied on this technique to save its May parades.

But, of course, sunshine was not the main reason why the DDR folk would sacrifice a bank holiday morning to go demonstrating. Every school, institution, company or organisation asked its people to turn up at the designated meeting place in one of the many side streets. Though no one was forced to show their face, if you did not want to have to explain your absence the next working day, being out in the fresh air for a few hours and seeing our politicians up close was for most people the lesser evil. Some companies boosted the number of their participants by paying every member of staff turning up a fiver or tenner. A novel approach that may have been, but it was one that worked.

As kids, my brother and I loved accompanying Dad on the march, while Mum usually slaved away in the kitchen so lunch would be ready on our return. Naturally when we got older, we were required to join the parade separately under the banner "45th Polytechnical Upper School". Here is an entry from my diary for the 1 May 1982:

"The class was asked to turn up for the march today, but the only classmates I met were Heike, Silvia and Bettina. Not even our teacher, Frau Conrad, was there. Though we could have gone home then, we decided to stay put and go through with the march anyway. We got hold of some plastic carnations and small flags which had been handed out for waving. We walked past Erich Honecker. It was quite a laugh."

All the little things people could salute our leaders with on their walk past the stands, were called *Winkelemente* (waving elements) in DDR lingo, and they were handed out for free on the day. If you were unlucky, you were asked by your teacher or manager to carry a placard. Some were provided by the demonstration organisers others were made by participating companies or organisations. But regardless of their origin, all placards and banners had one thing in common – their mottoes were chosen from the 50 or so slogans that the Communist's Party Central Committee had pre-authorised and published. No one could make up their own motto and put it on a banner. Here are a few of the officially authorised gems:

"Three cheers for May Day – the fighting day of the international working class"

"For new achievements in the fight for peace and socialism under the banner of Marxism/Leninism"

"Microelectronic, robotics and new technologies – requirements for a powerful impetus in rationalization"

"Scientists, engineers! Achieve top results in research and production by working creatively"

"Without nuclear weapons into the new millennium"

"Protect peace by making socialism stronger."

But having to carry a placard was only a slight inconvenience compared to being asked to hold up a banner, or even worse a giant flag. If you were tired of lugging a placard around, you could easily lean it against a lamppost to blow your nose and then conveniently "forget" to pick it up when resuming the march. A banner, however, was harder to dispose of, because it required at least two bearers. And once you had walked pass the stands the banner had to be rolled up again and put back on a lorry. That made sneaking away virtually impossible. Just like when being asked to carry a giant flag. It was too big to be left standing somewhere and the wooden pole made it quite heavy. Carrying such a flag on a really windy day required a lot of strength and concentration.

One May Day, the march was just about to start, when a flag-holding colleague asked my grandfather whether he could quickly take over for a minute. The guy just wanted to go for a wee – allegedly. Grandad, always happy to help out, said yes. His colleague did not return. As soon as my grandfather realised he had been duped, he quickly passed the flag on with the same trick. God knows how often it changed hands on that day.

For me the best thing about May Day and the National Holiday was the festival atmosphere in the afternoons. Open-Air stages provided live entertainment, markets offered food, drink and all different kind of wares, while fun fairs kept kids and youths happy.

MAYTAMORPHOSIS

Ever since the eighth grade had started, the whole class had been looking forward to one day – Saturday 9 May 1982. It was scheduled to be the day on which we would have our Jugendweihe – an initiation, which would turn us 14 and 15 year olds into adults. Jugendweihe was an atheist version of the Catholic communion, Protestant confirmation or Jewish Bar Mitzvah. Its roots go back to the late nineteenth century, when freethinkers began to prepare their kids for life by marking their entry into adulthood with a ceremony and celebration. The idea was born in 1600 after the Italian Renaissance philosopher Giordano Bruno was burned by the Inquisition as a heretic. Rejecting religious dogmas, freethinkers believed that decisions in life should be based on science, logic and humanity instead. Within 300 years this movement spread to the United States, Canada, England, France and Germany. Seen as competition to their own philosophy of life, Hitler forbade the Freethought Societies in 1933. East Germany, with its mainly atheist population, rekindled the old Jugendweihe tradition in the Fifties, and it went from strength to strength from then on. In the Eighties more than 95 per cent of teenagers received this socialist blessing.

But before our Jugendweihe could take place, we had to put in the sweat and do some work first. At the beginning of the school year, the whole class had to go to the nearby Pioneer House. There we were told that the purpose of the Jugendweihe was to accept us in the ranks of the working class. To prepare us for the world we were about to enter, we would have to organise ten events on different themes. They went like this:

Theme 1: Socialism – Our World

Event 1: The Time In Which We Live

Event 2: What the People Have Created Belongs to the People

Event 3: We Are This State

Theme 2: What Does It Mean to Be Revolutionary Today?

Event 1: To Learn From the Soviet Union, Means to Learn How to Win

Event 2: Your Work, Your Responsibility, Your Honour

Event 3: You Need the Socialist Society – the Socialist Society Needs You

Event 4: Courage and Heroism in Our Time

Event 5: To Recognise True Beauty and Experience Culture

Theme 3: On the Path to a Happy Future

Event 1: We Understand the World and Change Things

Event 2: We Are Prepared for the Communist Tomorrow

Quite a mouthful for any teenager. Thankfully we were handed a brochure giving us some ideas about what events we could organise: a visit to a factory, museum, theatre, court or cinema possibly with follow-up discussions. A meeting with Russian soldiers or communist war veterans or maybe a themed trip to another city...

All in all, it was a lot of work on top of our normal class meetings and other planned activities. What did we do? We resorted to creative accounting. If the class wanted to see a play at the theatre, any play, it would be declared an event in preparation of the Jugendweihe and crossed off the list. But it is still a mystery to me how on earth we got away with visiting a fascist concentration camp near Berlin under the heading of "What the People Have Created Belongs to the People".

Visits to old concentration camps were a regular occurrence in school. We were made to see the atrocities that the fascists, backed by profit-hungry capitalists, were capable of. And every time we were appalled anew when we saw for ourselves the horror of the camps: the poor living conditions, the electric fences, the punishment and execution areas, the gas chambers and the crematoriums. On those visits even the class clown went quiet. Watching films shot on site by the Allies in 1945 depicting piles of dead people, huge warehouses filled with human hair, suitcases, glasses, dentures and shoes from the people that had been killed, made many of us shake our heads in disbelief. The museum displays of lampshades and book covers made of tattooed human skin were equally horrific.

Often some of us felt sick, occasionally a few girls cried. Usually my thoughts were all over the place: "Would I have fought the Nazis knowing that, if caught, I could end up in such a camp? What, if I had been posted here as a guard? Would I have refused duty? Would I too have gotten a kick out of mistreating inmates? How long would I, as a malnourished prisoner, have survived the daily exploitation by hard labour? Would I eventually have run into the electric fence because death would have looked more attractive than living another day through such hell?"

Concentration camps touched us very much emotionally. They made us determined to ensure that nothing like it would ever happen again but they didn't trigger feelings of guilt or shame in us. These camps were the remains of a time and system that was not ours. We lived in a communist state with a strong antifascist tradition. Many leading DDR politicians had spent time in Nazi prisons or concentration camps. We grew up reading books about the lives of individuals who belonged to the communist resistance in the Third Reich. In 1933 the German Communist Party had 300,000 members. One year later half of them had been executed or imprisoned. For communists the capitulation of Nazi Germany was an act of liberation. According to our teachers, the perpetrators lived in West Germany, the legal successor of the Third Reich.

For the third event ("We Are this State"), our class visited the parliament, the Volkskammer (People's Chamber). It was housed in the Palace of the Republic, a hugely popular multi-purpose building in the centre of East Berlin that was also home to a number of stages, halls, restaurants, bars and cafés. Nearly 180 metres wide, 85 metres deep and 32 metres high, the Swedes built it in cooperation with the DDR (yet another project Dad had worked on) and when the building opened in 1976 its construction had guzzled up one billion DDR marks (400 million dollars). We East Germans loved the cultural and gastronomical variety the Palace offered, though because of the 1,001 lights that illuminated the foyer it was rather disrespectfully called "Erich's Lamp-Shop". Having already been numerous times to the public part of the building we teenagers were naturally quite excited to set foot into the sealed-off section of the building that housed the parliamentary chamber. The white marble and bronze windows on the Palace's façade glistened in the sun as our class gathered around the small side entrance that was guarded by two soldiers. Next to the door, on the wall, was a small DDR emblem. Bronze lettering underneath it read "Volkskammer der Deutschen Demokratischen Republik". Of course, we had prepared ourselves for the visit. Hence, when our guide, a thirty-something parliamentarian himself, showed us around I only half listened to what he told us: "The Volkskammer is in session only two or three times a year... It appoints high-ranking state officials, such as the Head of State and High Court judges, and passes laws... Us 500 parliamentarians are part-time politicians who continue working in their normal jobs... We are elected every five years... All parties and big organisations can nominate candidates, however the Socialist Unity Party nominates the highest number of candidates... Over 50 per cent of the parliamentarians are members of the working class... This reflects the true democratic character of our parliament and makes the existence of an opposition obsolete... "

I soaked up the atmosphere of the place, although today I cannot really remember what the individual rooms looked like. Yet, still imprinted on my memory is the girl who had brought her fury bear-like Monchhichi doll with her. As we walked along the corridors of power, she repeatedly asked us boys whether we wanted to stroke her little bear. Very surreal!

The pièce de résistance of the tour was the parliamentary chamber. Here my memory returns. Behind the podium with its lectern as well as seats and tables for the presidency, was a giant DDR emblem permanently fixed to the wall. We were not allowed to enter the podium. Instead we could make ourselves comfortable in any of the cream-coloured armchairs which the majority of Volkskammer delegates occupied. We shuffled across the chamber's red carpet, quickly heading to what we considered were the best seats and tables. After a few minutes rest, we all gave the seating arrangements the thumbs up. The armchairs were a bit on the firm side, yet comfy. The guide explained: "Here laws are being passed via an electronic voting system." Someone asked: "But why do the seats only have 'yes' buttons." The guide replied: " 'No' buttons are not needed because all draft bills that are sent to the representatives have already been drawn with the benefit of the people in mind." My friend Lars and I we just looked at each other sceptically when hearing this. Oh, what a shining example of socialist democracy our People's Chamber truly was!

TAKING THE VOW

Initiation Day finally came. I had chosen my outfit for the big occasion weeks in advance: A plain, light-blue shirt made in DDR combined with dark blue corduroy trousers made by Wrangler (thanks to my grandparents) and my brother's old Jugendweihe jacket in yet another shade of blue. The ensemble was finished off with plain black shoes and a breast pocket handkerchief instead of a stuffy tie. It all seemed to go together rather well. But I did not have long to admire myself in the mirror that morning. Shortly after nine o'clock the doorbell began to ring constantly as uncles, aunts and grandparents arrived one after another at our place. Even my grandmother from Saxony had taken the trouble to travel the 250 kilometres by train to be with me on my special day.

As we arrived at the big "Kosmos" cinema in the Karl-Marx-Boulevard, all the eighth-graders from our school had to gather in the foyer while our families were taking their seats. Just as we were about to begin our collective entry into the auditorium, Rick, a classmate, took it upon himself to judge everyone's outfit. Mine was declared to look Russian (God knows why) while his apparently resembled a US style. If that was what he thought... I wasn't in the mood for arguing. Not on that day! And not with someone who wore a beige corduroy suit and a Colonel Sanders style bow tie. So I bit my lip, not mentioning that he reminded me more of a giant baby in a romper suit. Then the double doors swung open. Our entry into the auditorium was imminent. The talking among us stopped. We all tensed up. On a teacher's signal we began slowly walking down the aisle in double rows to our seats. The cinema was brightly lit. The huge yellow curtains covering the screen stood out from the dark blue of the seats and walls. Our families were standing and applauding us as we entered. A pity we were too excited to savour the moment. Instead of nonchalantly walking out there with million-dollar smiles, most of us only allowed ourselves brief looks into the auditorium before concentrating on the way again. None of the rehearsals had prepared us for the overwhelming experience of being the focus of a thousand people's attention. At least we knew that the front rows were reserved for us. As we reached our seats a scratchy recording of the national anthem blared out in a great fanfare. We could sit down. So far so good.

Then the festive programme began: There was a poetry recital, singing, dancing and a wind quintet playing a selection of classical pieces. After the first three acts, the director of a local company gave a speech about what it meant to become an adult before asking us to stand up. The actual ceremony was about to start. From his notes, the managing director read:

"Dear young friends,

Are you, as young citizens of our German Democratic Republic, prepared to work and fight for the great and noble case of socialism and to honour the revolutionary heritage of our people? If so, please answer: Yes, we do!"

That was the part I really dreaded. What if later in life I could not honour my vows? Making socialism stronger by learning and working well was one thing but fighting for it and maybe even risking my life? I wasn't prepared to do THAT. So, I went with an idea that had come to me during rehearsals a couple of weeks earlier and only mouthed the words while everyone around me contributed to the collective: "Yes, we do."

"Are you," the bold, heavily sweating man on stage continued, "as devoted sons and daughters of our workers-and-farmers-state, prepared to strive for higher education and culture, to become masters in your field, to learn constantly and to use all your knowledge and skills for the realisation of our great humanistic ideals? If so, please answer: Yes, we do!" (Once again I moved my lips but kept silent.)

"Are you," he went on, "as worthy members of our socialist society, prepared to work together in a comradely fashion, to base your actions on mutual respect and help, and to always combine the path to your personal happiness with the fight for the happiness of the people? If so, please answer: Yes, we do!" (Still not a peep from me.)

"Are you as true patriots, prepared to deepen the strong friendship with the Soviet Union, to strengthen the brotherly ties with the socialist countries, to fight in the spirit of proletarian internationalism and to protect peace and socialism against any imperialistic attack? If so, please answer: Yes, we do!" (If my classmates were prepared to that, good on them. I certainly wasn't!)

"We have heard your promise. You have set yourselves a noble target. We welcome you in the society of the working people, which in agreement and under the leadership of the working class and its revolutionary party, builds the developed socialist society in the German Democratic Republic.

"We hand you an enormous responsibility. We will support you at any time, in word and deed, to shape the socialist future creatively."

Phew! Thank God that part was over. We were asked to sit down again and could calm our nerves by watching a few more performances on stage. But just as we were getting comfortable, the second official part of the event – the handover of the Jugendweihe certificates and books – started. The only purpose of the certificates was to remind us of our big day. As for the book, its title was *Socialism – Your World*. My copy still stands unread on the bookshelf. I keep saying to myself that one day, I might be in the mood to read such articles as *Signals From Space* and *Computer – Friend or Foe of The Humans*. But stories like *Juri Gagarin: I Dedicate My Space Flight to the People of Communism* and *Sources of Marxism/Leninism* I will definitely never look at.

We had to go up on stage in groups of 15 to receive our certificates and books. My heart was pounding like mad as it was our row's turn to face the auditorium. After lining up on stage, everyone had to go individually to our head teacher, who was dishing out certificates and books with a handshake. My only thought while walking those few steps to him was: "I must not stumble. I must not stumble." I didn't, but some dopey girl from another class managed to trip over her own feet and hit the stage, rather ungraciously, face down in full view of everyone.

"To the special day of the Jugendweihe we wish you all the best and much success for your future life and contributions to our DDR."

Jugendweihe Certificate

Before the variety programme resumed, little Pioneers handed us flowers and that was it – now we had it in black in white that we weren't kids any more. But who did we fool? Except for now being addressed by teachers as

Sie (the more formal, grown up version of "you" in German) rather than *du*, nothing had changed. But then, what we were really after wasn't the ceremony but the party that followed and the presents.

IT'S MY PARTY

Over the years the customary Jugendweihe presents seemed to become bigger and bigger. In the late Eighties it wasn't uncommon for some parents to surprise their offspring with a spanking new moped for the occasion. Coming with a price tag of twice the average monthly salary, it shows the Iron Curtain was no effective barrier to the wave of growing materialism that had already swept western cultures.

My Jugendweihe wish was to collect enough money from the family, so I could buy my own radio cassette recorder and not have to use my brother's any more. By then, my musical taste had changed from classical to pop music. Mozart was out and West German Nena (*99 Red Balloons*) was in. I regularly listened to the weekly radio chart shows and wanted to tape the songs I liked. But the latest generation of DDR recorders, like all our technical goods, did not come cheap. The model I was after (Star Recorder R4100) cost 1,160 marks (464 dollars) – more than a month's salary. My parents generously contributed 500 marks, from other family members I collected 850 marks (340 dollars) on the day, the rest I had to come up with myself. Thankfully I had saved most of the money that I had earned on my school holiday jobs. Other Jugendweihe presents I got were: a four-volume-set of encyclopedias, records, a digital watch, books, an extra-slim, all-metal Sony calculator and lots of chocolates.

After lunch at home, I popped over to see my best friend Lars. I buzzed him on the intercom of his apartment building and he came down. We went for a walk and had a good chinwag about how the day had gone so far. When I returned home, afternoon coffee was served. Several cream cakes later, I decided to go out on a second round of visits, this time to check out other friends' presents. Before I even had a chance to ring a doorbell, I bumped into Silvio. He was a nice guy but also a big show-off. If you had been on a week's holiday somewhere, he would have been for two weeks, to an even better destination. His competitiveness drove me crazy. And even on the Jugendweihe Day, he could not resist trying to outshine others. "How much money did you get?," he asked before I could get a word in. "850," I answered, truthfully. "I got 860," he replied with a smirk. Sure! I was so angry with myself I hadn't asked him the question first. When Ingo and Christian, two more classmates joined us, we began doing the rounds:

"First we went to Lars. There we were given soft drinks. Then we headed to Bettina, where we each got a small glass of coffee liqueur. On the way to my place we were joined by Cordelia (sigh), Silvia, Sabine and her West German cousin. Mum served us Advocaat. Next we went to Ingo (pineapple punch), then to Sabine (white wine) and Ines (home-made cherry whisky and West German beer). As we walked down the stairs from Ines' place, I occasionally missed a few steps on the stairwell. Oops! Thank God I was holding on tight to the handrail. At Christian's flat we continued with cherry liqueur..."

Diary Entry

On the day, many parents would allow their newly declared "adult" offspring to celebrate with a tipple or two. When we finished our round of visits, we were tipsy and very giggly but not drunk. It was the first time I had ever really consumed alcohol and I was glad I shared the experience with my classmates on such a memorable day.

After dinner I met up again with classmates, this time at Viola's place where the ten of us finished another four bottles of white wine. It was then that it became evident some of us had had far too much to drink. It was a sight for sore eyes to see Ines, the stuck-up class beauty, kissing everyone goodbye and losing her balance when leaving the house. Lying on the pavement she shouted, "I want a photo of Viola's dad dancing to German rock music." No one knew why she made this strange request but it was hugely entertaining to see the ever so self-conscious and perfectly made-up Ines crawling around on all fours in the street with smudged mascara and lipstick slurring her words. Divine!

Shortly after midnight I arrived home. It truly had been a perfect day for me. As I laid in bed that night, I did not dare to think about where and when I would be able to buy the radio cassette recorder of my dreams. Many of my classmates also had a cassette recorder on their shopping list; hopefully finding the model I wanted wouldn't prove too difficult. I closed my eyes and slept my first night as an adult.

HAIR PLAYS THE MUSIC

There were two days to go until the big summer holiday started on 2 July 1982, and a decision needed to be made. I had just come from a career advisor and was toying with the idea of getting a crew cut. "What the heck", I finally thought, "it's just hair" and spent the rest of the afternoon at my hairdresser's, waiting to be seen without an appointment. The wait was worthwhile. The next day in school I was the talk of the class. The girls could not keep their hands to themselves and endlessly stroked my hair one after another. I could not have asked for a better return on my 7.50 marks (three dollars) investment. Bliss!

The last school day before the summer break was always a cool affair. As we had no lockers in school, all books and files had to be brought from home each day. But on the last school day we always travelled light – playing games or reading extracts from our favourite books meant we hardly had to bring anything. The summer of 1982 was quite a nice one, with loads of sunshine. One day my parents and I decided to take a little tour through the DDR in our new car, a red Lada. We headed down south and spent one day in Erfurt at a horticultural exhibition where Dad was lucky enough to get his hands on some blueberry plants that he had always wanted for our garden. He was hoping that one day they would be as productive as our gooseberry bushes were that year. Apart from preserving the usual 30 or 40 jars for winter, we sold about 20 kilograms to the supermarket, because no one in the family wanted any more. And as I had helped Dad to pick them, I was allowed to keep all the proceeds. The 16 marks (6.40 dollars) additional pocket money were not to be sniffed at.

The only drawback with our impromptu trip was, that we had not arranged for any accommodation. This was a mistake in a country that had nearly two million tourists a year but only 137,000 beds available. I was cool with spending a few nights in youth hostels but I think my parents had hoped for a little bit more luxury.

Things improved when we went to stay with my paternal grandmother. I did my usual round through all the town's shops and hit the jackpot. "Oli is happy, he has bought his recorder." is how Mum put it on a postcard to my grandparents in Berlin. What a gross understatement! I wasn't happy, I was on cloud nine. Finally I had been able to buy the radio cassette recorder, I had spent the past three months looking for in Berlin. And what a beauty it was, with its built-in mic, manual song fading facility and flash LED display. I happily parted with my 1,160 marks (464 dollars). More than 20 years later it still works like it did on the very first day – the sure sign of a quality (East) German product. The only disappointment was when, a year after my purchase, I saw the very same model in a West German home shopping catalogue that my grandparents had smuggled over the border. The price for it on the other side of the Wall was 200 Deutschmarks (80 dollars).

Records and tapes of selected international artists such as Paul Young, Eddy Grant, Phil Collins, Michael Jackson, Jennifer Rush, made it into our shops. In most cases, though, we only got them years after their original release in the west but that did not dampen the enthusiasm of music lovers. Anyone not on good terms with a shop assistant could kiss goodbye the chance of getting their hands on one of those albums. To make life easier for people without record shop connections, a DDR radio station had a weekly programme called *Duett – Musik für den Rekorder* (Duet – Music for the Recorder), which played western records without any talking between the songs. Thanks to the show, I got A-HA's entire first album on tape. Yet the majority of DDR youth, just like myself, simply taped their favourite western songs directly from West German radio stations. I was in taping heaven whenever I tuned into the two main West Berlin chart show programmes on Mondays and Thursdays. The early and mid-Eighties saw a trend emerge in West Germany that became known as *Neue Deutsche Welle* (New German Wave). Groups like Nena (*99 Red Balloons*) and Trio (*Da, Da, Da*) began to dominate the music charts. It had become cool to sing rock and pop songs in German, rather than English. The fact that the majority of East German songs had always been sung in German was ignored by me and my friends. For us, listening to DDR music was uncool. My brother, on the other hand, was not as biased as me and liked a number of East German groups. This was one of the main causes of our regular morning clashes – I liked to listen to "Radio in the American Sector" (a West Berlin station) while he preferred the music on "Berliner Rundfunk" (East Berlin). It was only after the DDR ceased to exist that I discovered its music scene was as diverse and interesting as the West German one.

For my birthday in September Mum made a strawberry flan and bought some cakes from the patisserie counter in the supermarket. Black Forest gateau, nut cream cake and coffee-flavoured cream cake were family favourites. As usual, Mum got a bit carried away at the patisserie counter. Even after giving doggy bags to guests it still took us a few days to munch our way through the leftovers. By the way, to reduce waste and save resources, the sturdy cardboard boxes which the cakes from the patisserie counter came in were reused. Supermarkets and bakeries handed them out for a deposit of one mark (40 cents). This might not sound too hygienic, but kitted out with a new doily and parchment paper after each use, they always were as good as new.

Looking back, my fifteenth birthday in 1982 was quite a good one. I got all the presents I wanted, and more: three books, a pair of imported pyjamas, the long-desired finger guillotine (not some gruesome self-mutilation tool but a great magic trick), a pencil case and writing set, three blank cassettes for my tape recorder, a carousel for their display and lots of chocolates and sweets.

The cassettes, a present from my grandparents, had been bought in West Berlin. There was no tape shortage in East Germany, but at 20 marks (eight dollars) for a blank 60-minute tape in our shops, I would not have been able to afford to tape all those songs that had caught my ear while listening to the West Berlin radio stations.

Two months later I was in for another surprise. In Germany, November 11th traditionally marks the beginning of the *Fasching* (Shrovetide Carnival) season which lasts until Ash Wednesday. On that day, we all went to school a bit dressed up. As the fingers on the clock turned to the 11th second, of the 11th minute at the 11th hour, out came the traditional jam-filled doughnuts to celebrate the occasion. That year, though, things were a bit different to a normal November 11th. As soon as the next lesson started our teacher told us, stern-faced, that Leonid Brezhnev had died the previous day and that, as a mark of respect, we would have to go home to change into more suitable clothes before school would continue. At least rather than spoiling the whole day, the head teacher had decided to break the news to us after we had our little celebration. We thought that was very considerate of him.

Thankfully the DDR had moved on since Stalin's death in 1953. In 1982 there was no public shedding of tears for the dead leader of the Soviet Union, no solemn-faced people sitting in silence on trains or buses. Except for us having to change outfits halfway through the day, it was a school day much like any other. The announcement of Brezhnev's death had not really caught us by surprise. The last time he had made an appearance in the news, he looked a shadow of his former self. The one thing that baffled me was that just two days earlier, we all had made fun about how old and senile the Russian Politburo members were. My friend Lars even had doubted that Brezhnev was still alive. His words were: "For the last May Parade they probably just got his embalmed body out, put it up on a stage and once in a while someone secretly pulled a string, to give the impression he was waving." We all burst out with laughter contemplating such a ludicrous ruse, when Lars continued: "But seriously, when he dies, I am going to buy everyone a drink." And only one day later Brezhnev snuffed it. Creepy!

MY MOTHER IS BIG BROTHER

The rest of the year did not promise to be very exciting. I called up an export/import company to check whether they would employ me after school and send me to college. I was asked to call back in three months time. Hardly the answer I had been after...

So the only highlight left before Christmas was our class day trip to, once again, the Baltic Sea. Cordelia raised a few eyebrows as she turned up at the train station wearing an oversized knitted hat and white leather gloves while holding a yellow plastic straw like a cigarillo. But then, that was exactly why I loved her – she defied the norm. Despite it being a cold and windy day up north, we all had lots of fun. For the first time in my life I had spaghetti ice.

When I saw it on a café's menu I just had to try it, though I was slightly disappointed that it was only made of vanilla ice cream and raspberry coulis; somehow I had expected it to be made of real spaghetti.

Class beauty Ines was probably the only one whose day was ruined. With her long blond hair always immaculately brushed, she was the first one in our class to use make-up. Showing off her womanly curves in trendy western clothes, Ines knew that she was a stunner. Out of my league anyway. The Alpha males in our class were usually all over her and she enjoyed the attention. To show off, she had brought her West German radio cassette recorder with her on the trip, and with the boys at her feet she allowed them to carry it around for her. This turned out to be a mistake, because as we ran to the station to catch the train back, Ingo, who's turn it was to carry Ines' recorder, stumbled. As he landed, face down, on the pavement, the recorder, having slipped from his shoulder, hit the ground and skidded for another meter. We all stopped in our tracks, looking at Ingo. No one said a word. As he got up saying: "I am alright, guys, I am alright." our eyes went to Ines. Her mouth was open wide in horror but to be fair, her first concern was that Ingo was okay and surprisingly, with the exception of a few abrasions to his hands, the fall left him pretty much unscathed. That was more than could be said for the cassette recorder. A closer inspection by the group revealed that the antenna had snapped during the fall, furthermore, one loudspeaker was broken. Considering how precious tape recorders were to us (even more so if one was a western make), Ingo was horrified by the damage his stumble had caused. Yet Ines, although far from being happy, graciously said: "Don't worry about it, I'll get it repaired... somehow." The girls, not in Ines' circle of friends, looked at each other smugly before we all continued our run. Arriving at the station, it turned out we had hurried unnecessarily, the train was delayed by 25 minutes. Whether the recorder was ever fixed, I don't know. I never saw it again. However, we all noticed that from that point on, Ines preferred to carry her things herself.

Many DDR people considered West German products to be superior to ours. Quality-wise, this was not necessarily always justified, but western products still seduced us with their fancy packaging. Take canned beer for example. Unavailable in DDR shops, those cans were, for us, much more than mere containers for an alcoholic beverage – they were western lifestyle in a tin. I knew people who collected empty beer cans. Getting hold of a West German car was somewhat harder. With very few being imported, most DDR car enthusiasts had to resort to drooling over pictures of the latest models, with Mercedes occupying a top place in the "Want-to-have" league. Many East German youths wanted to possess something associated with such an iconic brand; hence, it became a popular sport among teenagers to twist off the Mercedes stars from bonnets of visiting motorist's vehicles.

A friend asked me once whether I would help him to nick the star from a West German Mercedes' that was parked by his block. "What are you going to do with it?" I asked. "Umm, I don't really know," he said while scratching his head. "It's just cool having it, I always wanted one." The prospect of being caught by a policeman or the car owner for nicking a stupid metal star did not appeal to me at all. My friend had to steal it on his own. The next day in school he showed me the corpus delicti. "It was so easy to nick", he confided, "just one twist and pull". Then he quickly added, "and the owner was arrogant anyway." Apparently the Mercedes driver had cut off his dad's Wartburg a couple days earlier, so my friend considered it legitimate to take the long-desired Merc star from this car in return. There have always been westerners who behaved arrogantly or in a patronising way when visiting the DDR. Usually the bigger their cars, the more they looked down on us natives. So, occasionally East Germans liked to get their own back. Mum, too, once played a trick on a West German Mercedes driver and his wife.

In front of the entrance to our apartment building, like most others, was a *Specki Tonne*, a bin for kitchen waste. Its contents were collected once a week and used for pig feed. There were always some idiots who also put glass or other inedible rubbish in the bins, even though big labels stated clearly what the waste was to be used for. One day, a shiny Mercedes with a West German licence plate pulled up in front of our house. Mum and I looked through the net curtain to see what it was all about. In the car were a well-to-do middle-aged couple. The man at the steering wheel was fiddling around with the car radio while the woman, a member of the blue-rinse brigade, put on a giant white hat. She got out, grabbed a white plastic bag from the back seat and walked towards the *Specki Tonne*. Then the woman saw the notice on the bin and stopped. She seemed indecisive. What to do now? She looked left – no one was there. She looked right - no one was there either. So, off went the lid and her rubbish went in. Mum ran like a flash to the intercom and shouted: "Take your rubbish out of the bin immediately!" Already on the way back to the car, the western woman stopped in her tracks and looked around. She appeared frightened and baffled. God knows, what must have been going through her head at that moment. But judging by the speed at which the woman ran back and fished her rubbish out of that smelly bin, she must have thought the secret service was watching her every move.

Maybe she even thought that her life was at stake. It was a sight for sore eyes, as she quickly dumped the rubbish in the boot of her Mercedes before the car sped off with screeching tires. Mum and I cried tears of laughter. Westerners may have had every need tended to when flashing their currency in the DDR, but it did not buy them the right to be ignorant.

FARE PLAY

In early December, Lars and I decided to go to the annual Christmas market in the city centre. The German Christmas market tradition goes back to the fifteenth century when traders began selling seasonal produce for the coming winter months around churches to attract as many customers as possible. Over the centuries, the markets developed to what they are today: a mixture of stalls and rides springing up around the country every year with the beginning of Advent. Even in East Germany, it was a question of prestige for every big town to have their own four-week-long Christmas market. Going to one is a must-do for any German child or youth in the run-up to Christmas.

Spread over an area of 55,000 square metres, East Berlin's Christmas market was the biggest in the DDR. On average it attracted three million visitors in the four weeks it was open every year. It had everything a visitor could wish for: Ferris wheels, twisters, dodgem rinks, houses of fun, mirror mazes, ghost trains, merry-go-rounds, roller coasters (in later years even one with loops) and all other sort of fairground rides that spun you around or up and down in all different variations. Add to that lottery kiosks, shooting galleries, hooplas, coconut shys and an endless array of stalls offering all different kinds of wares, food and drink and you ended up with a place that appealed to everyone. As children, even when it was freezing cold and snowing, we could not wait to put on our long johns, hats, winter jackets, boots and gloves and go to the market. Usually, by the time our family arrived, the stalls and rides all had their colourful lights on and we would buy *Bratwurst* (fried sausage) candied apples, roasted almonds, gingerbread hearts, candy floss and *Quarkkeulchen* (fried dough balls covered in icing sugar). If we were cold, my brother and I would get nice steaming mugs of hot chocolate while Mum and Dad would opt for the equally warming *Glühwein* (mulled wine). The air was usually filled with Christmas songs, coming from loudspeakers, music from old-fashioned organs and the sounds of excited kids squealing with delight at the rides. Little stalls sold anything that might be a potential present: toys, handicrafts, books and electric items. Kids had a special blockhouse, called the "Pioneer Centre", dedicated to them, where many a time I made little presents such as candleholders, letter openers or keyrings out of wood or metal. The air inside the blockhouse was usually filled with the smell of wood that had been maltreated by kids with hot soldering irons for decoration purposes. Inhaling this evocative scent alone was worth paying the "Pioneer Centre" a visit. And with Christmas decorations everywhere on the market, (including a giant Christmas tree and an oversized advent calendar) it never took long for visitors to get into a festive mood. For anyone who needed more stimulation to get into the Christmas spirit, choirs were performing on the open-air stage. Unfortunately, the Christmas spirit did not extend to the conductors lurking around in the nearby underground station.

East Germany's public transport relied on people's honesty. In buses, trams and at all underground stations *Zahlboxen* (pay boxes) were installed into which the money had to be deposited. The boxes had a little window through which anyone looking could see how much money had been put in. A couple of pulls on the lever at the right hand side of the box sent the fare to the bottom of this contraption and a ticket was issued, valid for one journey. Even though the fares were heavily subsidised and affordable – ten pfennigs (four cents) for children, students or pensioners and 20 pfennigs (eight cents) for everyone else – fare dodging was still commonplace. So, it made sense that East Berlin's public transport company BVB used conductors to protect its revenue. Not all of them, however, were BVB employees. Some were part time helpers who received a cut from each ten marks (four dollars) penalty fare they issued. Those part timers were the worst. Overzealous and ruthless, they tried to issue as many penalty fares as possible and were very much East Germany's equivalent of a UK traffic warden.

When Lars and I came from the Christmas market, the plain-clothes conductors standing next to the cash boxes in the underground station were clearly visible. Upon reaching the pay boxes Lars and I put in the required ten pfennigs each. We took our tickets and walked off when a conductor stopped us. He claimed to have seen that we had only paid a pfennig per person. We suggested that he opens the box and to check for himself that we had paid the correct fare, but our request was refused. Teenagers like us were obviously considered easy pickings, but we stood our ground. The conductor did not budge. We were cold, it was late and just to get home we finally paid ten marks each, under protest, and not without writing down the guy's name so we could claim our money back. Taking into consideration that a fairground ride at the Christmas market only cost 50 pfennigs, the extra ten marks made it an expensive afternoon. The next day I wrote to the transport company demanding a refund, to no avail. It was my word against that of a conductor and though I was prepared to fight for my rights, my parents realistically pointed out that with no evidence I did not have a leg to stand on. Instead Mum gave me ten marks and told me to let it go. Grudgingly, I accepted, but from then on I got my own back by seizing every opportunity to make a conductor believe I had no ticket, just to show it to him after he had wasted five minutes trying to nab me. Revenge can be so sweet!

DAD'S GOING TO THE WEST (AND COMING BACK)

In December 1982 Dad was able to travel to West Germany. He was only in his early forties and still a long way off retirement age, which secured the average citizen a passport. His company worked on many projects beyond our borders and employees were regularly sent to the Soviet Union, Hungary, Yemen or West Germany to install built-in furniture in offices or hotels. Of course, our family was fully vetted by the Stasi before Dad was issued his passport containing an exit visa to West Germany and West Berlin. When doing background checks, the Stasi normally asked informants, neighbours or colleagues for character references. If they all turned out to be positive and the secret service did not have any detrimental information on their files, a person could be considered a *Reisekader* (travel cadre), which was the official DDR name for people who were allowed to leave the country on business trips. But regardless of how spotless your background was, if you were below the age of 26 and/or single, there was no way that your company would have sent you westwards. The age restriction was there to make sure that travel cadres were mature enough. Furthermore, they had to be married, preferably with children to give them an added incentive to return.

But the thought of defecting and starting a new life in the west never even crossed Dad's mind. His home was the DDR, that's where his family and friends were, that's where his job was. Why would he have wanted to give all of that up to be on his own in a strange country?

His first trip in December 1982 was to Cologne and Braunschweig. In later years he was sent to Helgoland, Hamburg, Hannover, Mainz, Wuppertal and West Berlin. It may seem strange that East German cabinet-makers, polishers and carpenters were needed in the west to help build and refurbish hotels and offices, but what cost-conscious capitalist would refuse highly trained and skilled German workers from the east who cost a fraction of their western counterparts? A West German company secured the orders, the DDR supplied the workforce. Both sides made their cut. This line of business was a nice little earner for our state, because workers were paid their normal salaries at home in DDR marks. Only a fraction of the Deutschmarks generated was passed on to them for expenses, so they could buy food and drink during a stay. 45 Deutschmarks (18 dollars) per day were paid to workers sent to West Germany. Those on business in West Berlin received only 15 Deutschmarks (six dollars) because they could bring their lunch and snacks with them from East Berlin, when crossing the border every morning. At least the daily allowance was theirs to keep, regardless of whether it was all spent on food and drink. Naturally my father and his colleagues always took lots of tinned food and salami with them whenever leaving the DDR so more precious Deutschmarks could be spent on things to bring home.

Most of the time, Dad and his colleagues went to the Federal Republic of Germany in one of the company cars, a Barkas van (a DDR make). Travelling by car allowed them to take a lot of provisions when leaving our country. However, the downside was that once in the west they had to pay for the petrol from their daily allowance. To keep the outgoings low, Dad and two colleagues once crossed the border with 25 litres of DDR petrol in cans. This turned out to be a costly mistake! West German customs pointed out that the allowance was only 10 litres and demanded import duties as well as an on-the-spot fine. Grudgingly, they had to hand over some of their scarce Deutschmarks to the West German authorities.

Normally, six to ten colleagues from the east worked together in the west, alongside local employees. Mostly the work involved kitting out hotels with furniture, but there were other jobs too. For example, revamping the offices of a West German newspaper or fitting a millionaire's house with wardrobes and cabinets. The owner seemed to have close dealings with the DDR, as nearly everything within the house came from the east. Even the fence was of communist origin, made of East German railway sleepers. It was easy to see why this guy was a millionaire – with summer temperatures hovering around the 30-degree mark, Dad and his colleagues were not offered any water, let alone a cup of tea or coffee, in the week that they worked there. Although, to be fair, on the last day, after the job was completed, the housekeeper handed the four workers little bags, each full of freebies bearing the millionaire's company logo and 500 grams of coffee. Whoopi-do!

Not everyone who Dad met in the west was so stingy. Some hotel owners did not charge the workers for meals, others gave them free access to their car pools. One morning, while staying and working in a hotel at the West German seaside, Dad and his colleagues found a small DDR flag standing on their breakfast table – it was the 7 October, East Germany's National Holiday. For the evening hotel staff had organised a skittles competition: the Federal Republic of Germany against the German Democratic Republic. The DDR came out victorious and the prize – bottles of champagne, wine and beer – was shared with the other side.

Unfortunately, other West German businesses were slightly less relaxed about the East German connection. One posh five-star establishment in Cologne insisted that all the "Made in German Democratic Republic" labels on their chairs were painstakingly painted over by hand.

One day Dad saw a nice sweater for Mum at a West German market. A look at the label revealed that it actually was an East German product. It was made by a very reputable DDR company, probably for export only. Dad liked it and bought it. However when Mum unpacked the sweater back home in East Berlin the label was gone – it must have been cut off by whoever had wrapped the thing up. But Mum wasn't too keen on this particular present. An East German sweater was the last thing she expected to receive from a trip to the west. On other occasions, the things Dad brought back were spot-on. Though his rather limited budget only allowed him to shop for clothes at C&A, I made good use of the T-shirts, trousers or jackets he got me. A pair of lightweight, olive-green summer trousers and a dark blue winter jacket with a huge zip-up pocket at the back were my two most favourite items. Treasured fashion accessories from the west were woven fabric belts and leather ties in different colours. My most favourite was a fluorescent-green tie, which always guaranteed that I would stand out from the crowd. I may only have had a limited number of fashion items from the west, but it was enough to pep up my humdrum East German wardrobe.

Food-wise, Dad came home quite a few times with 40 or 50 pots of different flavoured yogurts. DDR yogurt was only produced in apricot, strawberry, cherry and raspberry flavours which, when available, were firmer and more gelatinous than their softer, creamier western cousins. Flavours like hazelnut, peach and passion fruit, pineapple, banana, and kiwifruit were new experiences for us. It was also thanks to Dad's trips to the west that we first tasted kiwifruit and nectarines years before the Wall came down and the rest of the country had a chance to try them.

Yet the most depressing part of a business trip for Dad was always crossing the border, especially when taking the train from the Friedrichstrasse checkpoint in the heart of Berlin. This border crossing was integrated into a train station, of which three quarters could only be accessed by East Germans after passport control. Two West Berlin lines, which cut through East Berlin, stopped below ground. The overground part of the station was divided by soundproof metal. The platform and two tracks on one side marked the final stop for East Berlin's overground, while two platforms on the other side were only accessible to travellers coming from and going to the west. Guards overlooked the tracks and platforms from bridges above, while 140 security cameras monitored the entire checkpoint. Westward-bound trains were checked by guards with dogs, which were sent underneath the carriages to ensure that no one was trying to escape by clinging to an axle. The inside of carriages was equally thoroughly searched with a number of wall and ceiling panels being unscrewed to spot-check potential hiding spaces. Once the all clear was given, a border guard blew a whistle and only then were travellers allowed to board the train by stepping over the white line drawn on the platform. The train would depart five minutes later. After the last stop in

West Berlin train doors were locked to ensure that no one could leave or enter the carriages in case there was an unscheduled stop on DDR territory.

But the West German border police had their objectives too. Once Dad was bombarded by them with questions all relating to Mum. They were after her date of birth, first name, profession and so on. He refused to give them any details and was eventually free to continue his trip. Dad heard later that what he had experienced was a tried-and-tested method to detect spies travelling under aliases. And occasionally there were other surprises when crossing the border. Once the West German Red Cross welcomed East German travellers with free bananas. Though as nice as this gesture may have been intended, Dad found it degrading. East Germans had accepted that West Germany with its strong economy could not be beaten but that didn't mean that we hadn't developed a sense of pride for our fatherland's economical and social achievements. Being offered free bananas, one for each DDR passenger, made Dad feel belittled and patronised. Our living standard might have been lower, but we weren't poor and in need of handouts. Yet interestingly the majority of his fellow East German travellers happily queued for their free fruit without any signs of embarrassment. Dad could not bring himself to join them. Instead he walked past the Red Cross tables like a westerner and later bought his fruit in the supermarket.

Some of Dad's business-travelling colleagues also had no qualms about asking for hand-me-downs from West Germans. In their quest for freebies, they played the "I-am-a-poor-East-German" card when going out for drinks with their western work colleagues in the evenings. Sometimes they succeeded and were given second-hand clothes or household items that weren't needed any more. If anyone had reported this begging to the company's headquarters in East Berlin, those colleagues would immediately have been barred from business trips to the west. It certainly was an eye-opener for Dad to see how low people could sink, especially since some of them made a lot of money by working in the west for six weeks in a row, several times a year.

Each stay netted them a couple thousand Deutschmarks in expenses, only half of which were usually used for buying food and drink. The rest was saved or spent on things to take home. Those guys were quite well off by East German standards. Anyone returning from the west with loads of goods or a pile of hard currency was envied. Being in the position to bribe someone back home with Deutschmarks made it so much easier to get hold of hard-to-get items. Grudgingly, East Germans had to accept that without Deutschmarks they were second-class citizens in their own country.

Unfortunately, Dad could not rake in as many Deutschmarks as he would have liked. His expertise was in high demand in East Berlin, and his stays in the west rarely exceeded 14 days in a row. Only once was he really loaded.

His company had asked him to take 5,000 Deutschmarks with him, so the colleagues in the west could get paid their weekly expenses. I still remember the five 1,000 Deutschmark banknotes lying on our living room table the evening before he left. Imagine, 5,000 Deutschmarks! With a black market exchange rate of one to ten, that money was worth 50,000 DDR marks (20,000 dollars). Joe Bloggs would have had to work a little bit more than four years to earn such an amount legitimately and there it was, right in front of me. I could not take my eyes and hands off the banknotes. And while Dad successfully got the money to the west, another colleague of his once came close to losing the lot. One morning, the guy in charge of petty cash had to return to East Berlin. He got up late and raced from the hotel to the train station. In the rush he forgot to hand over a couple thousand Deutschmarks to a colleague and instead left them behind in his room, in their hiding place – under the mattress. He frantically called the hotel from East Berlin and, luckily, even though the room had been made up in the meantime, the money was still were he had put it the previous night.

I always found it weird when Dad had to go to West Berlin for the day. Sometimes he had to refurbish hotels there, sometimes he just had to cross the border to buy West German varnish for his company because it was better quality than the East German make. Whenever Dad was on such a mission he would get up in the morning and leave the house as usual, but while I was sitting in school during the day in East Berlin Dad was in glitzy West Berlin. He was still close, yet too far to be reached. It seemed too surreal. The older generation, like my grandparents, always saw Berlin as what it was: one city that had been divided. For me and many others born after the erection of the Wall, West and East Berlin were two separate cities. There was a curiosity to see what lay behind the Wall and if there was an opportunity to peep, we grabbed it. Otherwise, for most of us, the border did not feature in everyday life. The presence of the Wall was blanked out.

Our leaders also actively encouraged people to forget about the other Berlin, hence all our city maps sold were for "Berlin, capital of the German Democratic Republic" only. The space behind the border marking was left blank, with the exception of a few drawn trees, rivers and maybe one or two main roads. To the uninformed, the absence of houses and infrastructure seemed to indicate that West Berlin was a deserted nature reserve, rather than a bustling city. Thankfully we knew better, after all we could see their buildings behind the Wall and received western TV stations. Later work colleagues would tell me how confused they were on their first business trip to West Berlin because people there talked and behaved just like fellow East Berliners back home. For many it only sank in then that this was one divided city, not two separate ones.

Dad was more pragmatic about it all. His main concern was to deliver good results when working in West Berlin. At least the border crossings were great for doing some after-work shopping. Once Dad was a bit in trouble when handing back his passport at work. The woman from the company's travel department saw his returning day and time stamp and asked why he had come back a couple hours later than his colleagues. Thinking quickly, Dad replied that he had to go back to the hotel in which they worked, for a tool he had forgotten. Though the workers were required to return to East Berlin immediately once they had finished a day's job in West Berlin, no one wanted to leave the other side without doing a bit of shopping and sightseeing. One of Dad's colleagues even went to visit family members. To avoid future trouble, the workers began to agree the times at which they would go back to East Berlin. This way, everyone could still do their private thing for a couple of hours without fear of detection.

Surprisingly Dad and his colleagues never crossed the Antifascist Protection Rampart with any sort of guard. No DDR official watched their movements while abroad and none of the workers was ever required to spend their spare time with the group to make a potential defection harder. Unlike with our Olympic Teams and other official DDR delegations travelling to the west, there were very few restrictions on Dad and his co-workers. If someone wanted to leave the hotel in the evening and go for a stroll on his own, he did exactly that, although the workers usually decided to spend the weekends together. It was more fun (and cheaper) to do all the touristy bits in a group. Of course, there was always the possibility that one of the colleagues was a freelance informer of the Stasi. But that did not stop anyone criticising their fatherland or the company's managing director, and there were never any repercussions as a result. Anyway, the worst thing the Stasi would probably have done in such a case would be to revoke the offender's passport – hardly life threatening.

Because our secret service was not visibly present in the west, workers were required to feed it with information gained on their trips. Upon their return to East Berlin, every DDR business traveller had to write a *Reisebericht* (travel report) in which all incidents, positive or negative, and all remarks directed at the traveller while he was in the west had to be noted. Of special interest to the authorities was whether any movements of the West German army had been witnessed. Dad always used a set of standard phrases when writing his reports. He stated the obvious, emphasised positive events and never wrote anything bad about colleagues. The others must have used the same strategy, because the Stasi, which cross-checked all reports, never picked up any inconsistencies. If they had, the workers would, without doubt, have been invited to take part in a "clarifying" chat.

With Dad being in the west during the run-up to Christmas in 1982 Mum and I went to the pictures. We saw *Foul Play* a film from 1978 with Goldie Hawn and Chevy Chase. Western film imports always took a few years to find their way into our cinemas – the later a movie was purchased on the international market, the less the DDR had to pay for the rights. My diary entry says that the film was very entertaining (I'll have to take my own word for it, as I can't remember for sure). The 31 December was, on the other hand, probably anything but entertaining for our Communist Party leader. Western media reported a few days later that a drunken stove fitter had tried to assassinate Erich Honecker on New Year's Eve, while he was travelling in a motorcade on a country road. Apparently the stove fitter attempted to break into the convoy with his Lada to ram Honecker's Citroen. Escort cars foiled the attempt and pushed the intruder's vehicle off the road. As Honecker's car sped off, the stove fitter allegedly shot at a policeman before committing suicide. What a sensation! If true, it was the first time an assassination attempt had been made against an East German politician. But most mysterious was the reported use of a handgun. Though people could gain temporary access to weapons through shooting or hunting clubs, their access was very restricted. Nor were guns freely available in shops. Everyone wanted to know how this guy could have possibly owned a gun.

First our own central news agency kept quiet, hoping the storm would blow over. East German officials rarely responded to West German reports of events in our country, regardless of how true they might have been. Trying to get the upper hand by taking the wind out of the enemy's sails, was considered the wrong strategy. Why stir things up even more when in a few days all will be forgotten anyway? But not this time. As the speculation, fuelled by the West German media, grew wilder and wilder, the DDR's own Allgemeiner Deutscher Nachrichtendienst (General German News Agency) published a statement confirming only a drunken driver had seriously wounded a policeman before committing suicide on New Year's Eve. There was no mention of an assassination attempt, but judging by the delay in releasing this half-hearted statement, most people had already made up their mind about who they believed. In the media war between the Federal Republic of Germany and the German Democratic Republic, deciding whose version of events sounded more truthful was something we had to do on a daily basis. Most East Germans realised that neither side could be trusted fully and that the truth often lay somewhere in the middle.

For security reasons, the majority of our political leaders lived 35 kilometres from Berlin in a 165-hectare complex. It was hidden in the forest surrounding Berlin and did not show up on any commercial map. The members of the Politburo lived in 23 two-storey-houses, built in the late Fifties and early Sixties. The buildings were surrounded by a guarded eight kilometre long, two-metre-high wall, which was covered with camouflage paint. The monthly rent for the dubious pleasure of living in this ghetto was an average 700 marks (280 dollars) per house. One custom in Politburo City was to welcome in the new year twice – once at Moscow time and then again two hours later when German clocks struck midnight. Honecker introduced this strange ritual to the enclave to demonstrate the steadfast friendship with the Soviet Union. Pebble-dashed and poorly designed with dated interiors, the houses were anything but flash, even by East German standards. Their most attractive feature was probably the 700-square-metre garden at the back of each one. Only one home had been fitted with a private swimming pool, but it was not Honecker's. He and his wife occupied a smaller house (250 square metres) that had a kitchen, bath-, living, dining and guest room on the ground floor, and two bathrooms and a guestroom, as well as a massage room and study on the first floor.

Nearly 650 members of staff made sure that everything in Politburo City ran smoothly. There was a shop, a restaurant, a pool, a kindergarten, a petrol station, a greenhouse, a bakery, a hairdresser's, a laundry, a tailor and a GP's surgery. Housekeepers – 64 of them – took care of the individual households from seven o'clock in the morning to five o'clock in the afternoon. There were three in the Honecker house; everyone else had to make do with two.

Honecker always saw himself as a member of the working class. Born a miner's son in 1912 in western Germany, he dedicated his life to the communist ideal at an early stage. Instead of finishing his apprenticeship as a roofer, Honecker joined the Communist Party full-time in 1930. Hitler rose to power three years later. One of his first actions was to ban the Communist Party. Its members and sympathisers were persecuted. Honecker, like many others, continued his fight against the Nazi system from underground. The secret service caught him in 1935. Honecker was locked up in the town of Brandenburg, near Berlin, and in 1937 sentenced to ten years in prison, of which two years had to be spent in solitary confinement. At first he worked on a toy soldier production line in the prison. Later he was transferred to the compound's building maintenance brigade. As the war continued, the shortage of civilian men led to prisoners being used to clear away or repair houses in cities that had been damaged in allied air raids. In March 1945, Honecker managed to escape his command while working in Berlin. Fearing the consequences of being caught, he voluntarily returned to prison two weeks afterwards. The Soviet Army freed him at the end of April 1945.

As Head of State, Erich Honecker had a total of 26 secret service personnel assigned to him as bodyguards and drivers, but he still remained a low-maintenance man with fairly basic needs. He did not like fish, game, vegetables (mushrooms were his worst nightmare) or fruit, except for the occasional apple. Honecker started his day humbly with two buttered bread rolls and honey. His favourite lunch was also very simple: Kasseler (slightly salted and smoked pork loin) with Sauerkraut and potatoes. He liked to wear hats (straw ones in particular) and to go swimming in the nude (provided no strangers were around). Honecker was keen on hunting and watching movies. Apparently he had a penchant for mildly erotic films, with titles like *Emmanuelle* and *Lady Diamond* forming part of his private video collection. But he also had an interest in action movies, à la James Bond. Whenever Erich Honecker wanted to view some new releases, he marked his choices in a West German video catalogue and passed them coyly on to the Politburo member responsible for economy, who made sure that the videos were bought in West Berlin and delivered to Honecker later in the week. Whatever tapes our number one returned watched, were then sold again in West Berlin. This, rather unusual, set-up ensured that costs for the exclusive film delivery service were kept at a minimum.

So, no gold decorated palaces and excessive champagne-and-caviar parties for our leaders then. A West German managing director of a medium-sized company had a more glitzy lifestyle than our top politicians. Honecker often worked from eight-thirty am to eight pm and it has been reported that Erich's wife Margot would get very upset if she found a West German tin of something in her larder. Both preferred to holiday in East Germany. Though there was a national outcry when it emerged in late 1989 that the water taps in the party leaders' houses were imported from the west (how shocking) while one kitchen even sported a West German dishwasher (oh, what a luxury). The only thing people really could have been jealous of was the enclave's little shop. It sold many items that were imported from the west: food items, clothes, cleaning products and cosmetics. Here Margot Honecker bought the clothes for her husband. And if a particular item wasn't stocked, all 20 odd Politburo members and their families could order almost anything from a selection of West German home shopping catalogues at a very favourable exchange rate. Some families, though not the Honeckers, ordered things as if there was no tomorrow. Every year, goods totalling six million marks (2.4 million dollars) had to be imported to satisfy demand in this very exclusive shop.

Honecker's monthly salary was roughly 8,000 marks (3,200 dollars) and in 1989 his savings account showed a balance of 211,964 marks (nearly 85,000 dollars). His wife, being the country's Education Minister since 1963, had managed to save 77,502 marks (31,000 dollars) over the years. And how did Honecker's annual salary of 38,400 dollars compare internationally? Well, Ronald Reagan earned 200,000 dollars a year. I doubt that he would have wanted to have Honecker's lifestyle, let alone earn his sort of money.

LOSING THE TOUCH

Unlike North Korea's Kim Il-Sung or Romania's Nicolae Ceausescu our leaders were not into self-glorification. Erich Honecker's photo may have hung in offices, factories and administrative buildings, but there wasn't a single Erich Honecker monument or Erich-Honecker-Street in the entire republic. If anything, Erich Honecker could be accused of distancing himself from the common people. Living in his self-chosen ghetto he had to rely on family members or reports prepared by the secret service to find out about the everyday problems in the DDR. But those sources would have been flawed – his family members hardly had reason to complain and Stasi reports mainly dealt with specific incidents rather than assessing the people's general mood. Most of the letters of complaint that ordinary people wrote to Honecker never reached his desk. And should a regional party secretary ever have prepared a realistic report about the economic shortcomings in his district, it would have been watered down as it was distributed up the ladder of power. Controversial parts in a report would mysteriously disappear as each reader edited it before sending it to the next, more influential person. It also did not help that Honecker's cronies were doing their jobs overzealously on other fronts. When going to and coming from work in his armour-plated black Citroen, Honecker would be accompanied by another decoy Citroen, two police cars and several other unmarked vehicles. The Stasi made sure that the motorcade travelled without hindrance at speeds of 130 kilometres per hour outside Berlin and 70 kilometres per hour in the city. Secret service members in police uniforms used to block off potential traffic from side streets – an unplanned stop seemed to pose a big security risk. Not necessarily for Honecker, but for his chum Erich Mielke, the Minister for State Security and Chief of the Stasi. Even on occasions where Honecker explicitly insisted on no special security arrangements, side streets were still secretly blocked off. Only further down and out of Honecker's sight.

Honecker's mistake was to take the world represented to him as real. He never asked for impromptu stops when being chauffeured around. Taking a non-armour-plated Citroen so he could open the window and wave to the people was about the only concession Honecker made on trips to other towns. When Erich and Margot made private, low-key visits to their daughter's apartment in East Berlin's city centre, they had the chance to see their homeland as it really was. A pity they did not bother looking. On all other occasions Honecker's staff made sure that their boss saw only a socialist Disneyland. My grandparents lived on the *Protokollstrecke* (Protocol Road), along which the Politburo members were chauffeured to and from work five times a week. Coincidentally, this particular road was always the one where Christmas decorations were put up first in December, potholes were attended to most swiftly, public lawns were mown weekly, instead of monthly, and snow ploughs were sent to first when yet another blizzard hit the capital in the winter months. The facades of the buildings in need of repair were attended to much faster and houses were given a new lick of paint much more regularly compared to everywhere else. The fact that the painters often stopped work once they had reached the first or second floor was all part of the plan and did not bother anyone in charge. Everything was fine as long as all that could be seen from Honecker's passing car window looked presentable. Shops, too, benefited from their prominent location and received better and more regular deliveries – after all, the General Secretary of the Socialist Unity Party, Head of the State Council and Head of the Defence Council could not be subjected to seeing his people queueing. As a result of this policy a snack stall which served *Currywurst* (fried sausage with curried ketchup), was moved ten metres down a side street. Customers waiting to be served when the early evening rush set in were deemed both an eyesore and a security risk.

The good thing about Honecker's travels was that whenever he was about to visit a place, funds were made available for road maintenance. Houses too were done up if our party leader was scheduled to enter them. For many councils and individuals, a visit from Erich Honecker was the best that could happen to them. Projects that had been deferred for financial reasons were suddenly completed in no time. When a Politburo member made an announced visit to a factory, the charade continued. Halls were freshly painted, sometimes offices were fitted with new furniture. And if a big wig wasn't supposed to see unrenovated parts of a building, a giant sheet of fabric would block the view. Here is a popular joke about what might have happened had Honecker ever been too inquisitive during one of his visits:

Erich Honecker visits an industrial cattle farm. The director explains that the barns are home to 100,000 cattle. Honecker asks whether the amount of manure generated causes any problems. The director replies: "It may be hard to believe but we have invented a process that transforms manure into cheese. And the cheese we make here has all the characteristics of a high quality food item: it's firm to the touch, with a nice yellow colour and totally odourless." Honecker is impressed and asks for a piece to try. The director refuses but a crony cuts Honecker a slice. He takes a small bite which he spits out almost immediately. "That is absolutely disgusting." Honecker shouts. To which the embarrassed director replies: "Our scientists are still trying to find a way to eliminate the taste of manure."

When one of Honecker's grandchildren died of an infection at an early age, the grieving grandfather put a big, unique crystal vase on her grave, which was situated in a normal public cemetery. Of course, the vase was stolen. These things happen, but did anyone tell him about it? No one made a peep. Instead his cronies got hold of an identical vase which was always put on the grave shortly before he arrived and was taken away immediately after he left. Surely he could have handled the truth, but instead he was made to believe once more that he was the leader of a problem-free and crimeless country. When Honecker left his post in 1989 despised by two-faced former colleagues and comrades who had quickly trimmed their sails to the new system, he was suddenly faced with a reality that he did not know exist. That is when I felt somewhat sorry for this old man who did not understand the world around him any more even though it was him who had, with the best intentions, helped to shape it for the past 18 years.

A man walks into a registry office: "My name is Erich Shitbucket and I would like to change it to something less embarrassing." Says the clerk: "I do feel for you. Who wants to be called Erich?!"

NO MARTINA, NO MOVIES

While I was glued to the radio in early January 1983, listening to various West Berlin stations and waiting for my chance to tape Nena's brand-new song *99 Luftballons* (*99 Red Balloons*), I read in our *Berliner Zeitung* newspaper that DDR television was looking for teenage boys and girls to star in a TV production. Ever since my first appearance on national TV seven years ago as a spectator on a kids programme, I had been on the lookout for an opportunity to show off my acting skills. I traipsed to every audition I saw advertised in the press, but to no avail. I was never one of the lucky kids chosen to go through to the next stage. It made me even more determined to succeed this time. On the day of the auditions, I went first to the hairdresser's first. I hoped that a nice haircut would make the TV people rule in my favour, particularly if my performance wasn't up to scratch. I arrived in the producer's office at three pm and was the fifty-fifth person waiting to be seen. Two hours later there were 240 of us. Divided into groups of ten, we were told that this search was for the main characters in a love film. Then we were asked to couple up with a second group member. I had chosen a girl, my age, with a cute face and long brown hair. "I am Martina." she said confidently. "You are beautiful." I meant to say but only managed a coy "And I am Oliver."

Martina and I were one of the last couples to be called into the audition room to act out an impromptu scene. We were told to have an argument and come to an agreement because a record Martina had sold me was scratched and she now refused to give me my money back. Following the advice given by all the rejected kids, we screamed our lungs out before agreeing on a deal. Our performance must have gone down a storm – we made it into the second round. I felt very strongly that we would be one of the winning teams. Only a few weeks later the dream was over. Martina wasn't there the next time I came back to show more of my acting abilities. She must have turned up on a different day. I was devastated and paired up with some dopey girl instead. We were asked to show spontaneous emotion in the following scenario: For years I have taken the girl's money pretending to do the lotto for her. Instead I spent it on sweets. Now her numbers have come up and I have to come clean. Unfortunately, little Ms Dopey did not show any emotion during the scene. My motivation went out the window. We were both rejected outright. It made me so jealous seeing the other kids who made it, being photographed and given a script to learn for the next round. Later that year I applied for a few more roles but the opportunity to become a child actor had passed. Just like the chance of getting to know Martina better – I never saw her again.

JOBHUNT

In the ninth grade the time had come for every pupil to decide on their career path. If you were good in school, had working class parents, and wanted to become an army officer or teacher, you were very likely to be delegated by your school to visit the *Erweiterte Oberschule* (Extended Upper School) after the tenth grade to make your A-levels in a two-year course. The A-levels may have been a pre-requisite qualification for anyone wanting to go to university, but I was keen to have a job lined up after school first. For the time being the A-levels had to wait.

East Germany, just like West Germany, was a vocational training country. Virtually every company in the country was given a yearly quota for the number of school leavers that had to be taken on as apprentices or trainees.

For two to three years, school leavers learnt the tools of their chosen trade by spending time in college as well as on the job. I had decided in the ninth grade that I wanted to become a merchant for international trade, which was a very prestigious profession in the DDR. After all there was a chance of maybe being allowed to travel to the west on business well before retirement age (which was 60 for women and 65 for men). So I called up the Human Resources department of an export/import company specialising in glass and ceramics where a keen Herr Schulze invited me for a chat. After having a look at my half-term report card I was encouraged to apply at his company, the AHB Glas-Keramik (AHB is an abbreviation for *Aussenhandelsbetrieb* – foreign trade company). According to Herr Schulze, male applicants with good marks where in short supply that year. Suitably encouraged, I sat down the same day and wrote my application:

"Dear Sirs,

At the end of the school year 1983/84 I will be leaving the Polytechnical Upper School after ten years of education. It has been my wish for a long time to become a merchant for international trade. Through talks with my brother and uncle who both work for export/import companies, I have become very interested in this profession. In previous holidays I have already worked for another export/import company, which gave me some insight into the duties and responsibilities of a merchant. Furthermore, I was given a clear picture of this job on a visit to the Job Orientation Centre. In most school years I have received only good and very good marks and I would be very glad if I could start in your company in September 1984."

While on 1 March the rest of my class were spending their field day, at the headmaster's request, at some army barracks near Berlin to congratulate soldiers on National People's Army Day, I was busy working on my future.

I wrote my CV and went to school to pick up a teacher's assessment of me. Then I got Dad to drive me to Glas-Keramik where I handed over my papers together with two passport photos. One month later I received a letter informing me that:

"All received applications... have now been considered by the company's employment committee and a decision has been made. We are glad to inform you that your application, subject to the company's doctor confirmation, has been confirmed..."

Overwhelmed by happiness I started screaming and dancing in the corridor. But it was not just the export/import company's employment committee and the doctor who had their say in the selection process. The secret service played a part too. Foreign trade employees were very likely to meet western clients face to face, so the Stasi did not want to leave anything to chance and vetted all new applicants very careful. Just like with my brother before he joined the foreign trade and with Dad before he was allowed to travel to the west, neighbours and colleagues were asked anew for character testimonials and general opinions of the Fritzes: Are they a properly functioning family? Do you have any grievances against them? How do they behave in public? Has any of them ever stood out in a negative way? And so on and so forth.

Those were the sort of questions Stasi employees, usually disguised as CID officers, would ask. How do I know? Not only did neighbours and colleagues tell my parents about their brush with the Stasi, but over the years my parents had also been asked several times for their opinions on neighbours or colleagues. And Mum and Dad never said anything negative about anyone. If you had a conscience, and the majority of people did, it was an unspoken rule to speak only good about a person. Alternatively one could always claim not to know someone well enough to comment. Mum's boss had his very own way of dealing with Stasi enquiries. In March 1983 he was approached by two "CID officers" asking for information on his employee, Frau Fritz. Mum was by then shift manager in the administration department of a polyclinic. Brusquely he told the two gentlemen that he had no time for their request. "However", he continued, "Mrs Fritz is in the building. Why don't you go downstairs and ask her directly whatever it is that you need to know." He rang Mum, advised her that two policemen had a few questions for her and showed the two men the right way to Mum's room. They never turned up.

FEELING FRISKY

There was tension in the air as spring came to East Germany in 1983. But not any old tension, oh no, I am talking sexual tension here. By then everyone in our class was 15 or 16 years old and for many a quick kiss behind the school gym just wasn't satisfactory any more. We now wanted to fall in love and do the romantic lovey-dovey stuff we all had seen in the movies: going for walks while holding hands and kissing, sitting on park benches and in cafés while cuddling up and kissing and going to the pictures for some more holding hands, cuddling up and kissing. Also very popular was the "bringing-the-girlfriend-home" routine that usually culminated in snogging for half an hour while standing in front of her house.

My best friend Lars got together with Viola from our class and as I was friends with both of them, the three of us hooked up quite regularly. Usually we would meet at the table tennis tables nearby, where most of our class hung out after school. Often Lars and Viola would also come to my place where we listened to music and did for hours what all teenagers do best – talk. When we went for walks, we regularly headed to the Café Sonja, where a bowl of soup cost one mark (40 cents) and a cup of tea 43 pfennigs (17 cents). The food and drink there were hardly extraordinary, (one day their black tea tasted of caper sauce!) but everything was affordable. That was all that mattered to us. As I saw Lars and Viola often going arm in arm and holding each other's hands I began to feel a very strong longing. On 30 March, I wrote in my diary: "I want Cordelia back." Not that she had gone anywhere or that we had separated. The spark just seemed to have gone in the last year and we weren't spending much time together after school any more. But I was desperate to turn things around and began to put in a lot more effort. Nearly every second day I went to her place, asking whether she was coming out. Sometimes I was lucky, sometimes not (usually when there was something interesting on telly). But the rejections did not dampen my spirit. Especially after Cordelia told me one day that she always felt sorry for me when I came in vain. Winning Cordi back had become my main objective, as I confided to my diary:

"02.04.83: It's Saturday today. Mum, Dad and I wanted to go to the allotment but it's raining cats and dogs. I wanted go to Cordi but when we went out for a walk yesterday she mentioned that she was going to meet a friend today. She is constantly on my mind. Every second word I said today, seemed to be 'Cordelia'. I really have fallen for her big time and so look forward to Monday, when I will see her again. "

Cordelia even appeared in my dreams. Just a couple of days later Mum mentioned to me that at night she had heard me saying in my sleep: "Cordelia, you don't have to help me peel the rhubarb... just sit down and help yourself to some crumble..."

As if sharing my Cordi/rhubarb-dream fantasies with my family wasn't embarrassing enough, the most awkward moment during our affair was brought about by one of our teachers.

It was a lovely sunny day in June, when Cordelia and I went on another of our regular afternoon walks. This time our way had led us back to our school, where we made ourselves comfortable in front of the building on a bench facing the surrounding park. First we were both sitting, then Cordelia laid down, resting her head on my lap. We were talking for another five minutes when I finally began bending down my head. And just as my face was only centimetres away from hers we both heard a sharp: "What are you two doing there?" It was the voice of our German teacher, Frau Vogel, who had spotted us while trying to close a window on the second floor. Though we hadn't done anything, it only took me two seconds to sit up straight as a die. With faces as red as train signals, we looked up and both replied with one voice: "Nothing!" The teacher mumbled: "Oh, it's just you two." and closed the window. We broke out in nervous giggles and quickly got up to continue our walk. A perfectly romantic moment had been ruined. Frau Vogel, I hope you can live with that burden!

CIVIL DEFENCE

In the ninth grade, a huge burden was lifted from my shoulders. After five years, the class finally elected someone else as class monitor. Hooray! Her name was Barbara and she was also very good at school. Slightly smaller than me, with medium length hair and metal-rimmed glasses, Barbara was very smart and ambitious. She wanted to become a Doctor of Medicine. And while I had lost my enthusiasm and had become somewhat sluggish as the years went by, she was full of new ideas. It looked like everyone was going to be a winner: the class was happy to see someone else in charge for a change, Barbara had a role where she could prove herself and I could finally step down from the pedestal the teachers had put me on. I looked forward to letting myself go once in a while instead of being a perfectly behaved super-human role model all the time. Unfortunately, the role of the deputy class monitor and agitator I had agreed to take on instead did not prove to be as cushy as I had hoped. I was now responsible for keeping the *Wandzeitung* in our classroom up to date. The *Wandzeitung*, meaning "wall newspaper", was a board, draped in either red or blue fabric and dedicated to current news in the world, country and school. This *Wandzeitung* had to be redecorated regularly with the latest pictures and articles. What a pain! Another duty of the agitator was to promote the party line to my fellow classmates. When for example Erich Honecker tried to kick start the creation of a nuclear-free zone in middle Europe, I had to tell the class about it in my own words. Having to add personal thoughts to any news story I was briefing my classmates about made it impossible for me to just read out newspaper articles. Bugger! In the run-up to official class meetings, our teacher even handed me lists with political subjects that needed covering. One of these lists has survived:

1) General Assembly of the United Nations

2) Disarmament (prevention of a nuclear war, production freeze on nuclear weapons, ban on neutron bombs, ban on weapons in space)

3) Middle East Conflict (Palestine today, steps taken to keep aggressor Israel at bay)

4) What is known about Israel's latest actions in Beirut (killing of children, women and innocent people)

The ninth grade also surprised us with a new subject: Eight lessons in Defence studies scattered throughout the year. For the boys, these were followed by a two-week stay in a paramilitary camp somewhere in the sticks. The girls were allowed to "defend" the country in Berlin. This was supposed to prepare us for the eventuality of an enemy attack on our socialist fatherland. The lessons were held by a reserve officer, Major Ziegel, after the normal school day had finished. No one was particularly pleased about having to attend Defence studies, especially as it clashed with the weekly chart show *Hits For Fans*, which was broadcast by a West Berlin radio station every Monday afternoon. Many in the class, including me, liked to listen in to keep up to date with the latest hits and the movements in the charts. Though I hardly excelled myself in Defence lessons, one day Major Ziegel approached me and said: "Oliver, as you are the agitator of your class, I have chosen you to be the agitator of your platoon in the camp at the end of the school year. You will be required to sacrifice one day of your spring holidays to go to a training course." And as it apparently was an honour to be nominated for that post (yeah, right!) I really couldn't wriggle my way out of it. Mind you, I was quite proud when I picked up my olive-green uniform for the camp well before my classmates were given theirs. Not that mine was particularly well fitting, what my trousers lacked in length they made up for in excess space in the waist area, but I still wanted Cordelia to see me in this manly outfit. Unfortunately, my parents did not allow me to put it on for a show-off visit to Cordi. But the uniform top on its own I later was allowed to slip in. Worn as a jacket and combined with my civilian clothes it looked quite cool, or at least I thought it did. I confided to my diary how my one-day training course went:

"For the past few days I really wished I did not have to go today. I have spoken to Mum and Dad about it but they are right: it's too late to pull out. Now I just have to go through with it. Damn! So I got up at six am and Rick (my classmate) who has been chosen as a squad leader, picked me up. We took the overground train to Friedrichshagen and then walked for 45 minutes. The training place was heaving with officers who were all shouting at us. They created such a noise! The sports officer seemed particularly sharp-tongued. First we were given theory lessons by the agitprop officer, a big guy with thuggish lips who wore cheap NHS-type glasses. It was so boring! For breakfast we were given sandwiches, then a guy from the marine taught us accurate bed making, greeting an officer, marching, assembling and building a tent. For lunch we had yummy noodle soup with a bread roll and an apple. In the afternoon the agitprop officer from the morning gave us more theory lessons. Once he had finished we were free to go home. For the march back to the train station I had been chosen as squad leader. The first half of the march went well but then it became a complete disaster. First it began to rain and then I got the runs. Everyone had to wait for me while I quickly disappeared into the nearby forest. Thank God for the emergency loo paper supply I had remembered in the morning. As I emerged from the bushes, I was given a big round of applause. I was embarrassed beyond belief and everyone got soaking wet while waiting for me. Yet thankfully everyone could see the funny side of it."

Compared to the one-day training course, the two-week stay in a paramilitary camp outside Berlin in June later that year was a doddle. At least for me it was. Because of a sprained ankle I was exempt from all physical activities at the time. Separated from my classmates I was put on kitchen duty with "invalids" from other classes who were in the camp at the same time. It was the best thing that could have happened to me. No one was supervising us "sickies" and consequently we had the time of our life. In the mornings we got up late while the fit guys had to sweat at the mandatory outdoor gymnastics. Throughout the day we sat in the sun, read books or chatted while our classmates had to march, shoot, crawl, run around and were subjected to officers barking at them. "Sickies" did not even have to attend any of the theory lessons. All we were required to do was lay the officers tables and serve them, dish out lunch and ensure everyone behaved appropriately when taking their meals. Compared to what my classmates had to go through, the whole thing was a breeze.

Normally we wore white coats over our uniforms but when we were "off duty" it was the yellow armbands over the right arm uniform sleeves that gave us the freedom to wander around the camp, ignoring military procedures. One evening, I was on my way to visit my classmates when an officer crossed my path. As usual, I walked past without acknowledging him when suddenly a hand on my shoulder stopped me in my tracks. "Why didn't you greet me?" I was barked at. Mr Important must not have seen my armband. Thinking quickly, I followed my inner voice that urged me to have some fun and played stupid: "Oh, I didn't know I had to." The officer's head turned purple from rage. Shouting at me, he demanded to know my name and platoon number so that he could initiate disciplinary proceedings. I turned around properly so my armband became fully visible, pointed at it, gave him the name of the camp's big cheese and walked off. There was nothing he could do. The next day I made sure it was me who served that bastard his lunch. He got the smallest schnitzel and mankiest potatoes I could find when dishing up his meal. From then on his plate always was the one with the least amount of food on. All served by me with a friendly smile. He never spoke to me again.

I had to leave the camp two days earlier, to get back to Berlin in time to sign the employment contract with the export/import company that had agreed to take me on after school. When my family arrived to pick me up in our new red Lada, my grandparents, who had joined my parents for a day out, got the shock of their life as I approached them to say hello. I was still wearing the white coat, and they mistook me for the camp's doctor, fearing that something might have happened to me. God bless them.

It was a pity the remaining two days on which I had to join the girls back home for their Civil Defence course weren't half as cushy as the camp had been. We had First Aid lessons and were educated about how to behave should we be subjected to a nuclear blast: cover every inch of your skin, avoid wearing clothes made of easily flammable material, take shelter, lie flat longitudinally to the shock wave and shut your eyes. We also learned how to deal with the aftermath of a germ warfare attack: household items would become germ free when washed with Fit, the DDR's number one washing-up liquid. And how could one prepare for an enemy attack? According to our teacher, by quickly piling up sandbags in the attic to prevent fire spreading. Could Hiroshima have been saved if the Japanese people had put sandbags in their houses before the Americans dropped their nuclear bomb in 1945? It all just seemed so pointless. Even more so as the DDR hardly had any public bunkers. Mum only found out by coincidence that the windowless archive room in the *Poliklinik* (medical centre) where she worked would double as a public shelter in a state of emergency. But it was all very hush-hush and she was not allowed to tell anyone else.

Why have a bunker if no one knew about it? The truth is that the DDR could not afford to build enough shelters. Recent figures revealed that one million East Berliners would have had to scramble for a paltry 3,000 bunker places. And things didn't get much better for our elite either. The UK government bunker, for example, was designed for 4,000 people to survive for 90 days. West Germany's government bunker could have provided 3,000 selected people with shelter for 30 days. In the DDR a measly 350 top party, government and military officials could have had their lives prolonged for 14 days only. But then our bunker, a 20-minute drive away from Berlin, had only cost 150 million marks (60 million dollars) to build while the West German government forked out nearly five billion Deutschmarks (two billion dollars) for theirs. As for us teenagers on the Civil Defence course, we were asked to build a decontamination unit in the gym's showers, though none of us probably would have made it through the first minutes of a real nuclear attack. The entire exercise was ridiculous and very depressing.

"The imperialists have already unleashed two terribly bloody World Wars in this century. Despite the German imperialists having lost influence, power and might in these World Wars, they are not being prepared to come to the inevitable conclusions. Accompanied by anticommunist hate tirades and supported by NATO, they are preparing for an armed encounter."

Inferno Dresden by Walter Weidauer (Dietz Verlag, Berlin, 1983)

Yes, there was more to the Eighties than just shoulder pads, big hairdos and electronic pop songs. It was a time when no one knew how the Cold War in Europe would come to an end. As documents now reveal even West German politicians believed that the two Germanys would account for up to 90 per cent of the military targets in a European war. Every scenario seemed possible and so right to the end the DDR continued to test its air raid sirens up and down the country every Wednesday at one pm sharp. For me those always were the spookiest 30 seconds of the week.

PREDICAMENTS

The year 1983 was full of predicaments. I faced the first one fairly early in the year during one of our Free German Youth meetings in which members honed their conversational skills by asking each other political questions. I had to think up an answer to: "Can communist countries prevent a third World War?" I wanted to say: "Yes, by reducing their arms. Someone has to make the first step." But that answer would not have been politically correct and would have resulted in the teacher's intervention. So I opted for the easy option and replied: "Yes they can, but only if they constantly deploy new arms to keep a healthy military balance." Like everyone else in the room, I had given the answer that was expected from me. It made life much easier.

If the West German rock singer Udo Lindenberg had also decided, to at least occasionally play by the rules, it would have saved our government a few headaches. Over the years, Udo had come up with several songs that weren't popular with our political leaders. *The Girl from East Berlin*, for example, told the story of a western boy who fell in love with a DDR girl but because of the Wall they could not be together. Another song of his was about the Russian army invading West Berlin: *In 15 Minutes the Russians Will be on the Kurfürstendamm* (West Berlin's main shopping street). Even though one of the lines went "and the Russians actually aren't as bad as our newspapers always make out", our Politburo failed to see the funny side. The song was banned in the DDR. Just like his 1983-hit *Special Train*, sung to the melody of *Chattanooga Choo Choo*:

Excuse me, is this the special train to Pankow (an East Berlin borough).

I am a yodeler and want to play with my band there.

I take a bottle of delicious cognac with me,

which I am going to slurp with Erich Honecker.

Ernie (meaning Erich), I will sing for little money.

I believe you are quite cool

and I know deep down you are a rocker too.

Surely you like to secretly slip on your leather jacket,

lock yourself in the loo

and listen to west radio.

Hello Erich, can you hear me,

yodellio...

Our officials argued that the capitalist entertainment industry found ever more cunning ways of manipulating us in an attempt to make us turn against our government, but people could still not resist singing along to Udo's songs. As the years went by it seemed highly unlikely Udo would ever be allowed to achieve his biggest dream: performing in East Germany. But Lindenberg also had a side to him, that very much appealed to our politicians: He joined the protest, together with the West German Communist Party, against the stationing of Pershing II rockets in his homeland. It was a dilemma for the Politburo – should they condemn him or use him? After careful consideration it was finally decided that he would be allowed to sing three pre-agreed songs on stage during a televised performance at the *Festival of the Political Song* which was due to take place in East Berlin. As soon as Udo crossed the border from West to East Berlin in April 1983 with 123 West German journalists in tow, all hell broke lose. Thousands of screaming DDR teenagers tried to get a glimpse of Lindenberg on his way to the venue. Countless police officers pushed back the masses of fans who had no tickets to see Udo live on stage at the Palace of the Republic yet still wanted to be close to their idol. At first I too considered making my way to the city centre, but eventually decided against it. I preferred to watch Udo on telly than risk not seeing him at all, as no real fans were let into the venue. Instead, all 4,200 audience members had been carefully hand-picked and briefed to save their enthusiasm for Harry Belafonte who performed later in the progamme. What a travesty!

Udo was an unpredictable character so, just to be on the safe side, 300 Stasi agents were assigned to watch his every move in the DDR. On top of that, the whole event was televised with an hour's delay. If he had said something against the DDR on stage, no TV viewer would have ever known about it. Snip! But Udo behaved himself. Once again, our paranoid secret service had worried unnecessarily.

In September of the same year, thousands of miles further east, an unidentified airplane flew illegally over several military areas in the Soviet Union, which made the Russian army very tense. The Russians decided to respond to the incident with a warning to the west and shot down what they thought was an enemy spy plane. What a misjudgment that was! After the fatal order had been carried out, it became clear that the "spy plane" was a scheduled South Korean Boeing 747 flying off-course from Alaska to Seoul. A simple human error made by the pilot had cost all 269 people on board Korean Airlines flight 007 their life. The Soviet Union claimed that the Americans had detonated the plane themselves. According to the Soviet version, the CIA had used civilian passengers to cover up the real purpose of the flight: a spy mission. How ludicrous! But because it was the version given by our closest and biggest ally, the DDR news agency followed suit and broadcast this nonsense. Yet DDR citizens were no idiots and began asking questions. No one in my class believed a single word of our propaganda about the incident. So we argued with our teachers, who had to represent the official version regardless of their personal beliefs. I told one teacher that, the version given by the USSR didn't add up. I asked: "What motive would the CIA have to allow a US congress member (Lawrence McDonald of Georgia was one of the passengers) to board a plane that was about to spy over Russian territory? Not even a capitalist state would deliberately endanger the life of one of their representatives, especially when, as in this case, the man was a passionate anti-communist." As an answer I was given: "Well, that just shows you how ruthless the CIA is." The reply left me speechless. And I, the class agitator, was supposed to know all the tricks to successfully argue a case!

I faced my biggest personal dilemma later that year, when we were asked to write an essay at school. The subject was:

"How does the following poem (published in 1904) apply to our time?

Armed Peace

Out of the blue and near a node

fox and hedgehog meet on the road.

'Stop!' the fox shouts suddenly,

'don't you know the king's decree?

Isn't peace declared at all

and isn't it a downfall

in these days, to still be armed?

And before someone gets harmed,

hand me now your prickly coat!'

But the hedgehog is not fooled:

'First have your teeth extracted, then

we can gladly meet again.'

And quickly he rolls up at once,

to show the world lance after lance

His enemies he does defy,

armed, nonetheless as a peaceful guy."

I immediately knew what was expected from us and started writing:

"This fable is very topical because these days everyone mentions the word 'peace'. Unfortunately, the capitalists abuse the word, just like the fox. Politicians in capitalist countries talk about peace but don't really do anything for it. In fact the west steadily increases its number of missiles, all in the name of peace.

But sometimes imperialism lets slip its mask and shows its true, aggressive face. US Defence Minister Weinberger, for example, once said: 'There are more important things than peace.' In a recent TV documentary about the USA a factory owner declared: 'We should decapitate the Bolshevist chicken.'

I find such sentences depressing and awful, but they depict the true face of the west. The socialist countries, on the other hand, only deploy new arms to keep the military balance stable. Their aim is to prevent a Third World War. Unlike the capitalist weaponry, here symbolised by the fox's teeth, socialist weapons, just like the hedgehog's spines, are peaceful weapons and are only intended for self-defence. If the Soviet Union is as aggressive as the USA always makes out, why is it that the very first decree released by the newly founded Soviet state in 1918 was the 'Decree for Peace'? Furthermore, one should not forget that it was imperialism, not communism, that started two World Wars...

On one hand, the western media speaks constantly about the 'danger from the east'. On the other hand, the USA rejected one proposal after another for mutual disarmament made by the Soviet Union during the disarmament talks in Geneva. This just shows how deceiving the capitalist system really is. In socialism the cost of defence represents a huge economic burden. It ties up money and resources that could be put to much better use in other sectors. In capitalism, money is made from guns and bombs. The more weaponry that is produced and sold to the state, the more profit the capitalists rake in."

So far, so good. Many words with which I can still identify. But what was I about to write as a conclusion? What I truly believed, or what Herr Wolff, our German teacher, wanted to hear? I had to make up my mind quickly and, shamefully, put the following words on paper:

"Because of the ever-increasing aggressiveness of imperialism I welcome the stationing of Soviet SS-20 rockets on Czechoslovakian and DDR territory. I also agree with the Soviet Union's decision to walk out of the disarmament talks in Geneva. The power games the United States played there were no longer bearable. I will continue to fully back the peace efforts made by the Soviet Union and disapprove of the United States' war preparations."

I hated myself for not writing what I really thought: that I strongly opposed the stationing of nuclear weapons in the DDR and that I found it quite irresponsible of the USSR to stop talking to the USA. For the sake of a good mark, I had become an opportunist. And a good mark I was given. With spelling, grammar, neatness, presentation and ideas for this essay all rated "perfect", my piece was considered so exceptionally good by Herr Wolff that he even read it out at a teachers conference. I was ashamed of myself for having made such a lasting impression with an opinion that wasn't mine. I swore that I would never lie again, just to please someone. If I opened my mouth from then on I would say what I believed to be right and fair. If that agreed with someone else's opinion, fine. If it didn't, tough luck. This kind of attitude has, over the years, not always won me friends, but at least at the end of each day I can look at myself in the mirror.

MONEY MATTERS

One very hot summer's day, Cordi and I decided to cool ourselves down. So, off we went to get some ice cream from the parlour at the nearby park. At 15 pfennigs (six cents) a scoop price was no issue. If anything, the queue at the parlour was off-putting. Thankfully we were served quickly and with our ice creams in hand we checked out the wares of the private sellers at the nearby overground train station. They weren't little toothless old ladies offering worn clothes and second-hand shoes or dirty rags to make ends meet. The DDR had the highest standard of living of all the socialist countries and people that poor just did not exist in our country. I did see poor old dears at flea markets in Poland, and later in the Soviet Union, but thankfully no DDR pensioner had to spend their twilight years in such an undignified way. Even in a worst-case scenario, when living in a retirement home on a rock bottom minimum pension of 300 marks (120 dollars) a month, a DDR pensioner could still put money aside. Occupying a room and being looked after, including full board and medical care, cost no more than 80 marks (32 dollars) a month. No, the handful of sellers at the Frankfurter Allee train station were all in their twenties or thirties, trying to make a nifty penny on the side. Some offered flowers from their allotments but the majority tried to flog handicraft items. The one who caught our eye was a nervous looking lady with shortish black hair standing next to the snackbar. The golden belts she was holding in one hand looked cheap but the two sunglasses in the other hand were a totally different story. They were identical to Tom Cruise's eyewear in *Top Gun*. With their thin shiny metal frame, those glasses were screaming out: "Buy us!". Naturally, they weren't original Ray Ban Aviators. Little stickers just identified them as "Made in Italy".

To this day, I doubt that the glasses had ever been anywhere near Italy. The woman had most probably bought fake merchandise on a holiday to Hungary or Poland and was trying to recoup some of her travel costs. She wanted 50 marks (20 dollars) for one pair. That was a lot of money for teenagers like us. Even more so considering that I only earned 110 marks a week working during the school holidays. But as soon as Cordelia and I heard that the lenses were photosensitive, the pilot-style glasses began to look like bargains.

What was the catch? As we walked off, empty-handed because we did not have that much money on us, our minds started working overtime. Here is a little extract from my diary:

"Those sunglasses looked so cool. I think Harry in *Derrick* (a character from a long running West German police drama series) wears them too. Coincidentally, on our way home we walked past an optician. We went in and asked to see a range of glasses with photosensitive lenses. Prices started at around 100 marks and the frames they had did not look even half as nice as the one we had seen. We just can't get our heads around why the Italian sunglasses at the station were so cheap. For the rest of the day, we talked only about those glasses. After I took Cordelia home, I told Mum and Dad about them. The more I spoke about them, the more I wanted them."

The next day I had made up my mind. I went to the bank, withdrew 50 marks from my savings account, traipsed back to the train station and bought the glasses. It turned out that the lenses weren't photosensitive at all, they just had a graduated tint – dark at the top, lighter at the bottom. I finally knew what the catch was. But it did not really bother me. I still felt cool wearing them. Although they hardly made me look like Tom Cruise. At least I removed the brand sticker from the lens and did not walk around, like many other East Germans who wore imported sunglasses, with the vision in my right eye blocked by a logo.

Just as I was besotted with those darned sunglasses, many East Germans longed for life's little luxuries and were prepared to spend a large chunk of their savings on certain items. Whether it was an automated washing machine for 2,750 marks (1,100 dollars), a dishwasher for 1,300 marks (520 dollars), a black and white TV for 1,000 mark (400 dollars) or one of two DDR-made colour TV brands (61cm screen and weighing a ton) for either 4,400 or 6,250 marks (1760 or 2500 dollars!) – people splashed out on such things. So much so, that when it came to colour TVs and cars, among other items, production could not even come close to satisfying the demand. To relieve the situation, every company producing industrial goods was ordered to devote five per cent of its capacity to producing consumer goods. In addition, extra goods were imported. As a result, in the mid-Eighties, DDR shops sold brand-new Sanyo Walkmans for an eye-watering 660 marks (264 dollars) each. Too much for my budget. I settled instead on a no-name product Dad got me on one of his business trips to West Berlin. But many DDR citizens could spend silly money on desirable electrical goods because the general cost of living was very low. Just before the Wall came down in 1989 my parents forked out over 8,000 marks (3,200 dollars) for a brand-new colour TV (model:

Colour 40) that I had secured them through friends. With rents and public transport prices frozen at 1936 levels, free medical treatment, and rock bottom prices for services and everyday food items, a lot of money could be utilised that had been put into savings accounts. Many people liked eating out. If you went to one of the 30,000 restaurants in the DDR, you could most likely get a steak with vegetables and fries for a fiver (two dollars). And why buy a half-liter bottle of beer for 73 pfennigs (29 cents) in the supermarket, when you could get the same in your beloved *Kneipe* (pub) for 80 pfennigs (32 cents)? As a DDR citizen, you took those low prices for granted. Life was affordable and fairly cushy even if you had to queue for things like ketchup, strawberries or pork loin. Of course, people moaned about those nuisances, but no one had to worry about whether they could afford the roof over their head.

When Erich Honecker came to power, the first thing he did was to boost the country's living standard, calculating that a more motivated workforce would deliver better results and lead to a stronger economy. Yet as the state began to use more cash for subsidies and imported consumer goods, less money could be spent on new production plants. Old machinery had to run for longer. And then raw materials became more expensive on the international markets. But even with higher production costs, Honecker was determined to not raise consumer prices for existing products. Consequently the three per cent of the gross domestic product that was used to subsidise living costs in 1971 ballooned to around 20 per cent in the mid-Eighties. Yes, nearly a quarter of the state's total income was eventually spent to keep prices for goods and services ridiculously low. At the time, only a few economists and politicians knew that the state's generosity was ill-afforded and could not be sustained. Like many western countries, the DDR spent more money than it had available. An economic disaster was looming. Thankfully, in 1983 West Germany came to the rescue and gave us a loan of one billion Deutschmarks (400 million dollars), to be followed by another one for the same amount a year later. For the time being, the DDR had been saved. And as a gesture of goodwill, our state removed 60,000 automated Russian mini fragmentation bombs that were mounted on fences along a 450-kilometre stretch on the border with West Germany to deter illegal crossings (though 1.4 million landmines remained in place). Each fragmentation bomb contained 250 steel balls to cause maximum damage when exploding upon contact. But the biggest beneficiary of the loans was West Germany itself – it was one the DDR's main trading partners.

I remember that one day our shops were swamped with West German mugs. Hardly an essential item, but it made a statement: if we had money to import crockery, surely the DDR finances were in a tip-top shape, regardless what the West German media said.

FROHE WEIHNACHT & BONNE ANNEE
(MERRY CHRISTMAS AND HAPPY NEW YEAR)

Christmas, 1983, was just like any other Christmas. My parents got their artificial Christmas tree for the living room out of the basement in early December; my brother and I insisted, as usual, on a small, real fir for our room. Poor Dad! Sometimes he spent ages shifting trees at the makeshift Christmas tree stall nearby trying to find us a half-decent one. Year-in, year-out, we paid 2.25 marks (90 cents) for a 1.5 metre natural spruce. Unfortunately, the low price often showed. By the time the New Year arrived, you'd better not sneeze near the tree or it would lose all its needles. Not that Dad wasn't prepared to pay more for better quality, he just never saw Nordic firs and the like being sold. Most probably they were all exported. Thank God being East German also meant being good at improvising and so every year Dad made us a bespoke tree by drilling a few holes here and there in the puny tree trunk to rearrange the branches to our liking. Pure genius. Every single time, Dad's special treatment turned an ugly duckling into a beautiful swan.

Even though by 1983 I had outgrown the advent calendar stage, I still looked forward to Christmas Eve, which in Germany is traditionally the day when presents are exchanged. Instead of finding their presents under the tree, smaller kids are usually visited by Father Christmas, who asks them to sing a song or say a poem before handing out the gifts. My niece, for example, only realised at the age of 11 that Father Christmas was a mythical figure. It was always so sweet to see her defend his existence ferociously in arguments with her friends.

Christmas was about the only time in the year when we, as a family, would go to the nearby church and attend a service. We were not religious but liked to soak up the churchy atmosphere at that time of the year. And when we walked home from church and saw the lit Christmas trees in people's windows while snowflakes were tumbling down from the skies we really were in a Christmas mood.

Most Germans have a simple dinner on Christmas Eve – chicken soup is very popular, in our family it is sandwiches with cocoa. The feast comes on Christmas Day and Boxing Day. Goose is the traditional German Christmas fare, served with red cabbage or curly kale, potatoes and gravy. For the sake of variety, over the years we also had turkey, rabbit, duck, pork and beef; sometimes even two different meats at once. And then there are the cakes, chocolates, gingerbreads, nuts and nibbles eaten between main meals. All washed down with some alcohol while yet another Christmas movie is being watched on telly.

January 1984 was far too exciting a month to waste time thinking about how to shed the few additional pounds that I had gained in the previous weeks. France opened its cultural centre in the heart of East Berlin, following the opening of the DDR's cultural centre in Paris a month earlier. The Centre Culturel de Francais offered exhibitions, a library, a small cinema and French language courses. While it was forbidden for visitors to the DDR to bring western newspapers and magazines into our country, at the cultural centre French print media could be read freely by anyone who visited the library. It was easily accessible to members of the public yet hardly anyone bothered coming in. Whenever I browsed through the centre's selection of 7,000 books, there were never more than five people with me in the room – even East Germans chose English over French when learning a new language. I particularly liked to visit the centre's regularly changing exhibitions.

On one visit I asked the bored looking French receptionist for a road map of France on my way out. I had seen her handing one out a couple minutes earlier to another visitor, and I wanted one too. A pity her answer did not contribute to building French-German friendship. With a look of disdain in her eyes she snapped: "What do want a map for? You can't even go to France." Ouch, that was below the belt and truly hurt. But if she thought I was walking out of that place with my tail between the legs, she was very much mistaken. "Who says I can't go to France?" I bluffed. She began to look baffled. Good! Deadly serious, I continued: "Listen, you may not have attracted my uncle's attention yet. But that can easily change. If I don't get my map now you will be strip-searched every time you leave or enter the German Democratic Republic." It was common knowledge that western foreigners feared the attention of our security organs, as the army, customs, secret service and police where collectively known. So Madame finally handed me my map. I thanked her effusively and began to whistle *La Marseillaise* as I walked out. It had been a very educational afternoon for the both of us: I had seen an interesting exhibition and the French lady had learnt to be friendly to a teenager, even if he was only East German and bluffing.

CLASS OF OUR OWN

Our last year in school, from September 1983 to July 1984 was cool. The younger pupils looked up to us tenth-graders, which made us feel very senior. We even got a new subject: Astronomy. It was very interesting to learn about the scientific facts of our solar system and the stars within it.

We were encouraged to observe the skies at night and many of us felt we should have been introduced to astrophysics and stellar astronomy earlier.

Another new addition to daily school life in that final year was the sight of pupils turning up with western shopping bags. The teachers weren't particularly happy about this trend but they tolerated it as long as the plastic carriers were turned inside out. On days where we only had a couple of lessons, many of us, me included, shunned their leather cases and put their schoolbooks, writing pads and pencil cases in plastic bags instead. I much preferred one from Aldi that Dad had brought with him from one of his business trips. It was very satisfying being able to signal to other pupils: Look at me! I've got connections to the west. And as the months went by and my bag became more and more tatty I resorted to repairing little holes and tears in the plastic with sticky tape. This was a widely used technique to prolong the life of any bag, but since the fall of the Wall I have given up this typical East German habit completely.

One day the contents of my bag nearly got me into trouble. A theft had taken place in school and halfway through a lesson our teacher began searching our bags. Not that I had anything to do with the theft, but I knew that inside my bag the teacher would find a West German 20 Deutschmark banknote with which I had intended to fund an after-school Intershop shopping spree. Intershops were special shops in which western goods could be bought for hard currencies only. I had saved up some money that I had been given by Dad over time and wanted to buy a nice pair of capitalist shorts that day. Possessing Deutschmarks was not forbidden but how would the teacher react to me bringing that money to school? Or even worse, what if the nicked item was a 20 Deutschmark banknote, just like the one I had? I began sweating as the teacher made her way through the rows and came closer and closer. The thought of hiding the money quickly sprang to mind. But taking something out of the bag and putting it into my pocket would have made me look suspicious. In the end I just prayed that the money would not be found. My prayers were not heard. Our teacher saw the banknote straight away. Without drawing anyone's attention to it she just looked at me, mumbled: "But, Oliver..." and moved on to my neighbour. Phew!

However, this incident was quickly forgotten after the first issue of our monthly class magazine had come out. Founded in the tenth grade by me and five other classmates, the concept of a class magazine was quite unique in East Germany. I suppose the non-existence of copy shops in the DDR had something to do with it. The Stasi was too afraid of someone mass-producing anti-state leaflets. (At least our secret service was not as paranoid as the Romanian Securitate, which even went so far as to registering all typewriters with individual typeface samples.) Thankfully a parent offered to do the copying at work, so the five of us who had appointed ourselves editors could concentrate on regularly filling 20 pages that were completely free of politics. I wanted a magazine that was fun to read. So the bulk of the content was a mixed bag: bizarre news stories, jokes, easy-to-follow recipes, sports write ups, articles about interesting scientific discoveries, music-related stories (no DDR band ever got a mention) and lyrics to the latest western hits, as well as tips for all sort of situations in life. The literature page was my responsibility. I loved writing stories. First, I took it upon myself to introduce my classmates to the delights of Wellington, New Zealand. I may have never been there myself, but I did have a tourist map with photos and descriptions that I had bought at the Journalists Bazaar, which took place once a year in the centre of Berlin. At the bazaar, items donated by DDR media companies or journalists were sold or auctioned off in aid of the anti-imperialist international solidarity. Whether it be exotic food items from far-away countries, signed scripts and autographs, film props, rare records/books or even hard-to-come-by plants, the *Journalistenbasar* was definitely the place to go. Very popular was also the talent search studio where hopefuls could get tested to see whether they had what it took to be the newsreaders or station announcers of tomorrow.

I bought the Wellington map cheaply at the bazaar for 50 pfennigs (12 cents) and it proved to be quite a good investment. For two or three issues, I filled my literary page with a story that revolved around the sights and layout of the New Zealand capital. Once I had milked every single bit of information contained on the map, I embarked on a serialisation of the life of a fictional DDR teenager. *Das Mädchen Karla* (The Girl Named Carla) was always knocked together by me one day before the deadline and while it was hardly high brow fiction, it still dealt with problems that we could all identify with: not being taken seriously by adults, meeting the first love, being fancied by someone you don't fancy and so on. Our class teacher then, Frau Märker, a woman in her mid to late twenties who we all adored and considered a friend (some classmates even had a crush on her), paid me the nicest compliment when one day she asked which book I had copied the story from. She could not believe it was a product of my imagination. I was so thrilled. But our finest hour came when we claimed in our April(!) issue that Rod Stewart, allegedly on his way to a performance in eastern Europe, had been admitted to our local hospital after an emergency landing near East Berlin. The cover of the May issue then showed a photo of the four gullible classmates who had fallen for our joke, waiting in vain for Rod to make an appearance in the hospital grounds.

Despite the fact that all of our news stories were rehashed from other publications (mainly West German magazines and newspapers that had been smuggled into the country), our headmaster was so ecstatic about the project he even showed the magazines to an editor friend of his. While we were criticised for not concentrating enough on class-related issues, we received the thumbs-up for entertainment. Goal achieved! And our class cash box, to which everyone contributed one mark (40 cents) each month to pay for group activities, also received a boost – all the magazine's takings, around 30 marks

(12 dollars) a month, were handed over to Andrea, who looked after the class's finances. Happy faces all around.

I wish the same could be said for our last class trip later in June 1984. The trip itself was great. We went somewhere up north and stayed in nice brand-new, two-storey cottages with parquet flooring. Each cottage accommodated up to six people, and everyone made sure they shared a house with their best friends. We went on excursions and walks, played games or table tennis, had a scary night ramble through the nearby forest and organised the obligatory disco, which no class trip was complete without. All the usual stuff really, yet this time a new element was added to the trip – alcohol.

At family celebrations I occasionally had a small glass of Advocaat or cherry liqueur. I liked everything as long as it was nice and sweet. Many classmates bought beer but I opted for a bottle of apple wine when choosing my drink for our BYO disco. Not only was it cheap as chips with a price tag of just over one mark (40 cents), but its sugary fruitiness promised to be just right up my street. And indeed it was. The evening was rather hot and humid and I couldn't resist taking one sip after another from my yummy drink. The 12 per cent alcohol soon had more of an effect than I had bargained for. By the time the disco finished I was back in our cottage and pretty much a vegetable, incapable of moving. If the teacher had seen me like this, we would all have been in big trouble. I didn't black out, but my entire body seemed to be detached from my brain. I wanted to tell a joke, but my mouth only mumbled. I wanted to go to the girls in the next-door cottage, but my body did not want to get up from the armchair I was in. And where was that blinding headache suddenly coming from? To get me into bed upstairs, two of my friends had to pull me, while three were pushing me from behind as hard as they could. Thank God, the bowl I requested as I lay down was not needed. Predictably, the next morning I was very unwell. What shocked me most was the colour of my face when I looked into the mirror. It was a very unflattering shade of grey. I pledged to never drink myself into a stupor again. Ever!

DAD AND THE UNITED NATIONS

While I was licking my wounds and trying to keep my headaches at bay, Dad had troubles of his own. He had read in the newspaper that for the past six months we, the Fritzes, had been in breach of a United Nations resolution.

During the early to mid-Eighties, western car manufacturers started to put additional brake lights into rear windows. Dad noticed this trend on his trips to the west and liked the idea of improved visibility to following motorists. So he bought two motorbike brake lights, got his toolkit out and installed them into our car. And as our own motor industry was unable to incorporate this trend into its current production, many car-owning DIYers took things into their own hands and followed suit. But as more and more motorists personalised their cars in this way, fewer and fewer of those lights became available to motor bikers. Remember, we had a centralised industry and if a trend had not been predicted at a time when production plans were drafted and resources allocated a year earlier, then this trend simply could not be fed by our industry.

As a once abundantly available good suddenly became scarce, someone high up must have had an idea. They could have simple admitted that the manufacturer wasn't geared up to increase its production in the short term and asked people to have patience. But instead, a statement was released in all newspapers, in which car owners sporting additional brake lights were ordered to remove them immediately or risk being fined. It was claimed that the lights did not improve road safety, as they allegedly distracted motorists. Furthermore, we were informed that their installation was in breach of a ratified UN resolution on road traffic. For many East Germans it seemed a bit much that a government which did not allow public criticism of its representatives and free travel to the west started citing UN resolutions. But there was nothing that could be done about it. As Dad grudgingly removed his lights, western cars passing through our country still seemed to be mysteriously ignorant of the fact that they were in direct contravention of a United Nations directive. Mysteriously, the "Additional Brake Lights Act", as our family had nicknamed the resolution, only seemed to apply to cars registered in the German Democratic Republic.

FAREWELLS

The year of 1984 was a time of farewells. I finished school and our sportsmen had to wave goodbye to the prospect of winning at the Olympic Games in Los Angeles. All socialist countries (with the exception of Romania) followed the Soviet Union's lead and boycotted the games in retaliation of the American boycott of the Moscow games in 1980. The DDR did so grudgingly but had no other choice because of economic reasons: only if we complied would the Soviet Union promise to increase our delivery quota of much needed mineral oil. In 1984, a record 40,974 DDR citizens left their fatherland behind and started a new life in the west. This was nearly four times the number of people who had left in the previous year. Among them were 192 who illegally jumped the border, and 3,450 who did not return from authorised trips to the west. But most emigrants (383,000 people in 27 years) overcame the border to the west legally by going to their local council offices and applying for a permanent exit visa.

"A DDR citizen can be discharged from DDR citizenship when he intends to take residency outside the DDR with authorisation of the relevant DDR authorities..."

DDR Citizenship Law

"Applications for migration can be authorised when citizens of the DDR

a) have reached retirement age

b) are invalids... and it is proven that their ability to work will not be regained before reaching retirement age

c) have married, with permission of the DDR authorities, citizens of the FRG (West Germany) or West Berlin

d) want to reunite with their spouse who has migrated... from the DDR with the permission of the authorities

e) are juveniles who want reunite with a parent who has migrated from the DDR with the permission of the authorities..."

Secret order by the Interior Minister

"Making an application" became the euphemism for trying to get a permanent exit visa and leave the DDR for good. At one stage it was very fashionable for motorists who had "made an application" to attach little white pieces of fabric to their car aerial. Anyone with a black piece of fabric was letting the world know that their application had been rejected. Naturally our People's Police was not keen on such public displays and regularly ordered drivers to take down the fabric or risk a fine.

The authorities certainly weren't happy about people wanting to be released from DDR citizenship. They did all they could to persuade individuals to withdraw their application, and parents were the easiest targets. Understandably many of them stopped the application process immediately after being told that their kids would have to stay behind. And as there was no official legislation to regulate the authorisation process, any applicant was at every stage of the process very much at the mercy of the authorities. Each district treated applications differently. Some cities were very lenient when looking at individual cases, others did not allow people to even hand in their application forms. The best bet for a DDR citizen to get permission to leave the country for good was to marry a westerner. Any such wedding required the state's blessing. The Stasi or police would ask whether the western spouse intended to move to the DDR. If that wasn't the case (and most times it wasn't), the East German partner could usually move to the west. But once the authorities had made their decision, they wanted to get a person out of the country as quickly as possible. Often within 24 hours. And not everyone was allowed to take all their possessions with them either. As unnecessary as this final flexing of muscles by the DDR authorities was, many of those keen to leave were happy to comply with whatever demands the authorities made. Many, but not everyone.

Fearing that their applications for permanent exit visas might be declined, in January 1984 six East Germans took matters into their own hands. After visiting a film performance in the American embassy in East Berlin, they refused to leave and applied for political asylum. The tactic proved successful. Just two days later, a DDR solicitor drove them in his car over the inner city border to West Berlin. From that moment on there was a fairly high police presence around the American embassy. But it was not only the East German police and secret service who wanted to deter potential copycats. The Americans, too, had no interest in seeing a repeat of such an incident and also tightened security.

But there were a total of 131 embassies in East Berlin and just six months later, more East Germans took refuge on extraterritorial soil. This time it were 55 people in the West German mission. They also succeeded. As a result, the Stasi stepped up their security arrangements even further. Over night, pedestrians innocently walking past the West German mission were stopped by police and asked for their ID. It happened to friends, my parents and one day also to myself. After handing over my papers, the police officer, pretending to talk to me, spoke very loudly and clearly into the top buttonhole of his uniform:

"So, your name is Oliver Fritz, your home address is blah, blah, blah and your ID card number is blah, blah, blah. What are you doing here?"

I gave him my I-can't-believe-this-is-happening-to-me look and replied: "I am going to the hospital up there. That isn't forbidden, is it?"

And again in the direction of his top buttonhole, the officer loudly repeated: "So, you are going to the hospital?"

Slightly bemused I answered: "Well, at least that was the plan before you stopped me."

It was only when he asked why I was going to the hospital that I lost my temper and told him to mind his own business. "And do you know what?", I continued, "I also do not appreciate my personal details and this conversation being recorded." He looked at me, bewildered, and after repeating my words again he replied, still addressing his buttonhole: "I don't know what you are talking about. No one is recording anything."

"So, why are you then speaking into a microphone hidden underneath your jacket?" I asked. And chin down, still speaking into his mic he said: "I am not at all talking into a microphone."

Then the policeman was finished with me. My ID card was returned and I was asked to move on. Most probably a little speaker in his ear told him that I was clean. As I walked off I muttered in a low but audible voice: "Someone definitely needs to work on his recording technique!"

The DDR might have stepped up security surrounding western embassies in Berlin but it did not stop people trying to find ways out of the country. Only a little later more than 150 East Germans made themselves comfortable in the West German embassy in Prague. Among them our Prime Minister's niece, as the western media pointed out with glee. Those people too were eventually free to leave the DDR. Naturally, none of those embassy squatting incidents ever made it into our headlines. Only five years later, when the same was happening again, yet on a much grander scale, did our central news agency felt obliged to tackle the subject, albeit half-heartedly.

A FRESH START

In September 1984 I began my tertiary education. In the following two years, which were a combination of college and work, I earned my own money. Not a lot – 120 marks (48 dollars) per month in the first six months, rising to 180 marks (72 dollars) in the second year, but nonetheless my own cash.

As I was still living at home, I insisted on paying a token amount for board to my parents. The rest I spent, like any other teenager, on records, books, clothes or nights out. Any money left at the end of the month went into my savings account. However, there was also a downside to being employed and educated by a foreign trade company: one had to show exemplary commitment to the DDR. Our state wanted to be 100 per cent certain that only ideologically trustworthy members of staff were representing the DDR. And so the foreign-trade sector was swamped with hardcore communists and spineless opportunists. Thankfully, most of my new classmates at the Foreign Trade College where we learnt the ins and outs of international business relations turned out to be refreshingly different. With the exception of "Red Heike", a girl who was very politically active, everyone else in my new class seemed much more interested in tracking down the latest in disco rather than analysing the latest Communist Party press releases. Of course, during lessons we all projected the correct ideological image and hardly anyone ever raised a controversial point of view when discussing political decisions made by the government. However, when we were out of college and among ourselves we freely expressed our true thoughts.

In March 1985 our newspapers published letters from people who had left the DDR and now wanted to come back because they could not adapt to life in West Germany. Apparently 20,000 former East Germans wanted to return. (A total of 35,000 had left the DDR legally in 1984.) Western journalists immediately investigated this claim. In reality only 543 people made such a request. It still showed that not everyone could cope with moving from a collective society to a competitive society. But instead of using the return of those disillusioned people as proof of the DDR being the better Germany, our politicians decided to let the majority of their former citizens rot in the west. The only promise they were prepared to make was to looking more favourably at applications from families who wanted to return for the sake of the kids. In the end only 90 people were allowed back in. The point our leaders wanted to make was very clear: Everyone in the DDR should consider very carefully whether they really wanted to turn their back on our country. Resigning from DDR citizenship was an irreversible act and anyone doing so had forfeited their place in our society for ever. I and others in my class found such a blasé attitude unnecessarily harsh, but when this matter was officially discussed in college, teachers just disregarded our opinion as political immaturity and we could not get in another word edgeways.

Anyway, the period 1984 to 1985 doesn't stick in my mind for political reasons. For me it represents the time when I metamorphosed into a disco bunny. By then school discos seemed so yesterday, going to clubs was exciting and *fetzig* (cool). Saturday was usually the best day for it. Though in the years to come this often increased to five disco visits a week. Going out on a Monday, Wednesday, Friday, Saturday and Sunday was occasionally very tiring, but at least this way I did not miss any of my friends' antics, was always up to date with the latest gossip and never lost track of who was going out with who. I, too, was looking for Ms Right. Though Cordelia still was part of my life, we did not see each other on a daily basis any more and we began to build separate circles of friends. I guess we both were ready to brave the world and get life experience.

Part of that process was travelling without our parents. So when a list with available places for trips in the following year made the rounds at college I naturally applied. Not only were the offered organised holidays dirt cheap, but they were also especially tailor-made for people up to the age of 30. The organiser, Jugendtourist (Youth Tourist), was the central travel agency of the Free German Youth organisation. However, the catch with Youth Tourist was that you could not buy any of their holidays in the High Street. Oh, no! Jugendtourist allocated places for their tours to companies and institutions only. If something on their list caught an employee's eye, they had to fill in a form to register their interest. It was then up to the Free German Youth representative in the applicant's company to preselect and decide whose application would be forwarded to Jugendtourist for a final verdict.

"If a trip attracts more applications than there are spaces available, young people delivering outstanding results when working and studying, or taking on social responsibility or protecting our republic, will receive preferred consideration."

Jugendtourist guideline

There was a buzz at my college when one day it was announced that in 1985, to commemorate the tenth anniversary of Youth Tourist, a few spaces would be available on organised tours to France, Italy and West Germany. I knew that my chances of securing one of those rare spaces were very slim indeed. After all I was known not to agree slavishly with all political decisions. I applied anyway. I shouldn't have bothered because, in the end, no one from our school got to travel to the west. The whole thing had just been hot air. A few years later, a documentary on West German telly with the apt name *Holiday with the Enemy* showed the type of people chosen for those trips: reliable, hardcore communists with an average age of 30. After watching this documentary about a Jugendtourist group in Hamburg, I wrote in my diary: "Those bastards were even given 90 Deutschmarks (30 pounds) pocket money each!"

Getting enrolled in a youth exchange programme was equally impossible for the average young East German. In 1985, West Germany sent 35,000 young people into the DDR but we only sent 10,000 DDR girls and boys westwards. Economic reasons prevented our country from making more use of the exchange programme. The DDR had to pay the equivalent of 32 dollars for every person sent, while West Germany paid us only 8 dollars for each of their travellers because life in the DDR was so much cheaper.

I might not have been trustworthy enough to travel to the west but I expected my application for a Youth Tourist holiday to Poland to be processed smoothly. I could not have been more wrong. Gernoth, the college's Free German Youth representative, informed me one day that he did not approve my application because of my lack of enthusiasm in taking on tasks for the organisation. The two of us did not get on very well, so I accepted his decision and began making alternative holiday plans. However, when an even less-enthusiastic classmate had her holiday application authorised, I was ready to fight. "Today I will give Gernoth a bollocking." my diary reads for Friday 23 November 1984. Our meeting was so heated it ended with me storming out of his office, slamming the door shut behind me. I was not taking this injustice lying down. I got teachers involved and had meetings with senior youth organisation representatives. Everyone I talked to supported my application. Two weeks later a tight-lipped Gernoth informed me that my application had now been approved. Strike!

ON THE MOVE

In 1985, the year Mikhail Gorbachev took over the reigns in Moscow as General Secretary of the Soviet Communist Party our politicians were bathing in international recognition. The British Foreign Minister, Geoffrey Howe, arrived in East Berlin on 8 April. Then Erich Honecker went on a state visit to Italy. He even met the Pope. In June, the French Prime Minister showed up in the DDR. And in between there was an endless stream of West German businessmen and politicians pouring into our country, all wanting to shake Erich Honecker's hand, including the future chancellor of a united Germany, Gerhard Schröder.

I went on my hard won trip to Poland in August 1985, but I had to be very diplomatic when talking to my fellow travellers. Most were extremely loyal to the Communist Party. Our itinerary was packed with visits to various cities. Day trips to destinations like the concentration camp at Auschwitz or Hitler's command headquarters, Wolfsschanze (Wolf's Lair, a bunker complex in a mosquito-infested forest), were interesting additions to an otherwise fun-filled holiday. One day I was given the fright of my life. I was a *Popper* as the pop music enthusiasts were called at the time in both Germanys. We were easily identifiable by our all-matching, pastel-coloured outfits. Jumpers were slung around necks, sleeves of jackets were rolled up, loafers had little tassels, socks were pristine white and trousers were carrot shaped – big on top and tapered to the bottom. I also got a very good use out of the pair of red trousers and the seven differently coloured leather ties Gran had bought me in West Berlin. But the German *Popper* look was only complete with a matching *Popper* hairstyle: a layered cut with shaved neck and asymmetric fringe that forced you to constantly hold your head at a slight angle if you did not want one of your eyes to be covered by hair. Of course, I had this haircut too. And as I did some window shopping with my parted blond hair three Polish teenagers approached me in the street. They stopped, lined up, did a Hitler salute at me and laughed. I nearly had a heart attack.

In Germany, any public display of Nazi insignia, greeting or gesture was and still is a punishable offence. Given Poland's suffering in the Second World War I imagined their legislation to be very similar. What if police saw this display? What if the three guys would claim I provoked them? I certainly had no interest to see the inside of a Polish holding cell. So I quickly ran away. I chanced upon a flea market, and within it a stall selling old West German *Playboy* magazines. The photos of nude women and an article about how Boy George had apparently been given lessons at a tranny school were worth getting the magazine for on their own. Only the hefty price tag equivalent to ten DDR marks (four dollars) for an issue prevented the transaction. I rather used my limited funds to buy clothes. Some of my travelling companions preferred pattern charts instead. Many people in the DDR made their own clothes, and so pattern charts were big business. I too asked once a friend with a sewing machine to tailor me something. I had been looking, unsuccessfully, for a pair of light-blue insulated trousers (Berlin winters can get freezing). My classmate made me a pair out of bed linen which turned out exactly as I wanted. Being inventive in this way enhanced one's individuality, and could spawn new fashion trends. The huge number of girls who bought fabric nappies, dyed them in bright colours and wore them as stylish neck scarves showed everyone the way.

Cordelia too had one of those nappie-cum-neckscarves. She wore it on an ill-fated trip to Birkenwerder, a small town on the outskirts of Berlin. One of my classmates living there had told us about a new club called "audio b" – a video disco. Fancy that, being able to watch video clips or short films on various monitors while dancing! What would they think of next? We just had to see this new type of disco, even if it meant an hour-long journey on the train. To make the time pass more quickly (and to get us in the right mood) I had bought a half-bottle of Zinnaer Klosterbruder, a digestive liqueur. Like most East Germans we preferred our alcoholic beverages to be on the sweet side. And with a flavour of herbs, plant extracts, orange peel and gingerbread, the liqueur was an instant favourite. At first, Cordelia was embarrassed to drink out of a bottle in public ("I am a lady", she protested) but as time went by and the alcohol began to have an effect she eventually stopped hiding behind a newspaper when taking a sip. Halfway through the bottle (and the journey), what was considered delicious in the beginning, began to taste sickly sweet and disgusting. But we were determined to finish the bottle. And by the time the train reached Birkenwerder station, we had achieved our goal. Giggling we stepped off the train to meet our welcome committee, my classmate and his girlfriend. Unfortunately, it turned out that "audio b" had been booked that evening for a private function and was closed to the public. What were we supposed to do now? So the evening wasn't a complete write-off, we went to the local funfair. And as the four of us sat in the waltzing train I began to feel very queasy. Thinking that all I needed was something to eat, I bought myself a hot dog and did not waste another thought on my tummy's rumbling. A bad mistake!

The next ride was a twister. It twirled punters, who were sitting in bobsled-like pods, up and down a pole. Once up, Cordi and I were suspended in mid-air for a minute or so. Just as we were wondering whether there had been a breakdown, we were hurled back down. That proved too much for me. By the time we got off the ride, I could only take one step before the Zinnaer Klosterbruder and the hot dog staged a united reappearance. And as I was leaning over, fighting additional attacks of retching, I saw two girls approaching. They wanted to get on the ride Cordi and I had just stepped off, but stopped after seeing me. I looked at them, they looked at me and the puddle of sick at my feet, before one girl quickly said to the other: "Beate, let's take the ghost train instead." And off they went. When Cordelia came to see how I was doing, she pointed out that I had puked over the tip of my left shoe. She was not impressed. "Scheiss Osten." (shitty east) I mumbled as I made myself look presentable again.

DRESSING UP

Blaming the fatherland was the instant reaction of many DDR citizens when something went wrong. Your TV packed in just after the guarantee had run out? "Shitty east." you would say (provided you were not within earshot of strangers). And if you called the TV repair service and were told the next available appointment was not for two weeks? "Shitty east" would be your reaction after putting the phone down. No points for guessing the words on your mind when the engineer inevitably turned up late on the day.

Cordi and I also blamed our state for just about everything that went wrong. Somewhat unfairly perhaps, but then we were quite annoyed about the injustice of having to spend the best years of our lives on the wrong side of the Iron Curtain. Whether it was the shortage of discos, the production of low-quality products or the lack of travel opportunities to the west, a reason for complaint was easily found.

"Today Cordi and I felt like a walk in the fresh air, so we took the S-Bahn (overground train) to the forest. The journey was fun. We talked about the shitty east and how cool it would be to be "free". On the steamed up window we scribbled with our fingers abbreviations like I.W.N.S. – Ich will nach Schweden (I want to go to Sweden), W.I.D.H.D.M. – Wo ist denn hier die Mauer? (Where is the Wall around here?), D.H. – Dort hinten. (Over there.), N.L.N.W.H – Na los, nichts wie hin. (Let's go then!) When we left the train the whole of our window was covered in letters no one else (thankfully) could understand."

Diary entry

The DDR just seemed so stuffy and conventional; the west so colourful and exciting. Though we were also familiar with the downside of capitalism. Our media grabbed every opportunity to show portraits of West Germans who had slipped through the social net. What we didn't know at the time was that the photos in our newspapers of unemployed workers queueing at West German job centres were cropped to hide the flashy cars they still seemed to be able to afford.

Cordelia and I may have been very pro-west, but we were hardly in the same league as a colleague of Dad's who, after returning from visiting relatives, insisted that the streets beyond the Iron Curtain smelled of apples. West Germans going around spraying apple-scented air freshener in the streets? Cordi and I did not think so. But we did imagine everyday life on the other side to be less politicised and more open-minded. And there was the possibility of being able to travel the world and to buy all the latest trendy clothes. At the time, though, there was just no conceivable way we could get there. So we tried to make the most of where we were and zested up our lives in the DDR as much as possible.

Whether it was exploring where the tube goes after it pulls out of the last station, putting rude stickers on the backs of unsuspecting strangers in the streets, deliberately walking into tourists' holiday snaps or, even better, just taking a photo of their feet or bellies when being asked to capture them on film, we did it all. A favourite pastime of ours also was to gate-crash corporate parties. Nearly every Friday and Saturday, a different company would hire the banqueting hall of the Palasthotel (Palace Hotel) right in the centre of town, for their annual event. The Palace Hotel was a top international five-star hotel built in cooperation with a Swedish firm. It opened in 1979 in the heart of East Berlin and was another building Dad had worked on. His company had built and installed the hotel's wooden interior. The Palace Hotel breathed an air of sophistication without being flashy. Tinted and mirrored honeycomb windows interrupted a natural sandstone façade. The building's three wings formed a little courtyard that housed the hotel's secluded entrance. The lobby consisted of marble flooring, small palm trees, a brown wooden reception desk and matching leather armchairs and sofas with glass tables. All employees wore uniforms in the hotel's signature colour: brown.

Cordi and I were obsessed with this hotel, but it wasn't the décor that drew us to the place. What made it desirable to us was the knowledge that, while some of the incorporated shops and restaurants accepted DDR currency, accommodation could only be paid for with hard currency. We were fascinated by the hotel's cosmopolitan atmosphere. The hustle and bustle created by the many international guests would make us forget that we were still in East Germany. Here we could experience first hand how life in the west must be. Many times we (illegally) roamed the hotel corridors pretending to go to "our room". We were so excited when, for the first time, we saw an ice vending machine on one floor. I wanted a chocolate ice cream, Cordi felt more like a strawberry one. Imagine our disappointment when we realised that the damn thing only dispensed plain ice cubes. It did not deter us from coming back time and time again.

Doors to the hotel's banqueting hall usually opened between seven and eight pm whenever a company event took place. Employees arriving at that time had to show invites to gain access. Once everyone was seated the cold buffet was declared open and the hired band began to play. At half past eight the bouncers would join the fun inside leaving the doors unattended. So, Cordi and I could always stroll unchallenged into any party between nine and ten pm. After handing our jackets to the cloakroom attendant we would head straight to the buffet. Most guests were dancing by then, so finding seats with our laden plates never proved to be a problem. We helped ourselves to other people's wine, greeted total strangers as if we were old friends and no one ever exposed us as frauds. Our breezy confidence, and the fact that most of the people around us had been enjoying the booze, worked in our favour. We were not even challenged when we turned up inappropriately dressed:

"After playing all sorts of pranks on unsuspecting people for a couple of hours downtown, Cordi and I felt like going to an office party in the Palasthotel. The company celebrating there today really had a top-class buffet. Four times we helped ourselves, leaving the buffet with full plates each time. It showed that we had skipped dinner at home. I was a bit concerned that our casual outfits might give us away. Everyone else around us was very smartly dressed. A sea of suits, dresses, ties, bow ties and well-polished shoes everywhere. Some men even wore tails! And we were running around in jeans and casual tops. Earlier in the evening, we had put bright red stickers on our chunky boots, just for fun. But not a single person batted an eyelid about our outfits! As usual there was a band too. I wanted to dance but Cordi felt too full to move. Somewhat stuffed we went home at 23:15."

Diary entry

Even more popular than gate-crashing parties were the "Dress-Smartly-Days" which Cordi and I initiated in 1985. Every now and then, usually on a Sunday afternoon, would we put our best clothes on and walk around the East Berlin's city centre pretending to be westerners. If we couldn't travel to the west, then we at least wanted to be mistaken for people from the other side. We would adopt a nonchalant attitude and be very loud as we walked around all the familiar East Berlin sights, pretending to see them for the very first time while secretly monitoring the reactions of the people around us. Were they looking at us? Our act fooled lots of people. Fellow East Germans regularly approached us to find out what life in the west was really like. And we were happy to tell them. First Cordi and I would moan about the high rents and taxes we allegedly had to pay, then we usually talked elaborately about our trips to faraway countries. Whether it was Egypt, Morocco, the States or "just" Italy, Cordi and I let our imaginations run wild. Not in a million years could we have fooled a real West German with our limited knowledge of everyday life behind the Iron Curtain. But East Germans were such an easy target for us – we knew exactly how they ticked and just gave them the answers we would have wanted to hear. We were so convincing that fellow East Germans asked us regularly whether we wanted to exchange some Deutschmarks into DDR marks. We always pretended that we just had changed some money with someone else. If they would only have come five minutes earlier...

At first I thought my Russian Smena Symbol camera (available in our shops for 90 marks – 36 dollars) would give the game away. But none of the people I handed it to in order to take a photo of Cordelia and me cottoned on to us. Instead I was complimented about "the cool design" of the camera. First I thought people were pulling my leg but no, they were serious. A simple sticker with some Norwegian writing, which I had slapped on to cover the Cyrillic brand name, made people mistake my camera for a western model. East Germans were so gullible. Unfortunately, most of the collective naïveté and innocence vanished forever with the disappearance of the DDR. But a conversation like the following, which took place on one of our "Dress Smartly Days", could still happen today:

"Excuse me Sir, could you please take a photo of us two?"

"No!"

"Why not?"

"Because I haven't got a camera on me."

"I wanted you to take a picture of us with our camera."

"Oh, I see."

"Did you really think I would have asked you to take a picture of us with your camera?"

"I don't know."

"What do you mean, you don't know?"

"Yes."

Stupidity, so it seems, is at home in any political system. Idiots of all countries, unite!

RING, RING

In 1985, I decided to cash in on my German language knowledge. I put up a notice in a shop window and a few days later I got a telephone call from a sweet little couple who were looking for someone to give their son private lessons to improve his spelling and grammar. I boldly asked for five marks an hour (two dollars) and to my surprise they agreed without quibbling. The boy's obsession with dead flies aside (he kept his collection of them in the family's fridge), we got on rather well. And after a while, the two hours private tuition per week started to show: His school marks improved and so did my bank balance. Everyone was happy – except me whenever I was shown the latest addition to the collection of dead flies. Yuck!

The telephone, which we had only had connected in late 1984, made organising my spare time so much easier. When my parents applied for a line in 1980 things did not look too promising. Mum and Dad supplied the Post Office with several statements from their employers stressing the urgent need for both of them to be easily contactable for work reasons. The employee who the application was handed to laughed at them. "You can either leave those certificates here and we will chuck them or you can take them back with you now. It doesn't make the slightest bit of difference to us," my parents were candidly advised. Thanks to one of our neighbours who worked for the Post Office and pulled a few strings, we only had to wait four years for a line. To a westerner, that might sound like a very long time to get a telephone, but for a DDR citizen a four-year wait was nothing. My grandparents had to wait eight years for their phone. The average waiting time was ten to 12 years! By 1989 one million applications were waiting to be processed. Every year, 100,000 applicants complained about the long wait. I have heard of one woman who clocked up 41 years before she could finally make calls from the comfort of her own home. Surely that must be world record!

Around 60,000 lines were installed in the DDR every year. It would have taken twice as many just to take care of the urgent cases. Because of constant underfunding (70 per cent of all funds for telecommunications were allocated to the Stasi or the army) the whole civil telephone network was fairly old and inefficient. In an attempt to satisfy at least some of the demand for telephones at home, many lines had to be shared by more than one user. We found out that we shared our line with our upstairs neighbour. Whenever they were on the phone, our line was dead and people calling us would hear an engaged tone. It was inconvenient not to be able to make or receive a call at a certain time, but at least we weren't as hard done by as the people who shared their lines with companies and could not make any calls at all during business hours. Even with such compromises, only one in five DDR households had a telephone. Most people had no other option but to rely on public phone booths, of which (at least) we had many.

Although our constitution guaranteed the secrecy of telecommunications, it wasn't worth the paper it was written on. In Berlin alone the Stasi had over 400 members of staff working in its eavesdropping section named "Department 26". Employees were on duty in two shifts: Monday to Friday from six-thirty to 14:00 and 13:45 to 22:45. Saturday's work began at eight o'clock in the morning and ended at 20:00. During working hours, calls were taped manually; at all other times the recordings were made automatically. In the capital alone 20,000 lines could be monitored at the same time. In 1985 the Stasi listened into 580,000 calls nationwide, of which over 70,000 transcripts were kept and filed. Quite a high number considering that the average citizen avoided tackling controversial political topics on the blower. Instead, people concentrated on everyday problems and shortcomings. Serious criticism about the state or its politicians was another matter and usually only done when meeting someone face to face.

No one knew for sure the extent to which the secret service was listening into telephone conversations, but everyone suspected their calls were being monitored. And so it was quite common for people to annoy possible eavesdroppers in mid-conversation with erratic comments like: "A hip-hip-hooray to the hard working comrades of the Ministry of State Security." or "Will the third person on the line please cough or give us some other sign if we're not talking clearly enough? Thank you!" or even "Hey, you gormless dimwit, get off my line!" Since officially no one was listening in, no one could be offended, right? If there was a crackling noise on the line early in the conversation, one would automatically assume that a tape recorder was being switched on. Comments like the above were then randomly fired off every couple of minutes. Dissidents went one step further and checked whether they were under observation by arranging bogus get-togethers over the phone. Claiming that loads of people would meet at a certain date and time, all a friend had to do on the day in question was to lie in wait. If the

Stasi turned up before the alleged event to secure the area you knew your telephone had been bugged. And bugging a phone was so easy. Later models were even manufactured to Stasi requirements. The addition of just one little wire inside the phone meant that the comrades at "Hear and Peer" could also hear every word that was said inside your home, even when the receiver was on the hook.

Many people suspected that the clause in the "Telecommunications Decree" that asked people to answer calls by first stating their names was to make identification easier for the secret service. I believe it had more to do with old-fashioned politeness. The Stasi had other means at its disposal to identify the recipient of a call. Telephone observation experts and computers alike could identify phone numbers by simply listening to the sound individual digits gave off when dialled.

But the DDR-telecommunications network could also provide entertainment when it was least expected. On numerous occasions I got a crossed line when making calls. I never heard anything worthwhile. Somehow I always seemed to be eavesdropping on old ladies exchanging recipes and talking about their latest baking disaster. Occasionally I would frighten the old dears a bit by suddenly coughing loudly or asking one of them to please repeat the last sentence more clearly. Cruel jokes, I know, but at least (unlike the state), I did not tape any conversations. The Stasi left 99,600 sound recordings behind. In an attempt to keep costs down (new tapes cost 20 marks a piece), the secret service also used up western pre-recorded music cassettes that had been confiscated by customs. Someone's telephonic rant about the shortage of ketchup being immortalised on a KISS tape? The Stasi made it possible!

FRUSTRATING FRUIT

If patience is a virtue, as the saying goes, DDR citizens were virtuous beyond belief. People joked:

Two neighbours meet. One says: "We might be getting snow tomorrow." The other replies: "I'll give it a miss. I can't be bothered queueing."

In our family we have always bought lots of fruit and vegetables. Only once did I hesitate buying vegetables, when a private flower shop offered asparagus for 15 marks a kilo (six dollars). That was daylight robbery, considering that apples sold for 1,90 mark a kilo (76 cents) and cabbage as well as potatoes were yours for 30 pfennigs a kilo – the equivalent of 12 cents. Fruit-wise, the worst part of the year was always the stretch from January, when the several kilos of Spanish oranges stashed away at Christmas had been finished, to March when the first rhubarb was sold. Rhubarb may be classed a vegetable, but after two-and-a-half months of munching only on apples (and maybe, occasionally, bananas or grapefruits) we craved something different. Once the rhubarb was cooked with water, sugar and sago (optional) we did not care what botanical family it belonged to, as long as it tasted nice.

In summer, lots of supermarkets and greengrocers' set up makeshift stalls outside to sell their fruit quickly – Bulgarian peaches, Rumanian watermelons or DDR strawberries. Sometimes fruit shortages were only the result of shoddy logistics. One case is documented where in the Eighties 265 tons of plums had to be fed to pigs because the trade did not sent any lorries to pick them up. Unfortunately, more often fruit had to be bought for hard currency in capitalist countries because, increasingly, producers in socialist countries only sent third- or fourth-grade merchandise to their East German comrades. The ordinary man did not care where the produce came from, as long as it was available. And when it did hit the shops, it was bought in typical DDR-style – in bulk. It was not unusual to see people buying five or six kilograms of cherries in one go. Peaches were sold by the crate. We Fritzes did exactly the same. It was common sense, after all, to keep the gaps between queueing as long as possible. But the most dreaded moment for every queuing shopper was when the last bag of fruit was sold to the person right in front of them. Grrrr...

Even buying preserved fruit could turn into a disappointment. One of my diary entries reads: "Today I bought ten jars of Bulgarian pureed strawberries. Yum!"

Only to be followed by a second entry later that day: "Had to return all ten jars to the shop – the puree was mouldy. Yuck!"

Once again, our communist brothers and sisters in Bulgaria had delivered to us the rubbish they were not able to flog off for dollars to the west. Thanks to our family allotment, we rarely had to rely on commercially preserved fruit. Every year, our 100-plus jars of home-preserved gooseberries, plums, apples and pears lasted at least a winter – and were much more delicious than the commercial stuff.

" 'A Year of Despair – Britain's school leavers should be taking their first step into adulthood this month,' writes London's newspaper *The Mirror*. 'But a big hurdle lies in their way: Unemployment. In April, 1.2 million people below the age of 25 had no work, 37 per cent of all unemployed were younger than 25. In 1984, only 18 per cent of 16 year olds held jobs.' The newspaper comments: 'It is an irony that we begin the Year of the Youth with mass unemployment. It would be better to call 1985 the Year of the Youth in Despair.' "

Article in East Germany's newspaper *Young World*

In 1985, we foreign-trade greenhorns still had to go to college to learn the basics of the profession, but we also had to do weekly practice days with our employers. By working in different departments on a rotating basis, we all could make up your minds about where we would like to be placed after college. Naturally everyone wanted to go into a department that had client contact, preferably with westerners.

Work aside, the weekends were what we teenagers really lived for. Anyone not wanting to go out dancing was a bore. My favourite disco at the time was located on the second floor of the House of the Teacher (a sort of headquarters for....ermm, teachers). I had gathered a little gang around me. Unfortunately, whether it be Simone, Beatrix, Annett, Rudi, Heike, Jens, Grit, Bengs or Kerstin, I can't remember any of their faces any more. Though what still sticks in my mind are the girl's kissing abilities. Divine!

It may seem a bit strange that we went to the teachers' headquarters to go dancing, but in East Germany purpose-built discos were a rarity. Most nightly dancing places were normal cafés, restaurants, canteens or youth clubs during the day.

According to *Melody & Rhythm*, East Germany's equivalent of the *NME*, the purpose of discos was to "entertain,... inform and contribute to the crystallisation of sophisticated cultural and educational needs and consequently the development of socialist personalities". Whatever! In reality, all us teens and twens were after was dancing, having a good time, meeting friends and preferably getting laid. But in a country where propaganda labelled workplaces as "battle stations for peace" discos, too, had to serve a more serious purpose.

Capitalism was hollow and shallow; socialism was deep and meaningful! And so disc jockeys were referred to as record entertainers or disco presenters. Yet not everyone could call himself a disco presenter and earn some spare cash on the weekends. Oh no – like all artists, disc jockeys too had to impress a jury first to get a licence. And the level of licence granted (ranging from amateur to professional) determined the fee they could charge. In retrospect, I think it was quite a good idea to test people's capabilities first before letting them loose on an audience. At least this system ensured that a certain level of artistry was maintained at all times.

One rule for disc jockeys was that 60 per cent of the songs played had to be performed by artists from the DDR or other communist countries. The remaining 40 per cent could be from the west. Why was this rule in place? The DDR didn't want to pay exorbitant sums of money in royalties to the west. However, few disco goers gave a damn about the state's finances. We wanted to dance to the songs we were familiar with from the chart shows on West German radio and TV stations. DJs were occasionally checked out by plain-clothes inspectors from the licensing authority, so they used little tricks to ensure the masses got what they wanted without breaking the 60/40 rule too obviously. No disco presenter was prepared to risk losing their licence over this issue. The most popular ruse was to play lots of DDR songs very early in the evening, while a venue was still filling up. However, as soon as a place was packed and the dancing started, only western songs were on the play list. Another trick was to announce an East German song but to actually play a West German one. After all, what would a middle-aged inspector know about the latest pop bands?

Discos usually started fairly early in the evening. Often, doors opened at seven pm for an eight pm start. By nine pm, places were heaving with people. Club Cola (the DDR's answer to Coca Cola) mixed with brandy, whisky or vodka were the most popular drinks with clubbers. I preferred a more exotic cocktail called Green Meadow – Curacao with orange or apple juice. Though unlike dancing, gossiping and French kissing, I could also do without drinking when going out. In my experience, pulling girls was best done with a clear head. Speed was of the essence when making a move. By one am, just after the last slow dance finished, the neon lights would go on. This usually was crunch time for couples who had formed that evening. Would the switch on turn out to be a turn off? Thankfully I was spared such an embarrassing experience.

THE BIG BANG

New Year's Eve celebrations in Germany have, for a long time, been a noisy affair. At midnight the old year is traditionally driven out with fireworks. These days, shopkeepers have to come up with ever more clever ideas to shift maximum quantities of fireworks. Back in the DDR, shop assistants had to ration the pyrotechnics to make them last longer. In our family we preferred just watching the fireworks. Only a couple of times did Mum put on Dad's long johns and begin queueing in the cold at seven am to get my brother and me some pyrotechnics, while the two of us were still snuggled up in bed.

Considerable planning was required for a memorable New Year's Eve. If you wanted to go out on the 31 December you were well advised to make up your mind very, very early in the year. Parties in restaurants, cafés or clubs were extremely popular and most partygoers booked their seats one year in advance – often when leaving the previous year's New Year's Eve party. Yet, in 1985 Cordi and I only bought our tickets two months in advance – we were friends with a waitress in a small café near the city centre. The place was nothing special but the tickets were cheap and we did not have anything else planned for the last day of the year. On the night, the two of us were quite disappointed to see that we were sharing our table with a pensioner couple and a nerdy father and son. The ticket price of 20 marks (eight dollars) did not only include a three-course meal but also a quarter bottle of bubbly per person. By the time we had moved on to a newly ordered bottle of Bulgarian white wine we were already in a jolly good mood. We sang and danced, talked with strange accents and entertained our table with silly jokes. In the end the party was so much fun that we stayed right to the end until four o'clock in the morning.

Cordi and I might not have felt our best on that New Year's Day, but hangovers aside, 1986 got off to a promising start. In January, the Jugendtourist holiday tours for the year were announced in work places up and down the country. My company was allocated 13 foreign trips, each for two people. I immediately went to Cordelia and we looked up all the available destinations in her old school atlas. None of the tours were to the west. After careful consideration, we decided that I would apply for the trip to Hungary as our first choice (one week, full board for 400 marks - 160 dollars - per person), with the week in Bulgaria for 1,000 marks (400 dollars) being the second choice. In my diary that day I wrote, "The thought of us lying on the beach at the Black Sea gave us both big smiles."

In 1986, the conditions under which DDR individuals could travel to the west became less stringent. The person being visited no longer had to be an immediate family member and less important events, like a cousin's first day in school, were now accepted as valid reasons for travelling. It was a pity Cordelia and I did not have any relatives in the west. But even if we did have family there we would not have known about those changes. To avoid being inundated by too many applications for trips to the west, the new amendments to the existing travel directive were not made public at the time.

The general public only learnt about them when it was too late – after the DDR had ceased to exist.

It was the same with the truth about the full extent of the Chernobyl nuclear power plant disaster in April that year. While the West German population was warned to avoid mushrooms and milk for the foreseeable future, no such warnings were deemed necessary by the DDR authorities. Instead, our media ensured us that radiation levels in the DDR remained low. It was only a matter of time until people started joking that our border fortifications were obviously so good, they even stopped radioactivity move between the two Germanys. Whatever disasters happened in the outside world, East Germans did not lose their sense of humour:

Q: "Why are cucumbers imported from Chernobyl twice as expensive as home-grown ones?"

A: "Because of their glow-in-the-dark properties they can also be used as flashlights."

THE GLAND FROM ABROAD AND A
HOMEGROWN HITLER-STYLE MOUSTACHE

For a teenager like me, Chernobyl was far away and, besides, I was in a joyful mood. Not only had my company offered to take me on after college with a starting monthly salary of 650 marks (260 dollars) and 20 days annual leave, but I was also allowed to stay in Department 4. Department 4 was responsible for the DDR-wide import and export of mirrors and industrial glass, including laminated float and automotive glass. It was not the products I was particularly keen on, but the people working in Department 4. Like virtually everywhere in the DDR, professional rivalry among them was non-existent and on top of that they were a fun bunch to be with. Dr Dressler, the department's director was generous, well travelled, very sophisticated and always had a friendly word. Hannah and Dieter were the jolly chubbies with roaring laughs who liked their ciggies and booze. Dagmar was the single parent with a wicked sense of humour. Liane liked her make-up and was outrageously funny just being herself. Achim was the tall, skinny and overly camp departmental bitchy gay guy with a shrieking voice. Silke, Danuta and Verena were the cuties who liked to party. Babsy lived alone with her cat and always spoke her mind, but had a heart of gold. With Steffen, every conversation led to the subject of height – he was a bit on the smallish side. Kirsten can best be described as the DDR's own version of Bridget Jones and

Bärbel, my favourite, was a petite, slightly posh mother hen with a witty mind, who loved her only son to bits. She took an immediate liking to me. They were the fun people.

I tried to keep a healthy distance from colleagues like Marion, with her permed hair, frilly blouses and annoying communist views. But Marion's unshakeable believe in the victory of communism was nothing compared to Katarina, not only a colleague but also the daughter of the DDR's Foreign Trade Minister. When she was around, the slightest criticism of our state always led to an endless debate.

According to her, "instead of whinging about problems, it is up to us people to make things better." How I, a 19-year-old teenager, could have possibly changed our society to a more liberal and less security-conscious one she did not say.

I once had a huge row with her because a Free German Youth meeting scheduled for working hours had been pushed back to after work. Having already arranged my weekly visit to my grandparents for that day, I told Katarina that I would not attend the meeting. As soon as I had finished the sentence her pale face turned red with anger. The eyes, as usual surrounded by dark circles, looked at me with loathing. She demanded that I stand my grandparents up. Stand my grandparents up for a stupid political meeting? If she thought I was going to do that, she had another thing coming.

I heatedly told her what I thought of that idea: "The Free German Youth organisation will always be there. But my grandparents are already in their seventies. So it's them who I will be seeing tonight. Full stop."

One thing led to another and finally we had a shouting match par excellence. I suggested that she sticks her meeting. Our argument ended with her storming out. I had a lovely evening with my grandparents and nothing happened as a result of my decision. I mean nothing happened immediately, but incidents like these were closely monitored by supervisors and could eventually affect an employee's climbing of the career ladder.

One thing foreign traders were actively discouraged from was having close contact with western foreigners. Everyone who joined the company had to lay bare all their friends and family members living abroad. Employees were also required to report any future contact with foreigners to the Personnel Department. If, for example, a western tourist would ask me for directions in the street, I was officially required to take his name and address and pass the details immediately on to Human Resources. What a ludicrous request. During my employment with Glas-Keramik, I befriended many westerners outside of my working life. No one's details were ever passed on by me. Being desperate to make contact with people from outside of our small and insular country, I began to build up an extensive network of international pen pals over the years. It started with a West German magazine that Grandad had smuggled across the Iron Curtain. In it was an article about an American pen friend club. I wrote them a postcard asking for my address to be published in their newsletter, which they duly did – free of charge for a "poor" commie kid like me. From then on, a regular stream of international letters arrived in my letterbox. Nearly every day I got post from countries such as Algeria, Australia, Belgium, Bulgaria, Canada, Denmark, Ethiopia, France, Great Britain, Hungary, Japan, Spain, Yugoslavia or West Germany. These days, it's hard for anyone to imagine the excitement I felt when reading about my pen pal's everyday lives. Their letters were my windows to the world behind the borders of the DDR. Holding them in my hand was for me the next best thing to being with my distant friends. In my replies I was honest, without being overly critical, about the DDR. The last thing I wanted to happen was being responsible for Dad losing his business trips to the west.

I had no doubt that the Stasi was reading at least some, if not all, of my letters, yet it did not stop me from expressing myself truthfully. In a letter to Miki from Japan, I once wrote about how strange it was to have the Berlin Wall so close, knowing that right behind it people were also living normal lives, yet under a totally different political system. I never received a reply and thought my pen friend's interest in me had waned. Yet Miki called one day, asking why I hadn't answered her last two letters. During our conversation it became clear that "someone" had made one of my letters, and two of hers, disappear in an attempt to get us both jumping to wrong conclusions. Quite a clever strategy and no prize for guessing who that smart "someone" was. To avoid similar incidents in the future I started to pay an extra 50 pfennigs (20 cents) for every outgoing letter, to have them sent by registered delivery. Never again did a letter vanish.

I also exchanged little presents with my pen pals. Often I just asked for typical foods from their countries but once in a while I dared to put in a special request. Olives, for example, featured high on my wish list. Our shops only sold them once in a blue moon. In return, I sent out sweets, little books on East Berlin or arty items, like prints, etchings or photos by DDR artists. Exchanging music was another big thing. Over the years I posted dozens of tapes containing a compilation of my favourite tunes (all West German) and in return was inundated with regional pop songs from all over the world. Surprisingly none of the small packets coming or going were ever confiscated by DDR customs. Maybe someone at the postal-screening Stasi section "Place 12" had taken a liking to me...

There was one small packet I will never forget. It was from Miki and arrived a few days before my twenty-first birthday. After unwrapping it, I found myself holding a proper Nikon camera. It was a compact one, but still an expensive model. I saw it in a West Berlin department store selling for the equivalent of 100 pounds, when the Wall came down! I just could not believe a pen friend would send me such an expensive gift. Naturally my old Russian camera was shelved the very same day.

But not all pen pals were like Miki. Ammar from Algeria, for example, once sent me figs, yet instead of buying a packet or two in a shop he went for figs he had picked and dried himself. On opening the parcel I was greeted by dozens of unfamiliar looking yellow beetles. The whole lot went into the bin. The only thing I managed to salvage from the contents was some strange looking seed he had also included. According to his letter it was from a gland that was growing in his garden. A growing gland? It sounded disgusting and didn't make any sense to me but Dad planted the seed in our allotment anyway. Six months later a holly bush emerged. We followed Ammar's lead and for years the bush was known as "the gland". It took a long time for me to realise that Ammar must have misspelled the word "plant". Unfortunately, our friendship ended well before I got this moment of enlightenment. I stopped writing to him after he asked me to send him some Adidas sneakers and Adolf Hitler's book *Mein Kampf*. The book request totally freaked me out. He also did not seem to have grasped which of the two Germanys I was from. I too would have loved to own a pair of Adidas sneakers. Yet all I could get my hands on in East Germany at the time were a pair of white, no-name trainers with Velcro fasteners imported from France, costing around 200 marks (80 dollars). When wearing them I too did what every respectable East German teenager did at the time to give off the impression they owned a pair of fashionable (yet unavailable) high tops: I stuffed my trouser legs into the white tennis socks I was wearing. Voila, from a distance no one could see the difference. From a very great distance, that is. I was so proud of that look that I even went to a photographer to have a full-length picture taken. Aaargh! When I finally got hold of my first pair of Adidas trainers from Dad a year later I immediately stopped committing this heinous fashion crime.

On the subject of embarrassing photos, I have to own up to one more fashion faux pas: a Hitler-style moustache which I sported for a few months in 1986. It was in no way a political statement. I grew the tache to stand out from the crowd. And I did. Anything to avoid following the herd, that was my motto. Sometimes I even darkened it slightly with Mum's mascara. Worn together with my khaki outfit and thin black leather tie I must have looked quite fascist. Surprisingly the police did not stop me once. They were probably far too busy keeping a watchful eye on the growing number of skinheads. After a few months, my parents' nagging finally bore fruits and I shaved the darned thing off. I had become tired of constantly having to explain myself.

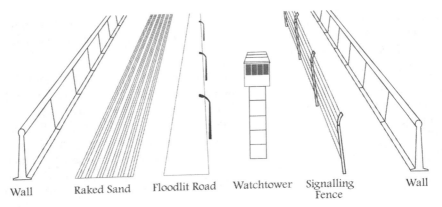

Wall   Raked Sand   Floodlit Road   Watchtower   Signalling Fence   Wall

Layout of the Berlin Wall

East Berlin street scene

During my short-lived moustache period

Omnipresent DDR apartment block: type QP 71

Cordi

In the 80s many DDR homes had picture galleries. Most of our prints were by Carl Spitzweg

My new baseball cap – courtesy of Nan

Cordi in front of 'our' Palace Hotel

On the set of a TV production

Protesters storm the headquarters of the Stasi in early 1990

Dad revisits the presidential palace and the wall he used to guard back in 1959

For more pictures please visit www.ironcurtainkid.com

What the DDR lacked in fashion sense it made up for in unenviable records, like that of alcohol consumption. East Germany was in the top of the international boozing league, up there with countries like Luxembourg, Hungary and Ireland. In the 1960s, the average DDR citizen drank four litres of spirits a year; by the late Eighties this figure had rise to 16 litres. (West Germany lagged behind with 12 litres.) On top of this, statistically every East German gulped down nearly 150 litres of beer annually.

Why did we drink so much? The easiest answer would be to say that they wanted to escape the dreary reality of everyday life. But this would not hit the nail on the head. Although alcohol consumption was not encouraged by the state, increasing alcohol production was a convenient way of tackling the problem of ever-growing personal savings. A 2007 survey by British bank Alliance & Leicester concluded that 29 per cent of British households had no money put away for a rainy day. In the DDR we took too much of it to the Staatsbank (State Bank). East Germans could not always spend their dosh on the things they wanted when they wanted them. People's net income increased annually by 4.3 per cent, yet the production of consumer goods only grew by a yearly four per cent. Many high-priced electrical items were in short supply, so more and more cash was put into bank accounts. In the mid-Sixties, East Germans had collectively saved 35 billion marks (14 billion dollars). By the late Eighties, this figure had risen to 150 billion marks (60 billion dollars), the equivalent of around 9,000 marks (3,600 dollars) of savings per person for which the state had to pay five billion marks (two billion dollars) in annual interest. The likes of Sambalita (passion fruit liqueur), Timm's Saurer (vodka with lemon), Kristall (vodka), Gotano (vermouth), Kruiden Schipper (digestive), Oldmaster (whisky) or Amitie (brandy) represented convenient ways to keep the level of savings at bay. Over the years it had become common practice for the Central Planning Bureau to get spirit manufacturers to boost their output when other industries indicated that they would not meet set targets for the production of consumer goods. If for example two million marks worth of refrigerators could not be produced for whatever reason, some other consumer product had to make up for the monetary shortfall. Alcohol was the ideal replacement. It was cheap to produce and offered a good profit margin. And as it was always available, consumers made good use of it.

Another reason for our high collective alcohol consumption was that we DDR folk were very sociable. Having many friends meant knowing many people who were able to help out with services or goods that were in short supply. And since private telephone lines did not exist in abundance either, friends met up more often for a drink, or two, or three...

Many East Germans even consumed alcohol regularly at work. Of course, the DDR's health and safety regulations strictly forbade that but it hardly bothered people. Being in employment in the DDR meant being virtually immune from getting sacked or being made redundant. The law was very protective of employees – one of the advantages of living in a state ruled by the working class. Every dismissal had to be sanctioned by the union and if a laid-off employee had no job to go to, it was up to the authorities to organise a suitable work place. Employees in return could resign anytime by just giving two weeks notice. They were also allowed to place job-seeking ads in newspapers, while companies could only advertise available positions in the print media in exceptional circumstances. No firm was to lure away workers from another employer by temptation. This policy forced companies to further and develop existing members of staff which led to many people staying for decades with one employer.

"The burden of labouring for parasitic exploiters has been replaced by the people working for themselves and the society."

The Law of Work

When it came to alcohol, my department at Glas-Keramik, was often also very merry. It was quite a regular occurrence for someone to get a bottle out in the afternoon two or three times a week. Sometimes there was a reason for it like a colleague's birthday or someone's promotion. On many other occasions, the department just got together for an afternoon of impromptu drinking. "Today, alcohol again!" I confided once to my diary after we had afternoon drinks for three days in a row. The department's most favourite tipple was Goldbrand – a 32 per cent by volume brandy. The 750-millilitre bottle sold for 14.50 marks (5.80 dollars). I wasn't particularly keen on brandy but usually that did not stop me from downing a few glasses. One day in the early spring of 1986, I bit off more than I could chew. Our department got together in the office to celebrate God-knows-what for the afternoon, and I emptied one glass of brandy after another. Three hours later I paid the bill for my binge drinking. I could only express myself in slurred speech and my limbs seemed to have developed a mind of their own. Embarrassingly I had become incapable of going home. My colleague Hannah took me to her place and called my parents to arrange a pick up. When they arrived Mum gave Hannah quite an earful. She wanted to know why no one at work had stopped me from drinking myself into a stupor. Even without Mum's anger, I had learnt my lesson. Never again did I want to relive such a hangover. Ever since then I have known when it's time for me to put the glass down.

I wish the same could be said about the DDR administration. The country's security paranoia was out of this world. Every company in the DDR, however big or small, had a security guard sitting at their gates. As forces in West Germany were apparently ready to strike at any given time, our state demanded constant vigilance from its citizens. However, most of our country's doormen were pensioners or early retirees. Take our company's concierge for example. How much of a deterrent to a deceiving and cunning enemy could a little lady in her late fifties be? The building I was working from had two separate entrances, one for employees and one for visitors. While the staff entrance gave you access to all floors, the visitor's entrance just lead to a reception area with a lobby and conference room where drinks and snacks were served. DDR suppliers could visit us in our offices, western clients on the other hand were not allowed further than the reception area. One day our concierge mistook a very plain looking West German client for a DDR supplier. Instead of sending him to the other entrance, she allowed him to visit some of my colleagues on the second floor. In an environment where employees had to flash their company ID card every time they were entering or leaving the building, this slip-up did not go down very well with the managing director. She was furious when she heard the news.

But what our concierge lacked in vigilance, she made up for in personality. If you heard a "Psst, psst" upon entering the building you knew she had had another clear out at home and was trying to flog you something. Once, she waved a pair of worn, brown men's shoes at me. Despite my immediate "No, thank you" as I walked past her window, she insisted that I try them on, "just to be on the safe side". Through gritted teeth I obliged. As it became obvious that the shoes were two sizes too big, she switched strategies and offered me a pair of used red stilettos. "Maybe for the girlfriend?" she suggested. I declined outright, but Mrs Concierge took it in her stride. I hadn't even left the area when I heard the next "Psst, psst!" and it was another colleague's turn to view her merchandise.

Guards were just one part of East Germany's security strategy. Another one was to seal managers' offices at the end of each working day. This way any unauthorised access could be detected the following morning. In addition, all employees had to lock their papers and files away when they finished work. Drawers, cabinets and rooms – nothing was to be left open overnight. To make sure employees followed security regulations, quarterly security checks took place after working hours. An unlocked drawer usually resulted in the line manager having a serious chat with the culprit the following morning. Strangely, no one in charge ever picked up on the fact that everyone hid their keys in the same place – the pencil holder on their desk. Any intruder would have had an easy time spying in our company.

"The shaping of the developed socialist society in the German Democratic Republic under the conditions of the intensified international class struggle demands that the protection of official secrets...in all areas of society is guaranteed and constantly perfected, which will contribute to a general strengthening of the German Democratic Republic."

Order for the Protection of Official Secrets – 1971

It is not surprising that in such an environment most companies even declared their internal telephone directory a classified document which was not to be made available to outsiders. *"Nur für den Dienstgebrauch"* (for official use only) was the lowest security classification and also the heading on my company's internal telephone directory. The next step up in the DDR's confidentiality classification league was the *"Vertrauliche Dienstsache"* (confidential official matter). The highest classification given to a document was *Geheime Kommandosache"* (secret command matter) – papers read and issued by the Politburo bore this marking. Anyone handling such highly confidential documents was quite disadvantaged. People privy to state secrets could forget being allowed any private contact with westerners, let alone being granted an exit visa for visiting the other side of the Iron Curtain upon retirement. For that reason, I was very happy with only having been entrusted with documents on a telephone directory level.

THE PRICE IS NOT RIGHT

I, like most DDR employees, saw a few things at work that were not to be made public. Some of our suppliers, for example, were operating under conditions that made you doubt whether the DDR really was a top industrial nation. The fact that high outputs were still achieved, despite leaky roofs and fifty-year-old production plants, speaks for the innovative workers, who were experienced improvisers. If, for example, a machine's transmission belt snapped and a new one had to be ordered, an old pair of tights would ensure that the production continued in the meantime. Repairs on imported machines were usually more problematic. If a spare part had to be bought in the west, the manufacturer had to apply for the allocation of Deutschmarks or dollars first. This was a very time consuming process that could leave a machine out of action for weeks. An unthinkable scenario for any managing director, even more so when export targets had to be met. Often, desperate suppliers would call us for help, and we would arrange for a friendly business partner in the west to get the required item. Twice I was handed bits of machinery in business meetings with a western distributor, free of charge. Such donations to keep the wheels of our industry turning were no act of charity but ensured that existing ties were furthered. Doing business with our country was very profitable for any western company. 60 per cent of East Germany's gross national product came from exports despite the fact that one-third of our goods and technologies fell short of international standards. Consequently, top quality items were sold to the west, while DDR citizens had to make do with seconds. Three very popular jokes at the time were:

The Politburo visits a light bulb factory. The managing director boasts: "Only five per cent of our production are rejects." Erich Honecker turns to the Minister for the Economy and asks: "Will that be enough to satisfy the demand in the DDR?"

Q: "Why do our streets have so many pot holes?"

A: "The DDR hasn't found a western buyer for them yet."

A toilet paper manufacturer only manages to reach 50 per cent of its annual production target. To appear in a better light, the managing director reports a 70 per cent success to the Ministry for Economy. The ministry increases the figure to 90 per cent when reporting to the Central Committee of the Communist Party. The Central Committee changes it to 100 per cent when providing the Politburo with the statistics. Erich Honecker finally gets the report on his desk, looks at the toilet paper manufacturer's figure and decides: "We will export 50 per cent of their production, the rest will be sold in the DDR."

One of East Germany's most famous brands, Meissen Porcelain, was produced mainly for export. Only second, third and even fourth quality items were sold in our country. Bed linen was another example. Some years we exported more than four billion sets, only to import the same amount later in the year to relieve a national shortage caused by people panic buying.

The DDR had deliberately chosen to operate a non-convertible currency, labelled funny money by westerners. The DDR mark's status allowed it to be free of manipulation by international financial markets. But our economy had to pay a high price for this convenience. East Germany's main trading partners in the west were Australia, France, Great Britain, Japan and West Germany. Because we couldn't pay for western goods with DDR marks, we had to earn Deutschmarks, dollars, francs, pounds or yen first before we could start buying from these countries. That required constant exporting of goods for hard currency, and the competition, particularly from Asian countries, was stiff at any time. Consequently, despite high production costs, our products often had to be sold at silly prices. In the early Eighties, if the average export item cost 100 DDR marks (40 dollars) to make, we could only sell it to the west for 50 Deutschmarks (20 dollars). In the late Eighties, things had taken a turn to the worse. By then 20 per cent of our production plants were over 20 years old and manufacturing costs had shot up. Now four DDR marks (1.60 dollars), instead of two, needed to be spent to earn one Deutschmark (40 cents). Selling below the cost of production doesn't sound very economical, and it wasn't. While typing contracts in the department selling Meissen Porcelain to West Germany, I regularly saw elaborate figurines with manufacturer's prices of 2,000 DDR marks (800 dollars) being sold for just 200 Deutschmarks (80 dollars). If anything good came of our rock bottom prices, it was that consumers in capitalist countries could regularly net themselves bargains. DDR clothes and electrical items were usually sold by western home shopping catalogue companies or department stores under their own brand names. The Ariete mixer, Model 64 ("Extremely powerful. Three speeds. Automatic whip expulsion. Ergonomic handgrip. Stainless steel whips. The real mayonnaise, home-made in only 90 seconds.") which my grandparents once bought in West Berlin came with Italian inspired packaging and a guarantee from an Italian company. They were quite surprised when closer inspection of the mixer at home revealed the logo of East Germany's number one electrical appliance manufacturer, AKA Electric, just next to the mark "Made in GDR".

But not all importers insisted on disguising a product's true origin. A few DDR brands might sound familiar to western consumers: Bechstein pianos, MZ motorbikes, ORWO films, NARVA light bulbs, Pentacon cameras, World Champion accordions, Germina sports equipment (also sold under the names Fanal and Turntex), Saxon watches, Foron knives, Veritas sewing machines, Erika typewriters or Plasticart/Playfix model kits.

East Germany was one of the biggest European furniture exporters and THE leading interior lights exporter. We manufactured many products for IKEA and, among other things, windows for West German cars. We even sold production plants to the west. Volkswagen and Daimler Benz (Germany's equivalent to Vauxhall) produced their car parts with machines "Made in GDR". Capitalist countries bought our leather, wood, eggs, meat, fish, sweets, beer and spirits. Earning hard currency definitely wasn't easy for the DDR. Even more so as lots of it was needed for the import of production plants and consumer goods. Western consumer goods were important to the government as they could be sold at a premium and got us East Germans to tap into our ever-increasing savings.

To achieve this, two different kinds of shops opened – Delikat (Delicious) and Exquisit. The purpose of the Delikat shops was to generate cash by selling high-quality foodstuffs (or what was perceived as such). Exquisit shops specialised in upmarket fashion and cosmetics. A factor common to both was that some of their prices were eye watering. A bottle of an ordinary Cotes du Rhone wine cost 35 marks (14 dollars) and a bottle of multivitamin juice sold for 7.80 marks (three dollars). Smoked eel topped the price league. Its kilo price was a whopping 190 marks (76 dollars). Tinned pineapple rings were also classed a luxury item. Tins sold for 18 marks (seven dollars) each. For someone in the UK earning 20,000 pounds, this would equate to them being asked to pay 30 pounds for 340 grams of pineapple rings. The Delikat shop near my workplace was fairly large and even had a Far East section, which I thought was great. Whenever I felt like cooking something from the Chinese cookbook Dad had bought me in the west, I could at least use original ingredients. Whether it was Kikkoman soy sauce, Nasi Goreng spice mix, seaweed or lotus root, this Delikat shop had it in stock. And just to make sure I did not miss anything interesting or rare, a quick browse in the Deli (as the shops were commonly referred to), became a daily lunchtime routine for me. But you could still draw blanks. One recipe I wanted to try called for tinned octopus; it was never imported.

Another lunchtime routine of mine was to pop into the many boutique-style Exqusit shops, which were also near my workplace. Their dark brown or black wooden interior combined with lots of chrome, piped music and indirect lighting gave these places a very sophisticated atmosphere. Some of the boutiques specialised in clothes, others in shoes, fashion accessories or cosmetics. Trendy shop-floor dummies sported the latest fashions. Strategically placed spotlights accentuated individual goods. Exquisit shop assistants were notorious for being rude and arrogant to customers. The secret to get their respect was to appear affluent. To help create this impression, I regularly looked down my nose at the most expensive items in store. In return, Exquisit shop assistants often greeted me upon entering with: "Nice to see you again.". Little did they know that my monthly take-home pay at the office was a modest 750 marks (300 dollars).

For a few years in the Eighties, most of my money went on clothes. I was definitely one of Exquisit's best customers. My love affair with the shops began in 1985 with a black silk French-made bow tie that cost 40 marks (16 dollars). I had no idea when I would ever wear it, but the moment I saw it lying on a cushion of tissue paper in its open box, sitting in a display cabinet in my favourite Exquisit store, I just knew I had to have it. I could hardly contain my excitement as I wrote out the cheque. That evening I tried the bow-tie on, looking at myself from ever angle in the mirror and imagining a life of James Bond-style parties where everyone and everything was beautiful. Over the years, my spending at Exquisit spun out of control – first a pair of light-blue swimming trunks for 67 marks (27 dollars) before going on a holiday to Hungary, then a pair of black leather gloves lined with lamb's wool for 105 marks (42 dollars) to beat the cold Berlin winters. A black Finnish winter jacket with mock fur trim and a husky print on the back for 400 marks (160 dollars) was the next must-have item. Two fleecy polyester scarves – one turquoise and one yellow – followed shortly afterwards (60 marks each – 24 dollars). For a trip to the Soviet Union, I just had to have a dark blue travel bag for 265 marks (106 dollars). To stand out in meetings I wasted 188 marks (76 dollars), or 25 per cent of my monthly net pay, on an Austrian-made leather-bound notebook. I can't remember what possessed me to buy a leather-covered hip flask for the same amount only shortly afterwards. I never used it – unlike my pair of silvery trousers for 240 marks (96 dollars) which I wore three to four times a week, especially when going out in the evenings. Their metal-look fabric was a head turner wherever I went. One of my best purchases ever!

Over the years, I bought at least 20 shirts at 135 marks each (54 dollars), five pairs of trousers (between 150 and 250 marks each – 60 to 100 dollars), 15 pairs of shoes (around 150 marks – 60 dollars – each) and five ties at 60 marks (24 dollars) a shot. My most treasured purchases were a dark blue tuxedo for 800 marks (320 dollars) and a pair of sleek, shiny black patent leather shoes that I spent a third of my monthly pay cheque on. After all, I needed something appropriate to match my very first Exquisit purchase, the bow tie, when going to a theatre or concert hall. The tuxedo was "Made in GDR" while the shoes were an Italian make. Now I really felt like James Bond, parading up and down my room at home looking at myself in the full-length mirror. My attire was proof that East Germans could be glamorous too, even if we had to pay through the nose for it.

One thing that I have to give the Exquisit shops credit for is that they were very generous if any of the purchased goods were not 100 per cent up to scratch. If, for example the colour inside your brand-new shoes rubbed off on your socks, you could easily recoup one third of the shoes' purchase price by complaining. I did it regularly. Occasionally, a shop assistant took a liking to me and even refunded me 50 per cent.

Despite regularly claiming money back for minor faults and imperfections, in some months my eyes were much bigger than my account balance. My bank was not happy whenever I made too many cheques payable to Exquisit – DDR accounts had no overdraft facilities. On those occasions, my punishment was that I had to wait for at least three months before I was issued a new chequebook once the old one had come to an end.

People joked about the Exquisit prices:

Erich Honecker visits a factory and asks the managing director whether all workers have received a Christmas bonus. "Of course" says the director. "And what did you do with the money?" Honecker wants to know. "I have bought a small house and paid the rest into my savings account." answers the managing director. Honecker is very pleased with such a sensible approach and asks the foreman what he did with his bonus. "I have bought a motorbike and paid the rest into my savings account," is his reply. Honecker likes the sound of that as well. Finally he asks a young worker: "And what did you do with your bonus?". "I have bought an Exquisit shirt," is his answer. "And what about the rest?" Honecker probes. "My mum kindly contributed the rest," is the reply.

No household had to pay more than five percent of its monthly income on rent but what fashionados like me saved on accommodation, we had to fork out on inflated prices when boosting our wardrobe. It was a paradox of the DDR that not a single price in the country reflected the true value of an item. You were either undercharged or overcharged for goods and services. My first rented apartment, a one-bedroom flat, cost 34 marks (14 dollars) a month. An imported, no-name, denim jacket from Finland, on the other hand, set me back 380 marks (152 dollars). Of course, no one forced you to shop in an "Ex", and it was possible to get dressed for much less in other shops. But if you wanted to pep up your appearance with a little bit of exclusivity and had no relatives in the west, then it simply had to be Exquisit. My friend Dörte, who I got to know at work while queueing in the canteen for sausages and potato salad at lunchtime, once bought a coat in Exquisit for 900 marks (360 dollars). That was an obscene amount of money for anyone to spend on a dress; even more so as she had only just finished high school. And to make matters worse, she never wore it. But her parents worked for the United Nations in Geneva (when younger she occasionally even got to go on visits to Switzerland), so she could afford to be a bit choosier.

I, on the other hand, got plenty of wear out of my Exquisit purchases. It was a pity that for the designer prices you only got no-name brands in return. Labels like Chicastyle, P.R.I.V.A.T.E, Jaques Greneta/Paris or Story Club were hardly Haute Couture.

My real addiction was to eau de toilette. I shunned the DDR fragrances, like La Grande or Wild River. Instead I collected imported bottles (average retail price: 50 marks – 20 dollars). To me they were the very essence of the high life. It was disappointing that men could not hope for top name designer fragrances – nevertheless, I never left home without a squirt of Sergio Soldano (a real stinker), a dab of Mascouline Or, a splash of Storm or a dash of R de Capucci. I had bottles in various shapes and sizes, mainly from Italy and France. And although I never added up how much I spent on them, I knew in the back of my mind that the sweet-smelling liquids in those little bottles on my bedroom dresser represented weeks of work back at the export/import office.

Most cosmetics sold by Exquisit were not exclusive by western standards. Men could buy Lynx products – hardly a boutique brand. And while the girls were able to get hold of Gloria Vanderbuilt fragrance and the DDR version of Yves Saint Laurent's Poison, much of the make-up offered was made by Bourjois, sold at Chanel prices.

If you had Deutschmarks at your disposal, you wouldn't waste your time in a Deli or an Ex but would head straight to your local Intershop. There you could get all the western goods you were familiar with from the commercials on West German telly. And no Chicastyle jeans or Sergio Soldano fragrance in sight. Instead, Levis jeans and Chanel perfume were sold. Being able to buy a few things in an Intershop was every DDR citizen's aim. Shop assistants there were given a 15 Deutschmarks allowance every month, but everyone else had to come up with their own ideas to get hold of some hard currency. I regularly asked foreigners in the streets whether they wanted to change foreign currency into DDR marks. I was not very good at it though, because most times I was too embarrassed to approach westerners. Yet I still managed to secure the occasional 20 Deutschmarks here and there, at a rather good exchange rate of one Deutschmark for three marks. Many East Germans were quite prepared to pay anything between five and ten DDR marks for one single Deutschmark. The black market rate for US dollars was one to 12, though the official rate was 2.50 DDR marks for one dollar. I spent whatever money I made in this way in an Intershop, or gave it to my grandparents to get me fashion items in West Berlin. We were taught in school how ruthless capitalists exploited the cheap workforce in Asia for profit maximisation. But then I discovered that the DDR was just as unscrupulous, when it came to making Deutschmarks. Two of my Intershop purchases bear silent witnesses to my fatherland's practice of buying cheap and selling dear. According to the labels, one sweatshirt was made in Indonesia, while a pair of shorts was manufactured in the Philippines. So much for socialism trying to make the world a better place.

WHEN CRIME PAYS

But who cares about morals when our ever-increasing living standard required funding by more and more hard currency coming into the country. Loans from western banks, which were also used to finance the DDR's social achievements, needed to be repaid. DDR economists had to come up with new ways of making money. One of them was the handling of West German rubbish. Waste disposal sites were created, fenced in and guarded to deter people from rummaging through the household rubbish West Germans had thrown out. Over the years, our state made 1.2 billion Deutschmarks (480,000 dollars) from refuse imports. Despite the security at the sites, wild stories regularly did the rounds about people climbing over the fences and finding new designer outfits and technical goods in perfect working order. As expected it was always a friend of a friend who was the lucky finder, never the storyteller. I believed all those "eye witness accounts" like I believed any other urban myth – not at all. (My most favourite myth was, where a couple comes back from a weekend trip to find their home has been broken into. Various things are missing but thankfully not the expensive camera. When a few weeks later the camera's film is being developed one of the photos shows the burglar's bare bottom with the wife's toothbrush in it – head first.) Another myth, and this time a typical DDR one, concerned people who had apparently complained about their Italian Exquisit shoes disintegrating when worn in wet conditions. Investigations by the authorities allegedly revealed that the importer, trying to buy as cheaply as possible, had mistakenly purchased so-called funeral shoes – one-use footwear which undertakers used to dress corpses. This story was so convincing that the Stasi even swung into action to investigate. They had to close their investigation shortly afterwards – this kind of profit maximisation never happened. In reality our state had discovered much more lucrative revenue streams.

There was the delivery of electricity to West Berlin, the treatment of West Berlin sewage or the sale of our blood (though not our sweat) to the west. Even weaponry seemed to be a legitimate way to make a bob or two. For seven years the DDR exported, very discreetly, old and new weaponry like machine guns, hand grenades, handguns, artillery, tanks and ammunition. Customers were countries Algeria, Ethiopia, India, Iran, Iraq, Mozambique, Nicaragua and Syria. This operation, though, was never seen as a major source of income. The turnover generated by weapon's exports between 1982 and 1989 was, at 250 million Deutschmarks (100 million dollars), not even a quarter of the amount we made with importing household rubbish.

Yet a rather more unusual income source was the so-called *Transitpauschale* (transit charge) – an annual amount payable by West Berlin because some of its underground lines cut through East Berlin territory. This was worth six million Deutschmarks, or 2.4 million dollars, each year. Furthermore, West Germany paid handsomely for its cars, ships and trains to use DDR infrastructure on their way to and from West Berlin. As it was an enclave, right in the middle of the DDR, the majority of westerners wanting to visit or leave West Berlin used East German roads or rail. In 17 years, this earned us roughly ten billion Deutschmarks or four billion dollars. But there was one more, rather shameful, export that provided the DDR with hard currency. We sold our "criminals" to the west.

Between 1963 and 1990 a total of 33,755, mainly political, prisoners, were driven (with their consent) by coach to West Germany. Occasionally East Germany also slipped in a few common criminals it wanted to get rid off. What an ingenious way to keep our country's crime rate down! The money the GDR demanded from West Germany was supposed to compensate for the education those prisoners had received as citizens of the German Democratic Republic. Until 1976, the amounts payable varied from person to person, with each prisoner being worth an average of 40,000 Deutschmarks (16,000 dollars). At the beginning of 1977, both sides agreed on an amount of 95,847 Deutschmarks (38,339 dollars) per person. However, to avoid international embarrassment, not a single Deutschmark ever changed hands. Instead West Germany delivered raw materials and industrial goods to the equivalent value. More than once, East Germany immediately sold the crude oil or uncut diamonds it had be given on the international markets. Over the period of the DDR's existence, goods worth totalling nearly 3.4 trillion Deutschmarks (1.4 trillion dollars) were sent eastwards to enable those prisoners to start a new life in the west.

It is said that the humanity of a political system can be judged by how well it treats its prisoners. In that respect the DDR, didn't cover itself with glory. The common convict in a DDR jail could only write three letters a month, which were censored, and was allowed to be visited for 60 minutes by a maximum of two people every second month. Pen and paper were not allowed in prison cells. During the day a prisoner could not lay or sit on the bed and at night hands had to be kept on top of the blanket at all times. Punishment for misbehaviour usually was the denial of visitors or a ban on sending and receiving letters. Lesser rule infringements were dealt with by a prohibition of watching television. Truly unruly characters could be put into intensified detention for up to 21 days. Imagine a cell without chair and bed, where a prisoner received just three slices of bread a day and would be given a hot meal only every third day.

Most convicts also had to work during their terms of imprisonment. Normal wages were paid for the work, however, 90 per cent of a prisoner's salary was kept by the prison to cover the cost of the stay. The remaining ten per cent was used to pay for court fees, fines or compensation. Any money left was put into savings for the prisoner to use after their release.

The DDR legal system differed substantially from the English system. All evidence – both against an accused and in their favour – was presented to a judge by the sole investigator – the Stasi. A defence lawyer's job was limited to ensuring that this presentation of evidence was balanced and contained a fair number of facts working in the defendant's favour. Prisoners and defence lawyers were only allowed to view the indictment a couple of hours prior to the start of a trial, but did not get their own copy. In many political cases, the Stasi handed down a sentence before the first hearing even took place. I am certainly glad I never made the acquaintance of the DDR justice system. But the DDR justice system also had some progressive elements. For example, house searches conducted by the police could only take place when two public witnesses, usually neighbours, were present. Petty cases did not go to court but were dealt with by a *Konfliktkommission*. This was a kind of ombudsman-jury headed by three volunteers which usually ordered offenders to pay a fine or compensation, or both, for any harm or damage caused. A *Konfliktkommission* judgement did not result in a criminal record.

In the Fifties and Sixties crime was considered to be a capitalist relic which would disappear altogether from our humanistic society as time went on. This turned out to be wishful thinking, yet over the decades crime rates did come down. In the Fifties, 870 crimes per 100,000 people were recorded; by 1987 this figure was down to 690 crimes. Compared to West Germany (7030 crimes per 100,000 people) and Great Britain (6750 crimes per 100,000 people) at the time, the DDR was a very safe country indeed. So safe that it was common for parents to leave their babies outside shops and department stores when going shopping. Murder was also rare. We had one murder per 100,000 people a year. West Germany's rate was five times higher.

The state also went to great lengths to take care of offenders who had been released from prison. No ex-jailbird had to worry about going flat hunting or writing job applications. Everyone was allocated accommodation and a working place on their release. Housing associations and companies were allocated ex-prisoners, and they had no say in the matter. Once it was Dad's team's turn having to integrate an ex-convict. His name was Ralf. He was in his early twenties, of medium height, a little stocky, with short brown hair and muscular, tattooed arms. Ralf never said what he did time for but more than once he mentioned that sex offenders came last in a prison's pecking order. Dad and his colleagues just put two and two together. In the beginning, Dad was sceptical about Ralf, but he seemed a good worker who helped out wherever a hand was needed. He even did overtime on a regular basis and never drank at work. Only when the team socialised after hours did Dad see a side of Ralf that made him feel uneasy. He would knock down one beer after another and, with the increased alcohol consumption he became loud-mouthed, complacent and arrogant towards women. Ralf's drunken arguments that women need to look up to a man and that every woman fancied him anyway, did not go down too well with female colleagues. No one was too surprised when a couple months later the Personnel Department informed the team one morning that Ralf would not be turning up for work again. The previous night he had been arrested for raping a woman. When Dad was subpoenaed as witness to the trial, he heard what had happened:

Coming home from the pub one evening, Ralf forced a woman, who was waiting at a bus stop, at knife-point to accompany him home. At the time he was lodging with an older lady. As Ralf and his victim entered the flat, he told the landlady that he did not want to be disturbed. After the poor woman had been raped in Ralf's room she finally managed to grab an empty wine bottle that stood next to the bed and clobbered her tormentor over the head. As Ralf lost consciousness, the woman ran half-naked into the street and screamed for help. The police arrived within five minutes.

Dad shook his head in disbelief when his and Ralf's eyes met on the day. Ralf quickly looked away. He insisted throughout the trial that he could not remember a thing as he was drunk. It did not help him. Unlike West German law, the DDR penal code did not consider drunkenness a mitigating factor. Ralf was sentenced to four years and banned from entering Berlin for five years after his release.

Towards the end of the DDR period, around 30,000 people were imprisoned – roughly 0.18 per cent of the population. While the UK keeps a slightly lower 0.13 per cent (78,000 people) locked up, the United States have a whopping 2.1 million prisoners. 0.78 per cent of the US population are behind iron bars – in percentage terms, four times more people than in East Germany.

BEING A PARTY POOPER

It was no secret that if you wanted to make a career in any of the state-owned companies, you had no choice but to become a member of the Communist Party. Naturally, I too was approached by one of the party's 44,000 full time employees and asked whether I would be interested in joining the two million members of the SED, the Socialist Unity Party. Hell, no! I was perfectly happy living my life without having to sit through two party meetings every month.

Although the Communist Party was always on the lookout for as many new members as possible, the application process was designed in a way that gave off the impression one was about to join a very exclusive club. Potential members had first to hand in a completed application form, two passport photos, a hand-written CV, two references and a detailed explanation why they wanted to join. Candidates then had to prove their worthiness for a year through the delivery of good results at work and extra curricular activities. After the probation period, they were invited to answer questions about themselves in front of a party committee which eventually decided, via a show of hands, whether the Socialist Unity Party should accept them as members. Successful applicants were then given a bunch of red carnations, along with their party membership book. The first month's membership fee was payable on the spot.

On paper the party was very choosy about who they took on board, in reality they had to reach recruitment targets. I must have looked like an easy target. But at the tender age of 18, I had no intention of committing myself to the party's course. What would have been the point? My membership would not have triggered any changes in the DDR. If anything, party members were expected to be less critical of our state than the average citizen. Following the official party line unconditionally was called "keeping party discipline" and demanded from every member. Members not publicly backing party decisions or, even worse, publicising political ideas and theories that differed from the Communist Party's official standpoint faced disciplinary action. The party wanted to appear united to the public at all times.

"The unity of the party, of the Politburo and of the Central Committee is our most precious possession."

Erich Honecker

Here is to show you what a sacred cow party unity was: When Erich Honecker was toppled by his Politburo chums in autumn 1989, he first put up a resistance. But the rule was that all Politburo decisions had to be made unanimously. To "keep party discipline" eventually he too voted in favour for his own stepping down as General Secretary.

While not very keen on becoming a party member myself, I certainly had no qualms about benefiting from the party. Every four years the SED held a party conference in Berlin, celebrating itself and its achievements. And to demonstrate to the people the success of its political work, additional goods were usually imported around conference time – whether it be bananas or new consignments of trendy western clothes sold at affordable prices in one of the Jugendmode (youth fashion) shops. For that reason the population liked the party conferences very much, but people couldn't resist poking fun, too. One song always making the rounds at party conference time was France Gall's hit *A Banda*, which had its German lyrics changed from:

Two oranges in the hair
and bananas round her waist,

Rosita wears
with her coconut dress.

to:

Two oranges a year
and bananas for the party conference,
the people shout: "Hooray,
communism is here".

Ok, the lyrics lose somewhat in translation but in German it all rhymes. Mind you the party conference delegates hardly had anything to laugh about. Sitting through endless speeches, all of which had to be pre-approved, was anything but a joy. So people came up with jokes like the following one:

A party member grabs the microphone during a party conference and spontaneously says: "I am comrade Schmidt and I have got three questions for comrade Honecker. Firstly, why can't we travel to the west freely? Secondly, why do we have to wait ten years to buy a new car? And thirdly, why don't our shops sell Spanish oranges all year round?" Erich Honecker, somewhat baffled, quickly replies: "Interesting questions. Let me answer them after a quick break." After the break another delegate fights his way to the mic and says: "I am comrade Petersen and I got four questions for comrade Honecker. Firstly, why can't we travel to the west freely? Secondly, why do we have to wait ten years to buy a new car? Thirdly, why don't our shops sell Spanish oranges all year round? And fourthly, where have those two Stasi employees taken comrade Schmidt to during the break?"

Reading the party speeches in the newspapers the following day was even more tedious than sitting through the actual conference itself. Little comments in brackets highlighted the reactions of the audience to speeches made on stage: applause, prolonged applause, prolonged applause with cheers, prolonged rhythmic applause with cheers, renewed prolonged rhythmic applause with cheers, renewed prolonged rhythmic applause with cheers leading to thunderous applause, renewed prolonged rhythmic applause with cheers leading to thunderous applause with cheers of hooray, renewed prolonged rhythmic applause with cheers leading to thunderous applause with cheers of hooray and intonation of the Internationale... Here is an extract of an Erich Honecker speech from the protocol of the Eighth Communist Party Conference in April 1971:

"Comrades! (*applause*)

Dear guests! (*lively applause*)

The Socialist Unity Party (*long applause*) has delivered good results (*prolonged applause*) with the development of socialism (*intense applause*) in the (*intense long applause*) German Democratic Republic (*prolonged strong applause*) for the Eighth Party Conference. (*rhythmic applause*) Every comrade from our party, (*strong rhythmic applause*) every citizen of our state (*thunderous applause*) can judge from their own experience (*frenzied applause*) that the way marked by the (*several minutes of frenzied applause)* Marxist- (*cheers*) Leninist party (*lively applause and cheers)* of the working class (*cheers and frenzied applause*) is correct (*cheers, joined in by all*) and successful. (*frenzied applause and enthusiastic cheers*) That is the purpose of socialism. (*cheers of hooray*) That's what we work (*general cheers and cheers of hooray*) and fight for. ('*Long shall he live, hip hip hooray!*')"

Reading such garbage always made me cringe.

Another tedious habit of our media was to permanently list a person's full name and title in a Byzantine style. It made official articles extremely hard to digest. Everyone in the DDR knew who Erich Honecker was but he was never referred to as just Erich Honecker. No, it was always, Erich Honecker, Head of the State Council, General Secretary of the Socialist United Party of Germany and Head of the Defence Council said this or did that. As if we all had collective amnesia, and were constantly struggling to remember who this guy was. Even worse was when he got together with leaders from other communist countries. Their titles alone would take up half the article. What a waste of paper. Just like all party conference reports. Only once did a sentence from a party conference article in the newspaper catch my eye. According to Erich Honecker, "with its revolutionary surge towards the new, the youth proves to be the builder of the socialist society."

Were we really? Somehow my surge towards building the socialist society was lacking.

I SPY WITH MY LITTLE EYE

The 155-kilometre-long Berlin Wall should have seemed the most normal thing for someone my age, who grew up with this construction. The truth is, it never lost its intrigue for me. After all, if it hadn't been for this damned

Wall I would have been able to visit the trendy fashion shops in West Berlin. But the Antifascist Protection Rampart was more than just a wall: it was two walls. They were an average 30 to 50 metres apart and packed with obstacles to make crossings in either direction virtually impossible.

White painted steel-reinforced concrete elements cut through Berlin for 45 kilometres, of which 37 kilometres were in residential areas. A total of 45,000 of these elements made up the Wall. Each one weighed 2.75 tons, was 3.6 metres wide, up to 4.2 metres high (depending on the location) and cost 359 marks (144 dollars) to make. Outside the city, high metal fences often replaced the walls facing our side. This was done for economic reasons but had no adverse effect on security. Every aspect of the border fortifications had been planned with (East) German efficiency.

Had a potential DDR escapee climbed over the first wall or fence, he would have been faced with a second barrier, the so-called signalling fence. A normal looking mesh wire fence that was interlaced with copper wire through which a low current ran. One touch would raise a silent alarm and enable the border troops to pinpoint any trespasser to a specific area. And with troops on their way, an escapee would then have to cross the so-called corridor of light (a brightly lid strip) without being seen and shot at. Over 200 watchtowers, each one permanently manned by two DDR border police guards, were dotted around the frontier to West Berlin to ensure that escapees did not reach the other side. Anyone trying to illegally cross the border on a section that could not been seen from a watchtower, would have been faced with an equally nasty surprise: guard dogs. However, the good news was that whoever managed to get past the dog/watchtower section was a great deal closer to making it to the other side. Running through freshly raked sand was not designed as an obstacle for escapees but as a control mechanism for the border troops to check whether someone had slipped through unnoticed. People could still get shot at while climbing the final, nearly four-metre-high wall, but soldiers were briefed to avoid shooting into a westwards direction. No DDR politician wanted having to deal with the issue of a westerner being accidentally hit by a stray bullet.

Over the years 5,075 escapees managed to illegally overcome the border fortifications to West Berlin. 3,245 people were less lucky. Their escape attempts ended in prison. Spring guns (mini fragmentation bombs) and mines were never installed on the Berlin Wall; nevertheless, between 1961 and 1989, 98 people died trying to cross the border between the two Berlins. Seventy of them were shot. Eight border guards also lost their lives. They were fired at while trying to avert breakthroughs. Gun use on the Berlin Wall was only prohibited for the border troops when foreign dignitaries made state visits to the DDR. If this had been common knowledge then, people trying to escape might have timed their attempts better, and it may have prevented a few deaths.

Some attempts to fly over the Wall in a hot air balloon or small aircraft were successful, but trying to go under the Wall was doomed to be a failure in the Seventies and Eighties. By then sewers were either bricked up and secured with sensors or blocked with metal bars. Tunnels through which three separate West Berlin train lines cut through our part of the city without stopping, had trip alarms and even laser alarm systems in operation. White lines on the tunnel floor and side walls indicated where the capital of the German Democratic Republic began and ended. Guards patrolled the 15 deserted and dimly lit stations that were closed to the eastern public and through which the western trains had to pass at reduced speed. Every time I stood in the street and felt an underground train from the other side of the Wall rumbling underneath my feet, I wanted so badly to sit in one of the carriages. I lost track of how often I walked past any of the 15 closed underground stations during lunchtime, looking down the steps overgrown with grass, hoping that a door might have been left open by mistake. Of course, nothing like it ever happened.

I really hated Hitler! Had he not come to power we would not have had a war. Then Germany would not have been divided and I would not have been stuck in the DDR. Life was just so unfair!

Once I witnessed some action on the border. I was on an overground train that came to a sudden halt while cutting through a small section of the frontier area. For security reasons, signals were usually not red on this part of the tracks. Perhaps someone had tried to flee and pulled the emergency stop in one of the other carriages. Only a couple minutes later, the entire train was surrounded by border guards – one man every three metres. The border to the west truly was a showcase of German efficiency.

I would never have dared to try to escape. It was far too dangerous. In my eyes, life in the DDR was not so bad that you had to risk your life trying to cross the border illegally.

Like many of my fellow citizens, I would have been happy enough with just being allowed to visit the west. As that wasn't possible I had to continue watching TV programmes or reading books and articles about it. Mind you I did get my hopes up when the west talked about France getting a socialist government in 1981. France becoming a socialist state? Like the DDR maybe? I wondered whether that meant we would be allowed to go to Paris? Unfortunately, the west's definition of "socialist" turned out to be different to ours and with France remaining a capitalist state, a holiday there was still out of the question. But at least I could dream about far-away countries. One East Berlin newspaper, the *Junge Welt* (Young World), even tried to convince its readers that dreaming about a faraway country was much more satisfying than actually going there. What a very convenient point of view...

One of my most preferred lunchtime pastimes was peeking at the west. For this I would stand about 30 metres in front of the famous Checkpoint Charlie, which was close to my work, and look straight through into West Berlin. A hundred metres down the road I could see people in the distance, another 50 metres further cars were driving past. It looked all so... normal. Just like the buzzing traffic on our side.

Once my colleague Danuta invited Cordi and me to her housewarming party. She had secured herself a nice rented flat near the Wall. Wherever possible, a hundred-meter wide strip of land in front of our side of the Antifascist Protection Rampart (increasing to 500 metres outside of Berlin) was declared a *Grenzgebiet* (frontier area). Only residents holding special permits had access to such a sealed-off area. Naturally every applicant's background was carefully checked before they were issued a permit. Any existing residents who were considered to be a risk for the security zone were lured away by newer or bigger flats elsewhere. Stubborn tenants faced eviction and were moved with force. And while, for obvious reasons, crime was virtually non-existent in the frontier areas, life there also had its drawbacks: For example, residents could not receive impromptu visits. For every potential visitor, an application for a temporary access permit had to be filled in well in advance, stating all their personal details and the time and date of the expected visit. Danuta's flat, in a Forties apartment block was bang next to the Wall. Surprisingly it was not in a sealed-off area. And as the flat was on the third floor, we even had a fantastic view to the other side:

"I too, just like all the other guests, had to have a look over the Wall, which in this part of town could easily have been mistaken for a simple factory wall. Surprisingly, Danuta's street continued on the western side, with exactly the same style of buildings as there were on our side. You could see people watching telly, or cooking in their kitchens. Someone over there was having a party too, just like us! Maybe even a housewarming party? A bus dropped off people at a bus stop, a drunk stumbled out of a taxi and some teenagers were shouting in the street and teasing each other. If it had not been for the western cars, you could have easily mistaken it for an East Berlin street scene. It all looked so normal and familiar, yet it was so far away and unreachable. It was such a strange feeling, it gave me the shivers!"

Diary entry

During the evening Cordelia and I both had knocked back quite a few glasses of sweet Hungarian white wine. When we left the party after midnight the two of us were quite tipsy. There was not a taxi to be seen anywhere, so we headed for the nearest bus stop, giggling and laughing. When we arrived, we found that someone had smashed the glass of the frame displaying the timetable, and as I fished out the paper in sheer exuberance to add some times of my own I suddenly felt a tab on my right shoulder. Quickly turning around, who was standing there right behind me? A policeman! The proximity to the border meant more policemen were doing regular rounds in the area. It had Cordelia in stitches that it looked like as if I was the one who had "vandalised the People's property", as this type of crime was officially referred to. Holding timetable and pen behind my back like a schoolboy who has been caught red-handed I quickly asked the Genosse Wachtmeister (comrade constable) whether he could be so kind to call for backup and get a colleague to chauffeur us home. He smiled but declined. After a quick look at our ID cards, and asking where we had come from he was off again wishing us a good journey home.

Policemen were not regarded very highly in the DDR. Constables of the Deutsche Volkspolizei (German People's Police) had a reputation of being a bunch of slow thinkers. They were the blondes of East Germany:

How does a policeman open a tin of mixed vegetables? He knocks on it and shouts: "You are surrounded by the German People's Police! Open up!"

Q: "Why do policemen have see-through lunchboxes?"

A: "So they know whether they are going to work or going home."

The new teacher wants to get to know her class of ten year olds: "What's your name?" – "Frank." – "And what do you want to become when you are grown up?" – "I don't know." – "Ok, never mind. Let me ask someone else... What's your name?" – "Petra." – "And what do you want to become?" – "I don't know." A boy raises his arm and shouts excitedly: "Miss, ask me, ask me, I know what I want to become." – "OK" the teacher says "What do you want to become" – "I want to become a policeman!" – "Good. And what is your name?" – "I don't know."

Policemen often sounded wooden. They always addressed or referred to people as citizen. "Citizen, can I please have a look at your ID card?" or "Citizen, can you please turn down your music. Another citizen has complained about the noise." were just some of their standard sentences used. All very politically correct, yet at the same time also a bit intimidating and somewhat old fashioned.

If the constables and Abschnittsbevollmächtigten (community police officers) were merely ridiculed, the Helpers of the People's Police were truly despised by most East Germans. After holding down their usual day job as train driver, roofer, shop assistant or whatever, they would put on a red armband emblazoned with the DDR coat of arms and suddenly be transformed into overzealous deputy sheriffs. Helpers had to assist regular police officers whenever extra hands were needed, for example as stewards for big events or for large-scale routine checks on motorists. They seemed to be driven by a desire for power. Why else would someone want to give up their free time and become an unpaid constable if it wasn't for getting their kicks out of bossing ordinary citizens around? What made police helpers so unpleasant was their mercilessness when it came to spotting any wrongdoing. If a pedestrian crossed the road on a red light, there was a fair chance that a police officer just gave the person a verbal warning. A helper would have imposed a five marks (two dollars) fine. Had I ever been approached by such a pompous idiot, I would have demanded to speak to a proper police officer.

GIVING 99.94 PER CENT

In 1986 I needed a confidence boost and decided to test my attractiveness factor. Once again I put a personal ad in the monthly youth mag *New Life*. More than 130 replies reached me within eight weeks. But I never answered a single one. Many letters began very promisingly, for example with:

"I am 1.71 metres tall, like to go to discos, passionately drive my moped, enjoy travelling and prefer camping. I always dress fashionably sporty, I am neither fat nor skinny, weigh 54 kilos, have medium-length brown hair with a few highlights in my fringe. But I am thinking of having the fringe restyled. All in all I am quite a normal girl."

or

"My favourite bands: A-Ha, ZZ Top, AC/DC, CC-Catch / My favourite actors: Jean-Paul. Belmondo, Richard. Chamberlain / My favourite films: The Thorn Birds, Fame / My favourite singers: Tina Turner, Madonna, Sandra, Bruce Springsteen..."

But when reading on all the girls I liked seemed to be more interested in the city I lived in, rather than in me. One reply even stated, rather bluntly:

"I would really like to visit you in Berlin... PLEASE WRITE!"

Gee, someone was obviously really desperate to get free accommodation in the capital. At least the girl was honest (or stupid) enough to let the cat out of the bag. And with that ulterior motive present in all shortlisted letters, I called it a day.

One piece of post I did not chuck was my polling card. For the first time I had been invited to cast my vote in the country's local elections.

"The citizens of the German Democratic Republic exercise their power through democratically elected representative bodies of the people."

GDR constitution

In reality, it did not matter whether anyone went to the polling station or not. DDR elections (also called "expressions of socialist democracy") left a lot to be desired by western standards. Our constitution stated that the Communist Party was the ruling party and no election was able to change that. According to our newspapers, we had a "democracy without opposition". Our politicians followed Lenin's point of view that a state ruled by workers and farmers was the highest possible form of democracy. This was called the Dictatorship of the Proletariat. Hence, votes were not cast for particular parties and their policies, but rather a candidate's ability to solve people's everyday problems on the thorny path to communism. The biggest hurdle for potential candidates was their colleagues. They had to decide before an election whether someone from among them was worthy of becoming a candidate. However, only candidates put forward by the coalition members of the National Front, an amalgamation of all major parties and organisations in the country, could be suggested. And that was as democratic as things got. Election Day itself was nothing but a formality, an opportunity for the people to declare their belief in socialism. The majority of voters followed two unwritten rules:

1.) They visited the polling station early in the morning.

This indicated a strong bond between the voter and the government. It wasn't uncommon for entire apartment blocks, streets or villages to go collectively voting first thing on a Sunday morning. (In Germany, elections always take place on Sundays.) People who did not go to the polling station were usually visited in the afternoon by agitators with mobile ballot boxes and hassled to cast their votes.

2.) They accepted all candidates on the ballot paper.

Most voters had a quick glimpse on the paper, folded it in front of the polling officers and put it in the ballot box – no marking was needed or expected. Anyone wanting to use the one voting booth present in every polling station to cross out candidates had to do the "walk of shame" first – the booth was always positioned at the furthest corner of the room. The names of the voters who went into the booth were secretly noted down, just in case the Stasi wanted to keep an eye on them.

Mum, rebellious as ever, regularly suggested to the polling officers they might as well stop handing the polling papers out and put them in the ballot box themselves. In the Eighties more and more East Germans began to make use of the ballot booth. My parents, too, started crossing out all candidates names out. By then using the polling booth had gained such a popularity it was not uncommon for voters to queue patiently in front of it waiting for their turn. Not that crossing out names changed anything, but it felt good to rebel against the system in whatever small way you could. Regardless of how many people rejected the proposed candidates, throughout the years the official election result always mysteriously came in at around the 99 per cent mark in favour of the proposed people. And the published participation figure was also never below 99.something per cent.

Only a small minority of the electorate ever made themselves familiar with the candidates standing for local election. Why bother if the vote is going to be rigged anyway? It was no surprise to anyone when the published election results for 8 June 1986 were very much in line with those from previous elections: 99.74 per cent of the electorate had turned out, of which 99.94 per cent had voted for the proposed candidates. 99.94 per cent! While no one doubted that the majority of the people had indeed backed the existing system once again, bumped up figures like those were an insult to people's intelligence and did not do the Communist's Party reputation any favours. Yet for the time being, East Germans let everything run its normal course, hoping that a DDR equivalent of Gorbachev would soon rise to the top and make such elections a thing of the past.

HYPERVENTILATING IN HUNGARY

In July 1986 it was not politics that was on my mind. Cordi and I were looking forward to our one-week Jugendtourist (Youth Tourist) holiday to Hungary, which I had managed to secure for us at work earlier in the year. When we finally met our group at the train station for the first time, we were shocked. Having to spend an entire week with a bunch of nerds was a daunting prospect. Upon boarding our overnight train the two of us broke away from "that yucky group", as I wrote in my diary. We bribed the train conductor to allow us to stay in an empty sleeping compartment for the entire 16-hour journey. The rest of the group had to spend the night in uncomfortable second-class seats.

When we got off the train near Budapest, Cordi and I were on cloud nine. Now we too were finally in the country that many East Germans loved so much. Hungary's liberal approach to its economy had resulted in an abundance of imported western goods and, what interested us most, was that many private boutiques offered their own designer clothes at moderate prices. If it wasn't already enough to be in love with the country, every Hungarian we met was friendly and hospitable. Things couldn't get any better. The only drawback was that occasionally we felt a bit like second-class tourists; a feeling many East Germans had when travelling to other socialist countries. Unlike the many West German tourists who visited Hungary, we could not bribe bouncers or illegal mini cab drivers with Deutschmarks. Instead, we often had to rely on people's altruism. No one wanted our DDR marks and there was a limit on how much money we could change into Hungarian forints – depending on the lengths of the holiday up to 500 marks (200 dollars) only.

Cordi and I had come up with three golden rules for a successful holiday:

1) Don't waste money on unnecessary items.

2) Buy as many cool clothes as possible.

3) Avoid being seen with the nerds from our group.

We did pretty much our own thing from day one and so hardly took part in any of the organised group trips and activities. Instead, the two of us hitchhiked to Budapest nearly every day, telling any driver who asked, that we were Swedish. Cordi and I saw ourselves as transnationals – westerners trapped in East German bodies. One evening we got into a situation in which we seriously feared for the wellbeing of those bodies.

After spending yet another day in Hungary's beautiful capital checking out sights and shops, Cordelia managed to flag down a flash BMW. Two foreign-looking guys in their twenties, who turned out to be Iraqis, were driving in our direction and happy to offer us a ride. We quickly jumped into the back seats and freely told them about how uncool we thought life in the east was. Cordi and I always revealed our true origins to westerners. Being short of Hungarian forints, we hoped for an invitation to a drink or dinner.

The conversation with the two guys, conducted in English went very well. But just as Cordi and I were secretly congratulating each other on our catch, we noticed that the area we were driving through looked somewhat unfamiliar. I asked the boys in the front where we were going and was assured that we were on the way to our hotel. However, the street signs were telling a different story – we were heading in the opposite direction. What was going on? Gulp! What were we supposed to do now? I quickly asked the driver whether he could stop the car as Cordelia was not feeling well and needed to get some fresh air. My request was faced with silence from the front. Our hosts, who had initially been so chatty, suddenly did not understand English and only talked to each other in their native tongue. Could this really be happening to us? I looked at Cordelia and she looked at me. Both our mouths were wide open. There was fear in our eyes. Desperately, yet as inconspicuously as possible, we tried to find something among our purchases that could be used as a weapon, if it should come to that. Was there any chance of me blinding them with the fluorescent shirt I had bought? Most probably not! Cordi's rummaging through her handbag wasn't too successful either and only unearthed two ballpoint pens. How pathetic! As it became darker, the roads narrower, the street lights more sparse and pedestrians virtually non-existent, Cordi and I secretly got ready for an emergency departure. Our belongings clutched in one hand we were each holding tight to a doorknob with the other hand – prepared to jump as soon as the car slowed down. When I realised that the road was about to cut through a forest ahead I started hyperventilating. There was a look of horror on Cordi's face when a couple of minutes later we turned into a pitch-black patch of forest! I already could see myself being clobbered over the head and lying motionless on the ground while Cordelia, having been dragged away, was screaming her lungs out for me in the distance. This definitely wasn't the holiday I had in mind when applying for a trip to Hungary! Thankfully Lady Luck was on our side, because as quickly as we had driven into the unlit forest, we reversed out of it and headed back into the direction from which we had come. God knows whether the two guys had only wanted to frighten us or whether they really had a sinister plan only to change their minds at the very last minute. We were just relieved about the outcome. Ten minutes later we reached an obscure disco at the other end of town. As soon as Cordi and I got out of the car, we took to our heels.

The next car we flagged down was a Lada – we did not care. It was a nice, safe-looking couple who had stopped to give us a lift. That was all that counted. We made it back to the hotel late on that day, but at least we had made it in one piece.

A SLIPPERY PURCHASE

There was one sure way to spot East German tourists abroad: No western car was safe from them. If they saw one parked in the streets, out came the camera and they would pose next to it, pretending it was theirs. Then again, maybe it was just Cordi and I who did that. I have countless photos of me posing next to a BMW, a Renault, a Mercedes, an Audi... Sometimes this obsession of ours could cause embarrassment, too. Occasionally the owners of the cars in question returned while Cordi and I were still going through our repertoire of "cool" poses next to their auto. Thankfully, they usually waited – slightly bemused – nearby for us to finish our photo sessions. Cordelia and I were very keen photographers. Most of our photos are in black and white as colour prints were ten times more expensive. But what the pictures lacked in colour we made up for in quantity. Every conceivable angle of a holiday was captured on film. One day Cordi's camera stopped working. I even have photos of her jokingly asking the first passer-by in the street to repair it for her on the spot. That is how we met Jay, a Canadian. To our surprise he managed to fix her camera. We three spent the rest of the day together, talking about our home countries and a nice friendship developed out of this incident.

As our Hungarian holiday was nearing its end, Cordi and I were really strapped for cash. With no DDR marks and hardly any forints left, the offer made by a passing gypsy woman to buy Cordelia's faux silver ring for 400 forints (20 dollars) was very welcome. Even more so as the ring only cost her two DDR marks (80 cents). Unfortunately, all the woman had was a 1,000 forint banknote. Although this would ring alarm bells for us today, back then we didn't even consider for a moment that it might be a con trick. It was only our empty wallets that prevented us from handing over good money for what must have been a fake or out-of-date banknote. With the little money we had left, Cordi decided to buy a nice juicy piece of watermelon from a street vendor. She gave me the piece she had chosen to hold while she handed over two hands full of change. But the wedge of melon slipped straight out of my hand and shattered on the ground leaving me holding only the cling film it had been wrapped in. Cordelia was furious and, to the amusement of the street seller, punched me hard in the chest. Maybe I shouldn't have laughed. All I could do was offer to buy her a melon back in the DDR. She was not impressed. But there was a happy end to our Hungary trip.

Boarding the train for our journey home, Cordi and I got the conductor to allocate us berths while the other members of our group made themselves comfortable on seats in second-class accommodation. Not knowing how we could pay for this little bit of extra comfort, a girl, who was already in the compartment that we had been allocated, became our saviour.

In desperation, Cordi and I asked whether she could loan us the 20 marks (eight dollars) per person that the conductor demanded, without a receipt, for a night's stay in the sleeper carriage. And we were given the money, no questions asked. People trusting each other – that was the good side of socialism. And yes, we did pay the girl back.

FACING THE ENEMY

As much as our propaganda depicted capitalists as enemies of the working class, our job as foreign traders was to establish and maintain business relationships with the west. In fact, the dealings with western clients was what made this job so interesting and desirable for many. Naturally I was very excited when I was allowed to attend a client meeting for the very first time. But as much as I had looked forward to my first negotiations, I was even more disappointed afterwards. My diary doesn't hold back:

"Because I already knew yesterday that Dieter would be taking me to the negotiations with Mr Mönning from Holland I put on my red leather tie this morning. The whole day I was so excited about going to the meeting that, when Mr Mönning arrived at two pm, my shirt was covered in giant sweat patches. Before we met the client, Dieter gave me the checked contract, which I had typed in the morning. He also suggested that I take a writing pad and pen with me: 'Just write something down occasionally. It will make you look more professional.' was his advice. Client meetings always have to be attended by two members of staff. As we walked down to the reception area he reminded me to not address the client as colleague or comrade, but as Mister. Mr Mönnink turned out to be a guy in his late forties/early fifties. Dieter asked what we wanted to drink. Mr Mönnink took a juice. I asked for a tea. As Dieter walked off to the receptionist to put the order through, I was left alone with Mr Mönnink. What was I to talk to him about? Thankfully he was quite happy to lead the conversation. I just agreed with everything he said – after all, a client is always right. At one stage he talked about how unfair it is for someone my age having to face an old hand like him. Then he threw his head back and started roaring with laughter. Out of politeness I laughed too. I was so praying for Dieter's quick return! In the meantime all of my shirt had become wet and was clinging to me like a second skin.

When Mr Mönnink wrote Dieter's and my name as the DDR negotiators in his diary, I felt very proud. I will now appear somewhere in his company's paperwork in Holland. As soon as Dieter and Mr Mönnink started talking about product parameters and specifications I hardly understood a thing. Following Dieter's advice earlier I put on an important face, nodded occasionally and noted down meaningless scribbles. When Mr Mönnink later had to call someone in his company, he spoke Dutch. It was the first time I had heard this language. It sounded nice. As the meeting was coming to an end an hour later, Mr Mönnink said to me: 'Mr Fritz, I have got something for you.' and out of his KLM briefcase (obviously a freebie) came a nice calendar depicting paintings of old Dutch masters. I was over the moon because it's always such a hassle getting a decent calendar in the shops. Dieter got a calendar too and he also took the packet of cigarettes Mr Mönnink had put on the table earlier. We wished Mr Mönnink a safe journey home. As Dieter and I walked back to our office he said to me: 'Just don't get too attached to the calendar. We will have to hand them in.' I could not understand why the calendars would have to be handed in. They bear Mönnink's company logo and are of no commercial value. But apparently the rule is that all presents, except pens, rulers and similar small items, have to be handed in to discourage corruption. So why did Dieter keep stumm about the cigarettes he had pocketed? Grudgingly, I later took the calendars to the managing director's office, probably never to see them again."

And as I suspected, I never saw them again. Officially client presents were used as prizes in the annual company lottery. Unofficially, much of the stuff handed over to the departmental heads or the managing director never surfaced again. A western client once gave my uncle Wolfgang, also a foreign trader, a gold-plated fountain pen engraved with his name. He handed it in, believing that the pen would be returned to him. It wasn't. Instead a Secretary of State signed papers with it during a meeting which my uncle also attended. Uncle Wolfgang could clearly see his name on the pen before it disappeared again in Mr Bigshot's top pocket.

My colleague Bärbel was the trader responsible for DDR glass exports to the Italian market. She was in her late forties, of petite stature and had a black bob. Bärbel was very sophisticated but attitude free and always up for a laugh. Clients, who liked her competence, regularly showered her with yummy Italian food items in meetings. Whether it was gourmet pasta, pesto, Parmesan or amaretti biscuits, for years she played by the rules and handed everything she was given over to the "Doc", our departmental head. This changed when one day she saw two pasta packets that she had handed in peeping out of the "Doc's" secretary's handbag. From that point on, Bärbel began distributing foreign food items among her closest colleagues instead. Thanks to her generosity, I came to experience my first taste of Parmesan cheese. It was a huge wedge bought by a client at Milan airport and, according to the price label, it was worth the equivalent of 40 pounds. Having never heard of Parmesan before (in the DDR you were usually served grated Edam with your pasta), I did not know what to do with it. The cheese tasted horrible on a sandwich. On toast it was not much better. Thinking it was off, I threw it in the rubbish. What a waste...

Bärbel was also in the lucky position to occasionally travel to Italy on business. Gee, was I envious of her. Well, not so much when she told us that once, when leaving a restaurant in Milan, her business partner had her handbag snatched by two guys on a moped. But everything else about that country sounded very nice indeed. Though sometimes Bärbel could get a bit carried away. Like when she called DDR supermarkets "giant rubbish containers" in comparison with Italian supermarkets. Maybe ours were not as colourful and varied, but rubbish containers? I wasn't too sure about that. Her juice story was equally strange, but believable. Apparently she gagged in a Milan restaurant after having a sip from her glass of orange juice: "At first I thought they were foreign objects in it," she told us, "But then I realised, it was juice with bits. Imagine, juice with bits in it!" We couldn't believe what we were hearing – DDR juice was always smooth. What would those capitalists think of next?

Conversations with Bärbel were always fun. I could listen to her stories about the olden days for hours. My favourite one was the story about someone nailing a smelly cheese to the back of a colleague's desk, who took a week to find the source of the foul smell. The practical jokes played in the Eighties were more refined: One day a colleague offered me some chocolate shapes. They tasted off and didn't seem to contain much cocoa. But I was doing our DDR food industry an injustice as I lamented the poor quality. It turned out I had been eating West German dog chocolates which, according to the packet, were designed "to give any canine a healthy shiny coat". Though non-poisonous for humans, I still rinsed my mouth with water for ages afterwards. Yuck!

One practical joke that could have backfired was when I provoked some secret service members outside our work place. Bärbel had noticed a blue Wartburg with a very long antenna. It regularly parked in the car park in front of our building. The car never seemed to change position and was always occupied by four men in their mid-twenties. One lunchtime I was walking past the car, when the front passenger door opened and I spotted a huge telephone mounted next to the seat. This was definitely no ordinary car. Its passengers must have been observing someone in the apartment block next to us, which housed normal DDR citizens, western diplomats and foreign journalists. Westerners living in the DDR used to joke that East German concrete was made of one third cement, one third spit and one third microphones. In my next lunch hour I positioned myself semi-close to the Wartburg, got my camera out and pretended to take photos of the car. What could possibly happen to me? There was no law preventing people from taking photos at public car parks. Yet I still did a runner when one of the Stasi guys quickly got out of the car and made his way towards me. Thankfully he gave up his pursuit after a few metres. The next day, Bärbel and I noticed that the blue Wartburg had been replaced by a brown Lada. The mighty Stasi obviously got a wee bit worried about having been spotted. I was very pleased with myself.

FAIR TRADE

Twice a year, the life of a foreign trader got very exciting. Being sent to Leipzig was supposed to be an honour. The city in the south of the DDR was the scene of the first mass demonstrations against the communist government in 1989. It was also the location for the DDR's largest trade fairs. Attending the spring and autumn fairs was either loved or loathed by members of staff. I loved it. Just like the Leipzigers who, for the two weeks a year that the fairs were on, benefited from a preferential supply of goods. Leipzig's international fairs simply were *the* place for foreign businesses to agree contracts with partners from the entire east bloc. In autumn 1986, companies from 24 capitalist, 12 socialist and eight developing countries displayed their wares in 73,000 square metres of exhibition space. The red and white labelled Russian Stolichnaya vodka still features a medal awarded by the Leipzig Trade Fair. None of my company's exhibits was ever awarded a gold medal – the rumour among foreign traders was that products which sold like hot cakes were not honoured in such way.

The opening of the fair twice a year was always a big event, with Erich Honecker and other Politburo members walking around meeting and greeting foreign politicians and managing directors and holding important talks. Once the Communist Party daily, the *Neues Deutschland* (New Germany) featured no less than 42 photos of Erich Honecker visiting various countries' stalls. The western media took this as a sign of vanity. Far from it, Honecker bored us with this photo collection because he did not want to discriminate against any one trading partner, so everyone he shook hands with had to appear. No wonder this particular newspaper was the least popular. The fair itself acted like a huge magnet to the general public. In particular, representatives from western companies were inundated with requests for brochures by private visitors. Whether it be brochures about fork-lift trucks, industrial lubricants or assembly lines, if it was printed on glossy paper, people pocketed whatever they could lay their hands on. God knows what they did with the brochures. Once, as I was making my usual lunchtime visit through the exhibition halls, I came across the stall of a Greek company that seemed to be attracting a huge crowd. As expected, a guy at the stall was handing out brochures. Curious about what all the fuss was about I took one too. It turned out that East German visitors were driven crazy by a pamphlet full of technical specifications about machines that made glass bottles. Didn't these people have a life? Or at least some dignity? I was truly appalled about how low people could sink. When I gave my brochure back to the Greek guy, his jaw dropped. He must not have seen anything like it happening at this fair before. He stared at me, with his mouth wide open until I turned a corner and disappeared out of his sight.

My horror at the grasping behaviour of my fellow countrymen inspired me to come up with a plan. To avoid being identified as an East German in future, I headed to the nearest West German stall, a steelworks company, to grab one of their brochures. Back at my firm's pavilion, I Blue-Petered myself a little company badge out of the steelworks company's logo. From then on, I put this badge on my jacket whenever I went for a lunchtime stroll around the fair. It did not take very long for other East Germans to approach me asking whether my stall was handing out free brochures. With promises of not only brochures, but also free ballpoint pens, rulers and bottle openers galore, I sent everyone to that steelworks stall with instructions to tell the girl behind the counter that Herr Berghofer had personally authorised the handout of a goody bag. It was a cruel joke, I know, but the opportunity was too good to be missed. The only person I felt sorry for was the poor West German receptionist, who at the end of the day was faced with the task of having to fend off a bunch of enraged East Germans demanding their promised freebies. What a sight that must have been!

On other occasions I did not even have to resort to a fake badge to give off the illusion of being a western exhibitor. My confidence was enough to gain (unauthorised) access to the Foreigner's Centre, a meeting point for westerners. Even though the colour of my fair pass, which had to be shown upon entry to the building, identified me as an East German exhibitor, I did not get stopped once. Instead I marched through the entrance with the kind of arrogant expression that westerners usually displayed when visiting the DDR. Once inside the building, you could buy for a few DDR marks what otherwise was strictly forbidden in our country – broadsheets from all major western countries. I usually got *The Times* or *The Daily Telegraph*. This way,

I improved my English and at the same time gained an insight into Britain that the *Morning Star* (mouthpiece of the British Communist Party), which could be bought from normal newsagents', did not give. It was quite a revelation to find out that everyday life in England was not at all overshadowed by unemployed workers fighting for survival and progressive people fighting for disarmament, as our schoolbooks suggested. To my disappointment, the DDR never featured in any of the issues I managed to get hold of. I would have loved to read what the media beyond West Germany thought of my fatherland, regardless of what crazy point of view they might have adopted.

Naturally the Leipzig fair also had its fair share of nutters. One of our American clients was a Mormon who, during his visits, regularly exchanged a substantial amount of dollars into small denominations of DDR banknotes and got his wife to distribute them to unsuspecting passers-by in the city center. Try explaining to an American eccentric that money was not the problem. If anything, more luxury goods were needed, so people could spend all the DDR marks they had already accumulated in their saving accounts. We failed to make him understand this point and so Mr Mormon continued, twice a year, to waste his cash on a pointless exercise. Though I am sure the Leipzigers on the receiving end still loved it.

My personal favourite was the spring fair in March, rather than the autumn one in September, because it coincided with the International Book Fair, which also took place in Leipzig. With no language barrier, the stalls of the West German publishing houses were always the most popular ones with DDR visitors. Dozens of people at each stall, all pushing and shoving and trying to get to the front, so they could browse through books that otherwise would never officially be seen in the German Democratic Republic. The book fair was the place where even I lost my blasé attitude and always joined the fight to get to the front. Unlike most other people, if I saw an interesting and non-political title, I could always ask Dad or my grandparents to get it for me on their next trip to the west. Unfortunately, I was never in Leipzig on the last day of a book fair. Rumour had it that many international publishers simply gave away all their sample copies to the visitors, to save themselves the return shipping costs.

Working at the fair was very stressful. But regardless of how busy a day turned out to be, hardly anyone wanted to miss out on the nightlife. Once the fair closed at seven pm, we usually had a few drinks at the bar in our pavilion to wind down. Martinis were my usual choice. Not that I particularly liked their taste. Far from it. But it was one way to satisfy my craving for olives – our shops rarely stocked them. The next stop on a typical evening was a visit to a bar or disco. Once I went with some colleagues to an international fashion show. From DDR couture to Yves Saint Laurent, the models presented all the latest trends. It was just a pity that most of the items never made an appearance in our shops. Regardless of whichever place or venue you wanted to go, making a booking was essential during fair time. If you didn't, there was every danger of being rejected at the door. And with so many international visitors in the city, many bouncers even expected a little Deutschmark-baksheesh before letting you in. Or at least a generous tip in DDR mark. One day, Cordelia visited me in Leipzig unexpectedly. Of course, we were after some entertainment in the evening. First we tried to befriend some foreigners who we expected would invite us for drinks or even dinner. In return we would have given them the usual insight into life in East Germany. But we did not meet anyone suitable.

So we went to the Restaurant Stadt Dresden (City of Dresden) looking forward to a nice meal at our own expense. There was just one hurdle, the bouncer would not let us in. Instead he asked: "How much are you prepared to pay?". Cordi, thinking that he was asking us how much we would spend once inside, replied: "Oh, we are very hungry." Mr Bouncer looked at her as if she was from another planet. To avoid further embarrassment, I dragged Cordi away, to the nearby Mokka-Milch-Bar, where, luckily for us, the bouncer let us in without making any monetary demands. It was packed, but we still managed to get a table – the last one, near the loo. Normally it's not the nicest place to sit, but in that particular establishment it was certainly the most interesting one. Most of the guests were darker-skinned foreigners who seemed to be in a constant rush to the men's loo. Many visitors went in with big bags and reappeared empty-handed, or vice versa. Then people, who we never saw going into the toilet came out of it. We could not make sense of what was happening in there. Shortly before we were about to leave, I decided to investigate. "Be careful!" Cordi urged me and we agreed that she should call the police if I didn't reappear within five minutes. I slowly opened the door to the gents, gave Cordi a final wave, walked in and found myself standing in a room that I had least expected to see: a loo, tiled, two by two metres big, with a toilet and basin. That was it! There was no sign of any people or bags. I even checked the walls for hidden doors. It was a big disappointment for us not having been able to discover the secret of the Mokka-Milch-Bar loo, so we assumed that it led to a hidden room where commanding Stasi officers met up with their foreign field agents. Naturally we could not prove our theory, but then what twenty year old could possibly have outsmarted our mighty secret service?

As Cordi and I took a cab home to my rented room in a private flat (all of Leipzig's hotels during a fair were usually filled with western visitors), we unwittingly had to give a last performance. The two of us were still discussing the obscure events at the Mokka-Milch-Bar when I noticed that the driver was watching us in the back mirror. He asked: "Are you guys from the east or the west?" Too tired to pretend, but too embarrassed to state the truth, I said: "Does it really matter?" As far as I was concerned that was as good as an admission of the shameful truth. After all, a West German would have had no reason to be ambiguous about his origins. But our cabby did not get it. He replied: "Sorry, it was stupid of me to ask. Of course, you are from the west." What? Cordelia looked at me, I looked at her. Obviously being dressed smartly and speaking without a regional dialect was enough in Leipzig to be mistaken for a westerner. Our breasts swelled with pride. Though the cabby seemed quite disappointed with us when we later left the car paying him in DDR marks.

CULTURE VULTURES

1986 ended on a somewhat sombre note. People were still speculating whether Dean Reed, an US American singer and actor who had made the DDR his homeland, really had died by committing suicide. Born 1938 in Denver, Colorado, Reed became a Latin American teen idol in the Sixties. He first moved to Argentina and then to Italy. He met his potential wife during an East German film festival and in 1972 moved to the DDR. Reed saw himself as a Marxist, fighting through his work for social justice and against imperialism, although he never gave up his US citizenship. In the Seventies, Dean Reed gave concerts (mainly in the east bloc) and made five movies in the DDR. His last production was *Sing Cowboy, Sing*. It wasn't too successful. In the early Eighties he began to suffer from depression and in 1986 he committed suicide by taking a sedative, cutting his wrists and driving into a lake. Tom Hanks has bought the film rights about Reed's life.

The year 1987 promised to be a very cultural year for us Berliners. Our city turned 750 years old and with East and West Berlin having separate celebrations, each side tried to outshine the other. Not that the DDR was ever a cultural backwater. The country's 134 theatres had 11 million visitors annually. An audience of around 60 million people each year attended events at 1,045 Kulturhäuser (cultural houses), local venues that hosted all different kind of events, such as variety shows, book readings, concerts, discos, plays, hootenannies and so on. East Germany also had cabarets – ten professional and hundreds of amateur ones. Going out for an evening's entertainment was extremely cheap. With the most expensive seat in a theatre costing around 15 marks (six dollars) there was no excuse for anyone to be ignorant of culture. After all, in East Germany spare time was officially called "a satisfaction of cultural needs". Cultural events were supposed to acquaint us with the ideas, values and philosophy of socialism. Hence, any creative output had to be free from blatant public criticism of the DDR. Instead, writers and performers often wove subtle political statements into their work with ambiguous wording, and so over the years East Germans developed a very finely tuned sense of reading between lines:

"I was born there, ...in the forbidden room. Now I am living in a big flat with many rooms, the forbidden room is one of them... It is quite small. I can walk around the walls. My life will be too short to see all of the other rooms, all gardens, all parks, all forests and all mountains, why do I want to see this room?"

The Forbidden Room by H. Schubert (*Schöne Reise,* Aufbau Verlag, 1988)

Any East German reading this extract would immediately, and as intended, associate the forbidden room with West Berlin. The flat with the many other rooms is, of course, the DDR.

Or take this sketch for example: An actress and an opera singer tease each other about their real-life personas being different to the characters they are playing on stage. This led to the punch line: "We are not the only miscasts in this country." The audience clapped frantically. Everyone had understood that this was a dig at the members of our Politburo.

The DDR's most famous and beloved entertainer was a chubby guy in his fifties with big square glasses and thinning black hair who always performed immaculately dressed in a tuxedo with red lining – O. F. Weidling. In 1984 he hosted a programme that was broadcast live in the presence of the entire Politburo. Hinting at the recent visit of West German politician Franz Josef Strauss, who had arranged a billion Deutschmark credit line for the DDR, O. F. Weidling joked on stage: "Construction work on our cathedral had finished, so Franz Josef Strauss could already view it... for a small fee." This remark had the audience in stitches. Yet making fun of the state's financial affairs on national TV was risky and Weidling knew it. Immediately he looked at the Politburo member in charge of economy and said: "Oh dear, comrade Mittag did not laugh. Hold on, he is smiling now. A load off my mind." Erich Honecker found the evening entertaining and wrote Weidling a letter afterwards congratulating him on his success, yet when the programme was repeated on television all of the entertainer's witty interludes were missing. It was his last appearance on TV. Weidling died a year later, aged 60, after a stroke.

Despite the word culture in their name, *Kraftsportkulturistik* (Power Sport Culture) – DDR speak for Bodybuilding – and *Freikörperkultur* (Free Body Culture), naturism to you and me, were hardly artsy. But they were both very popular pastimes. I don't think any other European country had more nudist beaches than East Germany. Skinny dippers had designated areas at the

Baltic Sea, at countless lakes up and down the country and even in some parks. On hot days, many Berlin lawns were regularly overtaken by nude sun seekers (including myself) and hardly any passer-by would bat an eyelid. Prudishness did not fit into the DDR of the Eighties. The procession in honour of the city's 750th jubilee, recreating everyday scenes of Berlin life, also had a water-themed float full of skinny dippers. State and party officials gave it a good look and cheer as it drove past their stand.

For those people who were after something more than just tits and bums in the anniversary year, there was a choice of 700 national events, 350 exhibitions and hundreds of guest performances by 467 artists from 44 countries. Jose Carreras, Carlos Santana, Shirley Bassey and Nana Mouskouri were just some of the stars bought in to give concerts. It was those guest performances by foreign artists that Cordi and I were most interested in – along with hundreds of thousand other East Germans. As soon as 1987's cultural events were publicised, the two of us applied for concert tickets as if there was no tomorrow. And so did many others. As officials later revealed, for performances of western artists it was quite common to receive up to 160,000 applications for every 6,000 tickets that were available. Our efforts were rewarded. Cordi and I managed to secure a ticket each for a performance by a western rock star – none other than Shakin' Stevens! Although I must admit, he wasn't our first choice. But, fuelled by rumours that concert tickets for some West German artist had apparently been sold on by touts for thousands of marks, we both believed we had a nice little earner on our hands. But things did not work out for us as planned.

The day Shakin's concert took place, a horde of touts tried to flog tickets near the venue. The only problem was, there weren't any buyers about. By the time we reached the entrance, desperate sellers were offering tickets for 15 marks (six dollars) – three marks below the official ticket price! Poor Shakin'! Cordi and I thought: "What the heck. We have got the tickets, so we might as well use them," and in we went. The multi-purpose hall was surprisingly packed. The two of us had to make do with a place that was furthest away from the stage. When the concert started at eight pm with flashing lights, some rumbling noise and fireworks, the majority of the 6,500 members of the audience began dancing and singing.

It was the first time we had been to a rock concert, and Cordi and I had just gotten into the swing of things when Shakin' disappeared from stage after an hour into the concert. A few minutes later he came back to play for another half an hour before he went off-stage again. "Must be the break." I said to Cordelia. It turned out to be the end of the concert. We were so disappointed!

The *Rock Salute to Berlin* got us much more excited. It took place in West Berlin yet still managed to create havoc in East Berlin. With the open air stage positioned near the Brandenburg Gate, close to the border, some loudspeakers were turned eastwards so fans in our part of the city could also enjoy the live performances of David Bowie, Eurythmics and the like. Bowie even greeted the "people behind the Wall" before starting his act. However, with nearly 4,000 East German youths gathering so close to the border, DDR security organs became very edgy and eventually dispersed the crowd. Cordi and I had expected such an outcome. We stayed at home, listened to the West Berlin radio station that transmitted the concert, and taped all songs we liked.

The unnecessary police action on the concert night had angered quite a number of youths who came back to the Brandenburg Gate on the following two evenings to protest. People shouted "Gorbi, Gorbi" (short for Gorbachev), "We want freedom!" and "Down with the Wall", and overran cordoned-off areas, throwing stones and tins at anyone representing the state. Police and secret service, fearing people might storm the border, quickly swung into action to break up the crowd. Protesters were hit by truncheons, some had to spend the night in jail. Poor sods. Afterwards, our media insisted the protests never happened. The fact that West German television stations had filmed the clashes and were showing the pictures on their news programmes did not bother our authorities at all. Instead any such reports were denounced as "fantasy products of western journalists". The DDR government was rapidly losing credibility.

WATCH OUT, STASI IS ABOUT

East Germany, like West Germany, had a National Service. In the DDR all healthy men aged between 18 and 26 had to serve their country in the military for at least 18 months to keep the military balance in Europe. 140,000 soldiers of the National People's Army, supported by the 390,000 Russians stationed in the DDR, faced the 490,000-strong Federal Armed Forces, which in return could count on the support of 225,000 American, 68,000 British and 45,000 French troops stationed in West Germany.

"The protection of the peace and of the socialist fatherland and its achievements is a constitutional right and honourable obligation of the citizens of the German Democratic Republic."
Preamble to the National Service Law

Army officials were keen to get soldiers who would serve for longer than the mandatory period. To reach recruitment targets, officers regularly went to schools to persuade boys to sign up for an extended military service. And if you wanted to study in university, like myself, serving your country for at least three years was a pre-requisite. Time and time again in school, I heard the argument that because the state provided each student with free education and grants, the least one could do in return was to help protect the fatherland for longer than those who didn't go on to study. Many probably would not have minded signing up, if there hadn't been the annoying rule that, for security reasons, no soldier was allowed to be stationed close to home. If you lived in the south, you had to serve the country in the north and if you lived in the east you were sent to do your "honourable duty" in the DDR's west.

However, one group of potential soldiers could outsmart the system: Berliners who joined the 11,400-strong *Feliks Dzerzhinsky* guard's regiment. Named after the founder of the KGB it was stationed in Berlin only. However on the downside, serving in *Feliks Dzerzhinsky* meant signing up for at least three years with the Stasi.

The regiment was part of the Ministry of State Security. Its duties were to welcome foreign dignitaries and to protect high-profile government or party buildings. Not having to leave Berlin for the service was a very tempting incentive. So I decided to give it a go. As long as I wasn't required to spy on people, I felt I could live with being on the Stasi's payroll for three years. Becoming one of the 0.2 per cent of conscripts who refused to do the National Service was never an option for me. The potential threat of being sentenced for up to five years in prison was too much of a deterrent. At least anyone not wanting to handle a weapon for religious reasons could always opt to serve in a construction battalion. Up to a thousand young men a year became so-called spade soldiers whose sole duty it was to build military structures. This was a unique setup among the east bloc nations for which the DDR was regularly criticised by its Allies. Other communist countries did not understand why their East German comrades offered such a soft option.

In 1985, I was called for inspection by the army and grudgingly declared my intention, in writing, to serve for three years:

"I, Oliver Fritz, ...agree to serve as a soldier for three years in the guard's regiment of the Ministry of State Security."

A month after signing the commitment, the Stasi swung into action. They did their customary gathering of information among our neighbours. "Hello Mrs Fritz," Mum was greeted one day by the guy living opposite us. "Is Oliver taking up a new job? Someone was here making enquiries about him." Then a few days later, our doorbell rang. A man in his early forties, medium build, with a chubby face, wavy ash-blond hair and a briefcase under one arm introduced himself as comrade Kauderer from the Ministry of State Security.

He asked whether he could come in. Pretending not to know anything about me I was asked questions about my life and my plans for the future. In return my parents and I wanted to know all about the implications of serving in this battalion. Would Dad still be allowed to travel to the west? And what about my grandparents? Would they still be able to continue their regular visits to West Berlin? The last thing I wanted was to disadvantage anyone. Therefore when comrade Kauderer asked me for names and addresses of two character witnesses, I became extremely cautious. Instead of revealing my best friends to him, I named two older work colleagues. Did Stasi-man really think I would be so stupid to subject my friends to his employers' scrutiny? Kauderer's disappointment over my answer was written all over his face. He made a second attempt to get the information he was really after: "Oliver, why don't you just give me the names of two people who are your age, friends you usually spend your spare time with?" I was tempted to reply with something like "Wouldn't you like to know who I am hanging out with?", but didn't. Instead I told him some rubbish about how "I just prefer the company of older people who I also trust to assess my complex personality more correctly." Comrade Kauderer definitely wasn't happy about this, but he moved on. "Do you have any immediate family living in the west?" he wanted to know next. His face lit up when I told him that we didn't.

After some more chitchat he got some forms out for me to fill in and promised to be back in a fortnight to pick them up. I offered to post the papers, but Kauderer insisted on picking them up. I gave in. Somehow, we all were very relieved to see the back of Mr Stasi that day. Two weeks later he was back, as promised. And when Mum showed him into the living room and offered him a seat on the couch he quickly said: "It's alright, Mrs Fritz. I am going to sit in this armchair again." At the time we did not think anything about it. It was only after he had left that we started to smell a rat. Well, Mum did. She suddenly shook her head and meant that something did not add up: "Why would Kauderer have remembered where he sat the last time? None of us did." Yes, why was he so keen to sit exactly in the same place again? We were wracking our brains until Dad came up with the answer: a bug. The following close inspection of the armchair in question and even of the underneath of the tabletop did not reveal anything suspicious. We were obviously too late. Kauderer must already have successfully recovered whatever listening device he had left behind on his first visit. Now we knew why he had rejected my offer of posting the forms. A family of four had been duped by Mr Stasi. We had to give the bastard credit for that.

Somehow comrade Kauderer must not have been too happy about something he had heard when secretly tapping into our living room conversations. One month later I received a letter, informing me that my application to join the guard's battalion Feliks Dzerzhinsky had been rejected. A second letter a couple of days later, this time coming from the Commissioning District Command of the Armed Forces, stated that I was now required to serve the three years, to which I had signed up for, with the border troops. I could not believe my eyes. I immediately fired off a reply in which I explained that my desire to serve for three years in some God-forsaken dump at the other end of the DDR was non-existent, and that my signed commitment was limited to the Stasi's guards battalion only. As expected, the army invited me soon for a "clarifying" chat.

The guy I had to see was comrade Lange. He was short, with a pointy nose and parted brown hair. As long as he believed he could still win me over, he was very friendly indeed. "Wouldn't you like to serve three years with the border police?" I was asked. I had made up my mind. No, I wouldn't. Even if it meant not being able to study. The border police was considered one of the most dangerous postings for National Service. Around 38,000 soldiers guarded the borders to West Germany and West Berlin (by comparison, only 1,000 men secured our borders to Czechoslovakia and Poland), and it was well known that border guards could not trust each other. It happened more than once, that a border guard was gunned down on duty by a comrade who was desperate to flee to the west. And I was not prepared to become the next victim. Nor would I have been able to shoot at anyone trying to flee our country. No, I was not prepared to serve for longer than the mandatory 18 months in such an environment.

When comrade Lange realised that all this sweet-talking did not work, he quickly changed his strategy. Suddenly I was accused of being against the DDR, socialism and world peace. There was now a danger of World War Three breaking out because of my decision to revoke my commitment to serve for three years. "You do want the DDR and with her socialism on German soil to prosper in peace, don't you?!" I was asked with a sharp undertone. Yet comrade Lange's hope that finally I was about to become putty in his hands was short-lived. Instead of turning into a nodding, spineless zombie who would agree to just anything, I stuck to my defences even more. Thanks to Mum's rebellious gene, which I had obviously inherited, I started a counterattack: "How dare you accuse me of being against socialism if I don't serve for three years", I shouted with such fury, it made comrade Lange jump in his seat. "That will have consequences!" I explained at great length how my workplace in the foreign trade was contributing to our state making precious dollars, Deutschmarks and yen on the international markets. "Money on which our economy heavily relies on so we can afford, among other things, a powerful and modern army. Civilian workplaces aren't called 'Fighting Places for Peace' for nothing," I lectured. "I know where my strength lies and where I can serve my fatherland best and I am very much bewildered by your attempts to talk me into something I would not be good at." Comrade Lange looked at me as if a poodle had just wet his leg. Divine!

Once at home, I immediately wrote a strong letter of complaint to the district commander about the disgraceful behaviour of one his subordinates. The secret to successful complaining in the DDR was to use as much propaganda lingo as possible so the recipient of your grievance had to assume they were dealing with an uber-communist who would cause more trouble if he did not get his way. Consequently, my letters of complaint never ended with "Sincerely yours" or "Kind regards". Instead they finished with "Socialist greetings" or, if I wanted to give off a particularly forceful impression, even "Communist greetings". Hardcore communists usually used such phrases in official correspondence. Certainly no one would have expected them to come from a teenager who got his kicks out of being mistaken for a westerner and whose most-used phrase was "Shitty east". My letter was successful. I got my apology and the district commander invited me in for a chat a month later. Here is how I recorded the event in my diary:

"I was welcomed by two fat army pigs, one of them being Colonel Giese, the district commander, who apologised again profoundly for the remarks made by comrade Lange."

"Mission accomplished", I initially thought, but then Colonel Giese also tried to convince me to serve for three years with the border troops. Every time I put a word in the second army official began writing in a notebook. This annoyed me so much, I got my own writing pad out and began taking notes. As expected, I did not have to wait long until Colonel Giese asked me, somewhat irritated, "What are you writing down there?" As if I was going to tell him! However, to demonstrate good will, I replied: "I am happy for you to read my notes if I in return can read the notes the other comrade, who I haven't been introduced to, has made." Naturally my offer was rejected. Good! Colonel Giese never found out that my four pages full of writing contained nothing more than meaningless scribbles. And nor was he successful in talking me into signing up for three years.

But the army did not give up that easily. On my way out of the building that day, I bumped (purely coincidentally, of course) into Stasi-Kauderer who invited me for a one-to-one in his office there. I was just in the right mood for a confrontation and followed him into a small room that had nothing in it except for a desk and two chairs. As soon as he shut the door behind me he was once again the Stasi recruiter I knew. "Oliver" he began "with you now having to serve at the border I am sure you will appreciate that especially in such a regiment vigilance is a necessity. Every soldier there is required to keep his ears and eyes wide open. What the Ministry of State Security would like you to do is give us reports about the general mood in the troop. You would have regular secret meetings with an officer and we would also train you so you can prepare secret reports with invisible ink and stuff."

How old did he think I was? The prospect of writing with "invisible ink and stuff" might have excited me when I was 12 but, being close to my twentieth birthday, my interests had somewhat moved on. "What do you say?" Kauderer asked. "Um, I am not sure," was my reply. "If there is one thing I really could not do it's spying on people." Playing stupid seemed the best option when dealing with the Stasi. Instead of rejecting their advances I wanted them to come to the conclusion that working with me would be a total waste of their time. "But we are not talking about spying," Kauderer quickly assured me. "It's all about creating a positive environment for the soldiers. If, for example, someone is not happy about his living conditions at home and we hear about it from you, we can boost that solder's moral by allocating him a new flat to rent." Seeing in my face that he was hitting a brick wall with his argument, Kauderer quickly added: "And don't worry, you wouldn't be our only source of information. We always cross-check reports." In other words, the battalion I was lined up for was heaving with Stasi spies. That was it. I'd had enough and just wanted to get out of there without losing face. So I said: "I am still not sure about the whole thing. Let me sleep on it and also have a word with my parents before getting back to you." Kauderer looked at me, his mouth and eyes wide open, as if I had just committed a terrible sacrilege. "Oliver", he hissed, "you can't speak to your parents or anyone else about what we have just discussed." He was getting annoyed with me. Great, I had found his weak point.

"Can't I?" I asked back innocently, explaining to him that we always discussed important things within in the family. But instead of giving up on me as I had secretly hoped, Kauderer became all buddy-buddy. Patting me on the back he said with a big cheesy smile, "Surely you don't need to ask your parents for permission", followed by a patronising, "You are a grown man now, not a child any more." I told Kauderer to give me his number and I would get back to him, but sensing that he had not yet bagged me, he changed his tactic once more. He gave me two stern warnings. "You cannot speak to anyone about this matter" he repeated before adding, "And don't think that you can wriggle you way out of your responsibility. Once we have set our eyes on someone we will not let go until we've got them." The phrase "let's wait and see" shot through my mind, but to keep Kauderer sweet I feigned interest and asked what our next meeting would be about. Now Kauderer was back in his element. "Well, first I will have to teach you conspiracy and for that we will meet at a tram stop near your home. When you get off the tram you will see me waiting nearby. But rather than saying 'hello' we will pretend to not know each other. Then you will casually follow me at a distance of 50 metres to a safe house. Once inside we will go through the different methods of how to gain information successfully and how to pass it on secretly." Meeting him at a tram stop and following him casually? Who did he think he was – James Bond? And who did he think I was – Joe Nerd? The Stasi might have successfully recruited 17,000 snitches aged 25 or younger, (1,700 of them even were under the age of 18) but not in a million years did I fit the profile for a teenage spy. I was not a loner, nor was I in need of a father figure.

When I left Kauderer that day he handed me a piece of paper with a telephone number in case I needed to rearrange our next meeting that was scheduled for two weeks later. My plan was to reschedule the meeting again and again until Kauderer lost all interest in me. To get the ball rolling, I dialled his number a day before our next get-together. "Hello?" someone barked down the line. "Yes hello," I barked back, "Comrade Kauderer please." "One moment." Then the noise of rifling through paper. "How do you spell that?" I spelled it out for him. "Sorry, I haven't got a comrade Kauderer in my directory. Have you got another name for him?" "Yes, he gave me Peter as a second alias." More rifling through paper. "I am sorry, but I can't find a Peter either. Has he given you any other name." "No, not really," I replied. "How many names is a person supposed to have?" "Sorry, but I can't help you then. Good bye." "Peter Kauderer" had obviously lost track about what cover names he was using at what time. Tough luck for him. Someone so stupid deserved to be stood up.

The next day, I went to the cinema. My tram went past the stop on which Kauderer was waiting for me. I could see him looking at his watch. I didn't bother getting off and continued my journey as planned. Kauderer, or whatever his real name was, never called me to find out why I had not made it to the meeting. Somehow he must have found out that I had not kept my mouth shut and had told Dad all about the Stasi's ham-fisted attempts to recruit me. Bugging our home while everyone was at work would have been easy for the comrades from "Hear and Peer". Or maybe he got wind of my attempts to avoid National Service altogether by gathering as many doctor's certificates as possible, so I would be excused on the grounds of poor health. A strategy, with which I eventually succeeded, thanks to a handful of helpful doctors. When the army's Medical Examination Commission informed me six months later that the forces had reclassified me as "permanently unfit" I felt like the happiest boy behind the Iron Curtain.

After the fall of the Wall it became known that the secret service kept a network of 12,000 informants among the armed forces, which were led by 2,000 Stasi employees from a department named "Administration 2000".

As for Kauderer, a couple of months after our foiled meeting, my parents saw him again on their way to the *Kaufhalle* (supermarket). He was coming from the nearby tram stop. They greeted Kauderer with big, knowing grins but he seemed to be in a hurry and just gave them a quick nod as he rushed past. A spotty teenager was following him "discreetly", 50 metres behind.

MOVIE MANIA

I might not have been made for a life as a spy or informant, but a good espionage thriller always did it for me. So it was a pity that we could only see James Bond movies on West German telly, as the DDR did not import any films which glorified western spies. But that doesn't mean the only films shown in our cinemas were bad communist ones. Some of the movies Cordi and I went to over the years were huge international blockbusters: *Close Encounters of the Third Kind, Crocodile Dundee, The Last Emperor, Fame, Tootsie, ET, The Never-ending Story, Rain Man, Out of Africa*, and *The Colour Purple*, to name just a few. Hollywood made us East Germans dream too. When Cordi and I came out of *A Chorus Line*, for example, nothing could dampen our spirits. The two of us sang and danced the whole way home. The fact that the temperature outside had dropped to an Arctic minus 30 degrees centigrade in the course of the evening had escaped our attention.

For many years my personal favourite was *On Golden Pond*. So much so, that I once even lugged my trusty cassette recorder R4100 into the cinema and secretly taped the German dialogue (most foreign films are dubbed in Germany) so I could listen to it again and again. But I was hardly as obsessed as Simone, one of my disco friends, who proudly claimed to have seen *Dirty Dancing* a whopping 150 times. She could recite lengthy movie scenes by heart. A nice girl, but unfortunately you could not talk to her about anything else but Patrick Swayze.

The only drawback with imported capitalist movies was that they were not the most recent releases. To save US dollars, the DDR always waited a few years before buying any film rights. *Beat Street* for example was released in East Germany a year after it came out in the western world. For *Blue Thunder* we had to wait four years. And *Woman in Red* found its way across the Iron Curtain three years after its first release. International film festivals may have provided us with a more up-to-date fare, but getting tickets for those events always proved to be very difficult. One time Cordi and I set our hearts on some screenings at the Norwegian Film Days held in the DDR. By the time I turned up at the cinema asking for tickets, every listed performance was sold out. All tickets had been snapped up within a couple of hours after opening. Shitty east!

On other occasions I was much more on the ball. In December 1985, an ad appeared in our daily, the *Berliner Zeitung*, placed by the state-owned television company. They were looking for new faces, so I sent a passport photo, along with a brief description of myself, to the station's casting agency. One completed questionnaire later I was taken on. I thought the world was my oyster, though I really wasn't sure whether it had been a wise move agreeing to do nude scenes if necessary. Thankfully no film director ever wanted to see me in the flesh.

Around 15,000 different TV productions and up to 20 cinema films were made in the DDR every single year, so fresh faces were always welcome. While things started off fairly slowly for me in 1986, by 1987 I was in business, making quite a bit of money on the side. Most of it was immediately spent on trendy clothes. A day's filming usually paid between 50 and 80 marks (24 to 32 dollars), but night shoots were the real cash cows. Sacrificing a night's sleep in return for 120 marks (48 dollars) always seemed a good deal to me. In the export-import company I made 40 marks a day and the work there was half as exciting. But I wasn't so stupid as to wave goodbye to my office job. It may not have made me rich but at least the income was regular. Film work was very sporadic. So I combined the two, and mostly filmed outside office hours. If I needed time off work, I drew upon my holiday entitlement of 21 days or used up accumulated overtime. And getting overtime was so easy, I earned it in my sleep. Literally! Countless times I went straight to work after finishing a night shoot, usually at four or five in the morning. Work started officially at seven am and the power naps I had before my colleagues arrived always boosted my overtime account nicely. The tricky bit was to wake up on time and to look busy before everyone else arrived. But I managed both, successfully every single time. In retrospect I should have won an Oscar for my performances at work.

UNIFORM ADVENTURES

Over the years I worked on more than 150 TV and cinema productions. I had parts as a construction worker, a tradesman, a ghost, a bear, a nosy member of the public, a courtier, a gardener... Yet most of the time I was being typecast. Being tall and blond with blue-grey eyes meant I was regularly asked to play either a soldier or policeman. Ironic, considering I wasn't fit for National Service.

Leaving the film set while wearing a uniform was, for obvious reasons, forbidden. I would never have dreamt of roaming the streets of East Berlin in a Russian or American armed forces outfit. But wearing a DDR policeman's uniform made it tempting for me to quickly pop out into the hustle and bustle of real life. One day, the filming inside a house had come to a temporary standstill because of a technical fault and I was absolutely ravenous as there was no catering provided on this set. "Now or never!" I said to myself, quickly grabbed my uniform hat and sneaked out unseen through the backdoor. With my chest puffed out and my hands behind my back I intended to make my way to the nearest bakery. I got 50 metres without any problems, then I saw a real policeman coming my way. "Oh my God" shot it through my head "what am I going to do? What is my rank? Will I have to greet him first? What if he asks something?" I suddenly felt very sick. My pulse started racing as I marched on with my head held up high. The two of us got closer and closer. "If hell is about to be let loose, then so be it." I said to myself just seconds before our paths crossed. Thankfully the feared showdown did not happen. We two constables greeted each other as we passed and continued walking. That was it! What a relief. I really had pulled it off. But there was no rest for the wicked.

Just as I turned into the main road, still marvelling at my excellent acting skills, I felt someone tugging my left uniform sleeve from behind. Fearing I might have been found out I quickly turned around to verbally attack whoever dared to challenge me. But who did I face? A small grey-haired lady who clearly was in a very distraught state. Before I could even ask what the matter was the words poured out of her: "Constable, constable you have to come with me. Quickly! There is a man, a bus driver, lying in front of the electrical goods shop. He is not moving and no one knows what's wrong with him. He seems to be unconscious. Maybe he is dead. You really need to come!" Why me? All I wanted was to get something to eat and show off that darned uniform. Being dragged into doing something about a guy who had passed out in the street could land me in all sorts of trouble. What if another passer-by had gotten hold of a real policeman in the meantime? What if the emergency services were already there? What if I was asked to take statements from people? Sneaking out in that uniform suddenly seemed such a stupid idea. What had I been thinking?

As we reached the lifeless body and I saw that there were only a few bystanders at the scene, my confidence returned. I quickly asked around whether anyone had seen how the guy went down but people just shook their heads. There was no blood anywhere and as I knelt down to check if the bus driver was still alive, he opened the eyes, raised his head and mumbled:

"Pissed today, pissed tomorrow and the day after tomorrow I will be pissed too." Then his head fell back and he started snoring. I don't know how I would have reacted if the guy had been dead. But since he was only drunk, the matter could, thankfully, be wrapped up quickly. I popped my head into the hairdresser's next door, ordered the employees to call an ambulance and I was off again. This time, straight back to the film set. I never made it to the bakery. Though I was still starving, my appetite for adventure had been satisfied for that day. Had I been caught on my illegal trip, I could have expected a fine of up to 500 marks (200 dollars)!

A very similar stunt on another occasion nearly got me arrested. The Free German Youth organisation was organising a Whitsun Festival in Berlin, with lots of cultural performances happening at different venues throughout the city. To create an olde-worlde atmosphere, I along with 15 other performers, was asked to roam the streets of the city centre in historic costumes. As expected, I was assigned the imperial policeman's uniform from the early twentieth century. The brief was to stay all day within the boundary of the Nicolai Quarter – an area that is a modern-day reconstruction of old Berlin. So far, so good, but come one o'clock, my lunchtime, I was curious to see what was happening elsewhere at the festival. After all, I was a member of the Free German Youth too. So I started walking down the main boulevard, Unter den Linden, looking left and right. After 800 metres I was stopped by a policeman: "Excuse me, what you are trying to achieve by wearing this outfit?" It took me a while to understand what he meant. Apparently my socialist "colleague" was worried that I was out to ridicule the DDR by suggesting it was as militaristic as the German imperialist empire, whose uniform I wore. Our security organs were always very edgy when they thought an anti-DDR provocation was taking place. As I tried to explain that I was wearing the outfit for financial, rather than politically motivated, reasons people started to gather around us to see what our arguing was about. To avoid creating a huge stir on the main road, the police officer asked me to accompany him to a side street where a patrol car and a colleague were waiting. Having had nothing to hide I followed him readily. Once there, my ID card was taken and enquiries were made over the police car's two-way radio. Ten minutes and 20 questions later, I was free to leave, even though the constable in the car made it quite clear that he would have liked to book me and did not agree with his headquarter's decision to let me go. I just smiled and shrugged my shoulders as I took my ID back, giving him my best "tough luck, pal" look.

The entire time I had been dealing with these two idiots, I was standing with my back to the main road. When turning round I was in for a big surprise. My dealings with the police had attracted spectators. Loads of them! Roughly two hundred people had been watching us from a short distance. As they saw me walking off, some of them started to applaud. The bystanders must have thought I was some kind of agent provocateur and patted me on the back and the shoulders with approving nods as I fought my way back to the main road. I could not understand why anyone would mistake my costume for a political statement. The only explanation I could come up with was that DDR citizens had adapted to reading between lines so well that sometimes events were given deeper meanings, even if there weren't any.

As I continued my stroll, a West German tourist approached me. He wanted to buy my police hat. As tempting as his offer was, I had to decline. While I was still pondering whether it had been wise to reject the 100 Deutschmarks (40 dollars) he offered, another two policemen blocked my way. They greeted me with a "humorous" opening line: "We have not been advised that there will be different uniforms to ours present in the streets." I did not laugh. Instead I lost my temper when I was asked for my motives and ID papers. I angrily told them that I was working for DDR State Television and that I was sick and tired of having to explain myself every five metres. They were not impressed by my speech. Once again, my papers were checked. Once again, I was free to go. I eventually made it back to the designated historic quarter without any more delays. When I collected my pay in the evening, the producer winked at me and said jokingly: "Ah, our runaway policeman is back." Apparently my thoughtless walk had caused a bit of a commotion at the TV station during the day. The security organs had called the TV station to check out the credibility of my story. I was embarrassed beyond belief.

The best job I ever had was when I secured myself a role in a series about the history of Carl Zeiss Jena, the high-quality optical lens manufacturer. I was one of the main characters yet never had to do any filming. In the beginning of the series I fought in the war, and later I fell for the fatherland. So all that viewers ever would see of me were the framed pictures that my screen wife had put on her grand piano in the salon. But those photos, including some wedding pictures, had to be taken first. On this occasion I was a high-ranking Nazi and as the costume designer and I were going through rails of film uniforms I realised, with horror, that these were all originals. Jackets, trousers and hats still had soldiers' ranks and names noted on their labels. Creepy. Somehow I had always assumed that Nazi uniforms used for filming, just like other historical outfits, were replicas.

After we found a costume that fitted properly, a swastika armband was slipped on for the final touch and the fascist officer they wanted was ready. All that needed doing now was to get me to my "wife" who was waiting with a photographer in a TV studio at another location. When the chauffeured car arrived to take us there, the assistant producer jumped into the front passenger seat, while I had the back bench of the Lada all to myself. We were in the middle of a lively conversation when, suddenly, all colour drained from the assistant producer's face. I was interrupted mid-sentence: "Oliver, your arm! Take your arm down!" While I had made myself comfortable on the back seat I had unconsciously rested my right arm on top of the back of the seat. This brought the swastika armband into full view of the traffic behind us. A definite no-no in a country that placed a high value on its antifascist credentials.

The entrance to the main broadcasting centre was guarded by police around the clock. Visitors were required to hand in their ID card in return for a visitor's permit. As our vehicle stopped at the boom gate, the production assistant quickly jumped out of the car to do the necessary paperwork in the guard's office. Under no circumstances was I allowed to be seen in public wearing a mustard-coloured nazi outfit. A couple of minutes later the assistant returned with my permit. However, the guard standing next to the boom, which now opened for us, made a terrible faux pas a moment later. He must have caught a glimpse of me wearing a uniform. And being chauffeured as well as having had someone doing the entrance paperwork, must have made him jump to the wrong conclusions about my persona. As we drove past the policeman suddenly raised his right arm and saluted me. God knows how my bright red swastika armband escaped his attention. He could have been in trouble had anyone else seen his salutation. Thankfully no one else had noticed it. I nonchalantly raised my left hand in acknowledgement of his greeting before we sped past him on our way to the studio.

Unfortunately, earning good money just for having a few photos taken was not a regular occurrence. On most occasions, cash had to be earned the hard way. Like the time when we were doing a World War One scene at an army training ground near Berlin. It was a hot summer's day. By ten am, the temperature had already risen to well above 30 degrees centigrade. Nice weather for running around in T-shirt, shorts and sandals, but unbearable while acting in a heavy uniform made of itchy felt.

After we had finished some scenes in the trenches, it was time for us to storm the enemy lines. First we were advised about where explosive charges, mimicking French shells being fired at us, had been placed on the field. Once we were familiar with their locations, we were given the timings: "Listen guys, the first explosion happens ten seconds after you have left the trench. The second explosion, five metres further down on the left, 12 seconds after the first one. The third explosion, three metres down on the right, 15 seconds later," and so on. "What happens," asked one of my soldiers, "if I stumble or can't run that fast? This old rifle weights a ton?" "Don't stumble! Move as quickly as you can, because the explosions will happen regardless." was the director's reply. Seeing the horror in all of our faces, we were quickly assured that the explosions were harmless. The ambulance on standby in the far distance was somehow painting quite a different picture.

After a few dry runs we were ready to do it for real. As per script, 20 of us boys jumped out of our trench and ran downhill towards an imaginary enemy. But for some reason the director wasn't happy with our performance, so we were asked to do it again... and again... and again. It was hell! The heat and the various explosions, which constantly showered us with sand, took their toll. Then we discovered that small particles from the explosive were burning holes into our uniforms. After the fifth take everyone in front of the camera went on strike. We were thirsty, exhausted and sweating like pigs. My mouth was full of sand that had been thrown up by the explosions and while throwing myself for the umpteenth time on the ground, I had bruised my knee on a rock. The others had similar complaints. A runner who turned up with a surprise crate of ice-cold drinks defused the situation a little. We only returned to battle after being promised a supplementary payment for our efforts. It took another three exhausting takes before the director was finally satisfied and called it a day. When I eventually saw the finished film, it hardly seemed worth our effort – the battlefield scene had been cut down to less than ten seconds.

BEING A PET SHOP BOY

DDR state television entertained the masses with two channels that were 100 per cent in line with the Communist's Party policies. It had 7,000 employees, of which 5,000 worked at the station's Berlin headquarters. Though only 28 per cent of DDR television staff were members of the Communist Party, no one could study journalism without being loyal to our political system. Critical minds were not welcome and had to find other career paths.

In 1972, 72 per cent of all East German households had a television set. By 1988, that figure had risen to 96 per cent, out of which half were colour receivers. By then, a third of the population even owned two or three tellies. State television broadcast 20 hours daily, out of which the average viewer watched between two and three hours. That's between 14 and 21 hours a week. By comparison, British viewers today manage 18 hours weekly.

What I particularly disliked on our television programmes was that productions were often too realistic – at least a third of all drama productions had to be set in the then socialist present. It totally escaped me why anyone who had come home from work would want to watch a film about a foreman or a shop assistant having to solve job-related problems. If anything, people wanted to be entertained and forget all about work. Yet the ruling Communist Party thought differently:

"The programme planning shall even more effectively... make people familiar with the values, advantages and abilities of the ruling workers and farmers. Thereby, the unshakable belief in the worldwide triumph of socialism and the pride in the DDR's socialist achievements has to be more emphasised."

Politburo resolution

Between 700 and 800 movies were shown on DDR television every year. We imported movies like *What's Up, Doc?, La Boom* or *Miss Marple.*. But our station's annual budget for western imports was only two million Deutschmarks (800,000 dollars). The average West German station could spend 20 million Deutschmarks annually on international film rights. Consequently western stations were very popular with East German viewers.

But DDR television wasn't all doom and gloom. We had some very popular easy entertainment. *Glück muss man haben* (One Has To Have Luck), for example, was a show involving different teams, each made up of a VIP and a member of the public, who had to answer questions. What made this programme so popular was that the top prize was a Trabant!

In *Wennschon, Dennschon* (In for a Penny, In for a Pound) eccentrics or weird record holders were introduced to the public. I remember seeing, for example, the fastest supermarket cashier, the oldest disc jockey and the friendliest security guard. But most popular was its parent programme *Aussenseiter, Spitzenreiter* (Outsiders and Frontrunners). A format in which the TV nation became acquainted with weird hobbies and collections or answers to strange questions. Viewers learned about the average length of a loo roll, how giraffes slept and where the geographical centre of the DDR was. We were introduced to a TV-addicted goat and saw the DDR's biggest privately owned clock collection as well as the country's oldest, fully functioning telly. Reporters visited the man who had to wait 16 years and two months before being allocated a subscription to a very popular weekly satirical magazine, a whistling baby and the car owner who could replace his Trabant's transmission belt in a record-breaking two minutes and 11 seconds. In *Schätzen Sie mal* (Have a Guess), participants had to estimate things such as, the number of bridges in our capital, the speed of a flash of lightning or the age of the oldest Siberian – at least one question of the quiz had to be related to the Soviet Union. The *Wunschbriefkasten* (Letterbox of Wishes) fulfilled viewers' requests for beloved TV moments while the *Rumpelkammer* (Junk Room) showed clips from old black-and-white movies. But our TV station's entertainment jewel in the crown was undoubtedly the big Saturday night variety show *Ein Kessel Buntes* (A Washtub Full of Coloureds). Broadcast six times a year from 1972 to 1989, and featuring artists from over 50 countries, 40 per cent of all viewers regularly tuned in to the programme. Five- or even six-digit dollar amounts were paid to top international stars who would appear on DDR television. To stretch the DDR's annual budget of 500,000 Deutschmarks (200,000 dollars) for western performers, fees were usually topped up with DDR marks with which goods like fur coats, porcelain or grand pianos could be purchased. Stars flocked behind the Iron Curtain in droves – Adamo (Belgian singer), Boland & Boland (Dutch singers), Cliff Richard, Abba's Agnetha Faltskog, Samantha Fox, Middle of the Road (Scottish band), Mireille Mathieu (French singer), Nana Mouskouri, Shirley Bassey and the Pet Shop Boys. They, and many others, made money not only in the north, the south and the west of the globe, but also in the east.

Once I had to pretend to be a Pet Shop Boy. No, DDR television did not try to pass me off as the real thing. Hammering away at the keys on a silent keyboard, I was merely a stand-in for Chris Lowe during rehearsals. International stars can hardly be expected to wait on stage while spotlights are being set and the producer decides on the best camera angles. Being a stand-in for quiz or variety shows was fun, easy money and gave me the chance to get close to the stars. However, when the long-awaited real Pet Shop Boys turned up in the theatre for the dress rehearsals, disillusionment set in quickly. Before the duo's arrival the production assistant had already warned everyone working on stage and in the auditorium that, at the Pet Shop Boy's request, private photography was not allowed. When an electrician ignored the request and took a snapshot of the duo walking past, Neil Tennant jumped at the guy. The surprised electrician legged it, only to be chased round the auditorium by a big bloke from the group's entourage. When the culprit was finally caught, he had to hand over the film. Amazingly, no one from our production team intervened. I guess the Pet Shop Boys had to be kept sweet. Even official photos could only be taken with lots of kerfuffle. Because of a bald patch Neil Tennant did not want to be photographed from certain positions. Over the years, I have come close to many national and international artists but in my experience Neil Tennant was the biggest diva of them all.

I AM READY FOR MY CLOSE-UP

The first time I was asked to be a stand-in I did not know what to expect. Friends and family members made wild guesses about what might be required from me. Suggestions ranged from being a body double in a sex scene to having something thrown at me. I became much calmer when I learnt that I literally had to stand-in for a similar-looking actor on some test recordings. For a couple of hours, I was filmed in different lighting conditions, sporting a face covered in white make-up. And that was it. Another easy job over. However, getting rid of the make-up afterwards proved to be a real difficulty. The cleansing oil the make-up artist used did not cut through the thick layer of face paint. I finally managed to get rid of two thirds of the make-up with water. The rest continued to stubbornly cling to my face and neck, leaving an unappealing thin white layer behind, making me look like a ghost. I did not want to be seen in public like this. So I got the make-up artist to slap some dark brown make-up onto the white base and from a distance I looked normal again. At least so I thought. Only at home did I realise that close-up I could have been mistaken for a model coming straight from the Barbara Cartland School of Make-Up Application. God knows what Ingo, an ex-classmate of mine who I had bumped into on the way home, had made of my appearance. I never saw him again to ask.

Another time, a health programme wanted to film different parts of my body to illustrate various medical conditions. Filming started quite late, at seven pm. First they did various shots of my face and me sleepwalking around the studio in my pyjamas before I was asked to take off my top. Footage of my naked upper body was needed. For this, every visible millimetre of my skin was painstakingly covered in make-up before the cameras began rolling again. By the time filming finished, it was one o'clock in the morning. The TV studio corridors, otherwise buzzing with people, were deserted when I went back to my dressing room. My steps were echoing eerily as I walked the endlessly long passageways. As suspected, my make-up artist was long gone. How was I supposed to remove the caked-on make-up from the back by myself? I could not manage it, and so had no other choice but to slip into my private clothes with large areas of my skin still covered in gunk. Despite a quick shower at home, the next morning my pyjama top, duvet cover and bed sheet all carried large brown stains. Mum was not too happy with me, considering that she had only changed the bed linen the previous day.

The greatest fear for television executives were live broadcasts. The slimmest possibility of someone being able to make a derogatory comment about socialism while on air had to be eradicated. So the majority of programmes were recorded. And if that wasn't possible, like the news for example, a policeman was put on guard at the studio's entrance door during the recording. It's a pity that no incidents ever happened, our news would have benefited from a bit of spicing up. The worst offender was the programme in the 7.30pm slot, called *Aktuelle Kamera* (up-to-date camera). It was a half-hour programme that usually started with reports on workers' achievements and figures that were supposed to be evidence of the health of our economy. Then followed reports of DDR politicians visiting or welcoming international dignitaries, sports news and a brief section on world affairs. Viewing figures for this programme were tightly guarded. Why? In the 1980s the already low viewing figure of ten per cent had fallen even further to an all-time low of between three and eight per cent (other programmes on DDR television were watched by an average of 40 per cent). Sadly, nothing was done to improve the situation. People instead got their news from one of the ten TV stations or 24 radio stations run by the enemy behind the Iron Curtain.

WAR REQUIEM

East Berlin's most exclusive hotel was the five-star Grand Hotel. And grand it truly was. Built in cooperation with Swedish and Japanese companies and opened in honour of Berlin's 750th birthday in 1987, it was THE epitome of glamour and internationalism in our capital. Though, with prices starting at 70 pounds a night for a single room and going up to 1,200 pounds for a suite (payable in western currencies only), a stay at the Grand Hotel was out of reach for most of us easterners. At least we were welcome to spend our DDR marks in any of the hotel's many cafés and restaurants that could be accessed directly from the street. The hotel lobby was reserved for staying guests only. Anyone looking remotely East German was ushered out as quickly as they had come in through the revolving door. Still, several times I managed to sit undetected in one of the comfy armchairs, watching the world go by, while imagining how nice it would be to be able to afford such luxury. One day I got a telegram from my casting agent informing me that the Grand Hotel had chosen me to participate in one of their parties. I could not believe my luck.

Along with a handful of other guys and girls, I was asked to enhance the hotel's New Year's Eve bash as a "Bearer of Good Tidings". Dressed as gardeners, chimney sweeps, bakers and shepherds, we mingled with party guests on the night to create a cheerful atmosphere. I was a gardener. The trousers I had to wear were very tight. An older lady pinched my bum. Twice! I just smiled. At midnight, we marched around in a little parade, distributed lucky pennies and that was it. Job done! Afterwards, we could join the party in our own clothes as private individuals. I befriended several West Germans. By the early hours, the party had become very boozy. I left at four-thirty am, after a drunken guest put his hand into my half-eaten crème brûlée while vomiting into a champagne cooler. I still rated it the best New Year's Eve party I ever went to. Even more so, as I got paid a whopping 175 marks (70 dollars) for attending. Though I really could have done without the headache on New Year's Day.

What I named the "classical job" gave me a headache of a different time. One day we were filming a scene in East Berlin's concert hall in preparation for Benjamin Britton's War Requiem, which was to be taking place the following night. Cordelia and I had tried to get tickets for this concert, but without success. When I discovered during filming that the backstage pass I had been given was also valid for the night of the premiere, a cunning plan to see the performance for free began to take shape in my mind...

The next evening Cordi and made our way to the concert hall. I entered the building first, at the stage entrance. A couple of minutes later, I handed Cordi my backstage pass through a little window that, as I had noticed the previous day, could not be shut because of camera cables running to the outside broadcasting unit. Once she was in, we made ourselves comfortable in the canteen until the first bell went off. When we got up to go to the auditorium, I could no longer remember where the door that I had used on the previous day was. With Cordelia in tow, I walked up and down the stairs and back and forth along the corridors. But it was to no avail – nothing looked familiar. Then the second bell rang. And we were still wandering about backstage! Finally I found THE door. I pushed down on the handle but nothing happened. Someone had locked the damned thing over night. Panic set in. In desperation, we opened all possible doors to see if they would give us access to the auditorium. No such luck. After we had run into an endless number of broom cabinets and storage rooms, the third bell rang. The performance was about to start any minute. Finally a door opened to the auditorium. Cordi and I ran out. Oops! We could not believe where we found ourselves – on the choir balcony above the main stage in front of a sold out house. Eighty singers in black robes who had just taken their places and hundreds of spectators looked at us from their seats in confusion. What now? The conductor made his way to the podium. People began clapping. Time was about to run out for us. At least now I knew where we were in the building. We quickly run backstage again, up one floor and finally emerged in the upper balcony. Just as the lights were dimmed and the first few bars of the music were played, an usher quickly pushed us in the direction of two empty seats. We had made it! What a pity that, after all the effort we had put into getting into the performance, the music wasn't our cup of tea. We left during the break, but with a story to tell.

BROTHERS IN ARMS

Getting into the Concert Hall without tickets was one thing, infiltrating a party of international army officials was quite another. It was a cold Saturday evening in February 1987 and, after failing to get into a disco because of the long queue, Cordi and I were aimlessly wandering the streets of East Berlin.

As we walked past the Congress Centre and saw people inside dancing and helping themselves to a huge buffet, we knew we had found our entertainment for the evening. Unfortunately all three sets of entrance doors were guarded by big, burly men. We made our way to the stage entrance where a little old lady was on duty. "What can I do for you?" she asked in a frail voice. "I would like to see my brother Lutz Kerschowski who is performing here tonight." I replied confidently. Lutz Kerschowski was an East German singer, and I prayed to God he wouldn't be there. My prayers were answered: "I haven't got anyone with that name on my list, but let me ask someone backstage" came the reply from the porter's cabin and the lady went off on her search mission. Cordi and I were rubbing our cold hands in anticipation. With the back door now unguarded, we quickly let ourselves in, congratulating us on our brilliant plan. But we had both overlooked the guy standing right behind the door. He was big and had a little radio speaker in his ear. We were summoned to wait for the porter's return. Damn! Three minutes later we were back in the cold.

Resigned to calling it a night, we began heading to the underground, when we noticed that the front doors of the Congress Centre were not guarded any more. Hooray, the evening was saved after all! We quickly sneaked in and the buffet was one of the best we had ever seen. Row upon row of cold meats, salads and canapés were there for the taking. The pièce de rèsistance was a huge Brandenburg Gate made of butter. How very decadent! While I was still marvelling at the structure, Cordelia went over to take a huge dollop out of one of the gate's columns which she spread about three centimetres high on a small slice of baguette. I wasn't sure whether she really was about to eat that concoction. She didn't. After taking a small bite she loudly announced to me in a posh voice: "Uh, I don't like it. It's too... buttery." and dumped the piece of bread on someone's plate who had just gone for a dance. Then we raided the buffet properly. Every time our path led us past the damaged buttery miniature landmark we had to snort with laughter. As it turned out, Cordi and I had invited ourselves to a party thrown by the DDR army to celebrate the military cooperation of the eastern bloc. High-ranking officers from all communist countries were having a carefree evening. They sported so much bling on their uniforms, we regretted not having our shades on us. Cordi and I mingled a lot with other plain-clothes couples so we would not stand out too much in our preppy outfits.

After we had our picture taken by the resident photographer, Cordi noticed that the main doors were under guard again. The men must have been on a quick break when we slipped in. But before the feeling of how lucky we had been could sink in, an officer from the National People's Army approached us. He and his wife, arm in arm, were smiling. "What is this all about?" I muttered to Cordelia who was as clueless as me. A meter away from us, the guy saluted us, while his wife nodded agreeably in our direction. Our faces froze in cheesy smiles. Cordelia waved and I nodded back, before we quickly changed direction and walked briskly to the bar at the other end of the building. A couple of glasses Crimean sparkling wine did a good job of calming our nerves.

From then on, Cordi and I remained on the packed dance floor to avoid any similar incidents of mistaken identity. Fuelled by free alcohol, the crowd became very lively as the evening progressed. Even more so when the famous double act of Hauff & Henkler entered the stage. Many DDR citizens mistook this cheesy folk-singing duo for a couple, which they never were. Nothing could have been further from the truth. I was once present in the TV studio as a song of theirs was recorded. Before filming started, Herr Henkler entered the stage from the left, Frau Hauff from the right. Not a word was exchanged between the two. Ignoring each other she looked at an imaginary point in the far distance while he made sure that his watch chain and chunky rings would be visible to the viewers while playing the guitar. Their moods changed immediately as soon as the cameras started rolling. Suddenly, smiles overcame their faces, loving glances were exchanged and the air seemed to be full of chemistry between the two. True professionals – respect to them! That evening at the party, they also gave a very good performance, including one of their biggest hits: *Into the Trees, You Apes, the Forest is Being Swept.* The dance floor was a sea of moving uniforms and cocktail dresses.

On our way out at midnight, I patted one of the inefficient door guards on the shoulder and mumbled: "Well done, my friend." before hopping with Cordelia into one of East Berlin's many illegal minicabs. Regular cabs were hard to get without an advance booking because subsidised fares made them very popular. This was the hour for enterprising private car owners to jump at the chance to earn a few DDR marks on the side. Wherever a potential passenger tried in vain to flag down a licensed taxi in the evening, an unofficial cab would stop. The advantage in taking an illegal minicab was that the passenger could pay whatever amount he deemed appropriate. The driver was not in the position to demand any money. I always paid half of what a licensed cabbie would have charged. Our driver that evening wasn't too lucky. He was apprehended by a policeman for picking us up in a non-stopping zone and given a 20 marks (eight dollars) on-the-spot fine, payable immediately. Our fare, on the other hand, only came to a fiver. A raw deal for the guy but had Cordelia and I not pretended to be his cousins when he was questioned by the policeman, he would have faced a much stiffer penalty. The authorities were determined to stamp out the illegal minicab business. Thankfully, they never succeeded.

FAME

My office job was good for the pay cheque at the end of the month, but hardly the epitomé of cool. With television and movie experience under my belt, I felt that applying to East Berlin's (only) acting school was the next logical step. Convinced of my capabilities, I learned the audition song, poem and two scripts just three days before the big day. The poor preparation showed. My performance was unbelievably bad. But I was impressed by how cool the school's existing students were, as they tried to boost the confidence of us 30-odd hopefuls who were auditioning. They sang, tap-danced and sword-fought for our entertainment in the corridors during breaks. "The atmosphere there was just like in *Fame* – the movie." I wrote in my diary. A pity that all of us applicants that day were rejected.

I decided to channel my talents elsewhere. "How talented does one have to be to be photographed?" I asked myself as I saw the "MODELS SOUGHT" notice that had been put up on a shop's notice board by a photographer. I called the number, made an appointment and a week later I found myself sitting opposite Detlef, in his living room. Detlef, a skinny, blonde, camp guy in his late twenties, did not beat around the bush: He was looking for boys and girls who were happy to be photographed in the nude. Oops, that wasn't the path I wanted to go down. Pornography was considered degrading and forbidden in the DDR. Detlef assured me that he had arty nude photos in mind. Many magazines published those. The most prolific by far was *Das Magazin*. With a monthly circulation of nearly 600,000 copies, its aim was to "tastefully entertain and educate its readers". It published the first nude photo of a woman in 1954, the first naked man followed in 1975. In the late Eighties, its classified section became an El Dorado for sexually open-minded people, including couples looking for other couples or individuals seeking fun with members of the same or the opposite sex. *Das Magazin* was one of the most sought-after publications in the DDR.

So, I wasn't shocked at all when Detlef showed me examples of his work – tit, dick and bum shots. For my taste he just seemed a tad too keen wanting to add me to his collection. I asked for some time to think about it and never went back. Sorry, Detlef!

Instead, I joined a choir. Developing my singing voice seemed a much better idea. With our group's repertoire of historic and modern songs, we seemed to strike a chord with audiences. However as the months progressed, I was longing for some individuality. For one performance I swapped the obligatory black tie for a fluorescent-green leather one that Grandma had bought me in West Berlin. "Either the tie goes or you," the conductor said to me. The tie stayed and I went, straight to a fashion show organiser to become a dressman, as male models were referred to in DDR speak.

The fashion show troupe I joined was called *Kledage* and consisted of one boy and six girls who made it their goal to bring a bit of colour into socialist everyday life by showing fashion creations to an audience in a themed setting. Our routine was always the same: In the first scene the girls pretended to be shop display dolls. After I dressed them with different pieces of fabric they came to life and showed the audience how little it takes to pep up a look with accessories. The second scene was about the ever-popular sailor's theme. A nicely choreographed story performed to an Erasure song. A spy theme gave us the opportunity to strut around in business attire wearing sunglasses. In two more scenes I mimed a photographer and a thief. The show would end with clothes made of junk and elaborate, over-the-top, black leather outfits with matching giant hats. The programme offered something for everyone. And though we also sold clothes after each performance, the outfits we sported during the show were unique one-offs and not for sale. Once a guy from the audience pestered me after the show, asking me to sell him my grey stage jacket from the spy scene for an obscene amount of money. The jacket was my own, and as much as I wanted to, I couldn't sell it. That particular fabric, a Swiss import, was no longer available in the shops. Had I flogged it, I would not have had anything suitable to wear to match the rest of the costumes in that scene. I was in two minds as I sent the guy away but I had no other choice.

I may have never found true DDR stardom, but when I heard from my classmate, Silvia, that a new bar called Yucca had opened, and that it was attracting lots of important people, including diplomats, westerners and East German models, I wanted to check the place out. Cordelia was quite keen to accompany me to this refined establishment. So one Saturday evening we could be seen queueing at the bar's entrance door, next to which was an original red English telephone booth. But as exciting as the exterior was, once inside the place things went downhill. After we had handed over the ten marks (four dollars) entrance fee per person (normal discos charged one mark entrance), we weren't even allowed to sit on any of the comfy white leather sofas. Those were strictly reserved for westerners, or anyone else who was prepared to give a generous tip to the bouncer, preferably in a western currency. Cordelia and I had to make do with bar stools instead. Clutching our glasses of extortionately priced sparkling wine, we waited to see what would happen in this very Eighties environment, full of chrome, leather, plastic blinds, yucca palms and a dance floor that was lit from underneath. Two hours later, we had seen enough. Watching East German tarts throwing themselves onto West Germans, who in return behaved like they owned the joint, were one thing. But being treated like second-class citizens by the bar staff because we could not wave Deutschmarks or dollars at them was another. This place just wasn't us. The whole experience was degrading. Cordi and I were so desperate to go, we even left our second round of expensive drinks behind. Cocktails that tasted of cheese somehow weren't our thing. Instead we wrapped up the evening in a nearby café, watching a constant stream of East Berlin girls in fishnet tights and made up with Action (a youth cosmetics brand), heading to the Yucca bar. Many punters would waste their time. Anyone looking too East German or wearing sneakers had no chance of getting into the place. Cordi and I might not have liked the atmosphere at the Yucca but at least we had made it past the bouncer. If that wasn't a reason to celebrate, we did not know what was. Two bottles of Bulgarian red wine later we were much more at peace with ourselves and well on the way to recovering from our Yucca experience.

PIMP

Cordi and I were hardly shy of making the acquaintance of westerners. In our never-ending quest for contacts, we even roamed the corridors of the five-star Palace Hotel in the hope that guests would open their doors and say to us: "Come on in, you two and tell us what life in the DDR is really like. Let us become friends." We were so naive. Of course, nothing like that ever happened, but once while Cordi, our friend Sabine and I were in the city, we met two Swedish guys, Kjell and Mike. I am sure that when they invited us all to their hotel room in the Metropol Hotel (western guests only) they had more than talking on their minds. But talk was all they were getting from us.

The room was nothing special – a bed, a desk, a table, a couch. The usual. As Kjell and Mike only spoke Swedish and English, the entire evening's conversation was conducted in English, channeled through me as interpreter. When the alcoholic contents of the raided minibar began to have an effect at midnight, my translations became more and more vague. Kjell would talk to me in English for a minute or two, while my German translation to Cordi and Sabine would only last 10 seconds. So as not to lose face, I began to invent entire stories, just to account for the time difference. Cordi and Sabine really believed that riding mousse was Mike's most favourite pastime.

Kjell took a photo of us five with a delay timer on his camera before we left. He sent a copy of it to Cordelia. It showed us seated on the couch. A number of bottles and glasses can be seen on the table in the foreground. Mike, who is sitting on the right next to Sabine, seems to be very relaxed and is eyeing her up. Kjell looks slightly tense, as I form an impenetrable barrier between him and Cordelia. His hands are clasped and he sits on the sofa's edge with an unsure smile. While Sabine and I look somewhat bedazzled by the flash, the only person who gives the camera a big smile is in the middle of it all – Cordelia.

Many of the westerners we met did not know what to expect when visiting East Berlin. Often they were just after a quick glimpse behind the Iron Curtain. The less prepared they were, the more Cordi and I found them to be interested in hearing our anecdotes about everyday life. Not once did we hold back with our complaints about how boring and small-minded we thought the DDR was. Every westerner we waved goodbye to at the end of a day left well-informed. No one boarding a sightseeing bus in West Berlin and being chauffeured through our capital with a West German tour guide would ever have gotten the same insight into DDR life.

It did not happen very often, but sometimes even Cordi and I were left speechless. One Saturday evening we were sitting in the Palace Hotel's café with some time to kill before the hotel's own disco in the Sinusbar (Sine Curve Bar) opened at nine. Going to the Sinusbar was a great laugh. Watching young, attractive, part-time DDR prostitutes (who officially did not exist) chatting up hairy, big-bellied Middle Eastern businessmen twice their age was hugely entertaining to us. Often foreigners paid for our drinks hoping to get into Cordelia's knickers. Always a bad investment from their point of view, because all they ever got in return was a "Thank you" and a smile. I was regularly mistaken as Cordi's pimp, which had a fun element to it. I loved threatening her jokingly that the next time some guy was waving a big wad of dollars at me, I really would sell her for an hour or two.

Yet on this particular Saturday evening we never even made it to the Sinusbar because of a couple that sat down at our café table. Both darkish skinned, in their late twenties and English speaking, it was obvious that they were visitors to the DDR. It turned out that he was from Iraq and she was from the United Kingdom. The things she told us about England made our jaws drop. According to her, British people believed that the DDR was a dark, dirty, underdeveloped place. A jungle-like country where the people lived in mud huts. Her colleagues, she insisted, always looked in disbelief when they were told how modern East Germany was. She told us she was lucky to not have been arrested by the fascist British police for revealing the truth about East Germany. Cordi and I were shocked when we heard that. This was not at all how we imagined Britain to be. Maybe our media was right in its portrayals of capitalist countries and progressive people really were suppressed?! But we started to smell a rat as the lady went on how she liked DDR television because of its true-to-life programmes. How would she know? She did not even speak German! Either she was bonkers or a hardcore communist. Why else would someone from the west go on a two-week holiday in the German Democratic Republic, as she proudly proclaimed? The couple invited us to dinner in a posh restaurant the following evening. We did not bother turning up. No free meal was worth sitting through hours of lectures about how perfect our country was. For that we could have just watched DDR television news.

Instead, Cordi and I ended up in a café with a cheesy band playing live music. Ten minutes after we sat down, the waiter seated a couple in their late thirties with trailer trash appeal on our table. Both seemed to watch us as we ordered our bottle of cheap Bulgarian wine, and a little advocaat for Cordi. They ogled us even more as I ostentatiously placed a Pall Mall cigarette packet on the table. A colleague had given it to me empty. Refilled with some Czechoslovakian menthol cigarettes, it was an indispensable prop in our quest to fool people about our origins.

The two of us were dressed up, Cordi in a blue cocktail dress and I in a dark suit with wing-collared shirt and bow tie. It did not take very long for the couple on our table to engage us in a conversation. Cordi and I were just talking in posh tones about how enchanting we found the capital of the German Democratic Republic to be, when Mr Council Estate butted in with a remark about the weather. He, medium build with curly brown hair and a moustache, was a decorator. His name was Tommy and his charming wife was Vroni, short for Veronica. She was a cook's helper, slightly taller than him with an Eighties perm, glasses and a missing middle finger on the right hand. What class! After a bit of chitchat, Tommy wanted to know who he was talking to and, to avoid any misunderstanding, he asked bluntly: "You two are from the other side, aren't you?" In unison and without the slightest hesitation, we both replied: "Of course, we are!"

From that moment on Mr and Mrs Council Estate began to give us an earful about how dreadful life was in the east. It was just like when we were meeting (real) westerners. I was flattered when they said: "Oli, it's impossible to buy clothes like yours here in the DDR." But at the same time, I wanted to scream at them: "Look at me properly! Everything I am wearing tonight was bought in DDR shops." Instead, I bit my tongue and enjoyed the free bubbly they had ordered in our honour, one bottle after another. Happy about the free booze, Cordi and I poked each other under the table. But all that free bubbly came at a price: Besides telling stories about our alleged life in the west (which, thanks to our vivid imagination, was the easy part) we also felt obliged to dance with our table companions. That proved to be the real challenge, which became even harder as the evening progressed. Tommy and Vroni knocked the booze back as if there was no tomorrow. A few hours later they could not stand on their own any more, let alone make coordinated moves to live music. During the last dance, Vroni tucked her right hand (yes, the one with the missing middle finger) into the back of my trousers to keep herself upright, while Tommy made sure he was pressing as tightly as possible against Cordi. Secretly Cordelia and I pulled faces in horror whenever our eyes met behind our dance partner's backs. We felt it was time go home. Cordi and I left the café at two am, after we had managed to discourage Tommy and Vroni from accompanying us to a border checkpoint. Those two might not have been very sophisticated but Cordi and I realised on the way home that essentially they were no different to us – the desire to have contact with someone from the outside world was burning in people from all levels of our society.

WHAT AN HONOUR

It was not uncommon for visitors from capitalist countries to look down at us East Germans. My parents and I experienced at first hand how blasé westerners could be when visiting the DDR as we went to lunch in one of East Berlin's finest restaurants. Dad had been given a medal in recognition of his achievements at work. To mark the occasion he had invited Mum and me (my brother was doing his National Service at the time) to a restaurant in the prestigious four-star Hotel Stadt Berlin (City of Berlin) – a 150-metre, 37-storey skyscraper in the city centre. The restaurant was located on the thirty-seventh floor. Our table was next to the window. We indulged in culinary delights like Russian Eggs (hardboiled eggs topped with caviar), shrimp salad, frogs' legs, lobster soup with asparagus, veal, deer and trout fillets followed by a selection of ice creams and exotic fruit, flambéed with French cognac. But the perfect meal was slightly spoiled by a West German family on the table next to us. Two adults and two kids were loudly demanding to be served bangers with chips and ketchup. The problem was, there were no sausages on the menu. Long discussions with waiters followed. The suggestion to visit a more rustic restaurant on the ground floor was rejected. After the parents failed to control their two spoilt brats who were racing round the tables, the family was asked to leave. Screaming blue murder, they retreated. The diners were clapping.

When the bill arrived, Dad had to cough up 240 marks (96 dollars). It was a lot of money, considering that the average main course in an ordinary restaurant was around five marks (two dollars). But we felt that the culinary delights we had experienced had been well worth the price tag. For the American soldiers and their dependants on the other hand, who occupied the other tables in the restaurant, 240 marks were peanuts. They illegally exchanged their dollars into DDR marks in West Berlin at a rate of one to 12 and smuggled the money over the border. Being occupying Allies, they could not be searched by DDR customs, hence every day bus loads of soldiers invaded East Berlin to snap up heavily subsidised goods like bedding or kids clothing for next to nothing. The shopping spree usually followed a visit to the hairdresser's and a nice meal in a posh restaurant before heading home.

Dad settled the bill with part of his 2,000 mark (800 dollars) prize money that had come with his medal. It was called Banner der Arbeit (Banner of the Work) and awarded on the order of Erich Honecker not more than 1,750 times a year. East Germans may have been decorated with five million tons of medals a year, but their real motivation came from the accompanying financial rewards. The state set aside 40 million marks (16 million dollars) every year as prize money. And Dad got his fair share of those funds. Over the years, he was declared an Aktivist no less than nine times, and once a Verdienter Aktivist (Well-Deserved Activist), which took activism to a higher level. Three times, he was rewarded as a member of a Kollektiv der sozialistischen Arbeit (Team of the Socialist Work). And for working on so many buildings in the capital, he was given the Medal of the Builders of Berlin in Gold. Unfortunately, it was not made of real gold.

The government issued a total of 155 different types of honours. But this was nothing compared to what other institutions and organisations swamped our country with: 10,000 various rewards. Statistically, every DDR citizen was honoured ten times in his life. Dad was certainly well above average. Though he never got the most prestigious honour – the Order of Karl Marx. A pity, because this medal, made of pure gold, came with a handy cash payment of 20,000 marks (8,000 dollars). Had the GDR continued to exist, I am almost certain Dad would eventually have scooped that one as well.

PORN

In the same year that Erich Honecker encountered a milestone in his career, Cordi, our friend Sabine and I decided to treat ourselves to a summer holiday abroad. Honnie flew in his aircraft – an Ilyushin IL-62M – for an official five-day visit to West Germany where he was welcomed by chancellor Kohl with full ceremonial honours (2,700 accredited international journalists covered the event). We booked three seats on a one-way flight to Budapest with our national carrier, Interflug. Our first ever flight! We were so excited. Since a one-way flight came to 164 marks (66 dollars) per person we had decided to return to the DDR by train. A sleeping berth for the 15-and-a-half-hour train journey only cost 69 marks (28 dollars). A pity our virgin flight to Budapest was over in 90 minutes. We were so fascinated by the experience that we would not have minded if the flight had lasted twice as long. Interflug only had 47 airplanes and 7,000 employees, but it still served 51 destinations in 37 countries. And now we were part of their annual 2.35 million passengers. What an uplifting feeling.

This was Cordi's and my second trip to Hungary and, just like in the previous year, we found that people were so friendly. One hot day, with the thermometer showing 36 degrees Celsius in the shade, the girls and I were hitchhiking to one of Budapest's many open-air baths. Soon, a guy in his late twenties stopped. His name was Janosz. He spoke very good German and it did not take long for us to chat away like old friends. Janosz had been on his way to visit a friend in the city but he suddenly asked us whether we would like to drive with him to Lake Balaton instead. What a question. Of course, we wanted to go to central Europe's biggest lake in this scorching heat. On hot days, up to 1.3 million visitors flocked to the 600 square kilometres of murky water that is Lake Balaton. Janosz drove the 100 kilometres to the beach in no time and, once there, he even taught us three how to surf. We stayed at the lake all day, got sunburned and after he had driven us back to Budapest we literately had to force some money upon him as a contribution towards petrol. In return he invited us to his place that evening for drinks.

After freshening up, the three of us arrived at Janosz' place at nine pm. His one-bedroom apartment in a Fifties block was tastefully furnished. He even had a video recorder, which was quite a novelty for us. When the first VHS recorders, Japanese brands, were sold in East Berlin on a Friday morning, people had begun queueing on the Wednesday evening. If a video recorder changed hands privately, its price could be anywhere between 8,000 and 10,000 DDR marks – almost the price of a new Trabant.

In Hungary, however VCRs seemed to be quite the norm. We chatted with Janosz about this and that, had our first-ever Bloody Mary and watched a few short films on video. Our host tried to settle with Sabine on one side of his huge brown couch. She needed more time and wanted to stay a little bit longer with Cordi and me at the other end. Next thing I knew we were watching *Caligula*. Tits and dicks everywhere (on the telly, that is). I was spellbound. Mouth open wide, my eyes were glued to the box. Janosz tried to get us in the mood. After all, we were two boys and two girls. But he hadn't counted on our innocence. The girls tried to overcome their embarrassment by talking non-stop while I became more and more quiet, watching telly. Yet poor Janosz misunderstood our reactions. Instead of going down a gear he went up one, thinking that the old chestnut *Caligula* was not hot enough for us. "Do you want to watch a porn film?" he asked. The girls stopped talking and looked at each other, shocked. You could have heard a pin drop. "Yes, please." I replied eagerly. Cordelia punched me hard behind Janosz's back as he was looking for the tape. "Ouch! What was that for?" I asked her quietly. Janosz looked up briefly before popping the tape in the machine. Cordi mouthed the words: "Stop him! Do something – NOW!". But before I could say or do anything we were already being treated to the sight of a horny couple copulating near a river. What followed was a different position, every 60 seconds. I never thought that some of the positions shown were even possible. The movie was quite an eye opener for me. However, after ten minutes it was evident that all the uuuuuuuing and yeahhhhhhhing on screen was not doing anything for the girls. Drinks in hand, both sat there as stiff as boards, blushing as they admired the window drape's intricate crochet work. Reluctantly, I asked Janosz to turn the telly off. When the stereo was switched on instead, the atmosphere became much more relaxed again. Until four o'clock in the morning we talked and danced. All in all it was a great evening – and on top of that very educational.

NEWS FLASH

"The old year is coming to an end. The new year is just around the corner. We look back at what we have achieved so far, but we also focus on what the future will bring."

Those were the opening words of Erich Honecker's New Years Eve speech in 1987. Little did he know that a disaster was looming. In January 1988, a train collided with a Russian tank that had been abandoned by its crew and was left on railway tracks during combat training. Six people dead, 33 wounded, one locomotive destroyed and nine carriages wrecked were the sad statistics of this accident. When the little DDR charged the mighty Soviet Union 14.7 million marks (5.9 million dollars) for the rescue operation and damages, people inappropriately joked:

Q: "What is the latest must-have item for any train driver?"

A: "A bazooka to clear the tracks ahead!"

1988 surely was a funny old year. In May, West German chancellor Helmut Kohl visited the DDR with his family for a private three-day holiday. Their trip to the southern cities of Dresden, Erfurt, Gera, Gotha, and Weimar was so secret that not even the West German media found out about it. Kohl rejected the DDR's offer to provide him with bodyguards. Instead, he wanted to keep a low profile and make contact with normal people in everyday situations, just like any other tourist. Of course, the Stasi secretly tailed him and plain-clothes Stasi officers inconspicuously tried behind the scenes to keep DDR citizens away from him. But it was impossible to stop all contact. Shop assistants and waiters could not believe their eyes when they found themselves serving the West German chancellor.

Another surprise in 1988, this time for all DDR citizens, was that old rules did not seem to apply any more. For decades, the state had tried to persuade us to see the Soviet Union as a friend whose lead we should follow. Slogans like "To learn from the Soviet Union means to learn how to be victorious" were bread and butter for our media. But the DDR stopped following the Soviet lead when Gorbachev began to introduce his policy of glasnost (openness) and perestroika (political and economical reform). As one of our Politburo members put it in an interview with a West German magazine: "Would you feel obliged to decorate your apartment just because your neighbour is decorating his?"

Such comments enraged many East Germans who had hoped our country would become a little more liberal. When Romanian communist leader Nicolae Ceausescu was presented with the prestigious Order of Karl Marx by Erich Honecker, we analysed this blatant error of political judgement at work for days. Obviously it was time for Erich Honecker, by then already 76 years old, and his Politburo chums, to be replaced by younger and less senile politicians. People were joking:

Q: "What has got 104 teeth and four legs?"

A: "A crocodile."

Q: "What has got 104 legs and four teeth?"

A: "Our Politburo."

Later that year, some Russian publications and films were even removed from our shelves and screens because they had dared to portrait socialism as a less-than-perfect society. By then, many East Germans wondered where it all was going to end. Upsetting our closest ally, the guarantor of our very existence, did not seem a particularly wise move. For our country to be alienated by the rest of the world, with probably only Romania and North Korea on its side, wasn't exactly a prospect relished by many East Germans. Opposition groups began to form under the roof of the church. Not to get rid of socialism but to make our country more democratic by addressing problems publicly. Yet the Communist Party wasn't going to have any of it. It announced that "neither now, nor in the future, will we make compromises with people who want us to mainly talk about mistakes, shortages and failures." The Stasi continued to treat critical citizens as enemies of the state.

Once troublemakers had been identified they usually were intimidated. Following a person in an obvious way or photographing them in public were two methods used by the Stasi to shut critics up. Sometimes a "clarifying chat" at a police station with a short stay in a cell did the trick. On other occasions, parents were threatened that their kids would be taken away by forced adoptions if they went to jail. The Stasi was a creative organisation when it came to dealing with enemies. It placed fake "For Sale" ads for hard-to-get items in newspapers, including the phone number of a person it wanted to intimidate, so victims would be inundated with calls from potential buyers. Or it ordered goods in victims' names. Leaving them to deal with angry sellers demanding payment. But the Stasi could also destroy someone's reputation by not doing anything at all. If you were part of a dissident group and everyone else but you landed in prison, what did that indicate to others? If none of the Stasi's dirty tricks deterred someone from provoking the authorities, the next step was usually prison. In severe cases, even the loss of the *Heimat* (homeland). Quite a number of dissidents were given the option either to go to jail in East Germany or to relocate to West Germany. Others were stripped of their DDR citizenship and forced by the Stasi to exit the DDR within 24 hours. Put on a train to West Germany, they had to leave friends and family behind and were not allowed back into the country. Even tourist visits were out of the question.

In 1988 it was obvious to many East Germans that a general dissatisfaction was brewing among the DDR population. For the time being at least, the Stasi was able to keep the lid on things.

"Neither the donkey, nor the cow can stop socialism now."

Erich Honecker

MEAT AND FEW VEG

While Cordelia and I were very much in favour of the Soviet political reforms, we still disliked the Russian soldiers stationed in the DDR. Even more so when, during a walk in the woods at Easter, we were faced with the sight of a dead sheep, covered in blood, with one haunch missing. The hastily trodden out campfire nearby was littered with Russian cigarette stubs. The perpetrators must have felt very secure. Cordelia was disgusted. If soldiers of the Red Army had no qualms about killing our sheep willy-nilly every time they felt hungry, how did ordinary Soviet citizens behave in their own country? We were soon find out, as we started our two-week trip to Yalta on the Crimean peninsula in late April 1988.

Staying in a modern 16-storey, four-star hotel near the beach with a fantastic view over the Black Sea was just magical. Even though the summer season had not yet begun and we could not go for a swim in the sea because it was still freezing cold. We swam in the hotel pool instead. The only downer was that some hotel guest went walkies with my brand-new Adidas flip flops that I had left next to the pool as I went into the water. To cheer me up, one of the group members told me the following joke:

Back in the DDR a young man puts his bicycle in front of an office block and walks off. A policeman says to him: "You can't leave your bike there. A Russian delegation will be arriving shortly. Replies the guy: "Thanks for the warning, officer, but the bike will be safe – it's locked."

Our hotel was home to both eastern and western tourist groups who were all subjected to the same rigid Soviet institution – the *dezhurnayas* (women on duty). Placed on each floor, these mature ladies functioned as points of contact – and watchful guards. The one on our floor never seemed to leave her post. Day and night, she sat in her chair behind that table next to the lift. Even at three o'clock in the morning (we set our alarm to double check) her watchful eyes did not miss a single movement on the floor. Amazing!

What surprised us was how economically weak the USSR seemed to be, compared to the DDR. As we went for a stroll into town, Cordelia and I were asked by little kids whether we had any *guma* (chewing gum). We didn't. While we were still talking about how such begging would never happen back home a little *babushka* (grandmother) approached us, pointing at Cordi's back. "How much for the rucksack?" she asked. It took a while until she understood that the rucksack, which contained Cordelia's personal belongings, wasn't for sale. Grandma was miffed, but not heartbroken as she walked off. During the course of the afternoon we were stopped a total of 18 times. People wanted to buy our tops, shoes and trousers, right there in the streets. We were asked for stereos, pop posters and records. Very persistent admirers of my baseball cap and Cordi's shades, could only be fended off by demanding a ridiculous 1,000 roubles (760 dollars) per item. Once we reached the town and had a look in the shops, we knew the reason for the people's behaviour. Had DDR shops been as empty as their Crimean counterparts, East Germans would have taken to the streets in protest a long time ago. The only shops in Yalta with decent offerings were of the hard currency variety catering for western tourists. Cordi and I both set our eyes on some red T-shirts with the hammer and sickle emblem. However, at 19

US dollars each, they were way beyond our reach. "One day" we promised ourselves, "we will have enough hard currency to buy whatever we want."

On 1 May, all guests at our hotel were invited to take part in the May Day demonstration. I am not aware that DDR hotels ever asked their guests to participate in marches but then the Soviet Union always struck us as a more patriotic country. We could feel the pride lingering in the air as Cordi and I went into town. War veterans were showing off their medals, groups of women walked through the streets arm-in-arm, singing melancholic folk songs while kids ran around in their Pioneer uniforms. The city centre was a sea of red flags, behind the stand holding the local dignitaries were giant paintings of all members of the Politburo in Moscow. But, instead of joining our group walking past the stand behind a DDR flag (far too embarrassing), we joined the Finnish tourists from our hotel. Cordi and I had drunk with them the previous night in the hotel bar reserved for westerners (payments in hard currency only), and when they saw us again they greeted us with a big cheer. Thankfully no one from our group noticed our "defection". It certainly would have raised an eyebrow or two among our fellow countrymen.

The following day we visited a local market. It came as a bit of a shock seeing little old ladies selling a mishmash of possessions, including old clothes, shoes, cookware and home-preserved fruit, just to make a few roubles. It was only then that we realised how comfy and cushy life in the DDR was. Appalling hygiene conditions in the market also made you wonder whether the Soviet Union really was a superpower. Stalls without any refrigeration selling fly-ridden animal parts wrapped up in newspapers would have been closed down in a flash by health and safety officials back home. But in the USSR, it seemed to be standard practice. Cordi and I felt like we were in a third world country. "If this is the future of socialism we better regress to capitalism!" commented Cordelia as we were discussing the day's events over long drinks and a few Russian Eggs (hard-boiled eggs topped with caviar) at the bar on our hotel's private beach.

Only once were we jealous of the locals. Going to board a bus on our way to a tourist attraction, Cordi and I thought we had found an easy way to multiply our roubles. In the middle of a car park, a guy, surrounded by a few other men, was clumsily moving around a little ball under one of three upside down cups. One of the onlookers pocketed one 20 rouble banknote after another. Bystanders encouraged us to also cash in on the player's ineptitude. But Cordi and I had both left our purses in the hotel. Having missed out on this opportunity, the two of us were grumpy all day. Even the boat trip which took us past the holiday houses of all eastern-bloc party leaders could not cheer us up. It was only when shell-game con artists arrived in the DDR after the fall of the Wall that Cordelia and I realised how lucky we had been on that day back in May 1988.

The USSR certainly was a strange country. Even as fellow communist brothers and sisters, we could not leave the district in which we were staying without a travel permit issued by the local authorities. But we could freely buy West German newspapers at the hotel shop. Cordi and I made good use of this opportunity. If DDR customs officials had discovered all the western newspapers we smuggled into East Germany on the way back, we would have been in a lot of trouble.

We may not have been able to watch any western TV channels while on holiday but, for one reason or another, the hotel seemed to attract a string of western television crews during our stay. First I managed to get interviewed by ABC, which was shooting some footage for *Good Morning, America*, then a British team filmed our group's dinner table and the one next to us, which was occupied by our Finnish friends. I guessed it was to show how differently guests were being treated. While the westerners were served strawberries as dessert, we had to settle for blancmange. Slightly unfair perhaps, but hardly shocking. But regardless of everyone's origin, all hotel guests got the same main course, which day in, day out, consisted of minced meat and not a lot of vegetables. At least the way the mince had been prepared changed regularly. But whether it was grilled, boiled, fried or baked mince, 14 days of the same food left us all longing for something different. Upon my return home, Mum's welcoming words still ring in my ears today: "It's so nice to have you back. As a surprise I have made your favourite – a big batch of *Buletten* (fried meat balls)." As much as I wanted to eat them, I could not stomach yet more mince. Thankfully, Dad and my brother came to the rescue. I opted for some leftover carrot stew instead. I never thought eating vegetables could be so satisfying!

ROMY

Over the years, I identified less and less with my work at the export-import company. Even the slightest constructive criticism of the DDR would cause a huge stir if the wrong people were present. By contrast, the atmosphere on the film sets was so much more relaxed. I tried to spend as much time as possible away from the office. When I was given the chance to appear in a FRG/GDR co-production about a West German singer travelling through our country, I immediately jumped at the opportunity. Having to perform a convincing stage fight turned out to be the highlight of this job. Surprisingly the director was happy with the second take. Had I not gotten the giggles earlier, he might even have settled for the first shot.

Unfortunately, there were also some cringe-worthy moments while working on this series. Travelling through the DDR in a West German television production van with Munich licence plates made people in the countryside regularly wave at us as we drove past, as if we were royalty. I felt ashamed and embarrassed.

Thankfully, all of the West German crewmembers were attitude-free, including the main character, singer Katja Ebstein and her director/husband Klaus Überall. It was quite a star-studded production and, one day, Heinz Rennhack, a very popular East German actor and comedian, turned up on the set. "Who is that good-looking girl he arrived with?" I asked myself. As filming always means waiting around I started a conversation with her. Her name was Romy and she was Heinz Rennhack's daughter. I wanted to see her again. We exchanged numbers and called each other a few times. But our romance was short lived. One day, her dad decided to not return from a performance in West Berlin. Afraid that continued contact with Romy might end my dad's trips to the west, I discontinued all contact. It wasn't an easy decision to make. I wrote bitterly in my diary (which I had painstakingly covered with pictures of exotic beaches from a West German travel catalogue; beaches I never really hoped to see): "The DDR is nothing but a giant prison. Something just has to happen!" And something did happen. Romy was allowed by our authorities to follow her father. Along with her mother she moved to West Berlin.

MISO

I was 21 and my hormones were playing havoc. I was chasing girls big time. Whether it be Jeanette, Annette, Heike, Doreen or Judith, the grass always seemed greener with the next one. During the course of the year, my disco gang had changed venues and was now at home at the Busche, a purpose-built canteen which, in the evenings, became a gay disco. The girls loved it because none of the boys there tried to grab their bums. And I liked it for exactly the same reasons. With lesbians being my only competitors, I could be sure that the girls I arrived with would not leave with other boys. And when occasionally a guy made a pass at me, it wasn't anything I could not live with. In fact, I found it quite flattering hearing from someone of my own sex that my face or bum looked cute. Explaining that I was a lady's man stopped the guys pursuing things further. Though some still gave me their telephone number anyway, "just in case you change your mind!". No harm done and happy faces all around.

The most entertaining person by far at the Busche (the name of the place was derived from the street it was in: Buschallee) was without doubt a guest known only as Susie Butterkeks (Butterbiscuit). This overweight, camp guy with a slight lisp and shrill voice entertained the whole joint. But as much as I liked Susie, when he entered a Busche strip contest I felt that I had seen far more of him than I had ever bargained for. I was not alone with that opinion.

Overall my life was pretty well sorted in 1988, until a fateful Sunday in July. Bruce Springsteen had played in East Berlin in front of 160,000 fans earlier that week and I, like a million other DDR teenagers, had taped the country's biggest rock concert ever from the radio. I was on my way to the city centre. Listening to the recording and playing around with the new walkman Dad had bought me in West Berlin, I somehow managed to forget to get off at the right train station and missed the car that was driving our fashion show troupe to a gig down south. With unexpected spare time on my hands I went on a walk instead and bumped into a girl that seemed to know an awful lot about me. She asked me a series of personal questions: "How was your holiday to Yalta? Are you still doing the film work? What is Cordelia up to? Which disco do you go to these days?" That girl seemed to know me inside out. The only problem was, I did not have a clue who she was. I could have sworn I had never seen her in my life before. Too embarrassed to ask where I knew her from, I resorted to giving vague answers. As we parted five minutes later she said: "I will give you a call next week." before dashing off into the opposite direction. She never rang. To this day I am convinced the Stasi must have been behind this encounter, trying to find out what I was up to and who I was hanging out with. Maybe Cordi and I were under scrutiny because we had said "shitty east" once too often.

I continued on my way, still trying to make sense of what had just happened, when I heard a splat. My blue-and-white, marine-style sweatshirt from the west was sporting an unsightly streak of runny bird poo. Could the day get any worse? Thankfully, the familiar Palasthotel was nearby and, after a quick dash to the lavatories on the ground floor, the jumper looked like new again. I made myself comfortable in one of the lobby's brown leather armchairs, while I waited for the giant wet patch to dry. A few minutes later my attention was caught by a guy who, with his short black hair, could have passed as a member of Bronski Beat. He had just arrived with a busload of American tourists. Only a few years older than me, he seemed to be their tour guide. I was amazed. There was no way a DDR-twenty-something would have been entrusted with such a responsibility at such young age, let alone be allowed to travel the world. I was envious and, at the same time, seriously impressed by how routinely the guy seemed to be doing his job. He obviously wasn't a novice at this. Young East Germans like myself would have killed to be in his shoes, yet he made it look like it was the most normal job in the world. Which, of course, for him it was. Naturally, my staring did not go unnoticed. Once he briefly looked back from a distance with a smile and a nod. A friendly gesture, but somehow it embarrassed me massively. My ears began to tingle. I quickly looked away. My face was heating up, beginning to resemble a giant beetroot. I jumped up and sprinted to the exit.

Back at home I could have slapped myself for making such a fool of myself. But as my confidence returned, I was determined to get to know this guy better. What were his views of the world? Did he take his freedom to travel for granted? Where else had he been to? What were his thoughts on my fatherland? Questions were flying around my head. At a visit to Europe's biggest variety theatre, the Friedrichstadtpalast, that evening, I could hardly concentrate on what was happening on stage.

Arriving at work the next morning, I first called the hotel to find out when the Americans were departing. I was devastated to hear they had just left. Damn! All day I felt miserable. I was in such a foul mood that I decided to treat myself and went shopping after work. It was a muggy day and walking around town was no fun. I bought a straw hat (that I never wore). As I left the boutique, what did I see driving past but the very same bus the Americans had arrived on the previous day! The receptionist I spoke to in the morning must have gotten the wrong end of the stick. The group obviously had only left for a day trip. I quickly went home and, after a bite to eat and a refreshing shower, I made my way back in the sweltering heat to the Palasthotel. The sky was full of black clouds as I entered the building.

There I was then. Sitting in the lobby, nervously waiting for this guy to show his face without really knowing how I would approach him. The last thing I wanted was to give the impression that I was making a pass. When he walked out of the lift 20 minutes later, all my confidence vanished. I quickly looked away. Yet through the corner of my eye I could notice that he had registered me on his way to reception. A few times he walked up and down the lobby and then went into a lift, only to emerge a few moments later going back to reception again. He was obviously in the middle of sorting out a problem. Shyly, I continued to pretend to look at everyone else in the lobby but him. Finally one of the elevators took him to the sixth floor and that was it. He did not seem to come back. Had I blown my chance? I was angry with myself. Two minutes later, which seemed like an eternity, he was back. It was a case of either now or never. I grabbed the bull by his balls and waved him over. His name was Miso. He was Slovenian and a tour guide for a Yugoslav travel company that organised bus tours through Europe for Americans. He seemed a friendly guy and I had the distinct feeling that this encounter was about to become a very interesting one. We made ourselves comfortable on a two-seater in the hotel's own Kaminbar (Fireside Bar), ordered two beers and I fired away my million questions about him, his job and impressions of the countries he had been to so far. During the second round of beers, the thunderstorm that had been lingering around Berlin finally reached the city centre. Huge raindrops were battering the hotel's bronze tinted windows. Yet the two of us hardly noticed. We were too preoccupied with finding out more about each other's lives. After the third round, I felt an electric charge going through my body. It seemed to be heading to my heart, but where was it coming from? Somewhat irritated I looked down at myself, as Miso answered a question. Sitting next to him, with our hands resting on the couch, our middle fingers touched ever so slightly. Yet this purely coincidental and hardly noticeable contact was undoubtedly the cause of the charge I felt. I could "cut the connection" by pulling my hand back. When our fingertips touched again the tingling sensation resumed. I did not understand. What the heck was going on?

SLEEPLESS NIGHTS

And then it clicked. While Miso was still talking about his travels, I was having my "coming out". I was gay, of course. Now I knew why lately my relationships with the girls weren't very stable. Unconsciously I must have been looking for something they could not give me. But on a more pressing note, I had to ask myself, how this evening was about to end? My heart began pounding. To calm down, I ordered a fourth round of beer just before the bar closed at one o'clock. Half an hour later our glasses were empty yet again. I could feel the mellowing effect of the alcohol. What next? Instead of going home I wanted to continue chatting. Miso suggested: "Why don't we go up to my room? Let's raid my minibar!" After unsuccessfully roaming the corridors of the Palasthotel with Cordelia for years I finally had the chance to see one of the rooms for myself. Great! But at what price? I became scared of the unknown... and curious at the same time.

Curiosity won and a couple of minutes later I was sitting with Miso on the leather couch in his room. The black furniture combined with glass table and comfy looking beige armchairs created a very contemporary Eighties ambience. And while I was hiding my insecurity with meaningless babble, Miso moved to plan B: the yawn-and-stretch technique. Twenty seconds later I felt his arm resting on my shoulder. Woah, woah, woah, woah! This was a tad too fast for me. I quickly jumped up pretending to look at some hotel brochures on the writing desk. When I sat down again his arm moved in close for a second time. Quickly I found something else in the room that required close inspection. After we played this game a few more times Miso gave up. He made himself comfortable on the bed while I spread out on the couch. Instead of shagging senseless we talked about our lives, values, achievements, dreams, hopes and wishes until six o'clock in the morning.

Miso was sound asleep when I came out of the bathroom after having a refreshing shower. A touch to his arm woke him up. As I was about to leave for work we hugged silently, Miso nudged my right shoulder slightly with his fist. I shivered as I stepped out of the hotel. The sky was cloudy and a strong wind was blowing. The temperature had dropped overnight by more than ten degrees. A little orange road sweeper was cleaning the footpath surrounding the hotel. Sadly, Miso was leaving Berlin the very same day. He and his group were heading down south, towards Czechoslovakia, the next country on their itinerary. Thankfully he had told me that his next tour would bring him to East Berlin in only a month time. I had 30 days to fully come to terms with my newly found sexuality.

To most East German city folk it hardly made a difference whether you were gay or straight. Homosexuality was legalised in East Germany back in 1968. West Germany followed a year later; Russia not until 1993 and Scotland only in 2000.

East Berlin, just like any other big city in the DDR, also had gay meeting places such as bars and discos. Newspaper articles, TV programmes and sex education books painted a picture of normality when reporting on homosexuality or answering questions put to them by young and confused gay and lesbian readers.

One year later, in 1989, the first gay-themed feature-length movie, appropriately named *Coming Out*, had its glamorous premiere in East Berlin. It was so well received by the public that screenings up and down the country were sold out for weeks.

Meanwhile on a hot Sunday in August 1988, the thermometer showed 30 degrees centigrade, I could be found sitting in the Palasthotel's lobby yet again. Having accepted my newly found sexuality, with the support of my parents, I was waiting for Miso's arrival. I had just refreshed myself with a Czechoslovakian Eau de Toilette named Chaz (a real stinker) when Miso's bus pulled up at the front door. Half an hour later in his room we had a long and silent hug. Then I showed him some Berlin sights that were off the beaten track before the two of us went for dinner at the newest addition to the East Berlin culinary scene – an Italian restaurant. Foreign cuisine was a huge hit in the DDR. I had to book our table at several weeks in advance. Some twenty years later I have forgotten what we ordered but I still remember that Miso seemed unusually monosyllabic when I asked him during dinner what he thought of the dishes. On pressing further he coyly admitted that, though as nice as everything tasted, the flavours weren't particularly Italian. Perhaps the lack of basil and real Parmesan cheese had something to do with it. But for the majority of us East Germans it was, at the time, as close as we would ever come to eating in an authentic Italian restaurant.

Back at the hotel later, I marvelled at the view from Miso's room, number 7073, of a scenically lit DDR capital. This time, reception had allocated him accommodation on the seventh floor. Little did we know then that this romantic view came at a price. Rooms and suites on the seventh and eighth floors of the hotel were under constant surveillance by the Ministry of State Security. Specially trained maids rifled through guests' possessions when making up rooms. Strategically placed secret cameras and microphones meant the Stasi was at all times fully aware of what guests were up to in the privacy of their rooms.

A watchful hotel employee must have seen me approach Miso the previous month. Maybe the Stasi thought I was looking for someone to help me to escape the DDR. Maybe they wanted a record of us in a compromising situation for blackmail purposes. Or maybe the secret service was just after a cheap thrill. Whatever their motives, on that particular evening they did not get to see anything. It all might have started very promising for them with some cuddling and kissing, but things went pear-shaped when I stubbed my big toe on the bedframe. Immediately I was in agony. With the toe quickly swollen to twice its size, sex was the last thing on my mind.

I needed medical help. The problem was, I could not call the emergency services without getting Miso into trouble. Hotel guests were not allowed to take non-guests up to their rooms. And as I wasn't officially in the room, how could the ambulance possibly pick me up. What was I to do? I had an idea. Not necessarily a good one but I still dialled 115: "Medical emergency services, how can I help?" – "Yes, hello, I stumbled and now one of my toes hurts and is badly bruised and swollen. It might be broken." – "Can you walk?" – "Not really. All I can do is hop around on the other foot." – "Ok, we are going to send an ambulance. What's your name and address?" – "I will meet the ambulance outside." – "I need your name and address." – "Even if I would meet the ambulance outside?"– "Yes, I do need both your name and the address." – "I can't give you the address." – "Why not?" – "It's secret." – "It is what?" – "Listen, I am not at liberty to give you the address. Just send an ambulance to the street crossing Karl-Liebknecht-Strasse and Spandauer Strasse. I'm the one waiting next to the Palasthotel... Hallo?" The emergency services had hung up. How was I supposed to get to casualty? It was a quarter past midnight and I had hardly any money in my pocket. Miso stepped in and gave me a crisp 100 mark banknote, the smallest denomination in his wallet. 100 DDR marks were nothing to him. Having paid eight US dollars for it on the black market (at the official exchange rate it would have been 40 dollars) he insisted I take the money. But for a DDR citizen, like myself, 100 marks was a lot of dosh. 100 marks, gosh! In the office I would have had to work two-and-a-half days to earn that kind of money. And the cab was only going to cost me a tenner. Surely I could not keep the other 90 marks. Or could I? No, I couldn't. It would have made me feel cheap. I promised Miso to repay him before limping down to reception and asking the porter to call me a cab.

Having my toe fiddled with by a casualty doctor at one o'clock in the morning was definitely not how I had envisaged the evening turning out.

A QUESTION OF TRUST

The next time Miso was in East Berlin, leading yet another group of American tourist through my fatherland, the two of us went for dinner at the prestigious Café Moskau. Located at the main Karl-Marx-Boulevard right, bang in the city centre, this Sixties' building had three levels which housed a café, restaurant and nightclub. Its façade was decorated with a mosaic depicting scenes from everyday life of the different Soviet nations. The roof sported a life-sized model of the legendary Russian "Sputnik" satellite. Although, the restaurant had a very good reputation, it did not live up to it on our visit. The meal was too salty and the service sporadic. At least the Hungarian white wine was nice and sweet, just the way we East Germans liked it. The entire evening I had been pestering Miso with my questions about all the countries he had been to. Yugoslavians, unlike us East Germans, could travel the world freely. Yugoslavia was a hybrid. More liberal than the average communist state but far from being a capitalist society, it did not seem to fit into any bloc. And the lack of heavy fortifications on its borders with its western neighbours meant DDR citizens had to come up with a pretty good reason if they wanted to visit the country.

Understandably, I was very excited when Miso asked me that evening: "Oliver, why don't you come and visit me in Ljubljana? " I nearly choked on my vanilla ice cream topped with mixed tinned fruit. Did I hear correctly? I had tried once before to get around the DDR's rigid travel restrictions by pretending that my grandparents were so weak they needed a helper to accompany them on their travels to West Berlin. The only problem was that Grandma and Grandad, both by then already well into their seventies, were far too fit. I was denied the desired passport and exit visa. But this time things seemed different. After all, Yugoslavia was still one of our Allies. My mind boggled even more when Miso mentioned that the controls on the checkpoints to Italy were very slack and that we could easily make our way across the border for a day trip. But how would I be able to secure myself the desired exit visa to Yugoslavia? "Don't worry" Miso assured me "I will send you an invite." I knew that independent travel to the Soviet Union was possible upon receipt of an invitation and hoped the same policy would apply to private trips to Yugoslavia. "But how would I get there and would I be able to change DDR marks into Yugoslavian dinars?" was my next worry. The official reason for not letting us citizens travel freely was that the DDR could not afford to supply 17 million people with foreign currency, let alone settle their international travel costs in hard currency. With a smile, Miso brushed aside my worries: "Relax! I will get you the plane ticket and I will also cover the costs for your stay." – "So my visit to you would not cost the DDR anything?" I double-checked, just to be on the safe side. "Neither the DDR nor you would have to pay a penny." was his reply. Overjoyed by the possibility of holidaying the following year in Yugoslavia, I quickly ordered a bottle of Russian Crimean sparkling wine to celebrate the occasion. Surely nothing could go wrong now. My trip would have no impact on the DDR's finances, so there was no reason for the authorities not to let me go. That exit visa was mine for sure! Or so we thought...

A couple of days later I enthusiastically went into my local police station. I approached the uniformed guy behind the counter: "Good afternoon, I would like to know which documents you require to issue me with a passport and an exit visa to Yugoslavia" – "Why do you want to go to Yugoslavia?" – "Because I want to visit a friend." – "Sorry, but private travel to Yugoslavia is only possible when visiting relatives." – "Alright, if I can't visit a friend then I would like to visit a cousin of mine who also lives in Yugoslavia?" – Sorry, but it's not possible." – "Why not?" – "Because you can only travel if a very close relative like a parent, grandparent or sibling is celebrating a special occasion. You will have to supply us with relevant proof." – "But the trip would not cost the DDR anything. I would be provided with a plane ticket and my expenses there would be met too." – "Sorry, but that doesn't make any difference. You can't travel. Next please!"

My dreams were shattered. I was fuming. The entry in my diary reads: "I'm being denied an exit visa to Yugoslavia. Why? What is the state afraid of?" Only then did it dawn on me that our state's restrictive travel policy had more to do with a lack of trust in its people rather than a shortage of funds. "If the state does not trust me, why should I trust the state?" I asked myself.

The world I was living in began to crumble. I might not have agreed with everything in the DDR, but for me socialism had always seemed the morally superior society. With this illusion gone, I began to doubt the whole concept of socialism.

To rule out a hasty overreaction on my part I went to a travel agent later in the week and asked, sweet as pie, whether they could organise a trip to Yugoslavia for me. "Sorry, Sir" the blonde girl behind the counter replied, slightly baffled, "but without a passport and exit visa I can't offer you anything for Yugoslavia." From that moment on I wasn't embarrassed by my fatherland any more. Instead I hated it.

Cordelia, too, had become disillusioned. She wanted to visit her Italian pen pal, Carlo. He even tried to get the DDR embassy in Italy involved to secure her an exit visa, but to no avail. Just as in my case, the authorities would not budge. Cordelia too could wave goodbye to her hopes of being issued the coveted blue passport of the German Democratic Republic.

One day, Cordi even asked me what personal papers she should take with her should she attempt to escape the DDR. I talked her out of such a dangerous adventure. Although we had both long ago promised each other that, one day, we would live on the other side of the Iron Curtain, we had never managed to come up with a sensible plan of how to achieve that goal. Was marrying a foreigner the best way to get out of East Germany for good? Or was applying to the authorities for release from DDR citizenship the better option? I had also heard of some third world diplomats smuggling people over the border in their cars. How dangerous was that? And how lonely would we be in the west, having left our friends and families behind? The authorities would not have allowed us back in for visits, nor would anyone have been allowed out to visit us.

"Only today it has fully sunken in that I will never be able to set foot in countries like the US, Australia, Spain, France, Japan or even Yugoslavia. I want to get out of here, but do not want to leave my parents, brother or grandparents behind. What shall I do? I have to think of something! I don't feel I have to leave the country immediately but it will have to happen before I turn 30."

Diary entry

CHARADE

As I could not visit Miso in his native Yugoslavia, I had no other choice but to make the most of the time whenever his tours brought him to East Berlin, usually a couple of days each month. I organised hard-to-get tickets to a cabaret, we went swimming at the Swedish-built Sports and Recreation Centre, took in a classical concert, went up Berlin's famous television tower for cake and coffee and had a look at several exhibitions. But whatever I had lined up for us to do, I was always anxious that a seasoned traveller like Miso had seen much more exciting things elsewhere in the world. So I was all the more determined to make every one of Miso's stays in the DDR as memorable as possible. For his visit in October 1988, I had the idea of visiting a recently renovated baroque palace and the Russian Capitulation Museum, whose main feature was the hall in which Nazi Germany had surrendered in 1945. Unfortunately, I learnt that both attractions would be closed during his stay. Determined to get my way, I set out to change things. First I dialled the number of the Russian museum: "Capitulation Museum. Good Day." I was greeted by a female voice with a heavy Russian accent. In a high pitched voice I said: "Yes, hello this is Frau Schmidt. I am calling from the headquarters of the people-owned Travel Agency of the German Democratic Republic and would like to speak to the director in charge of the museum please." – "One moment." came the reply. Then I heard a woman say: "How can I help?" – "Yes, hello this is Frau Schmidt, I'm a secretary at the DDR's national Travel Agency and my boss, Herr Schulz would like to speak to you. Please hold while I put you through." I made a few clicking noises with my tongue. After a few seconds silence I began to speak normally: "Hello, Schulz here from the head office of the Travel Agency of the German Democratic Republic. I am in charge of new contracts and international relations and on Monday in two weeks time a Yugoslav delegation will be arriving in Berlin for the signature of a very important contract. Our Yugoslav partner has expressed interest in visiting the Capitulation Museum. Would it be possible to open the museum for us for an hour or two on that day?" First the Russian lady was reluctant to cooperate but as I went on to explain the economic importance of the contract she gave in. In the end she even offered to guide the delegation through the house herself. Great! And with the director of the baroque palace being an equally easy target, the itinerary for Miso's next visit was confirmed in no time.

He arrived in East Berlin accompanied by his colleague Istok, who turned out to be a godsend. With Miso's German non-existent and my English far from perfect, Istok was happy to take on the role of interpreter in our charade, making us look even more official.

On the day, Miso hired a dark blue rental car, a West German make, from the hotel. Suited and booted we headed to the Capitulation Museum first. The director, a middle-aged Russian lady wearing loads of make-up, showed us round the building and explained all the exhibits in great detail. We could even sit at the normally cordoned-off table, were the surrender documents had been signed some 43 years earlier. At the baroque palace, which was located in the grounds of the zoo, we were welcome by the deputy director. After his hour-long tour through the various salons, he let us sneak into the rehearsals of two Japanese classical pianists who were to perform there that evening. When we walked back to the car I felt very smug because no one had cottoned on to us. Admittedly, it was an elaborate ruse just to get into two museums. But we all felt it was worth the effort. Later in the evening Miso told me that walking into an open exhibition wouldn't have been half as much fun and exciting and memorable, as the afternoon we had. I could not have asked for more.

On one of Miso's later visits, I asked whether I could join him on his bus trip to Dresden, where he and his group were due to spend one night before departing from the DDR. He agreed. He even offered to put me in a big suitcase and smuggle me across the border to the west. Apparently customs officials had never displayed any interest in the group's luggage. I rejected Miso's idea on safety grounds. After the DDR went belly up, it emerged that all traffic to and from the west was secretly X-rayed at our checkpoints, to detect illicit passengers. My refusal to hide in the luggage compartment had spared the two of us a few years in DDR prison.

I felt like the king of world when I boarded Miso's bus for the 200-odd-kilometre trip to Dresden. First I was a bit uneasy with the group, which consisted of loudly spoken American pensioners. But I was quickly made welcome by the oldies. Jack, a septuagenarian from California, told me enthusiastically about his house and garden near the sea. Ethel was a small wrinkly old lady in Bermuda shorts and sneakers. She tried to persuade me to sell her the light-green autumn jacket I was wearing as we went for lunch: "That is exactly what my son had been looking for in the past few months," she pleaded. But how could I possibly sell my most favourite jacket, an import from Finland, when our shops no longer stocked it? I had to refuse her offer. With everyone in the group asking me questions about life in East Germany we reached Dresden in no time. As far as I was concerned, the journey could have lasted twice as long.

In the evening Miso and I had a romantic candlelight dinner in a nice restaurant close to the historic city centre. The next morning, I sadly had to go back to Berlin. Jack, Ethel and the rest of the oldies waved me goodbye as the bus sped away from the hotel's forecourt, leaving me behind in the cold. None of them noticed the single tear rolling down my right cheek.

PRAGUE

In just a few months I had developed strong feelings for Miso. When he told me by phone that in a few weeks time a tour would take him to Prague for a few days, I knew what I had to do – take some time off work and buy an international train ticket to surprise him.

I arrived in Prague at noon on a rainy day in mid-October 1988. At Cedok, the official Czechoslovakian travel agency, I was told that I would find the group in the up-market Hotel Central. When I arrived there at two pm, the receptionist advised me that everyone had just left for a sightseeing tour. So I made myself comfortable in the lobby, got my book out and waited…and waited…and waited. At quarter past six, I walked over to the reception desk again and asked the girl who had just started her evening shift at what time the group would return. "Which group?" she asked. "The Americans with the Yugoslav tour guide." – "I am sorry, but we haven't got any Americans or Yugoslavs staying in the hotel." – "WHAT?!" I shrieked so loud that everyone in the lobby stared at me. Miso was in Prague and instead of trying to find him I had wasted four valuable hours reading Charles Dickens' *Old Curiosity Shop*. Panic-stricken and angry I grabbed my suitcase and stormed out of the Hotel Central in a huff. I tried my luck at other hotels nearby but every receptionist I approached shook their head. "Think, Oliver, think!" I said to myself. Didn't Miso mention once the Hotel Ambassador? Hopeful, I went on my way, just to find out he was not staying there either. What was I to do next? I was cold, hungry and thirsty. I did not have enough money on me for a room and the banks were closed. The thought that I might have come all that way for nothing made me feel sick. But I quickly pulled myself together. Determined to find Miso, I got myself lots of change, occupied a public telephone booth and set out on a mission to call every hotel listed in Prague's telephone book. Miso was out there somewhere.

And Lady Luck was on my side. I hit the jackpot with the third call. He was staying at the four-star Panorama Hotel – a high-rise building in some godforsaken outer suburb of Prague. Miso was just tucking into his dinner at the hotel restaurant when I arrived. He was so surprised to see me he dropped his fork when I suddenly stood next to him. To celebrate my unexpected arrival Miso, I and Liljana, the local guide he had been allocated by the Czech authorities, had a couple of drinks at the hotel bar. The next day, while the group had a few hours free time, the three of us went shopping in the city. Liljana seemed like a very nice girl. She was slightly older than me, had long dark brown hair and was very chatty. We immediately clicked and had interesting conversations, from one Iron Curtain kid to another.

A short 48 hours later my time with Miso came to an end. After a quick hug in the hotel room, Miso got on his bus and headed off to the next stop on his itinerary, Vienna. I had to make my way back to East Germany. Life was so unfair! And it was to become even more so. When I arrived at the border checkpoint, Czech customs officials immediately singled me out. My ID card was passed to four different officers who all scrupulously checked every single page. I had to empty all my pockets and unpack my entire luggage. A small bottle of DDR tablets was carefully examined. One pill was confiscated for testing. A tub of hand cream was put through the X-ray machine. My personal diary, containing my innermost thoughts, as well as telephone numbers and addresses of all my friends and pen pals around the world, was photocopied. It was still warm when handed back to me. Yet the search continued and I was wracking my brain trying to figure out what they were after. A few minutes later the wanted item was found. Customs officials breathed a sigh of relief as they discovered Miso's business card. I had innocently used it as a bookmark. The card was confiscated. Obviously I had been expected. Somehow the Czech security organs had learnt of my little get-together with Miso. Which was strange, considering that I had told everyone at home, including my family, that I was going on a shopping spree to Czechoslovakia. Only three people knew what I had really been up to in Prague: Miso, myself and… Liljana. Suddenly, all her interest in me began to appear in quite a different light. And so did her refusal to give me her address.

Then the questioning began. Two stern-looking Czech officers demanded answers: "What was the purpose of your visit? Where did you go? Where did you stay? What did you do in Prague? Who did you meet? For how long have you known this person? What is the nature of your relationship with him? Why did you meet this person in Czechoslovakia? How often have the two of you met in the past?" and so on. I answered all their questions truthfully, after all I had nothing to hide. Half an hour later, I was free to go, but my joy was short-lived. DDR customs too rifled through my belongings and asked me virtually the same questions as their Czechoslovakian comrades. Another 30 minutes later, I was finally allowed to continue my journey home. I wrote in my diary as I was waiting for the next train to Berlin: "Every single piece of paper, however small, was carefully examined during the search. I am shaking like a leaf and need to calm my nerves. Those border pigs treated me like a criminal. What have I done to be treated as if I am a threat to the state? I hate the DDR so very, very much."

Later it occurred to me that the Czech and German authorities might also have been after a photo of Miso for their files. I did not have one on me when I was searched, but in the end the Stasi got their way. I'm sure it was no coincidence that my Prague photos took exceptionally long to come back from the centralised photo labs. I had to wait six weeks, instead of the usual two, for my pictures. Perhaps the Stasi department responsible for my file was temporarily short-staffed. Also did my medical file at the *Poliklinik* (Health Centre) mysteriously disappear shortly after my return from Prague. A couple of weeks later it turned up again. I guess by then the Stasi had found my GP's entry noting the prescription for the tablets which had aroused the suspicion of Czech customs officials.

Despite the Stasi's actions, I did not regret my trip to Prague a bit. In fact I was very happy that I had followed my heart, as a few week later Miso's itinerary changed and his new schedule did not bring him to the DDR any more. After a few more letters and telephone calls the contact stopped. With us being so far apart, we were destined not to have a future together.

HAVE I GOT NEWS FOR YOU?

In 1988 my colleague Rosch was looking forward to his first business trip to the west. He was a tall, intellectual guy in his late thirties and happily married with a child. Rosch went on a seven-day business trip to West Germany with one of our directors. Halfway through the week, a member of staff from HR, flanked by two strangers, stormed into our office and took away all of Rosch's desk draws. It set the whole office buzzing. No one bothered to explain why his desk was being raided. Rumours began to spread. A couple of days later, our departmental head informed us that "colleague Rosch has vanished during his stay in the Federal Republic of Germany." East Germans made seven million trips to the west in 1988. Rosch was one of the 7,292 travellers that year who did not return.

My departure from the foreign trade business early in1989 was in no way as dramatic as Rosch's defection. I just resigned and left. I did not want to work any longer in an environment where criticism of the state, however constructively intended, was considered blasphemy and adversely affected career advancement. Anyone demanding political or economical changes too vehemently was either branded an enemy of the DDR or, at the very least, a confused individual who was unwittingly playing into the hands of the West German capitalists. I considered myself to be neither. In line with most critics in our country, I did not want socialism to be abolished. All we were hoping for was a better, more perfect DDR. Gorbachev had introduced political reforms in the Soviet Union, why couldn't we do the same? Though, his economical reforms we definitely did not want to copy. When Dad went on a business trip to Moscow in early 1989, diners had to turn up with their own knives in the hotel restaurant. It was either that or eating the meals with a fork and spoon. At breakfast, Dad had to butter his bread rolls with a fork. For that to happen in East Germany was unthinkable. Our economy was sturdier than the Soviet's, but it hardly ran as smoothly as our media always tried to make out. Our shops were not empty, but neither were they filled to the brim with merchandise. And our authorities preferred to discuss serious shortcomings and political errors of judgement behind closed doors. The Communist Party wanted to appear infallible to the general public. No wonder that Gorbi, with his concept of openness, acquired cult-status among East Germans, and in particular, among the young people. We loved Gorbi whether our Politburo liked it or not. And it did not like our affection a bit.

During a Gorbachev visit to East Berlin, a couple of guys in their twenties stood next to me in the street. They were holding up home-made Gorbi posters. Nothing special, just blown-up photos of him on broomsticks. When Gorbachev and Honecker made an appearance, groups of young men, all strategically positioned in the crowd and wearing identical jackets, began to shout: "Erich, Erich, Erich." I, like the overwhelming majority of the masses, chanted instead: "Gorbi, Gorbi, Gorbi." Once the two statesmen had walked past, commotion set in. At least ten plain-clothes Stasi employees quickly closed in on the boys with the home-made posters. First their Gorbachev pictures were ripped apart then the youths were led away. I and other bystanders tried to intervene, but the secret service guys were having none of it and pushed us away. Gorbachev was the General Secretary of the Communist Party of the Soviet Union, the leader of the mightiest socialist country on earth, yet people were led away for showing his photo publicly in East Berlin. Something was very wrong. What would be forbidden next? My homeland was becoming stranger by the minute.

"In our society the Communist Party and the youth are one because socialism with its goal of peace and prosperity for all meets the ideals of the young generation and offers… the perspective of a secure future."

Erich Honecker

Despite such official proclamations, in the late Eighties we, the young generation, did not feel represented, let alone understood, by the oldies in the Politburo. Secret surveys prepared for the Politburo revealed that back in 1985, 57 per cent of young workers and 70 per cent of students identified strongly with the DDR. In 1988 those figures had fallen to 19 and 34 per cent respectively. Even worse, in the late Eighties only four per cent of the teens and twens saw DDR media reports as a true reflection of reality. Politburo members did not grasp that the youth of the Eighties was more critical and less patriotic than the youth of the Thirties, when the politicians themselves were young. Undoubtedly, DDR politicians had achieved a lot in their reign. We had no homelessness, no unemployment, free healthcare and free education. Rents, childcare, transport, basic foodstuff and clothing were all ridiculously low priced. But that wasn't enough for young people in the 1980s. We wanted more from life than cheap basics. West German radio and television acquainted us every single day with the latest must-haves. We too wanted to splash out on life's little luxuries – trendy clothes, exotic food, classy furniture, electrical gadgets and trips to other countries. Money wasn't too much of a problem for us. The real problem was that our economy wasn't geared up to meet an ever-increasing demand for goods. In the end, we wanted more than our politicians had ever promised. More than the country's economy could afford.

But according to our newspapers the DDR economy could not have been in a better state. Companies were constantly exceeding their set production targets and we had no major economic problems. Yeah, right, as if...

After leaving the foreign trade business I started a new job as a part-time newsagent. Many of my customers whinged about the state of our print media. Hardly surprising, considering that most newspapers contained the same articles, identical almost to the last comma. Yet strangely, it did not stop people from reading as many publications as they could get their hands on. In 1977, 17 million DDR citizens, living in 6.5 million households, read 7.5 million newspapers daily. By 1988, circulation had gone up by more than two million. It still wasn't enough to satisfy demand. On most days, the morning newspapers were sold out by noon at the latest. Thankfully we had the evening newspaper, the *BZ am Abend*, to sell in the afternoon. In total, 39 daily newspapers, 31 weekly or monthly newspapers, 545 national magazines and 370 regional magazines were published. DDR citizens were some of the most well read people in the world. Newsagents' sold 500 magazines and newspapers for every 1,000 people. According to the UNESCO the worldwide average is 192 copies.

The newspaper *Junge Welt* (Young World) targeted young readers. With 1.6 million daily copies, it equalled the combined circulation of the *Guardian*, *Independent*, *Times* and London's *Evening Standard*. The *Wochenpost* (Weekly Mail), a very popular newspaper, had no problem selling all of its 1.25 million copies every week. That's roughly the circulation of the *Sunday Times* in a country with less than one-third of the UK's population. If it hadn't been for a lack of paper, research showed at the time that the *Wochenpost* could have shifted twice as many copies. If people could not travel the world, they at least wanted to read about it. But the authorities were not interested in increasing the *Weekly Mail's* print run. In the late Eighties, a copy of the *Wochenpost* still sold for 30 pfennigs (12 cents), just as it did back in 1952 when the first issue came out. For political reasons, its retail price remained unchanged for 37 years, despite the production costs having gone up to 50 pfennigs in the meantime. On this title alone, the Communist Party, as the publisher, made a weekly loss of 250,000 marks (100,000 dollars). The short supply meant that newsagents had a nice little earner on their hands. Many customers regularly tipped me to ensure they would get their favourite newspapers and magazines on a regular basis. Once a customer was so desperate for a copy of the *Berliner Zeitung*, he gave me 50 marks (20 dollars) for a newspaper that cost 15 pfennigs (six cents).

Our weekly TV listings magazine, *FF Dabei*, was the DDR magazine with the highest print run, at 1.5 million copies (by comparison, *Radio Times* prints about 1 million copies). But the *Eulenspiegel* was by far my personal favourite. Its subscriptions were inheritable! With a circulation of 360,000 copies, it was the DDR's very own version of *Private Eye* (200,000 copies) – a satirical weekly, though not as bold as its British counterpart. Criticising the Communist Party or, God forbid, a member of the Politburo was off limits. Yet the magazine still managed to put its oar in when it came to exposing human weaknesses, bad habits, poor service, faulty products, wasted resources, shortages of goods or minor injustices and inconsistencies in our country.

Other publications did not dare go as far as the *Eulenspiegel*, which occasionally even had an issue pulped before it got distributed, because a cartoon or article was deemed a tad too critical. But unlike in Romania and the Soviet Union, the DDR had no censors working alongside journalists signing off articles. Instead, the editors-in-chief were held responsible for the content of their publications. If they did not want to be demoted, they had better make sure nothing too critical found its way into an issue. Weekly briefings by the media department of the Communist Party kept editors regularly updated with the latest topics that had to be avoided, or required pushing. And just to make sure that guidelines were followed, voucher copies of every issue of every magazine and newspaper had to be sent to the propaganda department of the Central Committee of the Communist Party before distribution commenced.

A popular joke among journalists then went like this:

Erich Honecker visited a farm. One of the photographs chosen for publication in next day's newspaper shows him in a pigsty. Three editors argue about the most appropriate caption: "Honecker among pigs," the first one suggests. "Too vague," says the second one, "but what about: Honecker, surrounded by pigs?" The third one shakes his head. "It still needs to be more precise. I suggest: Erich Honecker, second from left."

WHAT A DRAG

One of the highlights in my life as a teenager and twen was calling the Rock Telephone of West Berlin radio station, RIAS 2 (Radio In the American Sector). Using a false name, over the years I requested many songs during phone-in programs. Because of the limited number of telephone lines available between the two Berlin's I usually called from home, as it was more comfortable than standing in a phone booth. Sometimes it took twenty or even thirty minutes of constant dialling (not pressing buttons but using a real dial) just to get through to the west. Once I called from work, where we also listened to RIAS 2. I was over the moon when my request (*Wherever I Lay My Hat* by Paul Young) was played half an hour later.

In early 1989 I was 21 years old and felt it was time to move out of home. Flats for rent were a rare commodity. Years of underinvestment, resulting from the low rents, meant many old apartment blocks were crumbling in the Eighties. I went to the local council but my application for a flat was rejected outright. Because I wasn't part of a young married couple or a single mum with kids, my completed form was filed, rather than actioned. And as if that wasn't bad enough, Erich Honecker publicly proclaimed in January 1989 that the "Antifascist Protection Rampart (the Berlin Wall, to you and me) will exist as long as the conditions that led to its erection remain the same. It will stay, whether it be another fifty or a hundred years."

A few days later I saw an old pith helmet in one of East Berlin's antique shops. Its price tag read: 120 marks. I was tempted to get the helmet but then decided against it. "What's the bloody point." I thought, "There is no way I will ever be able to go on a safari." Life had become depressing with no prospect of political change on the horizon. My state of mind even began affecting my film work. Once I forgot my lines in the middle of a scene. To buy extra time to think, I began fiddling around with the bottom of my jacket while nervously clearing my throat. Immediately the production manager stopped the recording. I was told to get on with it and reminded that "we are not making a Woody Allen movie here." The entire country seemed edgy then. Even foreigners living in the DDR were nervous, though for different reasons. A Parisian guy who I met in a café was working at the French embassy in East Berlin. One day he invited me to his place for dinner. He lived on the fifth floor of an apartment block reserved for western diplomatic personnel. Yet I was not allowed to go near the windows to enjoy the view over Berlin. He was scared of being blackmailed by the Stasi, which was also the reason why we could only talk with the stereo blaring in the background. I did not understand what this was all about. An hour later I was wiser. It turned out he was married with a daughter and liked to meet men whenever his wife and child were holidaying in France. This wasn't what I had in mind. I made my excuses and headed home to two hot reads which my grandparents had managed to smuggle for me into the country from behind the Iron Curtain. *Joy of Sex* and *More Joy of Sex* were two books that fascinated me for many, many years.

My part-time newsagent's job allowed me to live out some of my professional aspirations. Inspired by Miso, I decided to have a go at becoming a licensed freelance sightseeing guide. I was very hopeful as I handed in my written commentary for a tour I had devised through East Berlin to a panel of judges. When I received it back someone had written on it with a red marker: "Oliver, you have noted down too many historical details, and forgotten the present and future. Where are your notes on Berlin, as the capital of the German Democratic Republic? Berlin, the City of Peace? You also have totally ignored the social aspect of the government's program to improve general living conditions by building new apartment blocks...

You need to have more facts and figures for the Berlin of today. Remember, the DDR will celebrate its fortieth anniversary in October!"

Even a simple guided tour through the city had to be infused with politics. Under those circumstances I did not want to become a guide any more. I was not prepared to turn a sightseeing tour into a propaganda show. Instead I tried becoming a compere. An old hand taught me the tricks of the trade – every freelance artist in the DDR needed to pass a test before being let loose on an audience. This procedure ensured the maintenance of high entertainment standards. But my tutor warned me that being an entertainer also had its dangers. One political joke on stage too many and I could wave goodbye to future engagements. Knowing my big mouth, I left the course before the training finished and I could encounter any trouble. I was yet again on the lookout for something interesting to do, and an ad in our newspaper, the *Berliner Zeitung*, caught my eye:

"Berlin's Cultural Management Division is seeking show talents! For a forthcoming event in the restaurant Ahornblatt (acorn leaf), show talents of all genres are invited to apply to..."

Hmm, that sounded good. But what could I do? To secure myself a place in the finals I had to come up with something unusual. Then it struck me – a drag performance! I chose a song from the film *Cabaret*. My plan was to prance around the stage made up as a cleaning lady. For weeks I practised steps at home in front of a full-length mirror, while holding a broom in one and a bucket in the other hand. The performance ended with me kneeling down and taking off my wig. Quite pathetic, really. Surprisingly, I managed to make it into the second round from which the final acts were chosen. On the big day I was up against a professional drag performer. The other guy, a chubby chap in his early forties, had to present his act first. He wore a frilly white dress, a pink feather boa and a blond wig. His performance was very static and he had not bothered to shave that morning. The judging panel honoured his performance with moderate applause. Then it was my turn. As soon as my music started all of my senses were solely focussed on the stage. I had to concentrate on my steps: one, two three, four, five, six, and one, two... Four minutes later it was all over. The applause I got was twice as loud as the reception for my predecessor. Yet the faces of the judging panel seemed to express pity rather than enjoyment. There was that unmistakable "You-are-very-brave-to-show-us-this-crap" look in everyone's eyes. Or was I mistaken? Unfortunately, not. The other drag act was selected for the variety show. I decided to obliterate my sorrows at a nearby ice cream parlour with a Schwedenbecher (Swedish sundae) – a concoction of vanilla and chocolate ice cream, apple sauce, advocaat and whipped cream. As the waitress took my order she asked whether I would be interested in modelling clothes for a friend of hers. I was, and the photos from that fashion shoot certainly made me look much better than dressing up as a cleaning lady.

THE END IS NIGH

In an average year, people wrote at least 750,000 complaint letters annually to various government bodies and party institutions about injustices or shortages they had encountered. In the Eighties, this figure rose to over a million. In 1988 Erich Honecker alone was sent 29,000 letters of complaint by disgruntled citizens. The State Council, by law the highest institution in the country, was swamped with something between 60,000 and 100,000 complaints. By early 1989, a third of the population had, just like me, given up hope of domestic political reforms in the near future. More and more people began to shun political activities and concentrated on their private life instead. In 1987 105,000 citizens were released from DDR citizenship and given permission to move to West Germany. A year later 113,500 applicants wanted to move to the west. In 1989 it only took seven months for 100,000 applications to flood in, out of which 46,000 were approved. Even members of the Communist Party were fed up. Around 60,000 of them cancelled their memberships between January and November 1989. The party expelled them after they had already left – it made the statistics look better. The 30,000 new members recruited in the same period could not hide the fact that the heyday of the East German Communist Party was over.

The real heroes of that time were the dissidents. A colourful collection of idealists, intellectuals, hippies and eco freaks would best describe them. They took on the state by organising events under the cover of the church. Financially and morally supported by West Germany, the DDR church was a fairly powerful institution in its own right. With eight million Protestants and one million Catholics (out of 17 million citizens) the power of the religious institutions was not to be underestimated. The church gave singers or writers a platform to present critical songs or texts to an ever-increasing audience. Young people, especially, began flocking to these gatherings. It was refreshing to see problems of our society being addressed. Underground activists even used church facilities to print leaflets denouncing pollution caused by DDR factories. It was truly remarkable that more and more people began to stand up for what they wanted – a government that was in touch with the masses. There was tension in the air as local elections were held on 7 May, a sunny Sunday. As usual, the number of candidates on the ballot papers exactly matched the number of available seats, yet this time more voters than ever went into the polling booths, under the watchful eyes of polling officers. Instead of just folding the paper and accepting all candidates as in previous years, people crossed out every single name in protest. I did too. Would the government get the message?

Secret opinion polls done by the Communist Party before the election suggested that up to seven per cent of the voters would reject the candidates outright. Honecker gave the order that he wanted to see genuine election results. But old habits died hard. Regional party secretaries still wanted to outshine each other. Just like in previous years, polling stations were given targets on how many "yes" votes had to be reported. This time things were different, though. Christian groups and dissidents in particular had announced in the run-up to the election that they would show up in polling stations in the evening to witness the public counting of the votes. To save face, plans were put into place by the authorities to keep the exact numbers of "yes", "no" and invalid votes under wraps. Some "troublemakers" who intended to be present at the counting were refused entry to polling stations or given wrong times and turned up too late. Those who were able to observe the vote counting, and a record number were, faced polling officers who made "no" votes disappear or counted them as "yes" votes.

There was a collective outcry when the returning officer finally announced that 98.85 per cent of the votes (at a turnout of 98.78 per cent) were in favour of the proposed candidates. People felt they had been taken for a ride. Too many East Germans were dissatisfied with the DDR's political inflexibility for such a positive result to be genuine. A figure of 80 per cent of the votes in favour of the Communist Party would have been believable to most DDR citizens. But claiming a 98.85 per cent win was just defying belief. No East German expected the Communist Party to lose the elections. What enraged us was how blatantly the results had been rigged. Dissidents took to the streets in protest on election night. Police and Stasi quickly broke up these gatherings, making good use of their truncheons. In the weeks following, the authorities were swamped with complaints from election observers. No one in charge seemed to care. All complaints were rejected as unsubstantiated. In return, dissidents and Christian groups reported cases of electoral fraud "against an unknown person/persons" to the police. None of the reports was investigated; instead applicants were victimised. Many protesters were, more or less openly, watched by the Stasi. Anyone considered a serious troublemaker was given the option of either leaving the DDR westwards within 24 hours or facing a jail sentence. Yet all these measures could not prevent protests up and down the country. In big cities on the seventh of each month groups of people began to protest against the vote-rigging.

In early 1989 it had dawned on many East Germans, especially the younger ones in their twenties and thirties, that political reforms in our country were not coming soon. As a result, they began to apply en masse for their release from DDR citizenship and permanent migration to West Germany. When it became apparent that the authorities would not approve so many applications, people began to look for alternatives. The exodus to Hungary began after West German radio and television stations reported that the Hungarian government had, on 2 May, started to dismantle its border fortifications to Yugoslavia and Austria. Quite a number of my old schoolmates packed their bags and left so quickly I did not even get a chance to say goodbye. The western stations informed us in great detail about the latest developments in Hungary, while our media ignored the subject completely. It was the usual game. What the west hyped up, we played down.

Meanwhile, East Germans wanting to start a new life in the west continued to flock to Hungary. However, many would-be migrants were not aware that fewer border fortifications did not mean fewer guards. East Germans who were caught trying to get from Hungary to Austria illegally were sent back to the DDR with a special stamp in their ID card. A prison sentence was assured for anyone identified in this way. Unable to get to the west and not prepared to return to the DDR, East Germans abroad began turning to West German embassies. First in Budapest, later also in Prague and Warsaw. People hoped to be able to get to West Germany that way. The other Germany had always insisted on being the sole representative of all Germans. It had no qualms about its embassies issuing West German passports to East German citizens. But the passports on their own were useless. Westerners had to apply for visas when travelling behind the Iron Curtain. And only a traveller who had entered a communist country as a westerner could leave it as one. Changes of nationality half way through a holiday were (naturally) not recognised by the communist border police. East Germans holding newly issued West German passports found themselves trapped. In protest East Germans refused to leave the West German embassies in Hungary, Czechoslovakia and Poland until a political solution had been found for their problem.

Then the Tiananmen Square massacre happened in Beijing. The Chinese army had violently ended student protests calling for more democracy. Officially, 200 people were killed and 8,000 injured. But eyewitness estimates put those figures much higher, with up to 2,500 dead and 30,000 injured. Our media praised this bloodshed as a successful repression of a counter-revolution. The headline in the newspaper *Neues Deutschland* got many thinking:

"The German Democratic Republic and China stand side by side during the struggles of our time."

The warning to potential protesters in the DDR was clear: don't demand changes in the way the DDR is run. This prompted even more East Germans to pack their bags and go on "holiday" to Hungary, Czechoslovakia or Poland, with no intention to return to their fatherland. By the end of August, thousands of people had left the DDR. Some had managed to illegally cross the border between Hungary and Austria, many were lying low and still waiting for their chance. Less-adventurous East Germans made do with the cramped conditions in the West German embassies. Our Politburo reacted to these mass defections by saying nothing. The silence was prolonged when Erich Honecker was admitted to hospital in July that year. In August he had a gallbladder operation and in his absence, the Politburo did not want to make any decisions. No one was prepared to stick their neck out. Instead, our media was advised to ignore the exodus. West German television and radio stations were rubbing their hands with glee.

It did not take long for the first problems caused by the defections to be noticed. Thousands of migrants had left empty workplaces behind. Workers on production lines were missing. Public transport companies struggled to keep buses and trains running. There was a shortage of doctors and nurses. One day my dentist was on her own – her nurse too had migrated. As much as the shortage of workers made everyday life harder in the DDR, it was, at the same time, very exciting to see that the Iron Curtain could be overcome in Hungary. A little voice in my head said: "Being able to see the west well before retirement age, wasn't that what you and Cordi had always dreamed of? Grab your chance while you still can.". For the time being I ignored the voice. Hoping that our government would soon be offering unrestricted travel for all, making a migration via Hungary unnecessary,

By early September, 3,500 East Germans were refusing to leave Hungary to go back to their homeland. DDR officials tried to sweet-talk them to return, but to no avail. Instead they preferred to stay in camps run by the Red Cross until Hungary would allow them to go the west. Hungarian politicians urged their East German comrades to find a solution. But this drew a blank and so Hungary took the matter into its own hands. At midnight on 11 September 1989 Hungary officially opened its border to the west for DDR citizens. Within three days, 15,000 East Germans defected to West Germany via Hungary and Austria – two months later the figure had climbed to 60,000. West Germany granted Hungary a loan of 500 million Deutschmarks after they opened their borders. Erich Honecker wrote in our newspapers:

"The DDR is the greatest achievement of the revolutionary German workers' movement. It is a state with a functioning, effective socialist society and considering the human rights granted within it, it will also stand the test of time when facing the challenges of the Nineties."

Meanwhile, these jokes did the rounds:

Erich Honecker is flying home from a state visit abroad. From the air he sees a brightly illuminated East Berlin. After landing, Honecker tries to find out the reason why all the lights in his beloved capital are switched on. He walks through the streets but there is no one to ask. East Berlin is deserted. As he goes to the Brandenburg Gate he sees a hole in the Wall. Next to it is a hand-written note: "Erich, you are the last one. Please turn off the lights."

Erich Honecker is visiting a kindergarten. A little girl hides behind her teddy bear. Honecker bends down: "And who are you?" The girl replies coyly: "I am Ming of Laos." – "And do you know who I am?" Honecker asks. The little girl nods: "Yes, you are king of chaos."

Q: Which three catastrophes happened in 1912?

A: The Titanic sank, the Novarupta volcano erupted in Alaska and Erich Honecker was born.

Not the best jokes, perhaps, but they were told with such glee. On a more serious note, the question on many people's minds was how long our Politburo would continue to allow people to leave the DDR for good via Hungary. Would unrestricted travel for all East German ever be on the cards or was a declaration of martial law round the corner? I wasn't keen to take a gamble. So I quickly applied for an exit visa and booked myself a one-way flight to Budapest. Would I have the guts to leave everything and everyone dear to me behind in the DDR? At the time I did not know.

TWO TRAINS, ONE DECISION

As my parents drove me to the airport in September 1989 I went over in my mind whether I had thought of everything: All my degrees and certificates I had secretly put into a hidden envelope, taped to be bottom of my desk, together with two notes. One was to my grandparents asking them to smuggle the papers to West Berlin and to hand them to a friend there. The other one was addressed to my parents. In it, I explained that after careful consideration I had decided to defect and asked for their forgiveness for not having told them about my plan. The idea was that once I had decided for sure that I was not returning to the DDR, I would call Mum and Dad and tell them where to find the envelopes. That way the Stasi listeners would not have learnt of my defection and my grandparents would have had enough time to get the documents to West Berlin. Furthermore, my parents would have had enough time to distribute my personal belongings to other family members. Possessions of defectors were usually confiscated by the state.

Mum and Dad had been to Hungary just a couple weeks earlier. The family they stayed with offered to take them to Austria on a stretch of border that was not well guarded. My parents declined. They could not imagine leaving their family behind and starting from scratch again in another country. Now I was planning to do just that.

"You are coming back, aren't you?" Mum asked me at the airport. Two weeks earlier I had said in anger that I was through with the DDR and had no intention of waiting until retirement age to travel the world. What was I about to say now? With fake confidence I heard myself reply: "Of course, I will be coming back." The less my parents knew about my plan the better it was for them. Failing to report a planned defection was a punishable offence.

I gave Mum and Dad a final hug and made my way to passport control. My eyes were filled with tears as I turned around for a last wave and then handed my ID card to the border police officer for inspection. I had no idea when I would see my friends and family again. It proved to be a wise move not to take any of my qualifications with me. Being single, in my early twenties and travelling to Hungary on a one-way plane ticket with only a cheap train ticket for the return journey, identified me as a potential escapee. My luggage was rifled through and I was strip-searched. With no compromising paperwork found, I was free to proceed to the departure lounge. A guy and girl behind me in the queue, both in their late teens, were less lucky. Their trip was over before it began. Customs found school certificates in their backpacks and both were lead away.

I only discovered 19 years after the fall of the Wall, when obtaining a copy of my Stasi file, that while I was waiting to board Malev flight 815 to Budapest, the Stasi had secretly searched my checked-in suitcase. My diary, containing personal photos and sentimental notes, little keepsakes on scraps of paper as well as the addresses and telephone numbers of all my family, friends and international pen pals was painstakingly photographed, page by page. Even the most trivial things were considered relevant. A note from my parents (Dear Oli, have a nice day. Lunch is in the fridge. Take care when you are out. Love Mum and Dad), a Christmas greeting from my grandparents (Dear Oli, have a very Merry Christmas. All the best for the coming year. Love Nanna and Grandad) and possibly the unfunniest joke in the world (Q: "Do you remember the 100 marks I lent you last week?" A: "Yes, regularly and with pleasure.") made it all onto microfiche. Banality, captured for posterity.

While the Stasi was doing its dirty work in the airport basement, I bumped into the husband of a colleague. He was on duty as the DDR representative of Malev, Hungary's national airline. My seat number was quickly changed from 17B to 1A and the cabin crew was ordered to look after me as I was a "special guest". They followed the request to the letter. During the flight (unlike the rest of passengers) I was spoilt with an endless supply of sparkling wine and a visit to the cockpit. And I was so taken with the meal that I even forgot to worry about the loose screw on the wing that I had seen flying off in mid-air.

In Budapest, I set out to find accommodation for my week's stay. The travel agent got very annoyed with me. I rejected every hotel he suggested as too expensive. The amount we could change from DDR marks into Hungarian forints was capped and East German banks did not issue credit cards. I finally settled for a private room in a family home. When the travel agent photocopied my ID card, it became clear why all hotels he had praised as cheap were beyond my reach. He thought I was West German – if I had been, I would have received many more forints when exchanging currency. In Hungary the Deutschmark was five times stronger than the DDR mark.

For days I asked myself whether I was ready to step through the Iron Curtain. Wherever I went, whatever sight I looked at, I hardly took in my surroundings. Instead I was constantly weighing up the pros and cons of leaving my fatherland for good. Being able to travel freely and to buy what you want when you want it had great pulling power. But living alone in the west away from my friends and family did not seem a desirable prospect. And visiting the DDR would be out of the question. Illegal escapees were either refused entry to their former fatherland or at risk of being arrested at a border checkpoint, even as tourists. Yet, there was the possibility of meeting up in a third country, like Czechoslovakia, for example. Also, by earning Deutschmarks, I would be able to regularly send presents to everyone. But could presents and money replace the lost closeness? And what repercussions would my family be faced with if I left the DDR illegally? Dad's business trips to the west would come to an end, my brother would not be able to climb the career ladder, Mum would possibly be demoted from her managerial position and, who knows, Grandad and Nanna might even have had their passports revoked. Did I have the right to affect the lives of the people who I loved and cared for in such way? Or was I worrying too much and would everyone be alright? After all, thousands were leaving the DDR via Hungary. Surely the authorities couldn't bully all of these people's family members who had stayed behind? Or could they?

I finally decided that I was going back to the German Democratic Republic. For the time being, I wasn't going to join the 26,500 East Germans who had left the DDR via Hungary for good by the end of September. But as

I arrived at the Budapest train station for the journey home, my decision was put to a test. On platform nine was my train to East Berlin, ready for boarding. It seemed empty. I had an entire sleeping compartment to myself. As I looked out of the window I could see that the train on the next track was heaving with fellow East Germans. Did I get on the wrong train by mistake? When I asked a train conductor, he replied, with a cheeky smile: "It depends where you want to end up. We are going to Berlin. The train on platform eight goes to Vienna. From there it's only a stone's throw to West Germany."

For 15 minutes I sat in my empty compartment, mulling over yet again whether East Germany really deserved my return. If I was going to change my mind, this was the time. But I stuck by my earlier decision. Eventually the train to Vienna pulled out of the station without me. Had I done the right thing? As we reached the East German border, I began immediately to regret not having switched trains in Budapest. Instead of being grateful for everyone who returned from Hungary, the DDR border police were as grumpy as ever. After they barked "Passport control!" upon entering the compartment, I was asked questions about my stay in the People's Republic of Hungary. It was the crack of dawn, and not being quick thinking at that time of the day, my delays in answering were met with a stern face and a scrutinising stare. There was no "Good morning", no "Good bye", no "enjoy the remainder of the journey" – not even a smile. I guess I could consider myself lucky that customs did not search my belongings.

Back in Berlin my family welcomed me with warm embraces. Yet some of my friends were surprised to see me again. They had treated my earlier farewell as a final one. The next day I went to the police station and applied for a new exit visa to Hungary. When I received it in the post two weeks later, I began to relax. With my emergency escape secured, I could play the waiting game and see how things would develop, while our media blamed people's laziness for the dissatisfaction with their fatherland:

"Whether you are a miner, a baker or a construction worker: Socialism is only as good as everyone with their daily work has made it."

Junge Welt newspaper

CZECH THROUGH

Others were not as lucky as me. After being refused exit visas for Hungary, entire families went to Czechoslovakia instead and climbed the fences of the West German embassy in Prague. By the end of September, around 5,000

East Germans lived there in atrocious conditions, determined to leave their socialist fatherland behind. Not wanting to have any negative publicity overshadowing our state's fortieth birthday celebrations on 7 October, Erich Honecker allowed all embassy squatters to go to the west. However, to create the impression that the DDR government was still in control of the situation, escapees had to travel on trains that made a detour through East German territory rather than going straight to West Germany from Czechoslovakia. This way, they could officially be expelled.

"Politicians and the media of the Federal Republic of Germany uninhibitedly... mislead people onto a path that will end in an uncertain fate. The picture painted of life in the west is intended to make people forget the things the socialist society has provided them with and what they are about to give up. They will harm themselves and betray their homeland... Parents are making irresponsible decisions for their children who would have grown up well looked after by the socialist German state. All sorts of educational and development opportunities would have been open to them.

In agreement with the Czechoslovakian government, the government of the DDR has decided that everyone who illegally stays in the embassy of the FRG in Prague will be expelled from the territory of the DDR. This decision has been mainly made for the sake of the children, who have been forced into an emergency situation by their parents. The children cannot be held responsible for this irresponsible behaviour.

The renegades have treated moral values with contempt. They have excluded themselves from our society. One should not shed a tear over them."

Neues Deutschland newspaper

The last sentence was added by Erich Honecker himself. For weeks, our media remained silent and then such a statement was made. We East Germans were shocked and outraged by the ignorance of our politicians. Workers wrote a letter to a Politburo member:

"The majority of our colleagues do not agree nor believe our media's embarrassing... attempts to class the departure of so many of our people solely as the result of the enemy's work, depicting DDR citizens as victims and extras only."

Somehow Erich Honecker and his Politburo did not consider their subjects leaving the DDR en masse to be a major problem. Records show, that the Politburo bizarrely busied itself in one of its weekly meetings at the time with analysing the availability of onions in the city of Karl-Marx-Stadt. Maybe Honecker would have been less ignorant of the situation had his cronies not made him believe for years that the DDR was a picture-perfect place. In a private conversation, Honecker boasted to Gorbachev that for four hours, 700,000 Berliners had walked past his stand and waved at him in the traditional May Day parade earlier that year. Referring to this conversation, Gorbachev later confided to another DDR politician: "Honecker obviously saw himself as the number one of socialism, if not of the entire world."

For Honecker, the mass exodus was caused by external reasons outside the control of the DDR. And so our media began claiming that the west was inciting our people to leave by applying psychological pressure. The newspaper of the Communist Party, the *Neues Deutschland* (New Germany) even printed a ludicrous story about a DDR buffet car chef who had been kidnapped in Budapest by a West German people smuggler. Allegedly he was knocked out by a menthol cigarette a West German had offered him and only regained consciousness in the west. At work, we cried tears of laughter when reading this nonsense. Sure enough, after the DDR had ceased to exist, the chef came forward to admit the story had not been true. He had fled to the west but then had second thoughts and wanted to return to the DDR. Not everyone leaving East Germany was a dissident. In fact, the real dissidents were idealists and stayed behind because they wanted to reform their homeland and make it a better place to live. In September 1989, a group of 30 artists founded a political organisation, the New Forum. It was intended as a platform for discussions about political reform. But the state did not allow it to operate. The ruling Communist Party claimed to already represent the interests of all citizens. People in the south of the country, in Leipzig and Dresden, began to take to the streets in protest.

It is no secret that the majority of people leaving the DDR after the initial rush did it for economic, rather than political, reasons. The DDR's standard of living at the time was on a par with the UK. But why make do with that when West Germany had better living conditions? And since no one knew how much longer it would be possible to slip through the Iron Curtain, more and more people grabbed the opportunity with both hands. By the beginning of October, the West German embassy in Prague was again filled with East German escapees. Again, the DDR was prepared to wave goodbye to its citizens – this time to over 7,000 of them. Just like the previous lot all they had to do was board DDR trains that would take them to the west via a detour through East German territory. The only problem was that this time people knew which route the trains would be taking. East German tracks and train stations were heavily guarded by police and army, but it did not stop thousands of people trying to jump into the locked carriages as they drove past. For the first time in 35 years, police and civilians clashed violently, with injuries on both sides. A total of 224 people were arrested. Thankfully no shots were fired. East Germany's biggest planned media event of the year – the DDR's fortieth birthday celebrations – was about to take place, but would it really go as smoothly as our politicians hoped?

(A NOT SO) HAPPY BIRTHDAY

Leaders of all socialist countries and heads of worldwide pro-communist organisations and movements arrived for the much-hyped DDR birthday festivities. As Honecker waited at the airport for Mikhail Gorbachev's plane to land, he was asked by western journalists to comment on the mass migrations. "Is there a migration problem?" was his reply. Not even three per cent of the total population (around 400,000 people) fled the country in 1989 but wasn't every person who had left us one person too many? In nine months, more East Germans had turned their back on the DDR than in the previous 27 years. Between 1961 and 1988, while the 3,500 kilometre-long Iron Curtain was still holeproof, only 235,000 fellow countrymen had found a new home in the west.

If no one else in the DDR felt like celebrating, at least Erich Honecker was in a good mood about the forthcoming birthday bash. Not for long. At the traditional torchlight procession held on the eve of the birthday, many of the 100,000 youths walking past our Politburo and the international dignitaries chanted: "Gor-bi, Gor-bi!" The organisers cranked up the music from the loudspeakers to try to cover the shouts, but it could not drown them out completely. The young people especially had hoped Gorbachev could knock some sense into our leaders' heads and demand changes. He seemed to enjoy the shouts of support. Honecker, on the other hand, looked decidedly miffed. With a rigid smile he carried on waving at the passing girls and boys who were cheering not for him, but his guest.

The next day began like so many *Republikgeburtstage* (republic's birthdays) before. At ten o'clock the traditional military parade started. An hour later, Berliners began to walk past the stands that had been erected in the Karl-Marx-Boulevard for our leaders and their national and international guests. The same procedure as every year, yet this time something was different. There was tension in the air and more police than usual walking the streets of the city centre. Not to mention the casually dressed, young and fit, secret service lads standing at strategic points. Pretending to be bored, they scanned their surroundings very carefully. The Stasi assumed at the time that the DDR had 20,500 organisied dissidents, of which 60 were classed as "diehard provocateurs and enemies of socialism". On a big day like this, the Stasi did not want any of them to raise their head:

"The negative activities of the enemy have to be stopped by all means. Do not allow for surprises to happen. Prevent enemy activities by people who assume we are not present."

Extract of the Stasi's Order of the Day for 7 October 1989

Despite the DDR's closure of all frontier crossings between East and West Berlin to prevent troublemakers from the other side entering our capital, some western journalists still got in. A small number of them had been officially accredited to report on the birthday celebrations. Of course, they couldn't have cared less about the official programme of events. What they really wanted to capture was the groundswell of protest, which they must have sensed was about to erupt. And we East Berliners did not disappoint them. First we made most of the day and enjoyed ourselves. There was food and drink on sale at many of the stalls put up for the traditional birthday fete, and a number of stages showed various entertainments. Having gotten up late and skipped breakfast, I gobbled down a Grilletta (DDR name for hamburger), a slice of Krusta (pizza) and a Ket-Wurst (hot dog) before joining a few thousand of my fellow citizens on the capital's most famous city square, the Alexanderplatz.

It was heaving with people and come two pm public discussions about the latest political events began to spread. As expected, emotions ran high when our Politburo's passivity in recent weeks was talked about. Propagandists, sent by the Communist Party in an attempt to defuse any volatile situations, were fighting a losing battle. I listened to the arguments brought up by both sides but did not participate in any of the discussions myself. Too dangerous! There were far too many cameras around. Not knowing who was friend and who was foe, I decided it was best to keep my mouth shut. The risk of being filmed by the Stasi and later accused of public disparagement (up to ten years in prison) was too great. At three o'clock, the first clusters of people began to shout: "*Freiheit*" (freedom), "*Gorbi, hilf uns*" (help us) and "*Demokratie*". Then protesters, with an eye on the so far passive police, preventatively switched to chants of: "*Keine Gewalt!*" (no violence). Along with around 3,000 other Berliners, I began to make my way to the nearby Palace of the Republic, where government and Politburo had invited 4,000 national and international guests for an afternoon and evening of entertainment. Access to the immediate vicinity of the building had been blocked off by police. We positioned ourselves on the riverbank opposite the Palace of the Republic and began to shout: "Gorbi, Gorbi!". We could see how the guests inside the building were watching us. What a contrast it must have been for them, especially after they had just raised their glasses with Erich Honecker in celebration of the republic's fortieth birthday. If some of them had lost their appetite, it definitely couldn't have been on account of the menu. Dishes served included quails' breasts, marinated trout fillets, ox tongue terrine and turkey soup as starters; the mains featured veal fillet, beef fillet and chicken medallions. The dessert, aptly named "surprise", was a concoction of sponge cake, chocolate marzipan, meringue and various ice creams. Under different circumstances, it probably would have been very enjoyable.

As the time came for Gorbachev to head back to the airport and leave for Moscow, us 20,000 demonstrators made our way to the road to catch a glimpse of our hero as he drove past. We could not get close to the Soviet Union's number one politician. Policemen had locked arms and lined the carriageway, forming a human shield. Never in my life had I seen such a heavy police presence. I wanted to take a few photos of this spectacle yet every time I was about to hit the shutter release, a young men next to me, dressed in a DDR jeans outfit, began to jostle making it impossible for me to keep the camera still. Trying to embarrass him, I looked him straight in the eye and said in the most intimidating manner I could muster: "Are you queer, or what?" All cocky he smiled back at me. He obviously felt dead sure of himself, so I decided to expose him for what he really was. Terrified, but exhilarated, I began to point at the guy and said as loudly as possible to bystanders: "Careful everyone, there is a plain-clothes Stasi man among us." I had no idea what would happen next. Would his colleagues close in and take me away? Far from it. The guy looked around, but he must have become separated from his chums. His confidence instantly evaporated and he began to leg it. Before he could return with backup, I swiftly took my photos and went home. It was a good decision not to stay on. As the evening progressed, police and Stasi became much more violent. Around 3,000 men out of a 23,000-man security force on standby were used to keep 5,000 mainly peaceful demonstrators in check. With truncheons, tear gas, water cannons and stun guns our People's Police, supported by the Stasi, ended up fighting the very people they were supposed to protect.

Erich Mielke, an agile, stocky octogenarian who by then had been the Minister of State Security for the past 31 years, also kept a close eye on what was happening in the streets of East Berlin that evening. Mielke was a shining example of discipline and military correctness. On weekdays he would get up at six am sharp to go for a swim before being sped to the office at seven am. His breakfast always had to consist of two eggs (pierced and boiled for exactly four-and-a-half minutes), bread, jam, juice, coffee and milk. Whoever served him in the morning had to strictly adhere to a diagram that showed how the table was to be laid. Every single item needed to be in exactly the same place, every single day. Mielke clearly wasn't a man who liked change. His motto was: "We need to know everything." Indeed, most of the time his ministry did. But when things did not go according to plan, comrade minister Mielke lost his temper. Like the time when one of his officers defected to the west. In a meeting with other high-ranking Stasi officials the minister confided: "All the waffling about not to execute and no death penalty is a load of old twaddle, comrades – execute, even without court judgement." Mielke's unsophisticated roots also shone through on the night of the DDR's birthday. Seeing his troops faced with demonstrators, bystanders heard him shout at his men: "Beat 'em up, those pigs!".

A total of 547 people were arrested in East Berlin on 7 October. The next day, the demonstrations continued. Protesters sang *We Shall Overcome* and *The Internationale* as they claimed the streets. The *Sicherheitsorgane* (security organs) were as edgy as the previous night, and both sides clashed again. Another 524 people were taken into custody. On 9 October our media released the following statement:

"In the evening hours of 7 October, rowdies in Berlin tried to interrupt the fetes held in honour of the fortieth birthday of the DDR. They ganged up at and around the Alexanderplatz, in cooperation with the western media, and shouted anti-republican slogans. By staying calm, the Protective and Security Organs, as well as the visitors at the fetes, were successful in preventing the intended provocations from spreading. The ringleaders have been arrested."

There followed a flood of written complaints by ordinary people, organised protests and concerts held in churches in honour of the victims. By 13 October the state gave in to the growing public pressure and released the 1,071 arrested "ringleaders". Everyone involved in the protests was jubilant about the result. (Though later, 47 of the released people were ordered to pay a fine, while 33 received a minor prison sentence.) While the initial release of all arrested protesters in Berlin was undoubtedly a great success, the 2,385 demonstrators arrested in other cities continued to remain in custody. Again protests erupted. Demonstrations, sit-ins and human chains were staged up and down the country. Demands were made for the decriminalisation of arrested protesters, and the punishment of violent policemen and Stasi agents. A bishop publicly declared that an official apology was in order for the brutality shown by the security organs when arresting demonstrators.

By 13 October, 45,000 East Germans had left their fatherland via Hungary, the Czech Republic and Poland. For the first time since 1961, the DDR indicated that illegal emigrants who had problems settling down in the west were welcome to return:

"We will assist everyone who would like to return...to set foot again in their traditional native country."

Berliner Zeitung

THE FALL OF THE WALL

Despite the mayhem on the streets, in autumn 1989 good old Erich still thought his DDR was the best thing since sliced bread. Yet his Politburo comrades had finally come to their senses. In an attempt to restore domestic harmony, they got him to agree to the release of a statement a couple of days after the state's birthday celebrations:

"Socialism needs everyone. It offers a place and a perspective for all. It is the future of the up-and-coming generation. That is why it is not a matter of indifference to us when people who worked and lived here, have dissociated themselves from the German Democratic Republic."

Such a statement was too little, too late. Especially in Leipzig, the city that hosted the DDR's international trade fairs, more people than ever took to the streets to protest for free elections, free speech and free travel. What had started as small impromptu demonstrations after church service earlier in the year had developed into regular illegal Monday demonstrations with up to 150,000 peaceful protesters. Even the Politburo's decision to send Erich Honecker (by then 77 years old) and two of his colleagues into "early" retirement could not calm the masses. On the contrary! It wasn't long until 3,000 famous DDR artists demanded publicly:

"We are concerned about the current condition our country is in, the extensive exodus of many peers... and the unbearable ignorance of our government and ruling party... We want to live in this country and it makes us sick to see how attempts at democratisation are being ignored... We demand change. The time is now."

By the end of October, 300,000 Leipzigers were taking to the streets in their hometown, wanting to see a German Democratic Republic that truly deserved its name. On 4 November, the DDR's biggest-ever demonstration took place in Berlin. Between 500,000 and one million people (estimates vary greatly) took to the street that day to get the government to fully guarantee the freedom of speech, the freedom of the press and the freedom of assembly. DDR television broadcast the event for four hours. I was one of the protesters and the mood among us was fantastic. Only a month earlier, it would have been completely out of the question for the authorities to give their approval to such a devastating public expression of will. And now it seemed like the most normal thing in the world. Many of us wondered how far we might go in another four weeks. None of us could have imagined that the biggest change of all was only five days away.

Was our country really, finally, about to become a more liberal place or would the government eventually send in the military to restore the old order? No one knew at the time which way the dice would fall and so people continued to leave the DDR via Hungary. Every ten seconds, an East German arrived in the west to start a new life. Though not everyone was successful in taking such a step. West Berlin's unemployment figures soon showed that ten per cent of the city's jobless workforce were East German. While across the border more and more people were competing for fewer jobs, DDR companies became increasingly desperate for workers. To stop the continued exodus, the reshuffled Politburo decided to grant total freedom of travel for everyone. Our economists had no idea of how the hastily drawn up Travel Law could be financed. On 9 November at 18:58, Politburo member Günter Schabowski informed international journalists at the end of a press conference that: "Private travels to foreign countries can be applied for without the existence of prerequisites – reasons for travel or degree of relationship. Permissions are being granted on a short-term basis. Rejections will be restricted to special circumstances only... The People's Police have been advised to issue exit visas for permanent migration without any delay. Permanent migrations can take place on all frontier crossings between the German Democratic Republic and the Federal Republic of Germany." An Italian journalist asked comrade Schabowski when this new law would come into force. "Passports will have to be issued first," he replied, "but to my knowledge immediately."

The news was on in the background as I was getting ready to go out on that chilly Thursday evening with some friends from television. Not many East Germans, myself included, took much notice of Schabowski's announcement. He had been waffling for 58 minutes about how marvellous and in touch with the people our newly reformed leaders were. The new Travel Law was only mentioned in the final two minutes of the press conference. My thoughts were: "If this new law is revolutionary in any way, it would have been given top billing". I expected there to be some caveat, buried deep in the small print, that would still prevent the great majority of people from travelling to the west. There just had to be a catch, and undoubtedly the newspaper would explain it all the next day anyway. So instead of getting prematurely excited, I continued messing around with my hair and applied yet another layer of impenetrable hairspray so I would look the part at the disco that evening.

Coincidentally, we decided that evening to go to a disco that was close to the West Berlin border, in the city centre. Because it was midweek, the place wasn't exactly heaving with people. I was dancing with lovely Annett to Holly Johnson's *Americanos* when suddenly, at around quarter past nine, a guy ran in and shouted: "The Wall is open!" only to disappear again. The dance floor emptied immediately. Our group of three boys and two girls decided to check out the nearby frontier crossing. What a disappointment it turned out to be. As we arrived at the checkpoint on Invalidenstrasse, there was no sign of the Wall being any more penetrable than usual. Lit by unflattering neon light that emitted a low drone, the checkpoint looked familiarly deserted. Except for the occasional West Berlin car driving back to the other side, there was no other traffic. As expected, the group of us five youths hanging around near the entrance to the crossing for a few minutes did not go unnoticed by the checkpoint's personnel. Soon a border police guard walked casually into our direction and shouted, in a friendly, but determined voice: "Move on, please!" My friend Matthias immediately replied: "We don't want to move on. We want to go to West Berlin. Don't you know, the Wall is open?!" – "No, it's not!" was the stern reply. "Now leg it, or I'll do you guys for disturbing the public order in the frontier area." We were confused and probably would have gone back to the disco, if it hadn't been for a man who, as he ran past, shouted at us: "The frontier crossing at Bornholmer Strasse is open."

Bornholm Street wasn't too far away. We decided it was worth checking out whether the story was true. We quickly jumped into a tram and when we got off 20 minutes later we could not believe our eyes. Already, a kilometre before the actual border crossing, the streets were packed with people. Stationary cars jammed the surrounding roads for an even longer distance. Something was definitely about to happen here, if it hadn't happened already. We made our way at a leisurely pace to the crossing. Police tried to draw people away by announcing over loudspeakers that exit visas could only be obtained the next morning from all police stations, but the guys in uniform were fighting a lost cause – no one turned around. Didn't comrade Schabowski announce at the press conference that the new Travel Law was coming into force immediately? Thousands of curious East Germans had taken him at his word and wanted to see for themselves whether unhindered travel really was possible. The fact that a passport and an exit visa were needed first did not seem to matter. As we reached the checkpoint, its boom was still down. People shouted: *"Tor auf!"* (open the gate) and *"Wir kommen wieder."* (we will come back) but nothing happened. What none of the 20,000 travel-hungry East Berliners waiting at this checkpoint knew was that the 60 or so personnel inside were as clueless as the crowd about what was going to happen next. Schabowski's announcement had caught them by total surprise. The new law was only supposed to come into force at four o'clock the following morning. In desperate need of advice on how to deal with the situation at hand, the checkpoint commander called around, but no one in charge was prepared to give a definite order. Most party and government leaders were in late-running meetings and did not want to be disturbed. The lower ranks were stalling, trying to avoid having to make a decision. Finally, Stasi headquarters came up with a twisted plan. By ten pm checkpoints were ordered to allow the most provocative individuals to go through to the west, however passport control should place an exit stamp on their ID card photos. This meant they would unwittingly lose their DDR citizenship and not be allowed back into the country.

As the first people were selected by checkpoint personnel and invited to go through the gates, jealousy quickly spread among the rest of us who were left behind. I thought: "Why can they go but not me?" The selected few waved jovially at us before disappearing into the night behind the last barrier we could see, which did nothing to calm the masses left behind on the eastern side. With thousands of other people, I heard myself chanting: "Open the gate! Open the gate!" In the meantime, DDR television was pointing out that immediate travel was not possible, but the well-respected West German news program *Tagesthemen* (topics of the day) began its broadcast at 22:42 with the words: "...Good evening ladies and gentlemen, this 9 November is a historic day. The DDR has announced that its borders are immediately open for everyone. The gates in the Wall are open wide!" More East Berliners wanted to see whether this was true. Soon, around 30,000 people were packed around the checkpoint at the Bornholmer Strasse for their chance to go to the west. And the situation on other checkpoints in Berlin and the rest of the country was no different.

Well after eleven o'clock that night, the people at the back in the Bornholmer Strasse put more and more pressure onto the densely packed would-be travellers in the front. As the people in the first row began to get dangerously close to the re-enforced wire-mesh fence, the checkpoint commander finally gave the order to "flood" the crossing. Slowly the gate was pushed aside and people began to pour, uncontrolled, into the usually off-limits area. "Is this really happening?" I was asking myself as I set foot into the checkpoint. At one window, people were queueing to get a souvenir exit stamp with that momentous day's date in their ID cards. For a moment, I too wanted an exit stamp but decided quickly against it. Crossing the border anonymously seemed a much safer option. People tried to cheer up the solemn-looking uniformed checkpoint employees who watched in disbelief such an unprecedented event at their workplace. Perhaps they realised that evening what I hadn't – that soon their jobs would be obsolete.

After walking past several small buildings and fenced-off areas, the road became narrower (a tactic employed to make high-speed car escapes impossible). Then came a watchtower, an open boom and yet another fence. I looked for the white line on the road that would mark the beginning of West Berlin but couldn't see it. I continued walking towards the crowd which was lining the bridge ahead. Everyone who came through was applauded. And then, after passing yet another barrier at the end of the bridge I finally saw the white line which marked the border between two political systems. I wanted to treasure the moment of crossing it and slowly set my right foot over it. But just as my left foot was about to follow someone pushed me from behind and I ungracefully stumbled my way into West Berlin. Was I really in the west? I was unable to take it all in. I found myself hugging strangers and taking sips from bottles of sparkling wine that were going around. It did not take long until I too began to say the one word that was on everyone's lips that night: "*Wahnsinn!*" (madness).

The scenes I encountered at the checkpoint Bornholmer Strasse were repeated, with slight variations, on all border crossings in Berlin. Though it was mostly East Berliners who crossed the border westwards, some West Berliners too took advantage of the porous border that night and went for walks in the DDR's capital. The West Berlin mayor, Walter Momper, went onto East German territory to remind people to be considerate and disciplined. At the various checkpoints West Berlin policemen and East Berlin border guards worked together to try to keep people away from the roads as much as possible, so that cars could pass freely. Enemies became colleagues that night.

Once on the other side, I began looking for my friends who I seemed to have lost on my way through the checkpoint. Thankfully they turned up just a couple of minutes behind me. We jumped into one of the many waiting double-decker buses that the West Berlin city council had quickly organised to get people to the nearest tube station. To prove to everyone back home that I really had been in West Berlin, I took a promotional leaflet from a display stand on the bus. Coincidentally it was advertising performances by three East German artists in West Berliner clubs.

When we arrived in West Berlin's city centre we had a quick browse at some of the shop windows. As all the shops were closed, we decided to continue the evening the way it had begun – with a disco visit. None of us had any Deutschmarks to pay for entry, cloakroom or drinks, but when we told the owner of one club our story, we were let in for free and could order whatever we wanted from the bar. Around two am, all of us staggered to West Berlin's most famous shopping street, the Ku'damm. By then it was apparent that all checkpoints must have been flooded – the entire boulevard was tightly packed with people laughing and crying, some even managing to do both at the same time. Bottles made the rounds, special edition newspapers were handed out. "The Wall is gone!", one stated in huge letters, followed by "Berlin is Berlin again!"

Bystanders applauded every East German car that slowly made its way through the masses. Unsurprisingly, I lost my friends in the crowd but that did not really matter. Just like everyone else, I too found myself talking to total strangers. Emotions begged to be exchanged. It was a pity I could not share the moment with my parents. After a West Berliner had given me some change, I tried for 15 minutes to get through to the other side from a public phone – without success. Even at four am, all lines between East and West Berlin were jammed.

As I stepped out of the phone booth I could feel the night's drinks having an effect and kept my eyes open for a quiet place to have a wee. In East Berlin, lack of funds had created lots of parks occupying sites where previous houses had been reduced to rubble in the war. But West Berlin streets had one apartment block after another. And while DDR apartment blocks usually had unlocked doors allowing strangers access to communal courtyards, here in the west every single door I tried was firmly shut. The words profit maximisation and security consciousness sprang into my mind. In the end I gave up searching and took my business back behind the Iron Curtain.

On my way home I had a look in a 24/7 walk-in newsagent's. What a sight the shop was, with shelf upon shelf of publications. I had never seen that many special-interest magazines in one place before. There was even a separate over-18 section stacked with titles that left nothing to a reader's imagination. This area behind the beaded curtain was the most popular with DDR men. At five am, it was time for me to leave the West Berlin glitzy newsagent's behind and to head back behind the Iron Curtain to serve my customers back home. I was on morning shift and had to open the shop at six-thirty am. Standing in an overcrowded train heading to the checkpoint Friedrichstrasse, I wondered whether future visits to West Berlin would be possible. What if this had been a one-off, and the border would close again?

As the train approached the station at Friedrichstrasse, I had a good look at the border fortifications. Only 100 East Berliners took the opportunity that night to leave their fatherland for good. The majority of us dutifully came back, making all those fences and watchtowers on the border look pretty pointless. Yet the DDR border guards continued to diligently do their duty. East Berliners returning to their socialist capital had to have their ID cards checked. Would the border police guy make a big fuss because I did not have an exit stamp in my ID card? What if I was denied entry? Those thoughts were rushing through my head as I moved slowly towards one of the many cabins where the passports were checked. Then it was my turn to go behind one of the Formica doors that displayed a sign "Entry for citizens of the

DDR, FRG and Berlin (West)". It sprang open after the sound of a buzzer and I stepped into what turned out to be a little cabin. As the door fell back into its lock behind me, I shoved my ID through a little opening in the Plexiglas that separated me from the tired-looking uniformed border official who sat on an elevated stool. Only after having a glimpse at the mirror on the ceiling above me to make sure that no one else had sneaked in with me did he devote his attention to my papers. The guy, not much older than me, had a good look at my face before giving me my entry stamp. Then the buzzer went again and I was free to leave the cabin through the second door towards customs. I was sad such an unbelievable night was over, but at the same time somehow also glad to be back. Another traveller was less lucky. He must have been one of the poor sods who had been unknowingly stripped of his DDR citizenship by an exit stamp over his photo when leaving the country. I could hear him shout: "But I have to get back to my son. He is only ten years old and on his own." before three guards led him away. Presumably he was frogmarched back to the platform and put on the next train westwards.

As I arrived at home, for a quick refresh before work, I woke up my parents and told them excitedly about how I had partied at the Ku'damm last night. "Oliver", Mum said baffled whilst rubbing her sleepy eyes, "the Ku'damm is in West Berlin. What are you talking about?" – "Yes, that's why I am so hyped up. I was in West Berlin last night!" I shouted back excitedly. My parents just looked at each other in disbelief. It turned out, Mum and Dad had slept through the fall of the Wall. They had gone to bed at around ten pm, well before the border checkpoints opened. When I went to work it became clear that most of my customers were still partying on the other side of the Wall. I had no one to serve, except for a few pensioners and twiddled my thumbs. Even the rare weeklies, usually sold out within an hour after opening, were still available when handing over to the afternoon shift.

What a night it had been. I caught up with some sleep in the early afternoon before going back to a checkpoint for more border crossing action. People were queueing for several hundred metres. By then, border guards had resumed control. All travellers were issued free exit visas by policemen walking down the queue before people made their way to passport control and customs. West Berlin by day was even more exciting than by night – now the shops were open. Not that I could make any big purchases with the few leftover Deutschmarks Dad had given me. But I did want to grant myself one wish. So I headed to the nearest discount supermarket and strolled through the aisles until I spotted what I was after – tins of champignons. In East Germany they were a luxury (an imported tin from China cost more than ten DDR marks, that's four dollars!) and I wanted to satisfy my craving without feeling ripped off. The shop sold two different varieties: first-grade quality for one Deutschmark (40 cents) and third-grade mushrooms for 69 pfennigs. A difference of 31 pfennigs for one tin was quite significant to me

– I only had 2.70 Deutschmarks in my pocket. So I queued at the till with nothing in my trolley but a single, forlorn tin of third-grade mushrooms. Arriving back home, I immediately reached for the tin opener to indulge my mushroom fantasies. Disappointment set in as I fished oddly shaped bits out of the brine. I said to myself that looks aren't everything, as long as the mushrooms taste like first-grade ones. But they didn't. Their acidic, metallic aftertaste was disgusting. I chucked the whole lot and had learnt my first lesson of life in the west: unlike in socialism where prices were either subsidised or inflated, in capitalism you always only get what you pay for.

STASI CLAUS IS COMING TO TOWN

As much as the fall of the Wall was celebrated, West Berliners quickly became fed up with us easties clogging up their part of the city. Around 4.3 million East Germans visited the FRG and West Berlin in the first four days (only 10,000 applied to leave the DDR for good), nearly 11 million in the first fortnight. Parking spaces became scarce, buses and trains were packed (DDR citizens travelled free), pavements were heaving with people, shops, department stores and supermarkets had long queues. As did the banks and post offices, which paid every visiting East German their one-off "welcome money" of 100 Deutschmarks (40 dollars). The centre of East Berlin, on the other hand, was deserted on weekends. So much so, that West Berliners came to visit the capital of the DDR for some peace and quiet.

To ease congestion on the borders to West Berlin and West Germany fifty new checkpoints were opened, at a cost of 700 million DDR marks (280 million dollars). Reunification wasn't on the cards yet. According to a survey done in December 1989, 73 per cent of DDR citizens still preferred two separate German states. I was one of them. Somehow I was scared that a united Germany might turn into a Fourth Reich.

The winter 1989-1990 was a turbulent one. Too many of the old politicians clung to power. People took to the streets to demand more changes. First the Politburo that had toppled Honecker resigned. Then the government stepped down and finally the members of Central Committee of the Communist Party cleared their desks. East Germans wanted to see new faces to be convinced that changes were indeed permanent. Despite such high profile resignations, the Communist Party was still running the country. The party member who took over the position of Prime Minister, Hans Modrow, was liked by the public. In his previous capacity as a party secretary for the southern region of Saxony he and Honecker had a few bust-ups over the years. This undoubtedly had an impact on the later Prime Minister's popularity. Yet to be on the safe side, round tables comprising of members of all major parties and organisations, were set up to monitor the work of the government. Our media too changed drastically in those turbulent weeks. Freed from any censorship, we were surprised every single day anew with investigative news stories. Whether it be reports about Stasi activities or the lives of ex-Politburo members, the people were hungry for information. Viewing figures for our television news programme *Aktuelle Kamera* (up-to-date camera) increased fivefold. Suddenly, 50 per cent of DDR viewers watched DDR news. Anything to do with Erich Honecker especially seemed to catch the people's interest. First he was accused by public prosecutors of misuse of office, then of corruption and finally, and most bizarrely, of high treason. As if Honecker had planned to abolish socialism in East Germany, or had tried to assassinate a leading DDR politician. Honecker and his wife were kicked out of their house in the gated community near Berlin. A vicar offered them refuge in his house. Later they became guests of the Russian army stationed in the DDR, living in an army base. Just before reunification in autumn 1990 they were flown to Moscow. When Boris Yeltsin defeated Gorbachev, Honecker came close to being extradited to Germany. Instead he fled to the Chilean embassy. Many of the Chileans who fled their country after Pinochet's putsch in 1973 were now themselves politicians and felt obliged to repay the former statesman for the hospitality he had offered them two decades earlier. Honecker had to leave the embassy in 1992 after his stay began to affect political relations between Germany, Russia and Chile. Once back in Berlin, Honecker was jailed on remand and put on trial for his role in the shootings on the border between East and West Germany. Kidney cancer had taken hold of him, however, and the case against him was suspended. In 1993 he was free to join his wife in Chile, where his daughter and her family had been living for many years. In May 1994 Honecker died, aged 81.

When his ex-colleague, the Romanian General Secretary Ceausescu was sentenced to death in December 1989, I found it quite disturbing to see the pictures of his execution on telly. Thankfully, Honecker's reign had not given rise to the same sort of collective hatred. But then we East Germans never had to suffer like the Romanian people, who had to endure 12-degree temperatures in their homes in winter time, make do with five eggs a month, drink wine made of wood shavings or eat "ham" made from beans, blood and bone meal. The DDR's number one hate figure by far was not an individual, it was an organ of the state – the Stasi.

On 15 January 1990 a demonstration against the Stasi's continued activities took place outside its headquarters. In the late afternoon that day I could hear the protesters' chants from my newsagent's which wasn't far from the one-square-kilometre complex. When I had closed up shop for the day, I wandered down the road to see what the 2,000 or so demonstrators were up to. Standing in front of one of the many gates leading into the Stasi compound, people were cheering a guy who was demanding a speedier dissolution of the secret service. It looked like a tame event. But things changed quickly when some protesters began to symbolically brick up the gate and suddenly the steel double doors magically opened. Strangely, there were no Stasi guards around to keep any of the protesters at bay. I quickly joined the crowd which poured with great speed into the usually very heavily secured complex. There was no way that I was going to miss this once-in-a-lifetime opportunity to inspect the headquarters of our state's most secretive and most feared organisation with my very own eyes. It turned out later, that opening the doors and letting the public in was a well-orchestrated decoy by a mysterious insider who had stolen some pretty important spy databases for the Americans that night.

Unsure about how the Stasi would take our trespassing, people sought safety in numbers and stayed in groups. Most demonstrators stormed the buildings nearest the entrance. To get more personal space I followed some people to a building slightly further down the road. There was an eerie atmosphere in the air as I walked towards the doors. All buildings, with the exception of the ones that had just been stormed, were dark and not a single Stasi employee could be seen anywhere. My gut feeling told me that something was not right. I was scared that the Stasi might have been holding back their men waiting to open fire. My heart began pounding. I increased my speed to reach the safety of the building quicker but thankfully worried needlessly. Secret service employees later admitted, they were as scared to bump into us as we were to bump into them. Anyone still at work had locked themselves into their office and switched off the lights. In fear of being lynched, some even drew their gun in case protesters made it to their office. Thankfully all doors that I saw forced open gave way to empty offices.

The building I went to was like any other office block in the DDR. It reminded me very much of my previous employer, export-import company Glas-Keramik. Corridors in both buildings had linoleum and harsh neon lights. The offices featured plain wallpaper, pot plants and mix-and-match furniture. Some Stasi employees had decorated the walls near their desks with posters of communist faraway places like Havana or Tashkent. The only thing missing were pictures of family members on the desks.

For a while I followed a group of people that was led by a stocky guy in his late twenties carrying a crowbar. Cheered by the crowd, he opened the office doors with such ease as if he had done it a thousand times before. Maybe he had. Every door that went was applauded. As people poured into the opened rooms, locked desks and cabinet were forced open and paperwork was read. Commemorative plates celebrating DDR milestones and any other political memorabilia such as busts, glasses or miniatures were smashed. Everyone, me included, got caught up in the general excitement, but not knowing what or, more importantly, who would be around the next corner made me cautiously stay at the back end of groups of people.

As the evening progressed and it became clear that the Stasi would not retaliate against our intrusion, demonstrators became more boisterous. Offices were completely ransacked and the floors and hallways became littered with papers. Everyone seemed to be on a mission to find their Stasi file. Me too. What we did not know was that the organisation's central archives were housed in another building. Instead I read through index cards which listed personal details, right down to sexual preferences, of western businessmen who regularly visited the DDR. I am sure we all would have been shocked had we found some of the observation equipment that can today be viewed in museums: specially prepared shoeboxes, handbags, buttons, dustbins, tree roots and strap-on bellies could all be fitted with secret cameras. The Stasi's ingenuity knew no limits.

When searching in the basement for my files, I came across a stash of confiscated West German books, piled up into high stacks. I helped myself to a few interesting titles before proceeding to an equally well-stocked wine cellar. After squeezing one promising French red into my bag, my carrying capacity was exhausted. For me it was time to go home. As I walked up the stairs I came across Erich Honecker's autobiography lying on the floor next to a small (but too heavy to carry) Lenin bronze. I picked up the book to have a special memento of the DDR. A pity that near the exit a demonstration steward took the book off me again – the organisers condemned looting. With the other contraband out of sight in my bag I happily handed over the Honecker book and headed home, with a big grin on my face. Various family members received Christmas presents courtesy of the Stasi that year.

FATHERLAND, FAREWELL

By January 1990 the Communist Party had lost more than 1.5 million members. Yet our politicians still tried to prop up the DDR by creating a more liberal socialism. The problem was that people had had enough of social experiments. The following joke made the rounds at the time:

Q: What's the difference between "beautiful" and "crap"?

A: It's beautiful that socialism gets stronger every day. It's crap that we are the ones who have to do it.

In November and December 1989 alone, over 300,000 East Germans packed their bags and moved to the west. The DDR was indebted to other countries to the tune of around 20 billion marks (eight billion dollars). Peanuts, compared to West Germany's net borrowing on the international markets of 169 billion Deutschmarks (67.5 billion dollars) at the time. But our country was smaller and our economy somewhat less efficient. Economists predicted that attempts to clear the debt would result in a 30 per cent drop in the people's living standard.

Under these conditions, it was no surprise that the conservative Christian Democrats won in the 1990 March elections on their promise of a speedy reunification. They got 48 per cent of the vote. The left-wing Social Democrats came second with 22 per cent. The communists achieved a paltry 16 per cent. The DDR was heading for voluntary annexation by the Federal Republic of Germany. Hooray, finally we too would earn our living in Deutschmarks and not have to feel like second-rate Germans any more! But in the meantime we were still stuck with the DDR mark. And I wanted to buy lots of clothes in the west. What could I do? Unlike many, I did not consider smuggling goods across the border a worthy option. But one day my eye was caught by an ad in a West German magazine; "Seeking Male Escorts" its bold headline screamed at me. The text did not mention any involvement of sex so I sent off my full length (and fully dressed) body shot as required, together with a covering letter to an address in Hamburg. Two weeks later I received the invite for an interview. Deutschmark here I come!

I arrived in Hamburg by train and did some sightseeing first before I headed to the escort agency in the afternoon. As it turned out they weren't after witty and smart companions for their clients, as I had imagined. This was a recruitment drive for good-looking and willing rent boys who wanted to sell their bodies to affluent guests in the company's classy in-house bar. And the boss was so desperate to take me on. "Oliver, if you come here on weekends, I will line the punters up for you," he assured me, "I can guarantee, that for two days work you will get at least 1,000 Deutschmarks." I could not believe my ears. 1,000 Deutschmarks (400 dollars) for two days "work"? Exchanged on the black market this was equal to 4,000 DDR marks (1600 dollars) – four times the average monthly salary. It was a very tempting offer indeed but only as long as I did not think about how I was expected to earn the cash. I declined to be videoed introducing myself to potential clients in the nude and took the next train home. Instead I secured myself a part-time job in a West Berlin newsagent's to fund my long-desired shopping sprees at H&M.

On 1 July 1990 we East Germans finally got the Deutschmark – 20 billion marks were initially distributed. During the last month of our old currency, our shops, had fewer and fewer goods on display. There was a huge run on all subsidised items like children's clothes, shoes and food basics. Some people even put five or ten loaves of good old DDR bread into their freezers, so they would not have to waste their precious and long-awaited Deutschmarks on something so trivial. Our shops were grey and empty on Saturday 30 June. When they reopened on Monday 2 July, we suddenly had western-style supermarkets. What a transformation! Everywhere, row upon row of western goods were stacked high and garnished with loads of colourful advertising. The memories from the previous year, when supermarkets in the provinces had to take down shelves to appear well-stocked, evaporated. Up to 6,000 DDR marks per person could be exchanged, one for one, into Deutschmarks, any amounts above that were exchanged two for one. But with the new currency also came western prices and the competitive demands of a western-style economy. That was hard for the DDR industry, with its subsidy culture. Only 32 per cent of our companies were profitable. Many factories went bust because there was no demand for their products any more. East German consumers collectively spent their new money on the western brands they had seen being advertised on western telly for all those years. Eventually shops stopped stocking East German products. Unemployment in the east shot up. Newly opened sex shops made a killing. People were intrigued by dirty magazines and videos – pornography had been banned in East Germany. But porn was hardly an adequate replacement for a lost job. First voices could be heard wanting the old DDR back. But by then it was too late.

In autumn I went flat-hunting, DDR style. A friend had given me a tip that a street near my parents' building had a number of empty flats. I reported the vacant apartments to the housing authorities. In return I was allowed to move into one of the places. At 22, I had finally a pad of my own – a one-bedroom flat. On 2 October, one day before reunification, the tenancy agreement was signed. The monthly rent was still set at the old DDR tariff – 46 square metres for 37 marks (15 dollars). At midnight, the German Democratic Republic "voluntarily joined the jurisdiction of the Federal Republic of Germany", as the act was officially called. Four days before its forty-first birthday, the DDR ceased to exist. Overnight, we East Germans had become part of a different political system, with its own structures and legislation. Several newspapers and magazines explained the ins and outs of a western democracy and made us easties familiar with the lyrics to our new national anthem. I am still struggling to remember all of its lines.

LIVES OF THE OTHERS

From the many people who have crossed my path over the years I have only stayed in touch with a selected few. Lars, my best schoolmate, still lives in Berlin and is today partner of a management consultancy. Cordelia, my school love, married a colleague of hers in the early Nineties. They now live, with a pair of adorable twins, in Düsseldorf, former West Germany.

Dörte, my close friend from the foreign trade days, has settled with a husband and two kids in a small swiss town. She misses Berlin.

I googled Miso in 2005. He is still living in Ljubljana and now a director of the travel company that he worked for as a tour guide in 1988. Here is how he remembers our encounters back in 1988:

"I clearly remember seeing you for the first time, in your almost all-white outfit, resembling a marine cadet on his first day out. With the sun shining through the windows behind you in the hotel lobby there was something angel-like about you. A hint of innocence, maybe even some longing... You were curious about everything, wanted to know all about the world. There was this incredible wish to hear about my views on any topic. We talked about politics and life philosophies. You tried your very best to explain everyday life in the DDR. But somehow you were more critical about it than myself. I tried to point out some positive aspects and you always found the not-so-pleasant ones. You seemed embarrassed by your fatherland, probably longing to make it better. I felt this as a kind of pain you had... You never asked for presents. It was always me asking you whether you needed something from the west. In fact, you were quite reluctant when I clumsily tried to give you little gifts... Once you went to Dresden with me, on a bus full of elderly Americans. I remember the mixed emotions you showed – being curious yet at the same time, talking to them with a slight unease... Later you came to Prague to see me. We had a great time but I never found a way to contribute to the costs for your trip. It haunted me for a while... You are a long lost friend."

These days, we see each other at least once a year.

My grandparents have sadly passed away in the meantime. My brother is living with his family in Germany's west where he manages a company. My parents, now retired, followed him in 2008.

In November 1990 I found my match. I met Ward, a smart and sexy Australian, in former West Berlin, at a Mac Donalds, of all places! We have been together ever since.

A FINAL LOOK BACK

This was the Deutsche Demokratische Republik as my family and I experienced it, and many East Germans would have lived very similar lives. The majority of DDR citizens did not reject their fatherland outright. For 40 years, people grumbled about any shortcomings and got on with their lives. Reunification only became a topic in early 1990. Before then, all anyone had hoped for was a reformed, better-executed socialism. One of the Stasi's biggest mistakes was to brand critics as enemies of the state, when their input could have been used to create a more liberal DDR. Instead, the ludicrous, paranoid secret service preserved smells of dissidents in jars. It also secretly marked dissident paperwork with radioactive or UV-visible substances to find out who was getting their hands dirty. The Stasi's overriding goal was to gather as much information as possible on anyone and anything. In the late Eighties the Stasi had 90,000 employees. By comparison, the secret service of the reunited Germany operates with just 13,300 members of staff.

As the DDR came to an end, the Stasi kept itself busy with one thing – shredding files. Much of this was done by hand because the electric shredders, all of which had to be imported from the west, could not cope with 24-hour use and packed up, one after another. In the end, 45 million documents had become 600 million pieces of paper, all of which were filled into 16,000 sacks. The original plan was to burn these sacks in disused quarries outside Berlin. But, typically East German, there was a shortage of lorries in the last few days of the DDR and the sacks had to be left behind. After reunification, 15 workers, armed with tweezers and sticky tape, were given the task of reconstituting the shredded documents. It would have taken them at least 400 years to solve the world's biggest jigsaw puzzle. Thankfully then the E-Puzzler arrived – a computer programme that can recreate documents by grouping together scraps of paper based on their characteristics. The completion date for the job is now estimated to be 2012.

Despite the extensive attempt to destroy evidence in the final months of the Stasi's existence, the secret service still left behind intact papers filling 122,000 metres of shelves. Around 360,000 photos, 600,000 negatives, 24,000 slides, 3,850 videos, 730 movies and 99,600 sound recordings also survived. The state's obsession with snooping had cost ten billion marks every year, as much as was spent on education.

So far, two entries of my name have been found in surviving Stasi files. One in department HA VIII's archive. This department was responsible for observing foreign military personnel and securing transit routes through the DDR. The other entry was found in department HA XVIII's card file. This department monitored the DDR industry. When I started at the export-import company Glas-Keramik in 1984, I was asked to submit two passport-sized photos. One was for the company ID card, the other one, I assumed, would remain in my HR file. I was wrong. The second photo was glued onto an index card and, together with my personal details, sent to the Stasi.

But putting aside the state's constant mistrust in its citizens, the DDR's social achievements are undisputed. For example, one year paid maternity/paternity leave with a guaranteed working place to return to, reduced working hours for the same salary for one parent and an increased holiday entitlement for mums with two kids cost our state billions of marks. Alone, the nationwide summer camps for the children required funds of 40 million marks a year. Parents only had to contribute an average of four marks per child and week. Large families were exempt from payments altogether. Kids clothing, of which two-thirds of the true cost were subsidised by the state, was so popular with American soldiers that they regularly bought huge amounts of it on shopping sprees in East Berlin.

Our health service was entirely free of charge to patients – its upkeep cost 23 billion marks a year. Back in 1987, the DDR government used ten per cent of its income to pay for healthcare. Ten years later the UK spent only 6.8 per cent of its annual budget on the National Health Service.

Annually, a whopping 50 billion DDR marks (20 billion dollars) were used to keep prices for everyday goods and services artificially low. Every mark spent by customers on basic foodstuffs was topped up by the state with 80 pfennigs, to enable manufacturers and retailers to recover their costs. No one had to spend more than five per cent of their salary on rent. Children aged between three and six could go to kindergarten for a nominal charge, and 50 per cent of all pupils got their schoolbooks for free. Our national income per head, double the Soviet figure, was the highest among communist countries.

There is a part of me which is proud to have belonged and contributed to such a society. But I also remember the flipside of life behind the Iron Curtain: the Stasi's omnipresence, the need for an official and a private opinion and the unconditional commitment to the DDR that was a prerequisite for any successful career. The authorities' motto was: Who isn't for us, is against us! I was for the DDR but did not like the constant spoon-feeding and politicisation of everyday life. I wanted to go my own way, make my own mistakes and come to my own conclusions. It was a pity that too much individuality was frowned upon by our security organs. Someone trying to break the mould sooner or later attracted the authorities' attention. For me and my friends the DDR felt stuffy and small minded. We saw it as a place where nothing exciting ever seemed to happen. We wanted action 24/7 but we could not freely go where we knew the action was – the west. Instead we had to make life in the east as colourful as possible.

The average East German had no problem with pointing out the DDR's shortcomings to foreign visitors from the west. We felt flattered if anyone from beyond the Iron Curtain took an interest in our lives. Yet strangely, if a westerner began to criticise our homeland in a conversation many of us immediately turned into model citizens, passionately defending the state we may have criticised earlier ourselves. I too believed that someone not living in the DDR was not in the position to pass judgement.

The Berlin Wall was probably the most hated structure in the east and the west. Over its life span of 28 years, the Wall claimed 136 lives. At least when it was taken down in 1990 it helped to prolong life: Auctioned-off concrete segments with graffiti raised a total of 1.8 million Deutschmarks (720,000 dollars). The money was used to improve our health service.

As a teenager I often dreamt of finding a secret passageway to West Berlin. Today I live in the west for real. If the DDR still existed, I would not want to go back for good. I enjoy the personal freedom and individuality that capitalism offers too much, despite all its shortcomings. But I would visit the DDR often, to experience again and again the collective closeness, the low crime rate, the sheltered life in the slower lane and the humour that played on words and was often only unlocked by careful reading between the lines.

Resourcefulness was a key element in East Germany. Products came with functional rather than excess packaging. Ladders in tights were mended, small electrical items were repaired. Throwaway items hardly existed.

Our society was not driven by the desire of everyone trying to make a quick buck. Life was less commercialised. Instead of advertising billboards, we had pro-socialist slogans dominating the streets. "The state is me...is us...our state...my DDR" was one of them. It is the country's backwardness, and its collective innocence that I do occasionally miss.

On board a plane flying from Tokyo to East Berlin. The stewardess is addressing the passengers over the intercom: "Ladies and Gentlemen. Soon we will be landing in Berlin, capital of the German Democratic Republic. Please buckle up, stow your tables, bring your seats in an upright position and set your digital watches back by 15 years."

I am very grateful for having had the chance to experience two different political and social systems, each with its very own set of advantages and disadvantages. Better executed, communism might be a worthy alternative. But until such a day comes, I am happy to make myself comfortable in capitalism. For the time being, I'd rather be exploited by capitalists, than ruled by a dictatorship of the proletariat.

Bibliography

K. Hartwig – *Das Auge der Partei*, Ch. Links, Berlin 2004

C. Härtel/ P. Kabus – *Das Westpaket*, Ch. Links, Berlin 2000

S. Wolle – *Die heile Welt der Diktatur*, Econ & List, Munich 1999

W. Seiffert/ N. Treutwein – *Die Schalck-Papiere*, Goldmann, Munich 1991

H. Bögeholz – *Wendepunkte–die Chronik der Republik*, Rowohlt, Reinbek 1999

P. Bergner – *Befehl Filigran*, Paul Bergner, 2001

P. Bergner – *Die Waldsiedlung*, Paul Bergner, 1994

J. Ritter/ P.J. Lapp – *Die Grenze*, Ch. Links, Berlin 1998

A. Kaminsky – *Illustrierte Konsumgeschichte der DDR*, Landeszentrale für politische Bildung, Erfurt, 1999

T. Heyme/ F Schumann – *"Ich kam mir vor wie'n Tier" – Knast in der DDR*, BasisDruck, Berlin 1991

H. Bahrmann/P.-M. Fritsch – *Sumpf*, LinksDruck, Berlin, 1990

R.G. Reuth/ A. Bönte – *Das Komplott*, R.Piper, Munich, 1993

K. Bahnke/J. Wolf – *Stasi auf dem Schulhof*, Ullstein, Berlin, 1998

J. Kallinich/ S. de Pasquale – *Ein offenes Geheimnis*, Museumsstiftung Post & Telekommunikation, 2002

G. Schabowski – *Das Politbüro*, Rowohlt, Reinbek, 1990

S. Sommer – *Das große Lexikon des DDR-Alltags*, Schwarzkopf&Schwarzkopf, Berlin, 2002

T. Kunze – *Staatschef a.D*, Ch. Links, Berlin, 2001

L.A. Rehlinger – *Freikauf*, Ullstein, Frankfurt/Main, 1991

H-H Hertle/ K. Elsner – *Mein 9. November*, Nicolaische Verlagsbuchhandlung, Berlin, 1999

K. Polkehn – *Das war die Wochenpost*, Ch. Links, Berlin, 1997

F. Wolff – *Glasnost erst kurz vor Sendeschluss*, Böhlau, Köln, 2002

A.Mitter/ S. Wolle – *Ich liebe euch doch alle*, BasisDurck, Berlin, 1990

D. Schultke – *Keiner kommt durch*, Aufbau Taschenbuch, Berlin, 2000

H. Modrow – *Das große Haus*, Edition Ost, Berlin, 1994

T. Scholze/ F. Blask – *Halt! Grenzgebiet*, BasisDruck, Berlin, 1992

T. Stengel/ F. Tweder – *Deutsche Kulinarische Republik*, Eichborn, Frankfurt/Main, 1998

D. Dahn/ F.J. Kopka – *Und diese verdammte Ohnmacht*, BasisDruck, Berlin, 1991

N. F. Plötzl – *Erich Honecker*, DVA, Stuttgart/ Munich, 2003

J. Voigt – *Der Geschmack des Ostens*, Kiepenheuer, Berlin, 2005

T. Grimm – *Das Politbüro privat*, Aufbau, Berlin, 2004

G.-R. Stephan – *"Vorwärts immer, rückwärts nimmer"*, Dietz, Berlin, 1994

C.-H. Janson – *Totengräber der DDR*, Econ, Düsseldorf, 1991

K.Steffen – *Essen wie Erich*, Eulenspiegel/Heyne, Berlin/München, 1999

M. Gebhardt – *Die Nackte unterm Ladentisch. Das Magazin in der DDR*, Nora, Berlin, 2002